STATEMENT CONCERNING PUBLICATIONS OF RUSSELL SAGE FOUNDATION

Russell Sage Foundation was established in 1907 by Mrs. Russell Sage "for the improvement of social and living conditions in the United States of America." While the general responsibility for management of the Foundation is vested in the Board of Trustees, the responsibility for facts, conclusions, and interpretations in its publications rests with the authors and not upon the Foundation, its Trustees, or its staff. Publication under the imprint of the Foundation does not imply agreement by the organization with all opinions or interpretations expressed. It does imply that care has been taken that the work on which a manuscript is based has been thoroughly done.

To the Memory of

RALPH LINTON

and

BRONISLAW MALINOWSKI

*An Anthropological Approach
to Community Development*

COOPERATION

in

CHANGE

WARD HUNT GOODENOUGH

Professor of Anthropology
University of Pennsylvania

RUSSELL SAGE FOUNDATION
New York   *1963*

© 1963

RUSSELL SAGE FOUNDATION

Standard Book Number: 87154-344-3

Printed in the United States
  of America

Printed November 1963

Reprinted March 1965

Reprinted January 1968

Reprinted April 1969

Reprinted June 1970

Library of Congress
Catalog Card Number: 63–20667
Standard Book Number: 344–3

CONTENTS

5

FOREWORD

WHEN someone writes the history of efforts by great nations to aid in the development of smaller nations, he will be tempted to call it "How to Back Wrong Horses."

Such a title would not be a reflection on the purposes or philosophy of aid, but on the difficulty that has been encountered of selecting the procedures that will ensure success. Too often the agents of development discover that they are involved with groups in the developing nations who are opposed to the changes that development implies. Thus, they find themselves working to defeat their own aims.

Attempts to produce economic advance, to take one type of example, can result in the rich getting richer and the poor poorer. This has been seen to occur over a wide range of circumstances and types of people, from whole nations in places like the Middle East and South America to sections of the rural countryside in the United States where farm extension programs were intended to benefit all the people. Experience shows that it is easy for development projects to become identified with forces that are primarily against raising the standard of living, against access to economic opportunity, against general education, against the general improvement of health, against self-determination—against development, in short.

The recurrence of this paradox over and over again not only marks its importance, but also suggests that there must be perduring factors at work causing it. Some set of frequently occurring influences appears to be not merely deflecting development effort from its goal, but turning that effort back upon itself, generating bitterness, disappointment, and hostility instead of cooperation and good will.

Forces moving toward change, actual and potential, exist in all societies throughout the world. Sometimes these are triggered by aid programs, more often now they are well under way when the aid projects are introduced. In either case, these forces are the means for driving development; yet instead of being harnessed to

7

this end by the innovators, they are frequently resisted and fought with. Because they seem overwhelming and disorderly, they are held back; and from holding back, it's a short step to blocking at every turn. The flood then swells and instead of turning the wheel bursts the dam and sweeps wheel, mill, and all away.

If there are recurrent causal factors underlying this recurrent picture, it is also certain that they are exceedingly complex. Most thinking people recognize this today, even though starkly simple explanations are still current—explanations such as "mismanagement," "communism," "reactionary forces," "politics," "embezzlement," "thanklessness," and "stupidity," both individual and racial. More sophisticated and useful analyses have come from economics, political science, psychology, sociology and anthropology, but these explanations, too, taken one by one are at best only partial. The fact is that we are confronted by the consequence of social process, of recurrent transactions and patterns of human behavior, that manifest themselves symptomatically in all these ways, from "mismanagement" to "culture conflict." Although the behavioral sciences have uncovered a great deal of information about many of the relevant areas of motivation, interpersonal relations and mass trends, this knowledge generally lies scattered in many heads and in many books, with the result that it often fails to come to bear where it is needed.

In the present work, the product of over ten years of observation and reflection, Ward Goodenough does an extraordinary job of pulling diverse understandings together. While presenting a framework into which many useful details are fitted, the book is primarily a synthesis that provides a central grasp of underlying process. As such it holds interest for everyone who is concerned with the intricate human problems of our changing world, and who seeks a basis for making judgments regarding trends and policies. With clear writing the author builds logically from point to point, keeps technical terms to a minimum, and offers one of the most careful and systematic presentations of theory and empirical knowledge to be found in the literature.

But it is also a book for the specialist, for the professional and technical worker in the field of development, whether teacher, doctor, nurse, agronomist, engineer, administrator, or other.

Although the author points out that his work is not a "how to do it" book—not a Baedeker for the cross-cultural traveler—it is important to note that it contains innumerable points of practical guidance and suggestion that are readily translatable into action. It is focused on the common problems of those who work in cross-cultural situations and although drawing illumination in social science theory, it comes back again and again to these central issues.

In addition to being useful to those who are already in the field, Goodenough's work stands out as a teaching manual for those who are preparing for assignments overseas. It has its place both in the short and intensive courses for the technical expert who must be sent out in a hurry to meet immediate needs, and also in the longer range training programs of universities. The bibliography is a particularly useful tool. Taken together with two other books published by Russell Sage Foundation, *Human Problems in Technological Change*, edited by Edward H. Spicer (1952), and *Health, Culture, and Community*, edited by Benjamin D. Paul (1955), it constitutes an essential library and reference source that should accompany every worker in cross-cultural situations, or situations of rapid social change.

The book is not, however, limited to problems of application. It is also of serious concern to students of basic theory in behavioral science, and makes advances by bringing together and synthesizing with originality relevant theories from sociology and psychology as well as cultural anthropology. (In this connection, the reader's attention is drawn particularly to Chapters 10 and 11.) Because of this and because of the author's rich experience and observations as an anthropologist, the book is a major contribution to his own discipline.

There is one additional audience, the mention of which I have saved until the end for the sake of emphasis. This is the policymaker. In its most fundamental aspect the book presents an orientation, an orientation based on some of the discoveries and best established ideas of behavioral science at the present time. All its principles and all the particulars of its guidance stem from this. It is of very great importance that those whose task it is to make policy understand this orientation. Without such understanding the policy-makers will fail to comprehend what the field worker in development who does understand is trying to do. With lack of comprehension come lack of backing, misplaced criticism, and misplaced rewards and punishment. In such an atmosphere technical and professional competence in the management of human relations fades out or never flourishes and the potential of modern behavioral science finds no implementation. In the long run, therefore, the most significant audience for this book is the policy-maker, legislative and executive.

ALEXANDER H. LEIGHTON

Cornell University
April 28, 1963

AUTHOR'S PREFACE

EARLY IN 1952 Leonard S. Cottrell, Jr., and Alexander H. Leighton asked me if I would prepare a manual for people engaged in developing "underdeveloped" communities. The manual was to serve as a guide for dealing with the human problems that beset such work. Aided by a grant from Russell Sage Foundation, I went that summer to Arizona and New Mexico to confer with participants in Cornell University's experimental project in training people for development work.[1] There, with the help of John Adair, Robert Bunker, Henry F. Dobyns, Alexander H. Leighton, Solon T. Kimball, Tom Sasaki, and Edward H. Spicer, a preliminary outline for the book was drafted. The manuscript was to be completed in two years. It has taken ten years to finish. Instead of a manual, a much more general work has emerged.

Thanks to a fellowship at the Center for Advanced Study in the Behavioral Sciences, I was able to finish a first draft early in 1958. When I tried to pull it together and make a book of it, however, it became evident that what I had done was woefully inadequate. There was nothing to do but put it aside and begin over again, making use of materials in the first draft where appropriate. I had failed to come to grips with the fundamental problem: achieving cooperation among individuals and groups of individuals—each with different purposes and values and each with different customs and traditions—in implementing programs for change.

What does an anthropologist have to say that will help development agents deal with this problem with understanding and realism? The experience of anthropologists, in my judgment, does not permit them to recommend specific courses of action, but it provides an excellent vantage point from which to examine the problem and clarify its nature. Development agents themselves must discover techniques for applying to the specific situa-

[1] For an account of this project, see Bunker, Robert, and John Adair, *The First Look at Strangers*, Rutgers University Press, New Brunswick, N.J., 1959.

tions they encounter whatever anthropology and other pertinent sciences may have to teach them. As it took final form, therefore, this book became an introduction to the nature of the problem of cooperation in community development. It is offered as such.

Many people have contributed to the book. In addition to those cited in the text, I wish to express my gratitude to Clelland S. Ford, Samuel F. Sampson, and the many others who have commented constructively on the manuscript; and to Alexander H. Leighton for excellent counsel at all stages of writing. In addition, I wish to thank Irene Bickenbach and Karen Kummer for secretarial help and Peggy Figg-Hoblyn and Arthur M. Conning for research assistance. Above all, I must acknowledge the great contribution of Ruth Gallagher Goodenough, my wife. From the beginning she has played an active role in developing the ideas presented. She wrote sections of the first draft of the manuscript. She assisted in the review of pertinent literature and subjected the completed first draft to the hard appraisal that was necessary in order to see what was needed to make a book. On two occasions her participation approached full collaboration, but each time family responsibilities forced her to assume a more modest role. Nevertheless, she has made a major contribution, especially to the social-psychological interpretation of cooperation in change. Whatever merit this book possesses, she may justly take credit for a major share.

W. H. G.

Lima, Pennsylvania
January 8, 1963

INTRODUCTION

Chapter 1

THE BEGINNING OF A NEW PROFESSION

As long as humanity lasts, men will be reformers—or developers, to use the now fashionable term—endeavoring to change others in order to maintain or create desired situations for themselves, or to change themselves in order to accommodate to unyielding circumstance or to realize a new dream. Aware of the misery that frequently follows the efforts of even the best-intentioned reformers, we look unkindly upon "do-gooders" and "meddlers." Yet, when our own interests are at stake, be they material or emotional, we become reformers ourselves, rationalizing our actions as in enlightened self-interest, as for the good of others, as demanded by moral principle, or as in the interest of a transcendent value such as Progress or the Glory of God. Whatever else he may be, Man is also a reformer.

To accept this does not require that we be complacent about it. As reformers, too often we are inept. We defeat our goals or achieve them at unnecessarily great human cost. Better understanding of the reforming process and of human limitations within it may enable us to reduce our ineptitude. If we forestall unexpected and unwanted results more often, we may more frequently leave both reformer and reformed feeling that the change was worth its pangs. Our concern, then, is not with whether people should or should not try to change their own or their fellows' ways. We take it for granted that they will. We shall direct our attention, instead, to the problem of increasing the realism of our efforts at reform, thereby extending our control of the results.

More specifically, we shall be concerned with the particular kind of reforming known as "developing underdeveloped communities." And we shall concentrate on the problems that arise when a community undergoing change is in a client relationship with some outside person or group serving as a catalyst or helper in the change process.[1] Our observations will apply specifically to the situation in which the agent of change or development agent comes from a social group whose culture differs from that of the group he wishes to help—which we shall call the "client community."[2]

We shall use the expression "community" broadly, referring to any social entity in a client relationship with a development agent or agency. It may be a rural village, a metropolitan government, a tribe, an industrial organization, or a nation state.[3] These are, to be sure, very different kinds of social units. Nevertheless, the human requirements for getting the cooperation of the members of a power elite in helping them to develop an effective national public health service are not unlike those for getting the cooperation of a group of villagers in helping them to improve agricultural production or to develop a local irrigation system. The basic principles of cross-cultural cooperation appear to be much the same, however different the circumstances in which they are applied.

As our use of the word "cooperation" implies, we have a point of view toward the development process, one that reflects both ethical and practical considerations. This is not a book on "how to get other people to do what you want and like it." Imposition of one's will on others is often implied by such expressions as "reform" and "social planning." Because we don't like having our own lives arranged according to someone else's blueprint for us, we have ethical scruples against attempting to impose blueprints on others. As a practical matter, other people are likely to have similar objections to being reformed or subjected to somebody's plan. Development that is undertaken in the spirit of imposing our will on others or getting them to see the folly of their ways and the wisdom of our counsel inevitably meets with resistance. After all his efforts on behalf of others, the agent of reform is repaid with what he interprets as ingratitude. The truth is that to accomplish purposive change in another usually requires the other's cooperation. The question how to reform others successfully becomes more realistically the question how to cooperate in achieving a mutually more beneficial state of affairs. When we concentrate on the *human* problems of accomplishing technological, social, or other kinds of community reform, as we do in this book, we are forced to conclude that successful reform is not so readily accomplished by attempts to reform others as by helping others to reform themselves.

COMMUNITY DEVELOPMENT AND CUSTOMARY CHANGE

When we look at actual development enterprises, we discern two different approaches or emphases. One concentrates on changing the environment or physical conditions in which the community's members live, the other on changing their customary practices.

Much effort in development is aimed at altering the environment so as to change the physical circumstances of the client community. Dams are built to prevent floods and provide new irrigable lands. Draining swamps, building roads, all the projects that we refer to as "public works" provide further examples of this kind of development effort. Its object is to create new opportunities for economic or other forms of growth and development. Changing the physical environment may be accomplished with or without the community's participation. The assumption is that people will take advantage of the new opportunities in desirable ways once they have been made available. Development agents have found that when their clients actively participate in the work required to produce the physical changes, they are more likely to take advantage of these changes. As soon as the client community's participation is sought, cooperation between agent and client becomes essential to the project. In the last analysis, however, success is measured by the degree to which the changed conditions are exploited and by the desirability of the direction that the exploitation takes.

Environmental change is followed, of course, by some sort of change in customary practice. The client community may have to develop new ways of doing things in order to take advantage of the changed conditions. Or the consequent economic growth may lead to a need for legal reform and political innovation to keep pace with it. Indeed, environmental change is often undertaken as a device for provoking changes in customary practices, which were the actual target of development. One of the problems we shall have to consider is why people so often fail to respond to environmental changes in accordance with planners' expectations.

Often community development aims directly at changing some aspect of local custom. Instead of changing the environment to create new opportunities, the emphasis may be on introducing new techniques for more efficiently exploiting the existing environment. The purpose of the change in custom may be to free the community for growth and development by giving its members new technical knowledge and skills or by helping them to achieve more efficient ways of reaching communitywide decisions. Efforts to effect changes in customary practice range across the entire spectrum of human concerns—technological, political, economic, social, legal, ideological, and religious.

When change in custom is the immediate objective, the client community's cooperation is obviously essential. If its members refuse to change their customs in the ways deemed most advisable by development agents, there is little the latter can do to force them to change. They can force some kind of change, perhaps, but not the one they want. The need for cooperation is less obvious when environmental change is the main objective. But even here, customary change of some sort is likely to be the long-range aim, though not the immediate one. The usual reason for creating new environmental opportunities is to enable people to engage in new activities and to free them for economic, social, and political growth. Although cooperation between agent and community may appear to be a less immediate concern, in the end it becomes a problem here also.

Sooner or later, then, change in the client community's customs is an essential feature of nearly every development situation. The problem of cooperation in purposive change is largely a problem of cooperation in customary change. Customs and how they change will command our attention.

AGENTS OF CHANGE

Those who function as agents of change in cross-cultural situations engage in a wide range of activities.[4] There are government officers with authority to regulate the activities of members of communities within their jurisdictions. Examples are British colonial officers, United States Indian agents, and regional governors within some nation states. There are such civil servants as extension agents and directors of public programs of all sorts. Although the degree to which these officials and civil servants are empowered to initiate changes varies considerably, all are inevitably concerned with the problem of cooperation in some kind of change.

Educators are obvious change agents, especially in the world as it is today, where what is taught in schools is frequently at variance with what is taught in the pupils' homes.

Religious missionaries represent one of the oldest kinds of change agent. Under this heading we may include all those who actively seek to reorganize another people's way of life in terms of some ideological blueprint for personal or collective salvation to which they are personally committed, whether the ideology is that of Methodism, Communism, or Pan-Africanism.

Whenever any outside business organization establishes itself in a new locality, it inevitably functions as a powerful force for change. All those who make decisions regarding its operations in that locality, from its top management down to its line foremen, are agents of change. European plantation owners and managers in New Guinea, representatives of the American Arabian Oil Company in Saudi Arabia, the trader in some Hudson Bay outpost, all seek to modify the behavior of local people in ways advantageous to their business or industrial objectives. All are interested in averting changes that will be injurious to their interests. Many play powerful, active roles in local politics, whether openly or behind the scenes, in order to promote their interests.

A specifically modern development is the increasing recognition by nations and other communities that they can advantageously call upon specialists to help them initiate their own programs of purposive change. Economic, agricultural, and technical advisers and missions have become an established feature of international relations. Experts are being increasingly consulted by private and governmental organizations and by local communities. This is a significant development, because it has brought scientists face to face with the problems of change and has led them to begin to look upon these problems as worthy of systematic investigation and analysis.

Educators and missionaries, to be sure, with long experience in promoting change that requires the active and voluntary cooperation of others, have developed considerable wisdom and practical "know-how," which educators especially have sought to reduce to operational principles for teacher-training purposes. But their professional concern has been largely with the changing of children into adults. Up to now, certainly, government officials, religious missionaries, and business administrators have not tended to think of their professions or careers in terms of the roles they play as change agents. For most of them, their role as change agent is, or seems to be, incidental to some other job, such as saving souls, establishing law and order, or educating the young. Thus the police officer in our society sees himself as enforcing the law. His training is aimed at providing him with efficient techniques of enforcement in communities where law is an expression of the will of the vast majority of their members, where it is accepted by them as their own law for themselves and something that they can modify to suit themselves if it proves irksome. The law that an Australian patrol officer in the Trust Territory of New Guinea enforces is not likely to be an expression of the will of the local community's members. What he needs to know in order to perform his role as a police officer under these conditions is not a part of the usual police school curriculum. This is explicitly recognized in the special training program for such officers at Australia's School of Pacific Administration. Similarly, an Anglo-American teacher of Indian children in a reservation school is not training them for adult responsibilities in a society governed by the values of their parents. How well prepared is he to deal with the problems that face him as a teacher of alien ideas and values?[5]

With increase in the numbers of scientists and technical experts acting as consultants and advisers for programs of voluntary change, there has been increasing awareness of the special nature of the role of the change agent as such and of the need for professional training to help him play it.[6]

THE KIND OF PROFESSIONAL TRAINING NEEDED

Widespread interest in economic and social development since World War II has produced a sizable literature.[7] Much of it has been concerned with sorting out relevant problems and issues.[8] From technicians and administrators working as agents of change have come reports of their experiences.[9] And social scientists and others have undertaken baseline studies preliminary to development.[10] There have also been numerous appraisals of what is actually being done.[11] All concerned emphasize the critical role of "human" factors in determining the outcome of efforts at purposive change. They stress the need for a better understanding of the psychological, social, and cultural forces at work. In order to appreciate the impact of those forces in community development, let us consider for a moment the following hypothetical situation in which we imagine our own community as underdeveloped.

Suppose that one hundred years ago Turkey was a progressive and powerful nation. Suppose that by modifying and developing the Arabic tradition of medicine it had then achieved a state of medical sophistication comparable to that in which Americans pride themselves today. Suppose, moreover, that a group of forward-looking men in the United States government invited Turkey to send a medical mission to this country to give us the benefit of its know-how. And, finally, suppose that a Turkish mission and our government agreed that a pressing health problem and one in which dramatic results could be shown was the high death rate in childbirth, and that the Turkish mission should undertake to supervise the establishment of modern maternity hospitals and clinics and to train American medical practitioners to operate them.

What would have been the probable reaction of expectant mothers in 1850 to going to a hospital to have babies? What would their husbands have thought about it? How would church authorities have viewed the matter? What would have been the editorial reaction in the newspapers? Would such a project have had any chance of success, no matter how sound medically, if its planners failed to ask themselves these questions (and many more like them), to work out their answers, and to develop ways of coping with the problems that the answers presented? What would the planners and executors of this project have had to know about Americans, their customs, values, and habits of thought before they could answer these questions? It is not unreasonable to suppose that the success of the mission would have required as careful attention to problems of this sort as to those of a strictly medical nature.

With this hypothetical example we touch on only a few of the many human factors affecting the course of development programs. Because of their obvious importance, social scientists have rightly asserted that their several disciplines have vital contributions to make toward improving the effectiveness of change agents. Their concern has led, among other things, to several books intended to help development agents broaden their perspectives and discover more effective approaches to the conduct of their work.[12] In these, as well as in other publications, there have been two major foci of interest. One has been to illustrate for development agents the role of social and cultural factors. The other has been to review experience and draw up procedural rules. As a result of their efforts in the latter direction a number of principles have been formulated. Because they reflect actual experience, they are of special interest. We may summarize them as follows:[13]

1. Development proposals and procedures should be mutually consistent.

2. Development agents must have a thorough knowledge of the main values and principal features of the client community's culture.

3. Development must take the whole community into account.

4. The goals of development must be stated in terms that have positive value to the community's members. They must be something they, as well as the agent, want.

5. The community must be an active partner in the development process.

6. Agents should start with what the community has in the way of material, organizational, and leadership resources.

7. Development procedures must make sense to the community's members at each step.

8. The agent must earn the respect of the community's members for himself as a person.

9. The agent should try to avoid making himself the indispensable man in the development situation.

10. Where there are several agents at work, good communication and coordination between them and their respective agencies is essential.

Such are some of the practical lessons students and observers of community development have drawn from the record. But to state them and give them general lip-service is one thing; to put them into effective practice is another. Thus in one case where a relatively enlightened administration made what it regarded as a serious effort to win cooperation in a much needed program:

> . . . it sometimes took months to get acceptance by administrators of simple cultural facts which merely explained some of the opposition. It was infinitely more difficult to get agreement for modification, not of the objectives of the program, but of the procedures, that they might be somewhat more palatable. . . . If that was the situation under liberal policy and wise leadership, one can appreciate how much more difficult the problem will be elsewhere.[14]

There are, of course, cases where community development principles have been successfully applied. The Tennessee Valley Authority,[15] the development project at Etawah in northern India,[16] and Cornell University's experiment at Vicos, Peru,[17] are internationally famous examples. Official recognition of the value of these principles is very largely due to such cases. Growing acceptance, however, is not accompanied by a comparable rate of successful application. The same mistakes seem to be made again and again, and their analyses always lead back to reiteration of the same principles. It seems that professions of faith are not enough.

Several factors appear to contribute to this failure to profit in practice from the lessons already learned. The present state of knowledge is inadequate; what is known is poorly disseminated; and administrators and development agents are unwilling or unable to undertake the sometimes drastic modifications of their own established attitudes and habits that are required if present knowledge is to be successfully applied. Let us briefly consider each of these factors.

Inadequacy of the Present State of Knowledge

The operating principles so far formulated undoubtedly need considerable refinement. Sometimes they are couched in terms appropriate to the community or region with which their formulators have had experience and require restatement to be more generally applicable. Nor is a principle that has proved valid for one region necessarily valid for another, no matter how well formulated. For example, there is evidence that the dictum about working through a community's established leaders may not always be applicable.[18] Systematic testing of the lessons we think we have learned is badly needed.

Existing principles of community development, moreover, have been largely drawn from experience and have not been adequately related to general scientific knowledge. There has been a tendency to interpret the lessons learned in terms of social philosophies that derive their force largely from ethical values.[19] When appraised in the light of scientific theory, however, the lessons learned may take on a different meaning. Techniques that have worked in one community may fail when applied to another not because they were inapplicable but because what was really involved was not understood.

Finally, existing scientific knowledge does not allow us to answer all questions as to the psychological, social, and cultural forces affecting cooperation in purposive change. Indeed some of the answers that have been given in the name of science may not prove correct. Knowledge of the processes of social change is still sketchy.

Inadequate Dissemination of What Is Known

Many agents of community development lack an adequate background in the relevant social sciences. With it they would be equipped to view their work and their clients in ways that would greatly increase their sensitivity to the implications of their decisions. This lack is not due solely to their failure to appreciate the need for such background. The need is widely recognized. There are other contributing reasons.

For one thing, at the time in a person's career when he discovers the need for them, training opportunities are limited. Frequently, awareness of the need does not come until he is already engaged in community development work and discovering for himself the gaps in his background. Also limited are satisfactory training materials. Social scientists have not taken enough responsibility for disseminating their knowledge to change agents in a form suitable to meeting their needs.[20] In order to evaluate the effect of a particular course of action on a community's population, on their emotions, their customs, and their social and political processes, agents need concepts with which to make their own analyses of the situations they face. And they need training in using them. Relevant scientific concepts are often presented in connection with problems and illustrated by examples that have a tenuous connection, at best, with the concerns of change agents.

Agents of change have from time to time developed ingenious approaches to gaining their client's cooperation and dissolving resistance, but these are not adequately communicated to other change agents who might find them helpful in solving their own tactical problems.[21] This situation reflects the lack of professionalism among agents of change in their role as such, and the consequent lack of journals and other communication media that go with a self-conscious profession.

Interference of Agent's Established Habits and Attitudes

If we think about the procedural principles outlined in summary form on page 22 for a moment, it is evident that they have far-reaching implications for present practice in community development.

Field agents, administrators, and policy-makers all have their own customary ways of doing things that involve well-established habits and attitudes. It is not easy to change them. These habits and attitudes, moreover, vary from occupation to occupation. Observers have noted that agricultural extension agents are by the orientations of their profession better prepared to work in group situations and adapt themselves to others than are, for example, physicians or engineers.[22]

There is a tendency, also, even on the part of sophisticated Americans, to assume that cultural, social, and psychological principles, which they cite to explain the behavior of others, do not equally apply to their own behavior. An observation by Clyde Kluckhohn is to the point.

> Many educated people have the notion that culture applies only to exotic ways of life or to societies where relative simplicity and relative homogeneity prevail. Some sophisticated missionaries, for example, will use the anthropological conception in discussing the special modes of living of South Sea Islanders, but seem amazed at the idea that it could be applied equally to inhabitants of New York City. And social workers in Boston will talk about the culture of a colorful and well-knit immigrant group but boggle at applying it to the behavior of staff members in the social-service agency itself.*[23]

Furthermore, reluctance to carry through in practice the implications of what we already know and subscribe to is only natural if these implications have never been fully spelled out. If we begin to think about them for the first time only when faced with a practical decision and then find that they run counter to our established attitudes and ways of doing things, we inevitably dismiss them as "impractical." And under such circumstances there is a real sense in which they are impractical. If marked improvement in achieving successful cooperation in purposive change requires extensive reorganization of existing procedures and practices, such reorganization must be thought through in advance. Policy must take it into account and appropriate administrative procedures must be operative. No development

* Reprinted with permission of the publishers from *Mirror for Man:* The Relation of Anthropology to Modern Life by Clyde Kluckhohn. Copyright © 1949 by the McGraw-Hill Book Company, Inc., New York, p. 29.

program can be properly executed, for example, on year-to-year funding, which effectively precludes long-range planning and induces agents to try to get quick results in situations where attempts to get quick results may be disastrous. As things stand, the "right" course of action is too often dismissed as impractical because existing arrangements leave the agent with no apparent way in which he can implement it.

Our frequent failure to apply either the practical lessons learned or our scientific knowledge suggests a need for more professionalism in community development work. The need for professional training in order to help individuals achieve purposive changes in themselves is well recognized. One does not qualify as a psychiatrist, psychoanalyst, or psychological counselor by taking a "quicky" course on the subject. Some untrained individuals achieve considerable success in helping others with their problems, but their intuitive gifts do not make professionalism unnecessary. There have always been such persons; but significant advances in mental health have come only with modern professionalization. Some development agents have likewise been discerning and skillful. Nevertheless, helping a community to change is scarcely a less complicated matter than helping an individual.

There are many similarities between the approaches and problems connected with helping individuals to achieve psychological changes within themselves and those connected with helping small groups, industrial organizations, and communities to change, as Lippitt and his associates have shown.[24] They note that although the problems are increasingly complex with larger groups, there has been relatively little effort to learn to deal with them as compared with the intense effort to develop procedural principles and insights in psychotherapy and psychological counseling. Where the problems require, if anything, as much or more professional skill and training of change agents, such training has been neglected.

THE BEGINNING OF PROFESSIONAL TRAINING

An obstacle to professionalization is that agents of community development must have other kinds of technical or professional skill as well. Obviously, agricultural development cannot be accomplished by someone with a degree in human relations alone. To be competent in the fields of soil conservation, public health, or public administration, to take some more examples, requires years of technical training. The problem of professionalization here is akin to that in education. A schoolteacher must be in command of the subjects that it is his responsibility to teach. He can improve the likelihood that he will do a good job as a teacher if he also has a practical knowledge of child psychology and has been exposed to the pedagogical methods that teachers before him have discovered to be sound. Although there are disputes as to what constitutes a proper balance between professional training in subject matter to be taught and professional training in teaching anything at all, there are few critics of modern education who do not recognize the importance of both.

Recognition of the need for a similar combination of training for development agents in cross-cultural situations is gradually being implemented. Here and there training programs for religious missionaries, colonial officials, overseas administrators, and Peace Corps volunteers have introduced social sciences and related subjects into their curricula.[25] Just what should be included is, of course, still a matter of debate. Considerable experimentation will be necessary both in curriculum content and in the preparation of suitable teaching materials for some time.

But there is one point on which there already seems to be widespread agreement: the need for supervised practical experience with underdeveloped communities. Experimental field seminars conducted by Cornell University under the auspices of Russell Sage Foundation have demonstrated the educational value of shared practical experience under competent supervision.[26] As with teaching and other "clinical" professions, a significant portion of a person's training is to develop his ability to apply in practice the principles he has learned in the classroom and to develop the social skills and acquire the deeper understanding that can come only with experience. Nor can other aspects of training be entirely divorced from the accumulation of practical experience. Refresher courses and in-service training are recognized as essential to the process of creating effective development agents. From their experience, for example, Pal and his associates have observed:

> The development of persons into efficient cdws [community development workers] is easier said than done. Pre-service training is desirable, but there is no substitute for periodic in-service training. The time spent for the in-service training will be more than compensated for in the increased wisdom and skills of the workers. . . .[27]

This is only part of what is needed. Calling attention to the gross inadequacies in training and selection of United States personnel for overseas assignments, Cleveland, Mangone, and Adams argue that the capacity to work effectively in alien social and cultural settings requires a professional type of training, provided in part by colleges and universities and involving orientation and specialized knowledge, as well as internship experience. In their judgment, such a training program should include four steps:

> The first step is a liberal arts education adequate to the needs of a world in which the dividing line between "domestic" and "foreign" affairs has been permanently blurred; the study of foreign cultures and foreign languages should therefore be the rule rather than the exception. The second step is professional training in a subject-matter field—medicine or law, engineering or agriculture, journalism or military science, economics or public administration. Step number three is exposure to the special linguistic skills, area knowledge, and other kinds of understanding that are relevant to the first overseas assignment. The final step is the immediate orientation to the particular job to be done abroad.
>
> If the United States is serious about making sure of first-rate representation abroad, in private as well as public enterprise, there must be a conscious effort to build into the educational system *at each of these steps* the kinds of education and experience that develop the qualities of mind and spirit that make for success in work abroad.[*28]

If such a program is ever to be realized, it will be necessary to develop a body of new teaching materials to implement it. Such materials are beginning to appear. So far, they reflect a wide range of interests and points of view and aim to accomplish diverse purposes. Some deal with the general theory of economic, social, or cultural change, with varying concern for problems of application, mostly at the level of general policy.[29] Others provide distinctive and useful discussions aimed at giving the reader an appreciation of the importance of cultural factors in agent-client relations and also in the development process itself.[30] Still others deal with general principles of community development,[31] or with actual field techniques.[32] Specifically designed for classroom use are two books of readings[33] and two excellent casebooks.[34]

As for this book, it does not duplicate what is already available. It does not attempt to provide a detailed theory of social and cultural change, although it contributes to the development of such theory. Theory of change is not yet scientifically mature. Nor does it attempt to spell out what to do and what not to do in the field. It endeavors to introduce the reader to the range of things that bear on the problem of agent-client cooperation in customary change—the principal human problem in practice—so that he will be more sensitive to what is involved. Hopefully, it also provides a coherent point of view that will enrich subsequent, more detailed considerations of both theory and practice in community development. The reader will find its usefulness greatly enhanced if he has already had practical field experience. In any event and in the absence of such experience, especially, he is advised to make himself familiar with the materials in the two casebooks cited above and to refer to them in the course of reading this book. Other reading suggestions are given at the end of each chapter.

SUGGESTED READING

Foster, George M., *Traditional Cultures:* And the Impact of Technological Change. Harper and Row, Publishers, Inc., New York, 1962.

NOTES TO CHAPTER 1

1. For a view of the development worker as a "catalytic agent," see Foster, Ellery, "Planning for Community Development Through Its People," *Human Organization*, vol. 12, no. 2, 1953, pp. 5–9.

2. For the convenient expressions "change agent" and "client community" or "client system," see Lippitt, Ronald, Jeanne Watson, and Bruce Westley, *The Dynamics of Planned Change:* A Comparative Study of Principles and Techniques, Harcourt, Brace, and Co., New York, 1958, p. 10.

3. For another definition of community, see Murdock, George Peter, *Social Structure*, Macmillan Co., New York, 1949, p. 79. There it is defined as the maximal group of people living in face-to-face association. In *The Analysis of Social Change:* Based on Observations in Central Africa, Cambridge University Press, Cambridge, 1954, pp. 30–31, Godfrey and Monica Wilson state: "Communities are areas and periods of common life of more or less intensity. To facilitate the comparison of scale we distinguish between the largest community and extra-communal relations. The boundaries of community are the boundaries of many-sided relationship; extra-communal relations are one-sided and tenuous. The boundaries of community, like those of society, vary with the point of reference, and the exact line of demarcation is not always clear, but in cases in which the relevant facts are known it can be defined as falling within certain narrow limits."

4. This point is stressed by Harlan Cleveland, Gerard J. Mangone, and John Clarke Adams in *The Overseas Americans*, McGraw-Hill Book Co., New York, 1960.

5. Musgrove, F., "Education and the Culture Concept," *Africa*, vol. 23, 1953, pp. 110–125.

6. See, for example, Mosher, Arthur T., *Technical Cooperation in Latin-American Agriculture*, University of Chicago Press, Chicago, 1957, chap. 18. See also Cleveland, Harlan, Gerard J. Mangone, and John Clarke Adams, *op. cit.*

7. See the bibliographies by Sidney C. Sufrin and Frank Eugene Wagner, *A Brief Annotated Bibliography on Labor in Emerging Societies*, Center for Overseas Operations, Maxwell Graduate School of Citizenship and Public Affairs, Syracuse University, Syracuse, N. Y., 1961, and by Donn V. Hart and Paul Meadows, *An Annotated Bibliography of Directed Social Change*, Center for Overseas Operations, Maxwell Graduate School of Citizenship and Public Affairs, Syracuse University, 1961 (also included in Hart, Donn V., and Paul Meadows, editors, *Selected Abstracts in Development Administration:* Field Reports of Directed Social Change, Publication 3, Maxwell Graduate School of Citizenship and Public Affairs, Syracuse University, 1962). Journals devoting considerable space to these and related topics include: *Africa, Community Development* (formerly *International Review of Community Development*), *Community Development Bulletin, Corona, Economic Development and Cultural Change, Human Organization* (formerly *Applied Anthropology*), *Journal of African Administration, Rural Sociology, South Pacific, South Pacific Commission Quarterly Bulletin*.

8. Adams, Richard N., and others, *Social Change in Latin America Today:* Its Implications for United States Policy, Harper and Bros., New York, 1960, Vintage Books, New York, 1961; Batten, T. R., *Communities and Their Development:* An Introductory Study with Special Reference to the Tropics, Oxford University Press, London, 1957; Belshaw, Cyril S., *Island Administration in the Southwest Pacific*: Government and Reconstruction in New Caledonia, the New Hebrides, and the British Solomon Islands, Royal Institute of International Affairs, London, New York, 1950; Erasmus, Charles J., *Man Takes Control:* Cultural Development and American Aid, University of Minnesota Press, Minneapolis, 1961; Foster, George M., *Problems in Intercultural Health Programs*, Social Science Research Council, Pamphlet 12, New York, 1958; Foster, George M., *Traditional Cultures:* And the Impact of Technological Change, Harper and Bros., New York, 1962; Hall, Robert King, N. Hans, and J. A. Lauwerys, editors, *The Yearbook of Education, 1954*, Evans Brothers, Ltd., London, 1954; Hagen, Everett E., *On the Theory of Social Change:* How Economic Growth Begins, The Dorsey Press, Inc., Homewood, Ill., 1962; McClelland, David C., *The Achieving Society*, D. Van Nostrand Co., Princeton, N. J., 1961; Mead, Margaret, editor, *Cultural Patterns and Technological Change*, UNESCO, University of Columbia Press, New York, 1952, Mentor Books, 1955; Read, Margaret, *Education and Social Change in Tropical Areas*, Thomas Nelson and Sons, New York, 1955; Ruopp, Phillips, editor, *Approaches to Community Development*, W. Van Heeve Ltd., The Hague, 1953; Smith, Robert J., special editor, "Culture Change and the

Small Community," special issue of *The Journal of Social Issues*, vol. 14, no. 4, 1958; Symposium, "Economic Motivations and Stimulations in Underdeveloped Countries," *International Social Science Bulletin*, vol. 6, no. 3, 1954; Symposium, "Pitfalls of Point Four," *American Perspective*, vol. 4, 1950, pp. 113–145; Symposium, "Social Implications of Technical Change," *International Social Science Bulletin*, vol. 4, no. 2, 1952; Symposium, "Social Anthropology and Health Education," *The Health Education Journal*, vol. 15, no. 2, 1957; Staley, Eugene, *The Future of Underdeveloped Countries:* Political Implications of Economic Development, Harper and Bros., New York, 1954; Williamson, Harold F., and John A. Buttrick, editors, *Economic Development:* Principles and Patterns, Prentice-Hall, Inc., New York, 1954.

9. Allen, Harold B., *Come Over Into Macedonia*, Rutgers University Press, New Brunswick, N. J., 1943; Barker, Anthony, *The Man Next to Me:* An Adventure in African Medical Practice, Harper and Bros., New York, 1959; Hatch, D. Spencer, *Toward Freedom from Want:* From India to Mexico, Apollo Bunder, Oxford University Press, Bombay, 1949; Lilienthal, David E., *TVA: Democracy on the March*, Harper and Bros., New York, 1944; Rambhai, B., *The Silent Revolution*, Jiwan Prakashan (Regd.), Chawri Bazar, Delhi, 2d rev. ed., 1959; Wiser, Charlotte Viall, and William H. Wiser, *Behind Mud Walls*, Agricultural Missions, Inc., New York, 1951.

10. Allbaugh, Leland G., *Crete:* A Case Study of an Underdeveloped Area, Princeton University Press, Princeton, N.J., 1953; Banfield, Edward C., and Laura Fasano Banfield, *The Moral Basis of a Backward Society*, The Free Press, Glencoe, Ill., 1958; Houghton, D. Hobart, editor, *Economic Development in a Plural Society:* Studies in the Border Region of the Cape Province, Oxford University Press, Cape Town, 1960; Mukherjee, P. K., and S. C. Gupta, *A Pilot Survey of Fourteen Villages:* A Study in Methodology of Research in Rural Change, Agricultural Economics Research Section, Delhi School of Economics, University of Delhi, Asia Publishing House, London, 1959; Salz, Beate R., *The Human Element in Industrialization:* A Hypothetical Case Study of Ecuadorean Indians, American Anthropological Association Memoir No. 85, Menasha, 1955.

11. Adams, Harold S., George M. Foster, and Paul S. Taylor, *Report on Community Development Programs in India, Pakistan and the Philippines*, International Cooperation Administration, Washington, 1955; Adams, Richard N., and Charles C. Cumberland, *United States University Cooperation in Latin America:* A Study Based on Selected Programs in Bolivia, Chile, Peru and Mexico, Institute of Research on Overseas Programs, Michigan State University, East Lansing, Mich., 1960; Cochran, Thomas C., and Ruben E. Reina, *Entrepreneurship in Argentine Culture:* Torcuato di Tella and S.I.A.M., University of Pennsylvania Press, Philadelphia, 1962; Cumming, John, and Elaine Cumming, *Closed Ranks:* An Experiment in Mental Health Education, Harvard University Press, Cambridge, Mass., 1957; Dube, S. C., *India's Changing Villages:* Human Factors in Community Development, Cornell University Press, Ithaca, 1958; Epstein, T. S., *Economic Development and Social Change in South India*, University of Manchester Press, Manchester, England (Humanities Press, New York), 1962; Fisher, Glen, "Directed Culture Change in Nayarit, Mexico" in Edmundson, M. S., and others, *Synoptic Studies of Mexican Culture*, Publication 17, Middle American Research Institute, Tulane University, New Orleans, 1957, pp. 65–173; Gross, Neal, Eugene A. Wilkening, and others, *Sociological Research on the Diffusion and Adoption of New Farm Practices*, Kentucky Agricultural Experiment Station, University of Kentucky, June, 1952; Hayden, Howard, *Moturiki:* A Pilot Project in Community Development, Oxford University Press, London, Melbourne and New York, 1954; Jackson, I. C., *Advance in Nigeria:* A Study of Community Development in Eastern Nigeria, Oxford University Press, London, 1956; Loomis, Charles P., Julio O. Morales, Roy A. Clifford, and Olen E. Leonard, editors, *Turrialba:* Social Systems and the Introduction of Change, The Free Press, Glencoe, Ill., 1953; Mayer, Albert, and others, *Pilot Project, India:* The Story of Rural Development at Etawah, Uttar Pradesh, University of California Press, Berkeley, 1958; Orlans, Harold, *Utopia Ltd.:* The Story of the English New Town of Stevenage,

Yale University Press, New Haven, 1953; Pal, Agaton P., and Co-workers, *Siliman University Community Development Program:* Account of the Planning, Implementation, and Training of Workers of a Community Development Program, the People's Responses, Perception of the Roles of Workers, and Experiences of Each Worker, Siliman University, Dumaguete City, Philippines, May, 1959; Pearse, Innes H., and L. H. Crocker, *The Peckham Experiment:* A Study in the Living Structure of a Society, Yale University Press, New Haven, 1945; Reid, J. T., *It Happened in Taos*, University of New Mexico Press, Albuquerque, 1946; Selznick, Philip, *TVA and the Grass Roots*, University of California Press, Berkeley, 1953.

12. Batten, T. R., *op. cit.;* Cleveland, Harlan, and Gerard J. Mangone, *The Art of Overseasmanship*, Syracuse University Press, Syracuse, 1957; Cleveland, Harlan, Gerard J. Mangone, and John Clarke Adams, *op. cit.;* Erasmus, Charles J., *op. cit.;* Foster, George M., *Traditional Cultures:* And the Impact of Technological Change, Harper and Bros., New York, 1962; Hall, Edward T., *The Silent Language*, Doubleday and Co., Garden City, N.Y., 1959; Mead, Margaret, editor, *op. cit.;* Nida, Eugene A., *Customs and Cultures:* Anthropology for Christian Missions, Harper and Bros., New York, 1954; Read, Margaret, *op. cit.*

13. For statements of principles, see Batten, T. R., *op. cit.;* [Ensminger, Douglas], *A Guide to Community Development*, The Ministry of Community Development, Government of India, 1957; Hall, Robert King, N. Hans, and J. A. Lauwerys, editors, *op. cit.;* International Cooperation Administration Team III, *Community Development Programs in India, Iran, Egypt & Gold Coast*, International Cooperation Administration, Washington, 1955, pp. 7–8; Loomis, Charles P., "Extension Work for Latin America," *Applied Anthropology*, vol. 3, no. 4, 1944, pp. 27–40; Loomis, Charles P., and Glen Grisham, "The New Mexican Experiment in Village Rehabilitation," *Applied Anthropology*, vol. 2, no. 3, 1943, pp. 13–37; Mead, Margaret, editor, *op. cit.;* Richardson, F. L. W., Jr., "First Principles of Rural Rehabilitation," *Applied Anthropology*, vol. 4, no. 3, 1945, pp. 16–31; Tanous, Afif, "Extension Work Among the Arab Fellahin," *Applied Anthropology*, vol. 3, no. 3, 1944, pp. 1–12; Textor, R. B., and J. C. McCullough, *Manual for the Rural Community Health Worker in Thailand*, Ministry of Public Health, Bangkok, 1958.

14. Kimball, Solon T., "The Crisis in Colonial Administration," *Applied Anthropology*, vol. 5, no. 2, 1946, p. 16.

15. Selznick, Philip, *op. cit.*

16. Mayer, Albert, and others, *op. cit.*

17. Holmberg, Allan R., "Changing Community Attitudes and Values in Peru: A Case Study in Guided Change" in Adams, Richard N., and others, *op. cit.*, pp. 63–107.

18. Foster, George M., *Problems in Intercultural Health Programs.* Social Science Research Council, Pamphlet 12, New York, 1958, p. 31.

19. See, for example, Lilienthal, David E., *op. cit.* There are overtones of the same in Batten, T. R., "The Community and Development," *Corona*, vol. 3, 1951, pp. 330–334.

20. Since 1950 a few training materials have begun to appear, and the Peace Corps will undoubtedly stimulate the preparation of more.

21. Such is the conclusion of Ronald Lippitt, Jeanne Watson, and Bruce Westley, *op. cit.*

22. See the comments by Howard Kline in Cleveland, Harlan, and Gerard J. Mangone, *op. cit.*, p. 96; also the findings of Ozzie G. Simmons, "The Clinical Team in a Chilean Health Center" in Paul, Benjamin D., editor, *Health, Culture, and Community:* Case Studies of Public Reactions to Health Programs, Russell Sage Foundation, New York, 1955, pp. 325–348.

23. Kluckhohn, Clyde, *Mirror for Man:* The Relation of Anthropology to Modern Life. McGraw-Hill Book Co., New York, 1949, p. 29.

24. Lippitt, Ronald, Jeanne Watson, and Bruce Westley, *op. cit.*

25. Examples are the missionary training programs at Fordham University and in the Summer Institutes of Linguistics, the training received by cadets in the British Colonial Service, and the curriculum at the School of Pacific Administration for junior members of the administrative service in the Territory of Papua and New Guinea. Minimal training is also being provided in some Peace Corps curricula.

26. Bunker, Robert, and John Adair, *The First Look at Strangers.* Rutgers University Press, New Brunswick, N.J., 1959.

27. Pal, Agaton P., and Co-workers, *op. cit.,* p. 25.

28. Cleveland, Harlan, Gerard J. Mangone, and John Clarke Adams, *op. cit.,* p. 192.

29. Belshaw, Cyril S., *Changing Melanesia:* Social Economics of Culture Contact, Oxford University Press, Melbourne and Wellington, 1954; Erasmus, Charles J., *op. cit.;* Foster, George M., *Traditional Cultures:* And the Impact of Technological Change, Harper and Bros., New York, 1962; Hagen, Everett E., *op. cit.;* Hogbin, H. Ian, *Social Change*, Watts London, 1958; Loomis, Charles P., *The Strategy of Change*, Prentice Hall, Inc., New York, 1957; Wilson, Godfrey, and Monica, *The Analysis of Social Change:* Based on Observations in Central Africa, Cambridge University Press, Cambridge, 1954.

30. Foster, George M., *op. cit.;* Hall, Edward T., *op. cit.;* Mead, Margaret, editor, *op. cit.;* Nida, Eugene A., *Customs and Cultures:* Anthropology for Christian Missions, Harper and Bros., New York, 1954; and the two casebooks noted below.

31. For example, Batten, T. R., *op. cit.*

32. [Ensminger, Douglas], *op. cit.;* Textor, R. B., and J. C. McCullough, *op. cit.*

33. Hoselitz, Bert F., editor, *The Progress of Underdeveloped Areas*, University of Chicago Press, Chicago, 1952; Shannon, Lyle W., editor, *Underdeveloped Areas:* A Book of Readings and Research, Harper and Bros., New York, 1957.

34. Paul, Benjamin D., editor, *Health, Culture, and Community:* Case Studies of Public Reactions to Health Programs, Russell Sage Foundation, New York, 1955; Spicer, Edward H., editor, *Human Problems in Technological Change:* A Casebook, Russell Sage Foundation, New York, 1952.

Chapter 2

COOPERATION IN CHANGE: A PROFESSIONAL VIEW

FUNDAMENTAL TO THE PROBLEM of cooperation is some kind of conflict of interest. In community development it is the conflict between agency and community as to whose wants, views, and interests take precedence. Practically, of course, this conflict is usually resolved in favor of whichever party holds the power advantage. But any such resolution is likely to be more apparent than real. Courses of action and policies may be decided by the more powerful, but the conflict often continues, manifesting itself in noncooperation by the less powerful party. In one way or another, this conflict of interests is at the root of much community resistance to programs for change. It also raises ethical questions, the answers to which are associated with different philosophies of administration and human development. We cannot avoid these questions. A professional approach to development work must be built on a morally suitable and realistically practicable position concerning them.

Among administrators and planners there are different points of view concerning the extent to which the wants of a community's members are to be allowed to determine a program's objectives and the means to them. Because of our democratic tradition, those who would give high priority to the wishes of the community tend to justify this morally, in terms of ethical principles important in our own culture; while those who give high priority to what the planners want for the community tend to cite what they regard as practical considerations to make up for their moral handicap. They stress the need to be "practical" and "hardheaded," and look upon those who differ with them as "soft." We suspect that the decision as to who is practical and who is soft depends on how the moral cards are stacked in our own system of values. Practical reasons would probably be cited for respecting the local community's desires in a moral climate that glorified the state and subordinated private wants and satisfactions to the decisions of those responsible for the collective welfare. If what is moral depends on one's values, the issue still remains to be considered in practical terms. To what extent can one hope to accomplish one's objective without respecting the community's wants?

In part, of course, it depends on the objective. If it is to create a new set of conditions to which people must somehow adjust, much can be accomplished without attention to their wishes. If what is important is how they choose to react to these conditions or the kind of adjustment they make, then what the planner wants must be tailored to fit the values of those for whom he wants it.[1] If what is desired is that the community's members themselves undertake to change the conditions in which they live, what they want for themselves necessarily dominates the development situation. In economic and social development, as it is currently practiced, all three kinds of objectives are represented.

To accomplish objectives of the first type, all that is required is the power to do what is deemed desirable. The specific effect upon others is not a practical consideration at all, however ethically relevant. In this book we shall not be concerned with directed change of this kind.

To accomplish either of the remaining objectives requires thorough understanding of the people involved, though for somewhat different reasons in each case.

Where the desire is to introduce a plan for development and to try to get people to change their ways of doing things in the direction called for by the plan, as in health programs for example, what the people want for themselves and how the plan fits into it in their judgment can make all the difference between success and failure. On this matter Hoselitz has concluded:

> The problem of developing a group of skilled technicians is not a psychological question of the capacity of persons in underdeveloped

countries to learn, but a social problem: the creation of attitudes and material and psychological compensations which make the choice of such careers attractive. In other words, the question we must ask is not: "How can the people of technically less advanced countries learn the modern techniques?" but: "Will they learn them, and how can they be induced to want to learn them?"[2]

Here, where emphasis is on what the planners want, the wants of the community impose practical limits on what the planners can expect to achieve.

Where the desire is to mobilize the community to do something toward the achievement of its own wants, it is important to know what these wants are and their implications for the future. It is quite possible that, given opportunities to grow and develop, a community will do so in ways that bring it into conflict with the legitimate interests and desires of those who promoted development. Where emphasis is on what the community wants, the wants of the planners impose practical limits on what the community can reasonably expect to achieve.

All parties to a development situation, then, have their "felt needs," to use a term now in common use by development workers. Perhaps the most serious problem in development is the mutual adjustment of these needs. In this regard, it is worth noting that there has been much emphasis in community development work on ascertaining the felt needs of the local people and stimulating them to do something constructive to meet them. This emphasis has led to considerable disappointment on the part of change agents in some areas precisely because the results were not compatible with what they wanted for the community. It is regrettable that, disappointed because they failed to make their own wants explicit in their approach to development, some agents have decided there is little point to attending to the wants of the community or to giving its members an opportunity to help formulate their own development.[3] A decision to introduce the planner's wants for the community more directly into the development situation does not make the community's wants any less important from a practical point of view.

Our approach to human problems in community development, therefore, will be one that regards the planner's wants and the community's wants as both worthy of respect. We shall not attempt to establish any position as to whose are to prevail when there is conflict between them. In any case, these judgments will follow from the dominant values of the parties in conflict and the *de facto* powers that they have for implementing them. We can only hope to increase the perceptiveness with which planners and field agents make such judgments.

Regardless of how the conflict of wants is resolved, it is essential for development agents to know what the client community's wants actually are and to take them fully into account. Experienced development workers emphasize this point repeatedly. The record is clear that neglecting to take account of clients' wants is a major cause of failure in development programs.[4] Nevertheless, it seems often to be very difficult for agents and planners to give the wants of their clients serious consideration. Buchanan and Ellis,[5] for example, acknowledge that cultural factors affect the course of economic development, but see the customs of underdeveloped peoples mainly as impediments to the growth of industrial and entrepreneural economies of western type. They see western values as essential to development and any other values as something to be educated away.

> The depersonalization of economic relationships as a means of weakening cultural ties is perhaps more accurately regarded as a concomitant of the changes discussed than as an independent factor. Nevertheless, its importance needs to be underscored because, where the circumstances are such that economic relationships are strongly personalized, strictly economic considerations—for example, improvements in efficiency, acceptance of innovations, changes in the products grown or goods produced—are likely to be overridden by those of a socio-cultural nature. Thus, to depersonalize economic relationships is at once to weaken cultural bonds and beliefs and to promote efficiency.*[6]

Clearly, these writers regard anything that will promote efficiency as good. They are concerned with people only as instruments for promoting a particular ideal of material efficiency, as pawns in economic enterprise in which the wants and values of

* Reprinted by permission from Norman S. Buchanan and Howard Ellis, *Approaches to Economic Development.* Twentieth Century Fund, New York, 1955, p. 90. Copyright by Twentieth Century Fund.

the planners are all that really matter. To depersonalize is to dehumanize. Development undertaken in this spirit has little chance of success.

The frequency with which the client community's wants are slighted, or disregarded entirely, suggests that some general principle of human relations may be involved. Such, indeed, is the case. The principle of *ethnocentrism*,[7] the counterpart in intergroup relations of egocentrism in interpersonal relations, commands our attention.

EGOCENTRISM AND ETHNOCENTRISM

Everyone starts off in life with what we may call an ego-centered approach to the world. Gratifying his own wants and exploring and developing his own powers to manipulate his surroundings characterize a small child's preoccupations. Socialization, at first in the immediate family, and later in the larger community, is a process in which the child learns progressively to give way to the wants of others and to accommodate himself to the give and take of orderly group life. This accommodation is achieved in two ways. In one, the child recognizes the limits of what others will tolerate in his own behavior and respects them because of the sanctions others have the power to invoke. In the second, the child identifies with others as persons essentially like himself and comes to respect their wants as he respects his own. By putting himself in their place, he learns to appreciate the feelings of others. Insofar as he accommodates himself in the first way, he remains ego-centered; to the extent that he does so in the second way, he becomes other-oriented.

The great importance of being other-oriented is that it leads us to regard the wishes and feelings of others even in situations where we have the power to disregard them, as parents have the power to disregard the feelings of their children. Only by identification or empathy with others are we able to appreciate their feelings and respect them. But it exacts a price, inhibiting us from going ahead with the gratification of our own wants. It requires self-sacrifice. To identify with other people, therefore, may be rewarding under some conditions, especially where we have to live with them, get along with them, and establish positive emotional relations with them. But it may also be punishing, giving us a sense of deprivation and frustration as it prevents our enjoying other rewards. Often enough, it leads us to remove the conflict of interests from the arena of social interaction and push it down into the basement of our souls. There, whatever the outcome of the conflict, it is part of us that suffers. To the extent, then, that socialization does not make identification with others rewarding and desirable, we tend to remain ego-centered, concerned to manipulate others to our ends with few pangs of conscience, restrained mainly by what we have learned to be the practical limits within which we can do so successfully.

Consequently, an adult's social world consists of himself at the center, with an immediate circle of persons with whom he has strong identifications and to whom he is maximally other-oriented, and with a series of more remote circles in which the degree of other-orientation becomes progressively weaker. This has its counterpart in the phenomenon of ethnocentrism. The groups we have our strongest identifications with are those toward whom we are most other-oriented, to whose collective welfare and interests we are most ready to subordinate our personal interests. Those we have least identification with are the ones toward whom we are most ethnocentric, with whom we deal in terms of our wants and whom we judge as good or bad in terms of how readily they accommodate themselves to our expectations and desires.

There is a natural tendency in community development, therefore, for planners and field agents to be more concerned with what they themselves want of the community as they identify with it less. Development tends to be more community-centered when the community is "close to home" and more planner-centered when it is not.

Since, in any case, development calls for a considerable degree of cooperative interaction between community and agent, it requires a considerable increase in their mutual identification. Each must become less ethnocentric than before. An agent has the greater responsibility here, especially when his power position *vis-à-vis* the community puts little pressure on him to try to understand the community's point of view. Furthermore, it is easier for an individual to identify with a group than for a group with an individual. It is the individual who must take the initiative. An agent, then, coming in from the outside has to try to identify himself with the community, learn its outlook on things, to an extent far greater than he would normally ever take the trouble to do. Otherwise, he cannot interact with its members except in a self-centered way or achieve cooperation by means other than the exercise of power.

But what about planners and agency heads who remain out of direct contact with the community? In the normal course of events, simply by virtue of his increased interactions with the community's members, a field agent will develop a higher degree of identification with the community than will his organizational superiors. Consequently, field agents tend to be more community-centered; and planners and agency heads tend to be more agency-centered in their view of the development process. To the extent that decisions affecting the aims and methods of development lie with a field agent, they will be more likely to take the feelings of the community's members into account. To the extent that they are made by planners and agency heads, they will be more likely to express only the planners' desires without regard to the community's wishes. This is not a simple matter of information alone, but of identification, for it seems to be true even where information is equally available to both field agent and agency head.

As a consequence of this difference in degree of identification, serious conflicts can arise between field agents and directors of development programs. The latter tend to become impatient with attempts by field agents to use a community-centered approach to development, although they endorse such an approach in principle. Planners and supervisors have a special responsibility to recognize the natural bias which their removal from the scene of operations inevitably gives them. They must allow for the fact that their greater distance tends to make them less sensitive to human factors at the local level, however well informed they may otherwise be. It is in the field that the bulk of the human problems arise, and it is in planning and administration that there is the least sensitivity to them.

A final point of clarification is in order. In speaking of a community-centered approach, we are not referring simply to a willingness to like people and deal with them positively, important as such qualities are. Many people of good will mistakenly assume that "folks are folks" the world over and that cooperation is always therefore best achieved in an atmosphere of democratic informality, to take one example. For us to assume that the Bantu peoples of Africa will react to things as we do is to identify them with us, not us with them. We have to assume that there are many ways in which they are *not* like us, and we have to try to identify with *them*, see the world from *their* different point of view, and deal with them in the ways *they* consider conducive to cooperative relations. To get everybody together in a village in India, for example, and assume that by open democratic discussion in an informal and permissive atmosphere something constructive will necessarily emerge may be the antithesis of a truly community-centered approach. It assumes that how we want to do things is how others want to do them. Uncritically to export techniques suitable to a community-centered approach in the United States or Great Britain is to indulge one's ethnocentrism. To become other-oriented is to accept differences and to live and work with other people. If we cannot accept and work with other people as they are, identify with them as they are, we shall never succeed in putting into productive practice the lessons that we presume we have already learned from the record of our failures.

Our task, then, will be to explore as fully as we can just what a community-centered approach seems to imply for those who engage in development work.

THE PROBLEM OF RESISTANCE

The foregoing considerations have an obvious bearing on the problem of community resistance, which from the viewpoint of development agencies, is the major obstacle to achieving technical and administrative objectives. There are varying degrees and forms of resistance, ranging from apathy and inertia to open hostility. It may be expressed as simple noncooperation, as quiet sabotage under cover of pretended cooperation, as organized political counter-movements, or even by resort to destructive violence or armed uprisings. For the administrator and field agent, the problem to be solved is how to reduce resistance or forestall it and win the community's cooperation in carrying out a program.

From our point of view, resistance is a sign that there are unresolved problems in the change situation. These problems may arise from within the community itself for a variety of reasons independent of the way in which a change agent conducts himself; they may be inevitable by-products of the change process itself; or they may arise as a direct result of the agent's own conduct in working with the community. Whatever their source, coercion is likely to magnify these problems, although it may result in the temporary accomplishment of some purely technical objective.

Once convinced of the rightness of his program or given a time-table for which he is answerable to his superiors, an administrator will be inclined to resort to greater and greater coercive pressure whenever his efforts at winning cooperation by other means prove ineffective. Development projects that are undertaken for the best of technical reasons, with the welfare of the community as the prime consideration, and with sincere intention to enlist the community's voluntary cooperation, too frequently become transformed into police actions. When developing agencies have police or other coercive powers at their direct disposal, they seem ever ready to use them as their solution to the problem of resistance. The soil conservation and stock reduction program among the Navaho Indians is a case in point. There was no question of a need for stock reduction in order to halt extensive overgrazing and serious erosion of the land. The role of livestock in Navaho values, however, made a voluntary approach to reduction a delicate matter. Once fully alerted to the problem, however, agency personnel were pushed by a sense of urgency, and this made it difficult for them to be patient with Navaho objections. As resistance mounted and the possibility for voluntary cooperation declined, coercive pressures were increasingly brought to bear, including the use of court orders and the threat of imprisonment for failure to comply with what were now issued as program directives.[8]

Sometimes, to be sure, the subsequent course of events makes coercion appear to have been justified. Enforced planting of coconuts a generation ago in what was then the Mandated Territory of New Guinea provided a resource now widely appreciated. But it is safe to say that coercion is rationalized on the grounds that its benefits will be appreciated later far more often than subsequent events justify. And even when positive results are obtained, they are almost invariably offset in some degree by resentment of the coercion itself, a resentment that may seriously jeopardize the possibility of cooperation in the future. Coercion may get results, but rarely those at which it aims.[9]

We get insight into the meaning of resistance from psychiatry, where resistance to the therapeutic situation, to the therapist, or to discussion of certain areas in the client's experience is a common phenomenon. To overcome such resistance by coercive pressure would largely defeat the therapeutic objectives, if indeed it were possible so to overcome it. Signs of resistance have the important function of apprising the therapist as to what, for his client, is sensitive ground. Resistance shows up the sore spots, the problems with which therapy must eventually come to grips. In community development, also, resistance can convey useful information to change agents. This, of course, depends on their understanding the meaning of resistance in the development situation and their attitude toward the community and the development process. Whatever else resistance may indicate, it obviously serves notice that the conditions for cooperation between agent and community are in jeopardy. Because he is committed to implementing constructive change, it is an agent's professional responsibility, just as it is a psychiatrist's, to see that the necessary conditions for cooperation are met, insofar as it is within his power.

The several ways in which a development agent can effectively prepare himself to exercise this responsibility represent the professional requirements for his work. These requirements are:

1. An agent should be acquainted with scientific theory regarding human behavior. He needs to be sophisticated about human motives, the subjective factors so important in all human relationships.

2. He should have a clear idea of the nature and properties of what is being changed, in this case customs and institutions, ideas and beliefs. He must understand how these things function in human affairs, the processes by which they undergo change, and the effects of their change on people.

3. He must know how to gain accurate knowledge of the local situation, how to learn what the community's particular resources, customs, institutions, beliefs, and needs are. To do this, he must know what to look for and how to look for it. If he imposes on the local scene a stereotype of underdeveloped communities, he is not likely to discover what the realities are.

4. He must be free to conduct himself in ways that befit his knowledge of the local situation, his general understanding of function and process pertaining to human institutions and customs, and his professional objective as a development agent. This requires that he be aware of the forces and influences that inhibit his freedom of action: his own needs and motives, customs and values; the problems of living and working in a strange social and cultural environment; the organization of his agency; and the interests of other segments of the larger society or nation of which the client community forms a part.

5. He must know where to turn for competent help in order to enlarge his understanding and improve his knowledge of the local situation.

6. He must make his own operations as development agent an object of study. By making predictions and checking their outcome, by keeping a careful record of his experience and subjecting it to periodic analysis, and by explicitly formulating his conclusions and communicating them to others, he will contribute to the knowledge and understanding on which the practice of his profession must rest.

The body of this book deals with matters relating to the first four of these requirements. Part I provides a theoretical framework that can serve as a beginning for meeting the first and second requirements. Part II considers questions relating to the fourth requirement and, in its last two chapters, gives the reader a brief glimpse of the technical subject matter he must master in order to meet the third.

SUGGESTED READING

Batten, T. R., *Communities and Their Development:* An Introductory Study with Special Reference to the Tropics. Oxford University Press, London, 1957. See especially Chapter 5.

Tax, Sol, "The Freedom to Make Mistakes," *América Indígena*, vol. 16, 1956, pp. 171–177.

NOTES TO CHAPTER 2

1. See, for example, the refusal of the people of Viru, Peru, to use the new wells provided for them, as reported by Allan R. Holmberg, "The Wells That Failed," in Spicer, Edward H., editor, *Human Problems in Technological Change:* A Casebook, Russell Sage Foundation, New York, 1952, pp. 113–123.

2. Hoselitz, Bert F., "Non-Economic Barriers to Economic Development," *Economic Development and Cultural Change*, vol. 1, 1952, p. 16.

3. This problem has been discussed by David C. McClelland in "Community Development and the Nature of Human Motivation: Some Implications of Recent Research," a paper presented at the Conference on Community Development, Center for International Studies, Massachusetts Institute of Technology, December 13–15, 1957.

4. Similarly in industrial relations, it has been found that when management was unaware of, and went contrary to, the workers' sentiments in proposing a logical program in the workers' economic interest, the program could not be completed successfully. See Roethlisberger, F. J., *Management and Morale*, Harvard University Press, Cambridge, Mass., 1941, p. 64.

5. Buchanan, Norman S., and Howard S. Ellis, *Approaches to Economic Development.* Twentieth Century Fund, New York, 1955.

6. *Ibid.*, p. 90.

7. Sumner, William Graham, *Folkways:* A Study of the Sociological Importance of Usages, Manners, Customs, Mores, and Morals, Ginn and Co., Boston, 1907, pp. 12–15. See also Murdock, G. P., "Ethnocentrism," *Encyclopaedia of the Social Sciences*, vol. 5, 1931, pp. 613–614.

8. Spicer, Edward H., "Sheepmen and Technicians" in Spicer, Edward H., editor, *op. cit.*, pp. 185–207. See also Kimball, Solon T., "The Crisis in Colonial Administration," *Applied Anthropology*, vol. 5, no. 2, 1946, pp. 8–16. See the comment on coercion by David E. Lillienthal in *TVA—Democracy on the March*, Harper and Bros., New York, 1953, p. 195.

9. For a forceful statement of this point, see Tax, Sol, "The Freedom to Make Mistakes," *América Indígena*, vol. 16, 1956, pp. 176–177.

Part 1

THEORY

Chapter 3

WANTS AND NEEDS

W<small>HEN OUTSIDE ADMINISTRATORS</small> tour the communities whose welfare they have some official responsibility for, it is not unusual to hear them exclaim over conditions they discover, concluding with the statement, "What this place needs is. . . ." If they send someone in to study the situation more closely, they will receive a report detailing the conditions observed and closing with a set of recommendations to the same effect, that "What this place needs is. . . ." Such has been the start of many a development program. Because it is so easy to know what somebody else needs, but so difficult to persuade him to do anything about it, we tend to see the problem of cooperation as coping with apathy or resistance and to locate the source of difficulties in the attitudes of our clients. That difficulties may largely stem from our own assumptions about what they need is not likely to receive serious attention. What they need usually seems so obvious.

But a change agent and his clients do not usually want the same things or have the same view of the development situation and its requirements. This, we have seen, is at the root of the problem of cooperation in change. As development agents, therefore, we must have some understanding of human motivation. This is no simple matter, for students of behavior are still trying to arrive at a satisfactory theory of motives. Our discussion of wants and needs cannot reflect any definitive position, but it will present a framework that has relevance for the practical problems facing agents of change.

There are in this connection a number of questions for us to consider. We must try to understand why wants differ. As long as the wants of others remain inexplicable to us, we shall find it difficult to give them the kind of respect cooperation requires. We have also to see how wants relate to needs, if we are to reconcile the specific wants of a community's members with what appears to us to be required in order to enhance their well-being. We have to understand the relationship of wants and needs to customs and beliefs. Otherwise we will not be able to understand the conditions under which people resist efforts to change their customs and beliefs, or appreciate, for that matter, the source of many of their wants. Wants, needs, and their relation to customs will necessarily be an ever-present consideration throughout this book. In this chapter we shall try to deal with them in elementary terms and see what practical conclusions we can come to at this level of treatment. Our first task will be to define more clearly what we mean by wants and needs.

To begin with, when we speak of a community's problems as its members see them, just what do we imply? Obviously, what their problems are depends in part on the state of affairs they want to achieve or maintain, that is, their *wants*. Their problems also depend on how they perceive their present circumstances and what they understand to be the actions that will be effective in achieving or maintaining what they want. From their point of view, these actions and the conditions that make them possible are what they *need*. If they want a year-round water supply, for example, then they need a dam, aqueduct, or artesian well, and all of the things that their construction requires. If they have productive soil and want to keep it that way, then they need to use manure, crop rotation, or some other effective device their circumstances will permit. By wants, then, we refer to desired states of affairs, and by needs we refer to effective means for achieving or maintaining them.[1]

We may, of course, want something because we feel that we need it in order to gratify some other want. A youth, for example, wants an automobile because he feels he needs it in order effectively to pursue a number of goals. Thus wants and needs link together in chains such that any link (other than the terminal one) may be regarded as a want or a need, depending on whether we are looking at it as a goal or as the means to a goal. The great bulk of a person's specific wants, therefore, are things he feels he needs with reference to more remote wants. Some of his wants, on the other hand, appear to him simply as ends in themselves. The fact that wants tend to become needs and needs wants, according to how we look at them, does not make the distinction between them a meaningless one. Most human behavior is, after all, goal-oriented. People have purposes, whether well or ill defined, whether conscious or repressed, and organize their actions with reference to accomplishing them. In any situation there are both immediate and long-range purposes and there are courses of action and supporting conditions that are needed to achieve them. Wants and needs can be usefully differentiated and employed as conceptual coordinates in analyzing human activities.

WANTS

As we have defined them, wants may refer to particular arrangements in the world around us or to particular feeling states within ourselves. The ultimate referents for all our wants, however, are the feeling states within us with which we are content.

The reasons we value some feeling states and not others are complex and far from completely understood. Inherent in our physical makeup are tendencies to positive and negative orientations toward some of the many feeling states we experience, such as our negative orientation to sensations of nausea or pain. But there are no such tendencies with other feeling states. For example, we have no built-in approach or withdrawal tendencies relating to visual sensations *per se*, except to such things as extremes of light intensity. There are wide ranges of touch sensation that are equally neutral as far as our inborn reaction patterns are concerned. These originally neutral sensations acquire positive or negative value, or continue to remain neutral, according to how they become linked in experience with sensations to which we have biologically determined value orientations. Thus the ways in which people react to many presumably similar sensations vary according to the kinds of sensations they have already experienced and according to how these sensations have been mutually associated in their experience, as psychological experiments in conditioning have shown. So it is that some people are delighted and others repelled by the same foodstuffs; some, like certain North American Indians, seek hallucinatory experiences, and others, like us, avoid them. Even sensations to which we have automatically positive or negative orientation may by their associations acquire a degree of opposite value for us. Thus we may take a perverse pleasure in pain, as with the masochistic rites of some religious sects or the ritual self-torture on which some American Indian societies placed such high value.[2] No external arrangements or personal relationships to them, of course, have any value for us unless we learn to associate them with comfortable and uncomfortable feeling states within ourselves.

Given the wide ranges of difference in individual experience and in the kinds of associations that may result, we must expect people to show quite different orientations toward things and even, to some extent, toward their own internal feeling states. Since by wants we refer to the whole range of things internal and external to which we are affectively oriented, it is evident that no two persons are going to be the same with respect to all their wants.

People who grow up and live together in the same community will normally share a larger number of experiences and a larger number of associations than any one of them is likely to share with an outsider. If this is so, we expect that members of the same community will have more wants in common than they will share with outsiders, however much they differ among themselves. The members of a large, complex community will probably share fewer wants, for this reason, than will the members of a small, simple one. Certainly, we may expect an agent of change and one of his clients to share fewer wants with each other than either shares with members of his own community.

Differences in what people specifically want are frequently obscured by our tendency to interpret analogous wants as if they were the same. One man wants bread when he feels hungry and another wants potatoes. Because both wants are seen as means to a similar end, they are analogous, and we say that both men want food. Yet when people are without food and we give them some, they often reject it as not the kind of food they want. What some people prize, others abhor. To be sure, the analogies we observe between other people's wants and our own help to make their behavior intelligible to us. As we get to know them better and draw more analogies we feel we understand them better. In this way we get a sense that all people are, after all, very much alike. But while analogies help us understand each other, they do not provide common goals for joint action. Two hungry men will cooperate to get bread if they both want bread, but not so well if one wants only potatoes. On the other hand, people who want the same thing for reasons that are not analogous at all have a basis for cooperation in their common want. Common wants of the moment have made many a strange bedfellow.

Given great differences in specific wants, especially among people from different communities, it stands to reason that an agent must expect his clients to express some wants with which he cannot easily sympathize. They may, for example, want to spend all their earnings, beyond those needed for barest subsistence, on feasts and ceremonies. Or they may want to strengthen and maintain social distinctions of a sort that are repellent to the agent in the light of his own values. But this is no reason for dismissing his clients' wants as unworthy of consideration. It is with reference to *their* wants, not his, that they will decide to cooperate with him.

NEEDS

Given a desire for a particular state of affairs, the effective means for achieving it are whatever will transform the existing state into the desired one. What our needs are necessarily depends on the conditions we want and how existing conditions differ from them. Our nutritional needs, for example, depend among other things on what state of health we want, what body weight we want, how much energy we want to be able to expend, and how much our present condition departs from the one that is optimal for these wants.

For any set of circumstances, the actions and conditions, if any, that will satisfy a given want are presumably matters of fact, things that can be objectively determined. No one may have yet discovered an effective means for gratifying a want, but that does not mean that one does not exist. We are still looking for a means of preventing or controlling cancer, for example. It may turn out that there isn't any, but this remains to be determined by further research into its nature and causes. People have many wants that they are unable to satisfy, either because the effective means do not exist or because they are unavailable or remain unknown to them.

What people see as needed to gratify a want is not necessarily what is needed in fact. What they see depends on their cognitive knowledge: what states of affairs they have learned to discern, what they believe to be the relations between them, and what they understand to be the processes by which one state can be transformed into another. Their need as they see it may or may not be an effective means, in fact, for satisfying their want. Reciting incantations is not an effective means of preventing rain, for example. Since the cognitive knowledge of a change agent is not the same as that of his clients, there is likely to be a difference between them as to what they consider an effective means of achieving a goal on which they have agreed. And neither the agent's nor his client's view of what is needed will necessarily have any close resemblance to the view an omniscient observer would have.

In order to keep the different perspectives on needs clearly distinct we shall use the expression "felt need" to refer only to a client's need as he perceives it, whether it is realistic or not. His needs as others, including change agents, see them are his "observed needs." Neither should be confused with his "real needs": the most effective means that an omniscient observer would select for gratifying the client's wants.

People have a not unnatural tendency to assume that what they perceive to be needed to accomplish a particular goal is what an omniscient observer would also perceive. Agents of change, accordingly, often assume that what they see as their clients' needs are their real needs, given their wants. Technical assistance programs to underdeveloped communities are, of course, predicated on the assumption that change agents are technically better equipped to discern effective means of meeting certain wants than are the community's members. But it is well to remind ourselves that what we observe to be needed is not necessarily what is really needed at all. Agents may know better, but they rarely know best.

For a given set of conditions, moreover, there is frequently more than one course of action that will gratify a want. Which is most effective depends on how it affects conditions pertaining to other wants that one happens to have at the same time. For this reason we must qualify our definition of a need. In any situation, the need is for a course of action that will be of maximum net efficacy in relation to the gratification of all of one's wants. That is to say, for each want there is need for that one among the several possible means of gratifying it which will at the same time either maximally promote the gratification of other wants or minimally interfere with their continued gratification.

This implies, of course, that when two people have some want in common but differ concerning their other wants, any suggested course of action for meeting their common want will have a different net efficacy for each of them. What seems highly effective to one may strike the other as undesirable because of the effect he anticipates it will have on his ability to satisfy his other wants. This, it appears, is a not infrequent source of client resistance to particular proposals for change. Very often, for example, people will reject offers of help in achieving something they want very much because to accept them in the form in which they are made would have adverse consequences on their desire to maintain their self-respect. We never adequately anticipate, moreover, how a course of action will alter all the conditions affecting our other wants. Only after we have embarked on it, do we begin to discover its consequences. Whenever, in development work, an agent encounters growing resistance to a program for which there was initial enthusiasm, it means that it is interfering in some way with the gratification of other wants that are important to his clients.

It should be evident by now that even when we feel able to speak of someone's real needs, as we have defined them, we are not referring to something of an absolute nature. What a person needs depends on what he, or someone else observing him, wants and how his present circumstances relate to it. If this is so, how can we speak of any needs as universal to mankind?

There is a sense in which we may and, indeed, necessarily do speak of needs as universal. They derive their universality in part from the fact that all men share in the biological endowments that characterize Man as a species. These endowments make it possible for them to experience certain feeling states in common. In the presence of certain universal conditions of human existence, such as a long period of infant dependency and lifelong membership in social groups, all people are likely to have experienced a number of the same feeling states, though not with the same frequencies. By virtue of their common endowments, moreover, all people are likely to have similar orientations toward at least some of these feeling states. The wants that they thus have in common become associated with different kinds of specific objects as instruments of their gratification, to be sure, but all of these objects have certain common properties required by the nature of the want itself. To gratify our hunger, for example, we need something edible to eat. We can properly speak of a universal need for food in general, although we cannot speak of a universal need for any particular food. There are other needs, moreover, that derive their universality not so much from common wants but from the universality of the general conditions of wanting. All people, that is, *have* wants of some kind, and at least some of these wants they can gratify only by purposive action of their own. For some of them, moreover, whatever action is possible will, if taken, preclude the possibility of gratifying others of their wants. The actions people take, moreover, are in a social milieu where there are other people with competing wants of their own. If we ignore what is wanted and simply consider that there are wants and that they arise under certain universally prevailing circumstances, then it is evident that human beings require certain conditions if they are to gratify wants at all. These conditions, too, may well be called universal needs. We shall consider them along with the needs stemming from common wants in Chapter 4.

There is another sense in which people sometimes use the expression "universal human needs." Here, needs derive from what is believed to be a universal moral order that defines the goals toward which all men should work. Universal needs of this sort have a moral "ought" attached to them that is independent of human volition. Since there is no universal agreement as to what these moral orders are, and since their existence must be predicated on faith, they cannot provide a scientific basis for considering universal needs. From a practical standpoint, moreover, our personal beliefs concerning the moral order can easily become a cover under which we project our own wants upon our clients. Thus when we say that all people *need* to be free of pain, we are likely to imply that we ourselves have wants that cannot be gratified unless other people are free of pain. They may want to be free of it, indeed, but what we refer to as their need is very often a function of our own want. Similarly, when we say that infants need love, what we often mean is that we want them to grow up to exhibit the characteristics of persons who have been loved.[3] Many of the needs that we attribute to people for reason of our own wants and moral values may also be attributed to them by virtue of the universal conditions of human existence mentioned above. But if we use our own wants and values as the basis for determining what is universally needed by others, we reduce our effectiveness as agents of change. We will be likely to attribute such cooperation as we get to motives that our clients do not have, and we will tend to have false expectations about the things that will interest them. Some agents of religious change, for example, making assumptions about the universal needs of the soul in keeping with their own values, are notoriously naive about the motives that made converts of their clients.

From our point of view, then, when an agent of change decides that an underdeveloped community has certain needs, he must be careful to make clear to himself what his points of reference are. The community's needs as he sees them depend on what he wants for the community and on how present conditions appear to him to depart therefrom. What he wants for the community, moreover, is not unrelated to what he wants for himself. An agent's assessment of local conditions, furthermore, may or may not coincide with that of his clients, and his wants for them may have little relation to their wants for themselves. This means that he and his clients will be able to agree as to what are the community's needs only insofar as they agree regarding (1) their wants for the community, (2) their understanding of present conditions and how they differ from those wanted, and (3) what course of action is an effective means of transforming present conditions into those desired. Practically speaking, what a community *needs* for its development is not so much a matter of fact as a matter to be negotiated.

MULTIPLE PERSPECTIVES ON NEEDS

Determining a workable course of action for development requires reconciling several different pictures of what the community needs. When we try to schematize the problem, it appears that there are four perspectives which result from the difference in goals that an agent and his clients have for a community and the different views they have as to what would be an effective means of achieving each set of goals.

To illustrate the situation, let us suppose that a development agent has as his principal aim reducing the amount of sickness in a community. What is needed to accomplish this, he feels, is for everyone to use privies and to consult the physicians in a nearby clinic when they are ill. What the community's members see as needed to reduce sickness is to find out who the witches are who are causing it and to get stronger charms against them. The problem of sickness, however, is not their major concern at all. High in their scale of wants is to be able to live at a level of material comfort equivalent to that for which they envy other people. They see themselves at a disadvantage because they lack the qualifications for entry and advancement in the status system of the larger outside world where material comfort prevails. What they need, therefore, are educational facilities that will qualify them to escape from their present condition and enter that other world from which they are now excluded. The agent, however, sees their material well-being as best improved by increasing the efficiency of agricultural production in order to produce cash crops.

Reconciling these aims and ideas as to appropriate means might be accomplished by focusing on the development of school facilities, which is what the community's members see as needed to accomplish their objectives. Interest in improving agricultural production could be stimulated on the grounds that it would be needed to help defray the expenses of a school. In the school, principles of hygiene and an understanding of the causes of sickness could be taught as something one had to understand in order to achieve the goal of entry into the larger social order. This, incidentally, illustrates what it means to work in terms of one's clients' felt needs.

Schematically, then, there are four views of a community's need. There is the agent's view with his own goals in mind, and there is his view with his clients' goals in mind. Then there is the clients' view of what is appropriate to the agent's goals as well as their view of what should be done to achieve their own goals. When we take all four views into account, a major cause of failure in development work becomes obvious. Too often, as we have just indicated, a technical consultant appraises his clients' circumstances and draws conclusions about their needs with reference to only one of these four perspectives. Recommendations are almost invariably based on what the technical experts themselves want for their clients or assume *a priori* that their clients want.[4] To investigate what their clients want and how they regard their circumstances is, after all, beyond the competence of most technical experts in such things as health, agriculture, or irrigation. For this reason alone their recommendations are seldom related to what the community's members actually want or feel they need. Yet, their recommendations cannot be implemented programmatically unless their clients' wants are taken into account, as case studies so regularly show.[5]

In community development someone must take responsibility for assessing what is needed for programmatic purposes with all four of these points of view in mind. The only person who can do this is the development agent. Although a teacher may enlist the aid of other experts, such as child psychologists, it is ultimately his responsibility to respond to the emotional and other needs of his pupils and to adjust the method and pace of his teaching accordingly. Similarly, a development agent may appropriately enlist the aid of such experts as anthropologists or sociologists, but the responsibility for taking full account of his clients' wants and view of their needs is inescapably his. Whatever other professional qualifications he should have for his role as agent, the ability to exercise this responsibility must be counted as one of them.

Although practical reasons for being well acquainted with one's clients' wants and felt needs are now apparent, we are not yet ready to consider the more technical question of how a development agent is to go about discovering what these wants are. What people want is by no means always obvious either to themselves or to an observer. In order to know what people want, we have to know how to interpret their behavior. This requires an understanding of the relation between wants and behavior. Within the context of community development, of course, we are especially concerned with the relation of wants and needs to customary behavior, to the activities in which people habitually engage and to the beliefs that they habitually express.

SUGGESTED READING

Erasmus, Charles J., *Man Takes Control:* Cultural Development and American Aid. University of Minnesota Press, Minneapolis, 1961.

Galbraith, John Kenneth, "The Poverty of Nations," *The Atlantic Monthly*, vol. 210, October, 1962, pp. 47–53.

Symposium, "Economic Motivations and Stimulations in Underdeveloped Countries," *International Social Science Bulletin*, vol. 6, no. 3, 1954.

NOTES TO CHAPTER 3

1. Other theorists have defined "needs" differently. For example, in *A Scientific Theory of Culture and Other Essays*, University of North Carolina Press, Chapel Hill, 1944 (A Galaxy Book, Oxford University Press, New York, 1960), p. 90, Bronislaw Malinowski says, "By need . . . I understand the system of conditions in the human organism, in the cultural setting, and in the relation of both to the natural environment, which are sufficient and necessary to the survival of the group." Whereas for him, needs are the sufficient conditions for group survival, for us they are the sufficient conditions for accomplishing desired ends.

2. Bowers, Alfred W., *Mandan Social and Ceremonial Organization*, University of Chicago Press, Chicago, 1950; Lowie, Robert H., *The Crow Indians*, Farrar and Rinehart, Inc., New York, 1935.

3. Because the "needs" of others so often turn out to be reflections of the observer's wants, some social scientists prefer not to speak of needs at all, but only of wants. See, for example, Barnett, H. G., *Innovation:* The Basis of Cultural Change, McGraw-Hill Book Co., New York, 1953, pp. 98–100.

4. See, for example, the way in which the Anchau Rural Development Scheme was planned in Nigeria, as reported by T. A. M. Nash in *The Anchau Rural Development and Settlement Scheme*, H. M. Stationery Office, London, 1948.

5. See how clients' wants affected the outcome in Spicer, Edward H., editor, *Human Relations in Technological Change:* A Casebook, Russell Sage Foundation, New York, 1952. (Cases 2, 3, 6, 7, 10, 11, 12.)

Chapter 4

CUSTOM AND FUNCTION

WHAT INVITES ATTENTION to custom as a phenomenon is the contrasting behavior that one observes from society to society. If everyone lived in the same way, following the same conventions, there would be no noticeable differences to make us aware of what we call custom. At the same time, the fact of difference generates toward other peoples attitudes that prejudice the view we take of them and their customs. As we indicated in our discussion of ethnocentrism in Chapter 2, when people behave like members of our own community, we identify with them easily, whereas it is hard to identify with them or to regard them as in any way like us when they behave very differently.

The attitudes Europeans and Americans commonly exhibit toward other peoples and their customs reveal such ethnocentric bias. They reflect in this regard several points of view that were in vogue in intellectual circles in the nineteenth century and that the findings of anthropologists are only gradually dispelling.

One of these is the view that the world's nonindustrial and technologically simple societies represent stages of technological and cultural development through which our own ancestors once passed but which they have failed to outgrow. This presumed failure is usually attributed to an imagined natural inferiority of mental powers. Being at a lower or earlier stage of civilization they are more *primitive*. This view was common in scientific circles in the nineteenth century[1] and was widely disseminated among laymen with the popularization of evolutionary theory. Equally ethnocentric is the old view that the nonwestern peoples of the world have degenerated in varying degree from an original

61

high and noble estate still most perfectly represented in ourselves. Once widely held, this view of human differences lost ground as evolutionary theory and the idea of progress became popular. But echoes of the degeneration hypothesis still reverberate in some religious circles. Both views are, of course, greatly reinforced by the Christian assumption of religious superiority.

A third conception of nonwestern peoples expresses the other side of the ethnocentric coin. Those who are in intellectual revolt against the institutions of western society are inclined to identify themselves with exotic peoples, not simply with the object of understanding them, but in response to some private compulsions of their own. The lenses of romantic prejudice are those of ethnocentrism turned around. They distort equally in the opposite direction.

The last view is, however, much less common than those expressive of ethnocentric bias. Most of us assume that our customs are superior and, in one way or another, tend to patronize people whose customs differ. With this often goes the feeling that all we have to do is to expose people to our way of doing things, and they will, if they have any intelligence, quickly recognize its superiority and seek to emulate it. The following quotation illustrates this view.

> The New Guinea natives in their primitive condition have no culture worthy of the name. They are completely illiterate and have no understanding of hygiene. Consequently, the great majority of them, when first met by Europeans, are found to be dominated by witchcraft and sorcery; they are almost constantly embroiled in intertribal war; and they are very susceptible to common diseases— seen especially in high infant mortality, and a general tendency to skin diseases.
>
> The most noticeable results of contact with, and control by, Europeans are the improved social conditions brought about by the abolition of intertribal fighting and the rapidity with which they respond to community cleanliness and simple medical attention. In these directions both Missions and Administration have had remarkable results. It is claimed that these facts show how quickly these native races would respond to European care and instruction, once they could be fully reached through some common medium of instruction.[*2]

* Reprinted by permission from R. W. Robson, *Handbook of Papua and New Guinea*, *1954*. Pacific Publications, Pty. Ltd., Sydney, Australia. Copyright by Pacific Publications, Pty. Ltd.

Other people in the world, like us, tend to ethnocentric evaluations of human differences. Other things being equal, it is, of course, more practical to operate in ways with which one is familiar. Everywhere, therefore, people seem to be inclined to look upon their own customs as natural, most sensible, or best.[3]

The findings of behavioral scientists do not support these common, ethnocentric attitudes toward human differences. We have noted already that what people want depends in large part on the associations they have learned to make in the course of their experience. Similarly, students of behavior find that to a very large degree people do what they have learned to do. There are, it seems, no genetic factors that predetermine the exact forms human behavior takes. Biological heredity sets limits to what *can* be learned by an individual, but it does not determine what *is* learned. What is learned is forged from experience and necessarily varies with experience.

As members of a single species, all men appear to be equipped with similar capacities for learning. There are some individual differences in this regard, to be sure. It is not improbable that the distribution of these differences, as with some other genetic characters, varies from one community to another. But there are two things that are important to emphasize. First, it has not yet been possible to devise objective tests of *innate* mental capacities. All existing intelligence tests require the use of developed capacities based on learning and experience.[4] As yet, therefore, we have no objective measure of the differences between populations in regard to inborn abilities. Second, the subjective evaluations of field anthropologists agree substantially that whatever the differences between human populations are, they are not great. Although there may be far fewer areas of specialized knowledge in one community than in another, the number of things the average individual is likely to have learned in either seems to be fairly equal.

We conclude, then, that the established modes of action and belief, to which we refer as a people's customs, are something they have made out of experience, the distillates, as it were, of their history. And the fact that customs differ reflects different learning experiences rather than different genetic endowments.

CUSTOMS AND NEEDS

If customs are the product of learning, what we know about learning allows us to draw further conclusions about them. Experimental studies indicate that particular modes of action become habitual when they prove reasonably effective in gratifying recurring wants. Once these actions are perceived to be effective, there is a felt need to perform them whenever circumstances give rise to the wants with which they have become associated. The longer and more reliably they continue to gratify wants, the more firmly established they become as obviously appropriate ways of acting. Should they cease to be rewarding, they will tend to drop out of the individual's behavioral repertoire. The inference is that customs, as shared habits, must be gratifying in some way to the majority of a society's members (or of those who wield power in it) if they are to persist.[5] The known history of every society is replete with occasions in which established practices and institutions have been allowed to lapse when they ceased to gratify people adequately.

If the chronic or recurring problems facing us result from the way in which conditions tend regularly to depart from those we want, then our customs, as relatively satisfying solutions to our problems, may be said to answer our needs. They do not answer perfectly, of course; and, while gratifying some of our wants, they may actually work to frustrate the gratification of other wants in ways we do not suspect, as we shall soon have occasion to consider. That they persist, however, is *prima facie* evidence that we perceive them in our experience as serving desired ends.

There are a number of common problems to which every society must find solutions if it is to survive. This brings us back to the subject of universal needs briefly touched on in the preceding chapter. Among them, we noted, are those that reflect the universal categories of wants arising from the biological nature of Man, such as the various wants associated with states of physical comfort. Needs for food, shelter, sex partners, companions, and cures for ailments, for example, are felt everywhere. There are, moreover, the universal needs that arise because people have wants at all and can gratify them only by their own actions or the actions of others. The numbered paragraphs below, outline the universal needs that arise in this way.

1. In order to do something about their wants, people need to have sensory contact with their surroundings. They need a vocabulary of constructs by which to discriminate things around them, feelings within themselves, and ways in which they interconnect. They need to be oriented, in short, in terms of some coherent and internally consistent cognitive system.

2. People need to know what rearrangements of existing conditions as they discern them will lead to gratification of their wants. They need to know what courses of action will be effective. If people must rely on others to inform them, as all must, they need some means of communicating information; and if they must derive information from analysis of their own experience, they need some way of vicariously or symbolically recapitulating and manipulating experience and the discernments they have already learned to make. They need, that is, a means by which to reason.

3. People need power to alter conditions, either directly through their own skills or indirectly by commanding the strength and skills of others. If they must rely on their own strength and skills, they need opportunities to develop them. If they must rely on the strength and skills of others, they must be able to count on them when they are felt to be needed. To this end people need to be valued by others, to have their own needs a matter of concern to others; and, in varying degrees, they need by their own conduct to be able to affect the conditions that gratify or frustrate the wants of those on whom they must depend—to have power over them—so as thereby to control them.

4. Because people must rely on one another for help in gratifying their respective wants and, consequently, must live together cooperatively, they are faced with the problems raised by conflicting and competing wants. They need clear definitions as to rights, duties, and privileges relating to the exercise of their powers and the powers of others. In short, they need a social system.

5. People, finally, need to have confidence in the reality of their discernments, the validity of their knowledge, and the

adequacy and reliability of their information. They need confidence in the sufficiency of their powers and in the benignity of others who have power over them. They need to feel confident that others will abide by the rules of the social order. Above all, people need a sense of certainty that enough of their wants will eventually be gratified so as to give purpose to their past and promise to their future. The conditions we need in order to gratify our wants may obtain in fact, but if we do not believe that they do, we are not likely to take the actions they make possible.

Many things we regularly associate with custom have obvious connection with the broad categories of need just outlined. Beliefs, for example, relate to the needs for cognitive orientation, knowledge of means-ends relationships, and the sense of confidence. Language simultaneously meets the needs to transmit information and to reason. Educational practices serve to provide the needed physical and intellectual skills. Social customs, tabus, morals, and legal institutions all help to define rights, duties, and privileges, to rationalize them as just, and to give us confidence that people will do as we expect them to do. And many beliefs and practices of the sort we label as religious or magical help to promote confidence that our discernments are true and our knowledge valid, that we are in control of events where we need to be, and that our wants will eventually be fully gratified.

As the foregoing suggests, when we classify customs as economic, religious, recreational, political, and so on, we do not refer to the similarity of their particular forms but to the kinds of things they accomplish for people or are aimed at accomplishing. Such a classification, indeed, derives its universal applicability precisely because it reflects universal wants and needs without reference to the actual procedures by which they are satisfied. The commonality of interests that it reflects provides the basis for establishing the analogies between formally different customs, just as universal wants establish the analogies between felt needs. These analogies, as we have noted, give us the sense that all peoples, when one gets to know them well, are familiarly human. Hottentots are as offended by bad manners in others as we are. Sickness and death are a source of anxiety for everyone. There are no people who do not find it necessary to their mental well-being to relieve the humdrum round of everyday work with recreation and entertainment. All peoples, in short, have their codes of courtesy, morality, and modesty. All of them hold down competition between the sexes through a division of labor; regulate the consumption of raw materials and manufactured products through a system of property law; outlaw marriage within the immediate family as incestuous and value permanent marital arrangements; regulate their relations with one another by clearly defined mutual rights and duties; have dealings with the "supernatural"; and find it helpful in the face of recurring crises to invest them with drama and ritual.[6] For all of these there are common needs of some kind.

Because there are a number of common needs posing problems for which all people have had to find solutions, it does not follow that there is only one effective solution per problem. All people, for example, recognize certain acts as formally uniting a man and woman in what we would call marriage, but the form of these acts is highly varied. If an American man and woman become formally married at that point in the proceedings when the minister or court pronounces them man and wife, a man and woman of Truk in the Caroline Islands become formally married when the bride calls the groom to supper and he enters the house to join her and her family at the evening meal for the first time. To anyone who thinks of marriage in terms of American forms alone, the Trukese couple is living in sin. Yet each society is faced with the same problem: how to know when a man and woman are properly married; and each customary form satisfactorily solves it. With some types of problem the number of possible forms that will meet them is virtually infinite. This is especially true with problems of symbolism such as the one just illustrated, where almost any form, provided there is social agreement on it, will serve.[7] Where this is the case, the form a custom takes may be viewed as largely a matter of chance. The same need may be effectively met by customs of widely different form.

Although different communities have many needs in common, it is obvious that there are also many differences in the kinds of problem they must solve. Different natural environments not only pose different problems but also limit the possible solutions to similar ones in different ways. People must devise solutions with the resources available to them. On coral atolls, for example, it is impractical to keep domesticated animals on anything but a small scale, for land animals compete with man for the same food supply and do not provide enough additional food to compensate for what they consume. Customary practices that work well in one setting may not work well in another.

Once established, moreover, each custom becomes a part of the conceptual and behavioral environment within which other problems arise. As such, it will itself have a limiting effect on the forms that other customs can conveniently take. To illustrate this, we may reflect for a moment on our previous comparison between the ways in which Americans and Trukese determine when a man and woman are properly married. There is no reason why an American girl may not announce to a gentleman guest that dinner is served; but her counterpart in Truk must avoid any such action if she does not wish to be guilty of a *faux pas*.[8] The forms that Trukese customs relating to dinner guests can take are limited by customs relating to marriage. They are limited similarly by the form of Truk's many other customs. Customs, therefore, are only partially to be understood in terms of the problems they are directly aimed at solving. Their effect upon existing solutions to other problems, their net efficacy as we have called it, is an important consideration, also.

Indeed, one of the major problems facing the members of any society arises from the universal need so to integrate or systematize their various customs, beliefs, and values that they are reasonably compatible with each other. To cope with this problem all peoples have organized their customs into systems of behavior and thought, systems in which all the elements are interdependent in the sense that they all mutually condition the forms each may conveniently take. Thus in our own society, patterns of residential settlement and means of transportation to market and work have a limiting effect on each other. People make their residential choices with an eye to the transportation facilities available to them, and they appraise their transportation needs in terms of their residential locations. Our customary practices in regard to both residence and transportation are systematically interconnected. In India one thinks of caste organization and its relation to occupational specialization and the exchange of goods and services. Such systems, in turn, are geared to each other at least loosely in a single overall system, encompassing all the established customs and beliefs of a society's members. It is this systematic aspect of the whole that gives to every society a distinctive consistency which we colloquially term its "way of life."

It is not strange, then, that each of the world's societies should have distinctive customs, in spite of the universality of some wants and needs. On the contrary, it is the occurrence of similarities of form and detail, especially among people who are not in contact and in a position to borrow one another's customs, that is often more difficult to explain. In some instances, presumably, such similarities arise because the possible ways of meeting a common need are limited, so that on a purely chance basis more than one society will have hit upon the same one and from there have developed similar forms compatible with it.[9] The fact remains, however, that if at first sight it is the differences among societies that strike us as noteworthy, on closer scrutiny we often find the similarities harder to explain. Some of the major problems in anthropology concern explanations of this kind.[10]

There is a very practical reason for stressing the need-filling, want-gratifying role of custom in human affairs. Ethnocentrism leads us unthinkingly to appraise other people's customs from the standpoint of how well or ill we feel they would serve our own wants and felt needs. It is thus that we see their food as unappetizing or their rites as savage or barbarous. Such appraisals make it difficult for us to see customs as relatively efficacious instruments for meeting needs and gratifying wants. They incline us, too, to conclude that people who find satisfaction in some of the more bizarre things we see them do must be stupid or depraved. Other people, of course, whose wants and felt needs differ from ours, look at some of our customs in exactly the same way. We recall the utter disgust and horrified fascination with which people in the Gilbert Islands observed us frying and eating eggs for breakfast. As food, eggs are in their view like slugs in ours. If an agent of community development sees only the "harm" his clients' customs do from his point of view and fails to see the "good" they do from his clients' point of view, he will not be able to appreciate the reasons for their resistance to his proposals or to anticipate the points in the development process at which resistance will arise.

Important as it is, however, the fact that their customs are gratifying to people represents only a part of the story. It helps us understand their persistence as customs and some of the reasons people resist changing them. But it does not follow that people take pleasure in all their customs, nor are we to infer that customs are always adaptive as far as a society's survival is concerned. How, in view of what we have said, do we account for the persistence of customs that people find painful or unrewarding and that work against the collective welfare?

Customs That Do Not Gratify

We have said that if a custom fails to gratify people's wants or answer to their felt needs, they will tend to abandon it. Some conditions, however, impede this tendency.

The way in which a particular custom is integrated with other customs and beliefs into a larger system, for example, may make its abandonment a less rewarding prospect than its preservation. In our society, the great advances in medical practice of recent years present us increasingly with the spectacle of persons who suffer from painful and incurable illnesses having their lives prolonged, even against their own wishes, with the only result for them being an increase in the amount of suffering they must endure. We do not like this and wish that somehow it did not have to be. But we cannot condone mercy killings, because they are inconsistent with the great value we place on the sanctity of human life, a value we cannot compromise, so we feel, except at the cost of much that we find most rewarding in our way of life. The customs by which we gratify our more important wants and the beliefs by which we rationalize and integrate them provide a logic that compels us to adopt practices and cling to them even though they pain us. The desire for consistency in what we do often takes precedence over other wants. As long as a whole way of life provides sufficient gratification to let people feel content with it, they are likely to tolerate those of its unpleasant aspects that cannot readily be changed without seeming to threaten the whole.

The lack of known alternatives may also help to perpetuate practices with which people are discontented. Situations arise that produce a felt need to do something to alter them. If people do not know the real causes involved and seek to deal with these situations by trial and error, they may continue to resort to what they have hit upon, however ineffective, because they know of nothing better to do. When they are ill, for example, people resort to the cures they know or have heard about, although these cures may, like our own blood-letting practice of not so long ago, have actually harmful effects.

The fact is that we cannot face what we regard as crisis situations doing nothing. We want to do something, and we want to believe that the thing we know to do is the best to do, that it will really help achieve our desires. We will rationalize the experience that tells us a "cure" is ineffective in order to derive emotional comfort from its application when we are sick. When there is a sense of urgency, it is gratifying to have an action to perform, even though it cannot, in fact, serve any constructive purpose.

It is in this light, for example, that we may regard the practices to which anthropologists refer collectively as "couvade." Among some peoples, when a pregnant woman goes into labor, her husband simulates labor as well. He lies abed after the child is born receiving the attentions of his neighbors, while his wife and baby remain inconspicuous. However strange from our point of view, the couvade is a response to a deeply felt need. Childbirth is regarded as a crisis situation by all peoples.[11] The fear that the mother or child, or both, may not survive is likely to be especially acute for the husband. It is important that he have something to do that will help. That his behavior has little actual effect on the survival of his wife and child is beside the point. He believes that it does, and his belief gives him something constructive to do. Although he may doubt the efficacy of such action on quiet reflection, neither he nor his wife, nor his neighbors, will take a chance by failing to do the "right" thing in time of crisis.

As we know from our own experience, when we lack a really effective solution for a recurring problem and when, despite our rationalizations, we are aware of this lack, we tend to make a fad of each new proposed remedy, so long as its advocates present it in a manner that gives it a quasi-authoritative ring. An observer coming into a community may conclude that a widespread practice is a custom of long standing when it is actually the fad of no more than a generation or two, soon to disappear in favor of another one when some authority proposes it. But until the new one is offered, the existing practice will be religiously and devotedly pursued.

To sum up, customs that do not seem to gratify in any obvious way may provide gratifications that are not obvious. We have implied, moreover, that if we look at a custom only in relation to the ends that people say it is supposed to serve, we may miss observing the ways in which it actually gratifies them. Looking at it more broadly, we may find that a custom serves less explicit but more pressing felt needs, such as the universal needs to feel oriented in a consistent and orderly world and to have confidence in one's ability to take care of one's wants. With needs of this sort, we begin to touch on emotional factors in behavior. The appraisal of behavior as gratifying or not is so often in terms of material wants or social advantage that we easily lose sight of the important role that emotional gratifications play in reinforcing habits and customs. We have also been reminded that customs do not usually serve specific wants in isolation, but more often relate to many wants and felt needs at once, that it is their net efficacy which accounts for their persistence.

Customs That Work Against the Common Good

Customs, we have observed, do not always serve the interest of social survival. Sometimes they work against the general welfare so as to weaken a society's capacity to resist conquest by its neighbors. Or they may work to facilitate rather than hinder the spread of disease, rendering epidemics more devastating than they might otherwise be.

Often enough, this comes about simply because people are unaware of the chain of causal connections between their customary practices and their misfortunes. A sick person wants to be tended and nursed by his family, not be isolated from it in quarantine. If the germ theory of disease is unknown, to gratify this want is a reasonable thing to do, regardless of the illness. It seems reasonable to suppose that there is no custom whose practice does not have a number of side effects, and that no people can be aware of them all. Some of these side effects may be beneficial but others may actually work against the satisfaction of urgently felt needs.

There are times, however, when people are aware that their actions contribute to a state of affairs they regard as undesirable, and yet they continue in them, making no serious effort to alter their ways. The dangerously overweight person, for example, may know that he is shortening his life by overeating, but continue to overeat nevertheless. He does so, of course, because the wants he gratifies by eating are immediate and urgent as compared with the more remote benefits suggested by life expectancy tables. Another example is provided by the high rate of traffic accidents in the United States. We are well aware that there is a problem here and preach the need for caution in driving, but the accident rate continues to climb. It does so because the majority of people drive a good deal of the time in ways they condemn in other drivers but excuse in themselves. One reason for this may be that much of our life is regulated by the clock, and we try to squeeze so many things into a given time period that we are under constant pressure to violate speed laws, beat traffic lights, and pass other cars on the road. Many of us like a drink or two when we are out for the evening, though we know that it interferes with safe driving. There are undoubtedly a number of contributing factors. In any event, the situation illustrates that we are willing to jeopardize our lives and the lives of others in order to accomplish other valued ends. Preach though we do against unsafe driving, the rate of death and injury on the highways mounts year after year.

This example helps us understand why the women of Yap in the Pacific Ocean continue practices that have contributed, it is claimed, to the progressive depopulation of their island.[12] From their late teens to their late twenties, Yap's women customarily engage in numerous love affairs both before and after marriage. Since the responsibilities of motherhood put an end to these affairs, Yapese women do not want children until they are emotionally ready to settle down. If the analysis is correct, they regularly resort to induced abortion in order to avoid early motherhood. The result is a high rate of female infertility, many women being unable to conceive later, when they want children. This, it seems, accounts for the society's inability to recoup population losses following epidemics or other disasters. The pattern of life in Yap is evidently such that the period of active love affairs is valued by women as one of the truly high points in their lives. Because many individual women want to continue to enjoy the experiences they find so rewarding, they are willing to take certain calculated risks. The ultimate welfare of society is not an important consideration.

The reader can undoubtedly think of other examples from his own experience. They remind us that customs are not developed to meet the needs of society, but to meet the felt needs of individuals. Insofar as people's wants and felt needs include the promotion of the common good, they will be concerned to develop customs in keeping with the general welfare. But there is a limit to which people are willing to serve the needs of others or to subordinate their own wants and needs to what they regard as the long-range good.[13] People have even shown themselves willing to destroy their society and themselves in order to gratify a pressing personal want.

Customs that work against the general welfare or are injurious to a community's survival are, of course, prime targets of development projects. The fact that they are maladaptive, however, does not guarantee that people will be willing to give them up readily for different practices. Indeed, the fact that they have persisted in spite of their harmful effects is evidence that they are linked with the gratification of pressing wants. Any effort to interfere with them is likely, therefore, to produce considerable resistance. Contrary to what we might assume offhand, obviously maladaptive practices are among the most difficult to deal with in a direct fashion. Like our own practices on the highways, of course, they invite the application of legal force. Yet it is questionable that outlawing abortion on Yap would have much more effect on Yapese women than posting speed limits has had upon Americans. Indeed, abortion is already outlawed in the sense that its practice is felt to be bad and kept a strict secret. Clearly, any attempt to effect changes in custom, even where patently maladaptive, must appeal to people as individuals within the framework of wants and needs that are important to them. To rationalize proposed changes on the basis of the general welfare alone is likely to provide an inadequate basis for cooperation.

The persistence of maladaptive customs has called our attention to two things. One is the competition between wants, our inability to gratify some wants except at the expense of others, a matter to which we shall return later. The other is the tendency for customs to produce side effects of which people may or may not be aware.

THE SIDE EFFECTS OF CUSTOM

We have had a number of occasions to observe that customs are designed to accomplish something, to produce changes in existing conditions in order to achieve or prevent the loss of desired ones. The primary intent may be to affect material arrangements, social arrangements, the attitudes and feelings of other people, or the feeling states within ourselves. But whatever is intended, the application of custom is likely to have effects in a number of directions at once. Our customs regarding farming procedures, for example, alter the condition of the soil, of the water table, and of the flora and fauna, as well as the state of our food supply. Because these ramifying effects of custom figure prominently in problems of change, we shall have to consider them again and again in the chapters to follow. For the moment, we want to get in mind some of their more important characteristics.

Lauriston Sharp's account of customs relating to the use of stone axes among the Yir Yoront, an aboriginal people in Australia, provides an excellent illustration of widely ramifying side effects in the area of social relationships.[14] In this case, customs relating to trade, technology, and property had the effect of giving to older men exclusive ownership of stone axes. Stone axes were needed in all kinds of work in which women and younger men regularly engaged. Because they did not own any, they were constantly having to ask the older men for permission to use their axes. A result of the exclusive ownership of axes by older men was to make others dependent upon them. As Sharp goes on to relate, the introduction of steel axes directly to young men and women by European missionaries and employers undermined this dependency, a development that had important repercussions for the whole authority structure of the Yir Yoront community.

As in this case, the side effects of a particular custom often operate to the advantage of one segment of the community. This segment develops a vested interest in the custom's continued operation and is likely to be the main source of resistance to its change. The nature of vested interests is often obvious enough, but Sharp's analysis of the Yir Yoront reminds us that it is by no means always so. No one unsophisticated in the analysis of custom would be likely to discern the very important vested interests that may attach to simple household tools.

Sometimes a custom may have side effects of which people are entirely unaware and which are nevertheless beneficial from the point of view of their own interests and values. In Fiji, for example, the felt need for light in the evening used to be met by burning candlenuts. They did not give very much light and emitted a rather smelly smoke. Kerosene lanterns were adopted with pleasure by the Fijians as a superior solution to the light problem. Subsequently, they began to complain that thatch was no longer holding up as it once did, but was deteriorating more rapidly because of rot and insects. They continued, however, to be unaware that their old candlenut fires had helped to dry and fumigate their roofs.[15]

Such unawareness is by no means confined to scientifically unsophisticated peoples. In the United States the nursing and medical professions have found it helpful for their felt needs to keep to a minimum the contact between small children who are hospitalized and their parents. We are only beginning to discover the adverse effects of such practice on the emotional growth of children.[16] Here, of course, we have an example of side effects of which we have been ignorant and that are undesirable from the standpoint of our own wants and values.

Customs may also work to alter the very problems they were developed to solve. For example, in societies where it is customary for people to divide their land holdings equally among their several heirs, there arises in time a situation where individual holdings are likely to consist of many plots so tiny and so scattered that it is impossible to work them efficiently, let alone to subdivide them further. Ultimately, new customs governing inheritance must be devised to cope with a problem resulting directly from the workings of prior custom. The very application of custom to meet today's circumstances may produce a new set of circumstances for tomorrow to which prior custom may no longer be applicable. The record of human history is full of crises resulting from just this kind of interplay between custom and circumstance, leading to the breakdown of old forms and painful groping for new ones. The boom-and-bust cycles of our own recent economic history can be seen as by-products of just this sort of process. Moreover, many of the problems for which development programs are contemplated have arisen in this way, as the case record illustrates.[17] The necessity for changing long-established customs is often due not so much to their having always been inadequate to a community's needs but to their having become increasingly less adequate.

As the foregoing examples demonstrate, the side effects of customs may be such as to prevent potential problems from ever arising, or they may create further problems. In some instances these further problems are immediate and pressing, in others they mature slowly over a long period of time. In any event, the working of custom is frequently such as to create additional wants and felt needs which additional customs are developed to serve. Change in custom may, therefore, result in a situation where formerly useful customs become useless because the wants they gratified have ceased to exist. This is most obvious in the sphere of technology. The shift from horse-drawn vehicles to automobiles, to cite a hackneyed example, did away with the felt needs that were met by the blacksmith's art. Each change in custom, conversely, introduces new side effects, including new wants. The disappearance of domestic help from middle-class American households in recent years has stimulated a demand for labor-saving devices in the home. Much of the planning that goes into economic and other forms of development is, of course, devoted to calculating the effects of this kind that a specific change will produce.

Of great importance among the problems created by customs are the emotional conflicts their operation generates. In a familiar study Margaret Mead has emphasized that some problems relating to adolescence in our society are not present to the same degree in other societies where customs differ.[18] And other studies have described some of the emotional problems that specific customs of child-rearing help to produce. Thus Gladwin and Sarason, observing the emotional difficulties that Trukese men exhibit when they have to take responsibility in decision-making, connect these difficulties with the kinds of dealings Trukese children customarily have with adults and adult affairs.[19] To meet the emotional problems that child-rearing and other customs create, there may arise a number of beliefs and practices directly affecting the conduct of adult activities. A study by Whiting and Child, for example, suggests that the way in which children's dependency is handled in a community may have a bearing on the views the children hold later, as adults, concerning the causes of illness and the best methods of treatment.[20]

Obviously, we have a great deal yet to learn about the side effects of custom, especially those that are social and psychological in nature. Psychological side effects are necessarily a special concern to development agents, for resistance to changing a custom is itself an expression of its emotional importance. Certainly, the relationship between customs and their side effects offers a tremendous challenge to change agents. Any solution to existing problems will inevitably create other problems that did not exist previously. It is not sufficient to appraise the worth of a particular program in terms of the specific problems it is intended to solve. It must also be appraised in terms of the problems it is likely to create, which calls for analytical skills of a high order. We shall present a conceptual framework for making such analyses in Chapter 12. As scientific knowledge expands, giving us more insight into the relations between things, our ability to analyze the side effects of particular courses of action will continue to grow. But it can never be even close to perfect. Agents of change must always be prepared to have to deal with new problems following in the wake of change, problems whose relation to the changes that have occurred are quite unclear and that may seem, indeed, to have no connection with them at all. Furthermore, we must assume that even the best of solutions to present problems will eventually outlive its usefulness, having the effect of altering the problem it was designed to solve. If, in the course of time, customs change the ends they serve, absolutism regarding what is best is out of place in rational development planning.

FUNCTION AND MEANING

In the course of this chapter we have said that a custom's form is related to the wants and felt needs it is intended to serve and the way people perceive their circumstances. We have attributed the persistence of a custom to its ability to gratify wants and felt needs of some kind. We have also seen that a custom's form is related to the form of other customs with which it coexists. And, finally, we have observed that customs have many side effects, which among other things may work to prevent certain wants from ever arising or, on the other hand, to create additional wants and felt needs. On one occasion or another, anthropologists have used the term "function" to refer to all of these relationships, especially the utilitarian relationship of custom to need and the systematic relationship of custom to custom.[21]

It is, indeed, useful to have such a way of referring to the various relationships a particular custom bears to the total life situation (including wants, needs, and other customs) of a society's members. It is possible, as our discussion has shown, to see a custom as a function of recurring or ever-present conditions within the life situation and also to see the life situation, in equilibrium or change, as a function of the workings of custom. But we must continue to bear in mind that the view a society's members have of the interrelationships between their customs and their life situation is not the same as an observer's view of them. In order to avoid any possibility of confusion here, we shall reserve the term "function" to refer to those relations as they appear to an objective observer. If we think of a custom as a phenomenon in an immense natural process involving people, their actions, and their total environment, its relation to that process and to all the things involved in it is its function. From the standpoint of those who practice it, on the other hand, a custom may be said to have a *meaning*, by which we refer to the several ways in which they associate it with their wants and felt needs and with the various other features of what they regard as their life situation.[22]

The meaning of a custom to its practitioners may resemble an observer's picture of its function in many ways. Most atoll dwellers in the South Seas are fully conscious of the many problems that cultivating the coconut palm enables them to solve in the way of obtaining food, clothing, shelter, and even alcoholic beverages. An observer can learn much about the function of coconut cultivation simply by asking about its meaning. Function, however, always embraces more than meaning. And sometimes there is very little resemblance between the function and meaning of a custom. Indeed, there are occasions when a custom works in such a way as to make it very difficult, if not impossible, for people to be aware of functions that strike an observer as vital.

This can happen when a custom so thoroughly solves the problem that occasioned its development as to make people no longer aware of the problem. So long as there continue to be a few instances in which someone neglects to follow a custom, people will be reminded of the consequences of such neglect and thereby preserve their sense of need for it. But if the custom were religiously followed by everyone, the resulting lack of contrast would bring people no longer to feel the need or experience the want that the custom was developed to gratify. The custom would thus lose its power to gratify. When this happened, we would expect people to begin to neglect its observance and thereby to rediscover the problem it solved. But if a side effect of the custom's practice produced new wants that the custom's observance also gratified and that conditions did not allow people to forget, it could continue to be observed by everyone long after people had ceased to be aware of the needs it was originally designed to meet. This could happen, for example, if a custom came to be regarded as a distinctive feature of the community, setting it off from its neighbors. People would then want to follow it because it was a badge of their identity. The gratification of this want would ensure its continued observance after the original wants had disappeared. An illustration of just this sort of situation is provided by the custom of infant cradling as practiced by the Kwakiutl Indians of the Pacific Northwest.[23]

The Kwakiutl put their infants on cradle-boards and kept them there for the first two years of their lives. The cradle was so constructed and the child so bound to it that it markedly flattened the back of his head. There was an observable contrast between the Kwakiutl and some of their neighbors in flatness of head. This side effect of the cradle-board was given by the Kwakiutl as the reason for putting a child on it. No one would want a child to be ugly or to have the rounded head of a captive slave! To an observer there were very practical reasons for using the cradle-board. There were many hazards in the house and village to which crawling or toddling infants would be subject. The watchful supervision American mothers must give their toddlers when they are out of the playpen was unnecessary for the Kwakiutl mother, whose baby was safely out of harm's way on the cradle-board. Since a child did not come off it permanently until he had learned to talk and could be controlled by voice, a Kwakiutl woman had difficulty anticipating the possible accidents to which babies might be prone because they never occurred. She had, therefore, no habits of action or thought that would lead her to see a need for constant vigilance. Indeed, the cradle-board enabled her to carry on economic activities outside the home without concern for her child's safety. When the cradle-board was outlawed, the accidents it had prevented began to occur as babies fell into the fire, were bumped by heavy doors, or fell off piers and were drowned. Only after a number of such accidents could the existence of a problem begin to be recognized, and only after that could new solutions be tested until new habits were consolidated, habits that could be fitted at the same time into the economic activities in which women continued to feel it necessary to engage.[24] Thus the problems that the cradle-board was presumably developed to solve had disappeared from people's awareness. In time the custom of cradling acquired a meaning centering on considerations of physical appearance and social status, but its function continued to include the creation of conditions in which the chances of infant death or injury from accident were minimal.

With this example in mind, we see that the meanings people can attach to their customs depend on the opportunities they have to observe how they function. Such opportunities may exist because a problem is constantly recurring in experience and keeping a sense of need for the custom alive. Opportunities are also provided when a person neglects to observe one of his community's customs, so that the consequences of such neglect become evident to him and to his fellows. In this connection, we derive much appreciation of our customs from having to teach them to our children, whose nonconformity gives them meaning to us. Often, indeed, it is not so much the observance as the failure to observe a custom that reinforces its meaning for people.[25]

Both the meaning and function of customs are of obvious interest to change agents. In order to understand the sources of present problems in a community and in order to predict what new problems will emerge in the course of change, it is clearly necessary to know the functional relationships of its customs to one another and to human and environmental conditions. And in order to discern the points at which people are likely to be predisposed to resist or welcome proposals for change, it is essential to understand the meaning of their customs to them. The meaning people attach to their customs will account for their willingness to change them far more than will the ways in which they actually function.

SUGGESTED READING

Firth, Raymond, *Human Types*. Rev. ed., Mentor Books, New York, 1958.

Nida, Eugene A., *Customs and Cultures:* Anthropology for Christian Missions. Harper and Bros., New York, 1954.

NOTES TO CHAPTER 4

1. Eiseley, Loren C., *Darwin's Century: Evolution and the Men Who Discovered It.* Doubleday and Co., New York, 1958.

2. Robson, R. W., *Handbook of Papua and New Guinea, 1954.* Pacific Publications Pty. Ltd., Sydney, Australia, 1954, p. 33.

3. Paul, Benjamin D., "The Rational Bias in the Perception of Cultural Differences," *Economic Development and Cultural Change,* vol. 1, 1952, pp. 132–138.

4. For an extended discussion of this problem, see Anastasi, Ann, and John P. Foley, Jr., *Differential Psychology:* Individual and Group Differences in Behavior, rev. ed., Macmillan Co., New York, 1949, chaps. 21–23.

5. For a not too technical account of the fundamentals of learning theory and their application to custom from a behavioristic point of view, the reader is referred to Miller, Neal E., and John Dollard, *Social Learning and Imitation,* Yale University Press, New Haven, 1941. For a critique of the mechanistic assumptions of behavioristic theory, see Asch, Solomon E., *Social Psychology,* Prentice-Hall, Inc., New York, 1952. For a penetrating appraisal of the limitations of behavioristic psychology, see Chomsky, Noam, "*Verbal Behavior* by B. F. Skinner," a review in *Language,* vol. 35, 1959, pp. 26–58. A searching attempt to relate custom to psychological processes from a nonbehavioristic point of view is provided by H. G. Barnett, in *Innovation:* The Basis of Cultural Change, McGraw-Hill Book Co., New York, 1953.

6. Murdock, G. P., "The Common Denominator of Cultures" in Linton, Ralph, editor, *The Science of Man in the World Crisis.* Columbia University Press, New York, 1945, pp. 123–142.

7. This is most obvious with speech forms. Linguists agree that every known language is structurally as good a medium of thought and communication as every other. See, for example, Sapir, Edward, *Language:* An Introduction to the Study of Speech, Harcourt, Brace and Co., New York, 1921, p. 234. For a well-reasoned modification of this view, see Hymes, Dell H., "Functions of Speech: An Evolutionary Approach" in Gruber, Frederick C., editor, *Anthropology and Education,* University of Pennsylvania Press, Philadelphia, 1961, pp. 55–83.

8. The symbolic force of this act for the Trukese is clearly revealed by a woman who reports how her parents tricked her into marriage. "I came home one night and my mother called, 'Come and let's eat!' I came in and Richard was there. I wondered why he was eating with us. I sat down and my mother told me to call him to eat, so I said, 'Come and let's eat!' He was very happy at that because he thought I knew he wanted to marry me, but I did not. After we had eaten my mother called me outside. I went out with her and she told me that I was to marry Richard. She asked me if I wanted to and I said no. But she said I had called him to eat and that was that." Gladwin, Thomas, and Seymour B. Sarason, *Truk: Man in Paradise,* Viking Fund Publications in Anthropology, no. 20, Wenner-Gren Foundation for Anthropological Research, New York, 1953, p. 206.

9. Wide similarities of form in some aspects of family and kinship organization have been attributed to the limitation of possibilities by George Peter Murdock, *Social Structure,* Macmillan Co., New York, 1949. See also his "Common Denominator of Cultures," *op. cit.,* pp. 138–141. The "law of limited possibilities" was first formulated by Alexander A. Goldenweiser, *History, Psychology and Culture,* Alfred A. Knopf, Inc., New York, 1933.

10. A classic problem of this sort is to explain the presence in all societies of a custom prohibiting marriage with immediate kin.

11. There is no reliable evidence to support the contention made by travelers and other casual observers that so-called primitive peoples suffer less pain or fewer

medical complications in childbirth. Ford, Clellan S., *A Comparative Study of Human Reproduction*, Yale University Publications in Anthropology No. 32, Department of Anthropology, Yale University, New Haven, 1945.

12. Schneider, David M., "Abortion and Depopulation on a Pacific Island" in Paul, Benjamin D., editor, *Health, Culture, and Community*. Russell Sage Foundation, New York, 1955, pp. 211–235.

13. This limit varies from society to society in accordance with group identifications for reasons that are as yet unclear. Banfield and Banfield describe for a South Italian community a basic attitude which they call "amoral familism." It is expressed in these words: "Maximize the material, short-run advantage of the nuclear family; assume that all others will do the same." It follows that "no one will further the interest of the group or community except as it is to his advantage to do so." The authors conclude that this seriously limits the possibilities for economic and social development. Indeed, anyone who professes altruistic concern for others is reported to be immediately suspect. Banfield, Edward C., and Laura Fasano Banfield, *The Moral Basis of a Backward Society*, The Free Press, Glencoe, Ill., 1958, p. 85.

14. Sharp, Lauriston, "Steel Axes for Stone Age Australians" in Spicer, Edward H., editor, *Human Problems in Technological Change: A Casebook*. Russell Sage Foundation, New York, 1952, pp. 69–81.

15. We are indebted to Clellan S. Ford for this example.

16. Bowlby, John, *Child Care and the Growth of Love*. Penguin Books, Baltimore, Md., 1953. See also the symposium "Mental Health and Child Development," *Understanding the Child*, vol. 21, 1952, pp. 97–111.

17. See, for example, Spicer, Edward H., editor, *op. cit.*, Case 11.

18. Mead, Margaret, *Coming of Age in Samoa:* A Psychological Study of Primitive Youth for Western Civilization. William Morrow and Co., New York, 1928.

19. Gladwin, Thomas, and Seymour B. Sarason, *op. cit.*

20. Whiting, J. W. M., and Irving L. Child, *Child Training and Personality:* A Cross-Cultural Study. Yale University Press, New Haven, 1953.

21. For a review of the concept of function in anthropology, see Firth, Raymond, "Function" in Thomas, William L., Jr., editor, *Yearbook of Anthropology 1955*. Wenner-Gren Foundation for Anthropological Research, New York, 1955, pp. 237–258.

22. This distinction between function and meaning is essentially the same as the one drawn by H. G. Barnett, in "Culture Processes," *American Anthropologist*, vol. 42, 1940, pp. 30–31. See also Linton, Ralph, *The Study of Man*, D. Appleton Century Co., New York, 1936, pp. 402–404; also the distinction between "manifest and latent functions" drawn by Robert K. Merton, in *Social Theory and Social Structure*, revised and enlarged edition, The Free Press, Glencoe, Ill., 1957, chap. 1.

23. For this example and the point that it illustrates we are indebted to Clellan S. Ford.

24. Ford, Clellan S., *Smoke from Their Fires:* The Life of a Kwakiutl Chief. Yale University Press, New Haven, 1941, p. 160, note 6.

25. The existence of a small, lower class of "worthless people" among the Coast Salish, for example, may have provided the necessary contrast for reinforcing the ethical values of the numerically large, upper class of "good people," according to a suggestion by Wayne Suttles, in "Private Knowledge, Morality, and Social Classes Among the Coast Salish," *American Anthropologist*, vol. 60, 1958, pp. 497–507.

Chapter 5

CUSTOM AND VALUE

Customs derive their meaning, we have said, from the things people associate with them. Indeed, all objects, persons, and events, as well as customary practices, may thus be said to have meaning. Consequently, an inquiry into the meaning of custom requires us to examine the associations people have with things generally. For the present we shall confine our attention to essentially subjective associations, those having to do with how we relate things to our inner feeling states and to the gratification of our own wants and felt needs. How we orient ourselves emotionally or affectively to our customs and to everything else in our life situation depends upon such associations.[1] It is these that give things their subjective meaning, and it is with meaning of this kind that we shall be concerned in this and the next chapter.

Because it has to do with the gratifications and frustrations whose experience we associate with things, subjective meaning takes us into the realm of likes and dislikes, of sentiments and values. This is, indeed, a difficult and complex subject matter, for it is evident that people do not simply value some things positively and others negatively. They frequently value the same thing both positively and negatively at the same time, feeling, as they say, ambivalent about it; or they may value it in opposite ways at different times. Furthermore, among the things with which people have pleasant associations or anticipate having them, they attach greater value to some than to others. And to the despair of many a development agent, people often seem to value most highly objects, customs, and beliefs from which it is difficult to see how they can possibly derive any gratification at all—such, for example, as painful and medically dangerous

85

initiation rites or religious ceremonies calling for excruciating acts of self-torture. Strange as it may seem, moreover, it is a routine observation of psychological counselors that their clients tend to cling tenaciously to the very habits and attitudes that contribute directly to their unhappy emotional state. In community development we meet similar situations. Any insight we can get into what lies behind these phenomena will help us as agents of change to work more effectively with our clients.

PERSONAL SENTIMENTS AND COMMON VALUES

We start with the obvious fact that people do not value everything in the same way or to the same degree. Some wants and felt needs usually take precedence over others. If it were always possible to gratify any one want without interfering with the gratification of any other, of course, the matter of precedence and, with it, the relative weighting of wants would not arise. The fact is that our wants are often in competition with one another. This requires us to make choices, forcing us to decide which of our wants will be gratified and which frustrated. Correspondingly, of course, we order the activities and instruments by which we gratify them. We are less willing to part with things that gratify wants to which we give high priority, and we feel a greater need for them than for things that help to gratify wants of a lower order. In this way we graduate the things we value in scales.

At the same time, the necessity to choose between our wants forces us to experience frustration and self-denial. We have different value orientations toward those gratifying experiences to which we cannot easily attain as compared with those whose enjoyment is always available to us. The same grass may become greener and lusher by virtue of being on the other side of the fence, as the old saying goes. Or we may disdain what is not available to us. In one way or another we tend to be preoccupied with those wants that we feel are unfulfilled or of whose future gratification we are in doubt. Frustration and self-denial give rise to complicated cross-currents of envy, covetousness, hope, and anxiety, all of which significantly affect our choices and preferences.

It would be surprising if any two persons had exactly the same hierarchy of preferences or evaluated things relative to each other in exactly the same way. No two persons have experienced quite the same events or suffered the same frustrations; and different biological endowments tend to make different experiences out of otherwise similar events, as between normal and color-blind persons. Each of us, consequently, has his own personal sentiment system—the preferences in terms of which he would act if he felt himself free of all social restraint, if only his own inner sense of integrity were his guide[2]—and the corresponding private or personal value attitudes that he has toward things.

People who have grown up under similar conditions, to be sure, are likely to show less difference in their personal sentiments than are persons of disparate backgrounds. They will have developed their value orientations with respect to a common range of objects and events. Everyone will have evaluated the same things in relation to much the same other things. Although they may end up ranking them somewhat differently, there will be a number of things that all view positively and a number of other things that all find repellent.

People are unconscious of some of their sentiments. Otherwise they would never be amazed at the things they find themselves doing. They are also unaware that they share some personal sentiments with others. The reader has undoubtedly been surprised more than once to learn that some of his personal value orientations were not peculiar to him. The more intimately we live together, of course, the more opportunities we have to discover the sentiments we have in common. The broader the base of common sentiments of which we are mutually aware, the stronger the feeling that we are of one kind. For when we observe our fellows choosing as we would choose under similar circumstances, we feel that we understand them, that they and we have similar outlooks on life. We may even feel that there is a special bond of some sort between us.

For any community or social class, then, there will be some value orientations that are common to the personal sentiments of virtually everyone within it. They allow for the development of recreational, esthetic, and ethical traditions that have wide appeal. These traditions help to promote awareness of common sentiments, which in turn help to give people that sense of mutual identity without which there is no social group. This is especially true, of course, in the case of common sentiments that they do not share with members of other communities or classes. Such sentiments are especially important in giving to those who share them a consciousness of kind. The members of social groups, moreover, seek to promote this feeling by adopting customs and costumes that differ from those of other groups, and by prohibiting participation in those activities in which people in rival groups experience mutual identifications. No good Irishman wears orange on St. Patrick's Day. And that god whose worship provides the sense of communion among a group's members is necessarily a jealous god.

Common Sentiments and Social Cohesion

Small, unstratified societies tend to have a broader base of common sentiments than do large and socially complicated ones. The base becomes narrow even in small communities, however, if the individual members have widely differing experiences in the outside world, as may be the case, for example, when many of them go away from home for considerable periods of time to work in a variety of places in a variety of jobs. This helps to produce a feeling that there is much in one's experience which is not shared by one's fellows and cannot be understood by them, but which has had an important effect on one's personal sentiment system. An anthropologist is likely to be familiar with this sense of estrangement from his fellows after a period of field study in an alien society. He comes back having learned a language that none of his fellows can speak, along with ways of thinking and acting that are meaningless to his friends at home and, what is more, of only passing interest to them, though of intense interest to him. If he has no family or career commitments to keep him at home, he may soon seek a return to the field. Similar experiences of alienation from their fellows have been reported by both Japanese and Americans educated or employed overseas.[3]

The disintegration of formerly closely knit rural communities whose members are away much of the time may well reflect a progressive mutual dissociation of this sort among their members. A case in point has been reported by Ralph Beals, who notes the disappearance of a sense of community and increasing social disorganization in a village in Ecuador as its members devote more and more time to entrepreneural activities away from home.[4] The sense among a community's members that they have a number of sentiments in common, especially at the higher levels of their preference hierarchies, appears to be essential for community cohesion. For agents of change this is a matter of special importance in assessing a community's capacity for concerted action in carrying through a development project.

If the members of a community are to be aware that they have a number of sentiments in common, they must have ample opportunity to observe one another at work and play in a wide variety of contexts. To this end group activities are essential. By doing things together people are reminded over and over again of their common interests and values. By working in groups, even on tasks that require no cooperation, they reinforce in one another the values they individually associate with their work. Thus any social group whose members have a broad base of shared value orientations and whose way of life gives them recurring opportunities to experience the fact that these orientations are indeed shared tends to acquire some of the characteristics of a religious congregation.

This is especially marked when people find themselves reacting with their fellows in the same way to events that move them deeply. The experience of mutual identification people feel at such times gives them a sense of communion. This mystical experience is something people find highly gratifying, for once they have had it they usually seek to relive it again, directly or symbolically. Each war, for example, brings its new veterans' organization, and each new inspirational leader stimulates the formation of a new sect or congregation among those who have been moved by him. Public ceremonies that use awe-provoking or otherwise inspiring symbols acquire great positive value for just this reason. To the ancient Greeks, for example, attending the theater was to participate in a religious rite; nor are we ourselves unaware of the theater's potentialities in this regard. Whether it be by the theater, by church service, or by other means, every community includes among its institutionalized activities some that function to remind its members of their more important common values, to revive in them a sense of mutual identification, and thus to reconfirm their feeling that they are, indeed, a community.[5]

Group Spirit

What we have been talking about is obviously related to the group phenomenon known as *esprit de corps* or group spirit.[6] A general awareness of common sentiments is clearly indispensable to it. There is something more, however, that is necessary, and that is a general awareness of common commitment to certain goals and values as having top priority and, also, of common commitment to a particular course of action and to a particular leadership and social organization for implementing it. It also requires mutual confidence in one another's ability as well as willingness to do one's part.

When people consciously share such common dedication and mutual confidence, their capacity to endure the frustration of other wants is greatly enhanced. During World War II airmen who had experienced many bombing missions without showing signs of emotional breakdown frequently went to pieces when relieved of combat duty and sent home. Removal from their crew mates with whom they had developed deep emotional ties while sharing combat experience was shattering, for it was these ties that had sustained them through great strain. Returned home to a world in which their experience was meaningless, they were left without a sense of support, with emotional needs no one could satisfy.[7] In the Gilbert Islands, likewise, we were told that most instances of severe emotional disorder occur among people who are working away from home. Some individuals who have functioned adequately in the supporting environment of home, with its large circle of kinsmen and well-developed community life, break down when put in an alien setting in which they are subject to new stress and at the same time stripped of their usual resources for sustaining stress. It is established policy to get such cases back to their home communities as soon as possible. Being with family and kin once more seems most conducive to recovery. It would seem that when people are subject to little frustration and stress, they have less need to be part of a well-knit social group. On the other hand, the greater the stress they must sustain, the more important it is for their mental health that they operate as members of social groups with high *esprit de corps*.

A community whose members have strong emotional bonds with one another through joint participation in *traditional* activities is likely to be conservative, especially with regard to any changes that they feel may threaten existing ties. Few Americans can allow themselves to get excited about cricket as long as they continue to regard baseball as the national sport. A proposal to substitute cricket for baseball would certainly be regarded by many as an outrageous attack on a sacred American institution. Proposals for community development that threaten activities or objects having this kind of meaning for people are sure to be met with resistance. Such resistance will be active and energetic. Commitment to the preservation of threatened institutions of this kind, indeed, provides the ingredient needed to convert the existing sense of community into a fanatical group spirit. Concerted action in resistance is likely to strengthen further the community's *esprit de corps* and promote even more determined resistance to the proposed change.

But we should not conclude from this that group spirit is invariably a force against change. When established institutions fail to gratify people's wants and when participation in them fails to give people a sense of mutual identification, the discovery of common important values through participation in some new activity can unite them in working to realize shared hopes for the future. In such a situation the *esprit de corps* that develops in the context of the new may become a powerful force for change. It is this that gives people the capacity to persevere in the face of all sorts of obstacles, disappointments, and hardships. Without a deep sense of identity with others there can be no self-sacrifice for the common good. The very force that leads to organized resistance to change is also indispensable to accomplishing constructive change.

In stressing the importance of activities in which people discover and reaffirm their commonality of values and in referring to this discovery as a kind of religious experience, we do not mean to conclude, as some theorists have done, that maintaining the solidarity of the community is the sole or even principal function of religious institutions. Any kind of group activity may function in this way, whereas many activities we regard as religious are conducted in strict privacy for private ends. To perceive that *esprit de corps* relates to a kind of religious experience, however, does help us appreciate one of the important emotional forces in both conservatism and change and to understand what produces some of the religious overtones that accompany so many different kinds of activity and endeavor. Certain it is that such religious overtones are readily discerned not only when development projects are actively resisted but also when they are accepted and successfully carried through. The role of religious movements in the development process is a matter we shall consider at length in Chapter 11.

VALUES AND THE SOCIAL ORDER

We have already noted that competition between their several wants forces people to make choices leading to the formation of scales of preference and relative value. We also remarked that frustrations resulting from the necessity to choose produce affective orientations that complicate the weighting of values. Such psychological effects of the competition of wants will concern us shortly. This competition also has important implications for the organizational aspects of community life. It is to these and their implications for community development that we now turn.

Activities and Their Scheduling

In Chapter 3 we observed that people try to devise modes of action having a high net efficacy, in that they provide a wide variety of gratifications at little expense. So it is that many of the customary activities in which we engage are able to gratify not one but a number of our wants. And by limiting the occasions when we engage in them to those times when we experience the many wants they are capable of gratifying, we maximize the rewards to be derived from them. One need only think, for example, of the wants that giving a dinner party in our own society may help to gratify, such as being with congenial or stimulating people, paying one's social debts, impressing a business client, indulging one's appetite for drink and good food, getting the house thoroughly cleaned, and so on. As a number of such wants build up within us, we come increasingly to feel a need to give a party. Afterward we are likely to feel that we have managed to dispose of a number of matters at once.

Some wants, however, are such that the conditions permitting one of them to be gratified preclude the conditions for gratifying another. They give rise, that is, to mutually exclusive needs. Gratifying one frustrates gratification of the other. One cannot, for example, eat and sleep at the same time. A good many of our wants have this conflicting relationship to one another.

One way to deal with this conflict, of course, is to resolve it by choosing to gratify some wants at the expense of ever gratifying others, as when we take vows of celibacy or choose an occupation in which it is impossible to become wealthy. Another solution, and the one to be considered here, is to try to arrange things so that we can gratify our incompatible wants at different times, as when we spend some time at work and some time at play.

Scheduling of this sort is related, of course, to natural physiological rhythms, the satisfaction of one want freeing us for a time to attend to other wants. Having slept and eaten, we are ready to expend energy on activities relating to long-range purposes; but in due course we must give priority to eating and resting again. Scheduling, however, is much more than a simple response to physiological rhythms. Many different wants compete for attention in the work day, requiring us to budget our time. A Nakanai man of New Britain in the Territory of Papua and New Guinea, for instance, knows that he must not allow more than a month to elapse between taro plantings if he is to have a continuous supply of vegetable food. He tries to allocate the time he spends in hunting, house-building, trading, and warring with his neighbors accordingly. It is, indeed, a characteristic of every human community that a large portion of its members' affairs are conducted within the framework of established routines.

There are always some activities, of course, that remain unscheduled. This may be because the wants they gratify are not imperative, having at most a low priority, so that the activities in question can be worked into the scheduled routine as circumstances of the moment permit. On the other hand, the wants they gratify may be very urgent but arise unpredictably at quite irregular intervals, as in connection with illness. Therapeutic activities are not likely to be a part of the scheduled daily and seasonal round. This is the case, of course, with all activities that are aimed at coping with crises. The satisfaction of still other wants may be unscheduled because they become pressing only after long periods of time. When they reach a point where we feel an urgent need to indulge them, we may simply suspend the usual schedule by declaring a holiday. We cannot assume, therefore, that an activity's being scheduled or its rate of occurrence within a schedule is a reliable index of the degree to which people value it. They may cherish most highly an activity that is unscheduled and in which they seldom engage.

Taking daily and seasonal rhythms into account, then, schedules provide for gratification of otherwise mutually incompatible wants. In this way they are themselves a source of gratification. They acquire value also, in that they reduce uncertainty about gratification by making it possible to have fairly reliable expectations. Moreover, they relieve people of the necessity to make often difficult decisions as to who will do what, when. Finally, schedules help to space activities in such a way as to give the practice of each a fairly high net efficacy. Insofar as they accomplish these several ends in a gratifying manner, a community's established schedules will be positively valued by its members.

Because they resolve so many different problems, schedules often represent a delicate balance that allows for little alteration without serious dislocating effects. So many different wants are likely to be involved in the several activities within a schedule as to make it difficult for people to see how they can possibly alter it radically. This is a matter of obvious concern to development agents, for it would appear that proposed new activities are not likely to be adopted unless they can be readily fitted into existing routines. For example, incompatibility with household routines seems to have been an important reason that recent efforts to persuade housewives in a Peruvian town to boil their drinking water were largely unsuccessful.[8] Current efforts in some quarters to promote a return to breast-feeding infants in our own society are making little headway for similar reasons. However willing mothers may be to try breast-feeding, they cannot accomplish it successfully without neglecting their many other responsibilities within the domestic establishment and thoroughly disrupting their usual routines. On the other hand, in communities where people are acquiring many new wants whose gratification is frustrated by existing routines and schedules, there may be great dissatisfaction with things as they are, but a sense of helplessness because constructive change cannot be easily accomplished unless they scrap the entire schedule currently in operation. This raises the prospect of complete disorganization and creates a felt need for a new schedule, for social and economic planning. When the desire for such change is strong, totalitarian programs can be very appealing, as we see among intellectuals in many underdeveloped countries today.

These considerations apply with greatest force, of course, to those schedules and routines through which the various activities of different people and groups of people are synchronized or otherwise meshed so that common purposes to which all contribute are satisfactorily accomplished. Scheduling also enables people to pursue their own ends without disrupting the pursuit of other ends by others. This brings us to the problem of competition between individuals, whose regulation is a major function of any social order.

The Regulation of Interpersonal Competition

Selfishly, the ideal arrangement for each of us is to be always in a position that allows for maximal gratification of our own wants, whatever their nature. This requires among other things that we suffer minimal interference from others as they seek to gratify their wants. Each of us feels a need on occasion to restrict and control the behavior of others, to deny what would be preferable to them in order to make things more attractive for ourselves. Although each of us desires to be free of the control of our fellows, we are all united in the desire that our fellows be controlled. This common interest underlies every social order. The counter-regulation of our own conduct, though in some ways burdensome, is the price we have to pay for it.

How people regulate the competition among themselves is analogous to the manner in which they handle the problem of incompatible wants within themselves, that is, by scheduling the gratification of some wants and by denying or suppressing others. Thus every community has a set of rules by which people are required to conduct their affairs and interact with one another. The rules specify various rights, privileges, and duties, and indicate the combinations in which they can properly occur. These combinations constitute the statuses in which people are expected to operate.[9] The rules also allocate these statuses to specified categories of person, such as women, widowers, bankers, and so on, according to what other categories they are dealing with. Thus the rights, privileges, and duties of a physician *vis à vis* his client are different from those he has *vis à vis* another physician or a nurse in the system of rules governing social relationships in our society. That is, the physician, has a different status, depending on what category of person he is dealing with in his capacity as physician.[10] By classifying people into categories, by specifying what sets of categories (such as those of age, occupation, or class) are appropriate to what occasions, and by indicating the statuses that each of these categories has in relation to others, people endeavor to regulate conflicts among them resulting from their incompatible wants. The system of rules by which a social order is thus established not only provides a means of scheduling the gratification of wants, it also entirely disallows the pursuit of some wants by outlawing the conduct or other means by which to gratify them, as in the case of assault with a deadly weapon among ourselves. There is no society known to anthropologists, no matter how "primitive," that is without such rules, or whose social relationships are incapable of analysis as an ordered distribution of rights, privileges, and duties among well-defined categories of persons.

Every such system of rules gives expression to a set of what we may call public values. The rights and duties it defines are the moral code, specifying the things we may in all righteousness demand of others and they of us; and the privileges the rules allow specify the occasions when we may act selfishly, irrespective of how our actions may affect the ability of others to gratify wants of their own. The rules establish for a community a system of priorities and relative valuation not only with respect to wants and the means of their gratification but also with respect to circumstances and categories of person. The rules of eligibility to membership in the more privileged categories, moreover, also define the conditions by which to judge personal worth.

These public values reflect in many ways the personal sentiments shared by a community's members. But they do not necessarily coincide with all of the personal preferences people have regarding themselves and others or with their personal criteria for evaluating individual worth. People violate the rules or seek to subvert them often enough. Where personal values are at odds with the public ones, moreover, there is need of some inducement to persuade people to obey the rules. Where inducements are insufficient and the personal sentiments of enough people differ from public values in similar ways, a community will seek to modify its rules accordingly.

But we should not conclude that the demands which the system of rules makes upon an individual contrary to his private preferences necessarily lead him to want to do away with the rules. He may find them inconvenient or a burden on occasion, but he finds them much to his advantage on others, protecting him from being frustrated in his own wants by the actions of his fellows. The rules and the public values they express are themselves valued as something to which appeal can be made. Such frustration as a person must suffer from their operation enables him to demonstrate his own endorsement of them, to reaffirm his membership in good standing in the community, and, consequently, to claim his right to exercise the privileges of such membership without interference. The system of rules gives to every man a moral hold on his fellows, which he cannot afford to relinquish, even though he must subordinate his will to theirs on occasion in return for it and, indeed, deny himself forever the gratification of some of his wants and content himself with the furtive gratification of others.

Public Values and Personal Sentiments

It appears from the foregoing that we must consider the meaning of custom in the light of two different sets of affective orientations, one personal or private and the other public. The former is expressed by the choices we make or would make without regard to the demands of the social order in which we participate. These orientations may or may not be shared with others. The second set of orientations is expressed by the choices we make in conformity with the social order's demands. We automatically share these value orientations with others to the extent that we agree on the definitions and rules comprising the social order. Sharing public values is as much a matter of similar cognition as of similar feeling.

Within a community, the private orientations of its members may differ considerably and still allow them to profess the same public values. One person may rate fish low and another high among his food preferences; yet both may agree that it is right to serve fish on Friday. As this example implies, some people will find it easier to subscribe to the public values than will others. Differences in personal evaluation of the public values may also reflect different positions within the social order and the different degrees of privilege they allow.

Mention of privilege brings us to an important point about the interplay between public values and personal sentiments. Public values prescribe and proscribe certain kinds of behavior in certain situations, thereby establishing people's duties and rights. But within the limits thus set, the public values grant considerable freedom of choice. This constitutes the area of privilege, the things we may or may not do as we wish. How we exercise our privileges is necessarily a reflection of personal sentiments. We judge our fellows according to what they reveal of their personal motives and values in this way. For it is possible for someone to be absolutely correct by the standards of the public value system and yet behave in ways that are distasteful to many of his fellows. They may have no moral claim against him and yet detest him thoroughly. Similarity and complementarity in personal values, moreover, seem to be the grounds on which people discern those of their fellows whose company they find most congenial. So it is that privilege, the area of play between public and personal values, contributes to the apparent complexities and subtleties of social interaction. We cannot deal with people at all if we are ignorant of the public value system by which they operate. But we must get to know them intimately if we are to discover how to adjust our behavior to fit well with their personal values within the latitude the public system allows.

Because we justify our actions to others by reference to public values, these values tend naturally to become more highly rationalized and objectified than do personal sentiments. Myths, proverbs, holy writ, and laws enunciate and sanction public values. As we shall have occasion to illustrate in later chapters, many of a people's customary beliefs provide the axiomatic underpinnings for the values implicit in their social order. Personal value orientations, on the other hand, insofar as they differ from public values, tend to remain unverbalized. We often have difficulty objectifying them to ourselves, as is all too evident when we try to discover our real inclinations and motives in the arduous process of psychotherapy. But as psychotherapy also shows us, personal sentiments are no less important than public values for understanding people's reactions to the events around them.

Some verbalization of sentiments occurs, of course. Putting them in a form in which they become an object of scrutiny is, after all, a major concern of artists. Sentiments that are widely shared and that are among people's major preoccupations, for whatever reason, are likely to receive considerable artistic expression and to achieve clearest verbal formulation. Those sentiments that provide the basis for a sense of community, moreover, contribute to the "charter" of the social order. They are what the preambles to constitutions try to express, and serve to remind people of the "spirit" within which they are to exercise their rights and privileges as defined by the social order. So we may speak of a person as behaving in an un-Christian manner even though he is acting perfectly within his rights according to the rules of the social order. But the term "Christian," as thus used, is by no means easy to define so as readily to communicate to the uninitiated person just what is involved. Much close association with others may be needed before he can acquire a "feeling" for what is a Christian style of conduct.

Since there are often wide differences in personal values, a community's members are likely to exhibit not one but several styles of operation in the customary activities in which they engage. Their personal sentiments, aptitudes, and all of the other ingredients of what we regard as people's personalities incline them to model their conduct after one or another of the more prominent styles they encounter in the behavior of their fellows. Occasional individuals, of course, develop rather distinctive styles of their own. Such idiosyncracies of style are not likely to be of concern to agents of change, unless they characterize the behavior of a community leader. But awareness of the several more prominent styles can be important. Indeed, it is precisely such differences in style of thought and action as we label liberal and conservative in our own society, for example, that must be understood if one is to comprehend the course of events in our own public affairs.

The problem of getting along with other people may be likened to a situation where one is called upon to play in a musical ensemble. There is a score to follow, corresponding to the customary forms and the public system of meaning and rules. But it allows for all sorts of variations, cadenzas, and alternative harmonies and resolutions. How the others in the ensemble play within the range of freedom allowed by the score reflects their own musical inclinations, which are not haphazard and become predictable enough if one has a chance to play with them often and thus learn their personal styles. People with different styles of play will be likely to react differently to a proposal to change the score. They will tend to be negative about any change that they feel will "cramp their style."

It is obvious that an agent of change should know the cultural "score" that guides the thoughts and acts of his clients if he is to work with them successfully. But to be effective, it would appear that he must also get acquainted with their main styles of play and give them an opportunity to get acquainted with his.

PUBLIC VALUES IN COMPLEX SOCIETIES

So far we have treated the social order as consisting of rules of conduct that are accepted by a community's members. Acceptance requires that the public values which the rules express be reasonably compatible with personal values, especially those high on the priority scale. If these more important personal values are widely shared, and if there is wide agreement as to the nature of the problems people face, there is little difficulty in arriving at a consensus regarding the allocation of rights and duties. Under such conditions public values remain sufficiently compatible with personal ones as to guarantee their general acceptance. These conditions are most likely to prevail in small communities in which there is little social or economic differentiation and in which there is a broad base of common experience. But even here rival factions may arise.

Factions may agree as to what the system of rules should be and share their acceptance of public values, but vie with one another according to the rules to see who will hold the positions of maximum privilege that the social order allows. Such, for example, is the situation between our own political parties insofar as they compete with each other for the traditional spoils of political victory. Competing factions of this kind raise obvious problems for agents of change, for community development is likely to affect the conditions of their competition and the value in their own eyes of the prizes for which they compete.

Much more serious problems arise, however, when factional differences include disagreement as to what the rules should be, that is, disagreement, concerning the public values themselves. Disagreements of this kind are almost certain to arise in large communities encompassing socially stratified and economically specialized subgroups. Indeed, where there are many different groups within a community, each tends to develop its own system of rules and corresponding public values governing the conduct of its members in their dealings with each other. We see this in connection with social classes, castes, and different ethnic groups within our modern urban communities. Multiple public value systems occur in other types of social group as well. The rules and public values in the lodge, the local National Guard unit, the Church, the political party organization, and the so-called business community are often sufficiently different so that behavior condemned in one as immoral is condoned in a second and even positively valued in a third. Similar differences have been well described for Balinese society.[11] They are not necessarily conflict-provoking, provided certain conditions obtain. Since these conditions have important implications for the development process, we enumerate them below.[12]

1. *Where the same people are members of several different groups that do not have the same code of conduct, the occasions on which these groups operate as such must be mutually exclusive.* It would seriously interfere, for example, with the activities of certain kinds of fraternal organization in our society if they were to meet in the homes of their members. Just as it is necessary to schedule those activities that gratify mutually incompatible wants, so it is necessary to segregate the contexts in which people deal with one another in terms of mutually incompatible codes of conduct expressing incompatible values. In many communities, therefore, the rules and values shift from one setting to another, as from church to business contexts among ourselves.

This helps us understand why it is no simple matter in practice to tailor one's program to local values, even when there are honest efforts to do so. A program geared to fit one set of local values may founder because its scope is not confined to the settings in which those values are felt to be appropriate. A design for a community building drawn up with the values and customs of the men's lodge in mind, for instance, is likely to include some features that would make it unattractive as a place in which to hold church "socials." The different values of the several groups that might use such a building would all have to be considered. A case where very careful planning to introduce hybrid corn in a Spanish American community ended in failure for reasons of this kind is reported by Apodaca.[13] The extension agent appealed to the values of the farmer-producer perfectly, but ran afoul of the values of the consumer.

2. *The dealings that members of different groups have with each other must be confined to contexts that do not interfere with the conduct of affairs within their respective groups and must be governed by rules and values that are acceptable to members of all groups.* This requirement means that where there are subgroups of discrete memberships within a society, each with its own social organization and public values,

there must be an ordering of intergroup relations as well. These groups may be clans, business firms, different church denominations, castes, or political parties.

The public values reflected in the rules governing intergroup relations need not correspond with the values pertaining to conduct within any of the society's constituent groups. Thus the values implied by the traditional code of conduct between whites and Negroes in the American South are not duplicated in the codes by which Negroes govern their dealings with other Negroes or whites with other whites. In colonial areas, likewise, Europeans and their colonial dependents conduct themselves in dealing with one another in ways neither would regard as at all appropriate when dealing with their respective fellows. Intercaste relations in India also are different from those within castes, as are dealings within a social class in our own society as compared with dealings across class lines. In some of these instances, the traditional values governing intergroup relations are no longer acceptable to one of the parties concerned, with the result that we are now witness to a conflict as to whose definitions of rights and privileges shall prevail.

In no large, complex society do all of its subgroups have equal shares of privileges and rights, as when upper-class people deal with lower-class people, for example. This inequality is reflected in the traditional code governing the relations between members of different groups. Provided people's aspiration levels are adjusted accordingly, however, the social order may be accepted without question by the members of most or even all groups concerned. Under conditions of change, of course, new horizons and hopes may develop among the members of less-privileged groups. As this happens and their sense of being frustrated by the established organization of intergroup relations increases, social conflict inevitably arises.

This is of obvious importance to development planners and change agents. Communities that are selected for development are usually parts of a larger social order, and parts whose position in that order has been relatively unprivileged. As development progresses and people acquire new aspirations, they are likely to chafe against the roles they are expected to play by the members of other groups in the larger society. Those who belong to traditionally privileged groups, on the other hand, will interpret expressions of these new aspirations as "forgetting one's place" and as transgressions against the established order. Thus are the lines of social battle drawn. If community development is to proceed without such conflict as one of its results, all groups concerned must be prepared to accept change in their ways of dealing with one another and to make concessions to one another in the interest of keeping the change process an orderly one. Since this is rather unlikely, development agents have the responsibility of deciding whether the conflict that will result will serve their clients' interests and the aims of development or defeat them. To assume that careful planning and initial acceptance of development proposals by the several interested groups will be alone sufficient to prevent social conflict is to indulge in wishful thinking. Conflict emerges as a part of the development process itself and must be anticipated as such. Development agents cannot hope to avoid conflict. Their problem is to learn to understand it and deal with it wisely.

3. *The rules and values by which one group governs its affairs must not create among its side effects conditions that seriously interfere with the ability of members of other groups to pursue their affairs in accordance with their own rules and values.* This is, of course, a condition that is not easily achieved nor, once achieved, easily maintained. For as conditions change, they continually disrupt whatever accommodations to one another the several parties concerned may have worked out.

The contrast between simple and complex societies in this regard is noteworthy. In both alike, change in one activity usually requires adjustments in all the other activities with which it is functionally related. Automation in industry affects employment, for example. A single change may require reorganizing a society's entire schedule of activities. But in simpler communities, where there is little specialization of labor among individuals and groups, the compensatory changes are largely made by the same people in the same group that undertook the initial change. The chances that a new balance between conflicting wants and competing interests will be achieved without social conflict are relatively good. In complex societies, on the other hand, compensatory adjustments have to be made by individuals and groups other than those making the initial changes. Since they do not themselves engage in the activities for which change was originally deemed desirable, they have difficulty appreciating the reasons for the change and regard the adjustments they must make in the conduct of their own affairs as an imposition. The achievement of a new balance is no longer simply a technical matter for a single individual or group of individuals with common concerns; it is a social matter to be negotiated between groups with different stakes in the existing order, and each desirous that any necessary adjustments in the conduct of their internal affairs be made by groups other than their own.

We have already seen how development is likely to lead to conflict among social groups because changes in aspirations make the existing organization of intergroup relations no longer acceptable to one or more of them. At issue in such conflict is how relations among groups shall be conducted and what degrees of privilege will be accorded each. When conflict arises because the side effects of change in one group interfere with the conduct of affairs in other groups within the larger society, what is at issue is the degree of autonomy to be allowed each group to conduct its internal affairs as it wishes in accordance with its own values. Can industrial management allow labor to organize in its own interest, for example; or can labor afford to have no voice in management?

It is a truism that people resent interference by outsiders in the conduct of what they regard as their internal affairs, especially when it aims to alter conduct in ways inconsistent with public values and widely shared personal sentiments. Agents of development are themselves, of course, members of another group in the larger society or community of nations, and they are undertaking development activities because there are aspects of their clients' internal situation that they find disturbing. We must recognize that development efforts are themselves an outgrowth of one group's concern with the way in which another group is managing its affairs. Development aims, of course, to accomplish new adjustments by working within the framework of people's dissatisfaction with things as they are so that they will voluntarily undertake to alter their ways in a direction agents consider desirable from the standpoint of their own group's interests and values. In this way, it is hoped that differences among groups can be negotiated successfully and open conflict avoided. Thus conceived, community development represents a rather novel approach to an age-old problem in intergroup relations. The usual alternative has been, of course, for groups to seek to manipulate or persuade others, by force if necessary, to do their will, an approach that tends to increase intergroup friction and hostility.

This brings us to the final condition contributing to peaceful relations among different groups in complex societies.

4. *The members of each group must not feel compelled to impose their own or any other alien values and code of conduct upon the other groups.*

The "prohibition era" alerted us to the problems that arise when one group sets itself up as the arbiter of the values and morals of others. In most colonial areas also many of the ordinances emanating from colonial authorities are ignored or evaded at the village level, unless needed to keep up appearances and avoid punitive sanctions. Outhouses will be built but not used, to cite a familiar example. And in industrial management in our own society, things that are regularly done in practice in the shop often conform to a code of conduct and public value system subscribed to by the labor force but at variance with the system of rules set up by managerial officials and believed by them to be in operation. Whenever one group seeks to impose rules of conduct on other groups that are incompatible with the latter's values, systematic evasion results. Compliance can be achieved only by the exercise of constant policing and the use of punitive sanctions.

As representatives of an alien group, development agents obviously have to be circumspect when they seek to introduce ways of doing things that are out of line with their clients' personal and public values. Since the aims of development preclude the use of force, agents can only expect that their clients will fail to conduct themselves according to plan. Nor will indirect pressures short of naked force accomplish the desired results. The failure of this approach to development is well illustrated by the Creek Indians' unwillingness to go along with efforts by the United States Indian Service "to remold their political structure into greater conformity with that of the country as a whole."[14] As Opler's analysis in this example reveals, many important Creek values were associated with their own "town" organization, values with which the forms of local government desired by the Indian Service were incompatible.

A British effort in town planning has also proved disappointing for similar reasons. Faced with the problem of designing and building communities for population resettlement, the planners undertook their planning with upper middle-class and professional values in mind as to what constitutes a "good" community. Their model of the good community was one in which people of all classes would live side by side and mix freely. They identified the things they most valued with an idealized form of small town in a rural setting. Such models and values determined the goals of planning and thereby the "needs" of the new communities. The physical design of these communities was laid out with an eye to creating conditions that would invite people to live in accordance with the planners' values. What was intended to give people a fuller and happier life impressed many as an irritating infringement upon their personal freedom to live according to their own values and their own conception of the good life, which did not correspond with that of the planners.[15] By contrast, the resettlement of surplus population from the Gilbert Islands in the uninhabited Phoenix Islands of the Pacific Ocean was successfully carried through because the planning was done very largely by the settlers themselves, whose concern was to make the resulting communities, within the resources available to them, the kinds of places that they themselves regarded as agreeable to live in.[16]

In whatever guise it may appear, it is safe to say that the missionary approach to development, in which an agent's objective is to get others to live according to his values, can succeed only when the agent's clients have decided that these are the values by which they wish to live. This may happen when changing conditions have rendered the old social order and its public values a source of so much personal frustration as to produce widespread dissatisfaction with it. Otherwise, development planning aimed at transmitting the agent's values to his clients is almost certain to fail. But, one may ask, isn't it possible to educate people to see things our way? The answer remains the same: yes, *if they are willing to be educated;* otherwise, no. We are able to educate our children to the values of our society because most of them want to operate successfully within our society and are willing to accept its public values as a condition of their doing so. But when they reject our society, for whatever reason, our efforts to educate them regularly fail. It is not likely that adult members of other societies will be as willing as our children to be educated to our values.

This brings us back to consider the basic aims of community development. Whatever we think they ought to be, according to our own values, it is evident that some present fewer obstacles to cooperation in change than do others. If the object is to help people improve their present state of material and psychological well-being, then there is need to try to bring about changes in their social order and the values by which they live only insofar as they function to prevent improvement in one's clients' own sense of well-being. Otherwise, it does not matter what form their social order or its values take, either now or in the future. Even when thus limited, to bring about changes in personal sentiments and, through them, in public values is no simple matter. But if the object of development is to get people to live in conformity with a particular set of values, regardless of their effect on people's material and psychological well-being, or on the assumption that it will promote their "highest" well-being—that is, if values rather than living conditions are the ultimate end of development —then it would appear that the possibilities of obtaining the co-operation of one's clients are very limited indeed.

SUGGESTED READING

Firth, Raymond, *Elements of Social Organization.* Philosophical Library, New York, 1951, chap. 2.

Homans, George C., *The Human Group.* Harcourt, Brace and Co., New York, 1950, chap. 2.

Leighton, Alexander H., *My Name Is Legion:* Foundations for a Theory of Man in Relation to Culture. Basic Books, Inc., New York, 1959, chap. 7 and appendix A.

Linton, Ralph, *The Study of Man.* Appleton-Century Co., New York, 1936. See especially Chapters 7, 8, 15, 16, 24, and 25.

Kluckhohn, Clyde, "Values and Value-orientations in the Theory of Action: An Exploration in Definition and Classification" in Parsons, Talcott, and Edward A. Shils, editors, *Toward a General Theory of Action.* Harvard University Press, Cambridge, Mass., 1951, pp. 388–433.

NOTES TO CHAPTER 5

1. For developments in the psychology of association formation, see Rock, Irvin, "Repetition and Learning," *Scientific American*, vol. 199, August, 1958, pp. 68–72.

2. As Kluckhohn has put it, ". . . a value may be defined as that aspect of motivation which is referable to standards, personal and cultural, that do not arise solely out of an immediate situation and the satisfaction of needs and primary drives." (Kluckhohn, Clyde, "The Scientific Study of Values," *University of Toronto Installation Lectures, 1958*, University of Toronto Press, Toronto, 1958.) Thus conceived, values are not simply the choices people make but their bases for judging the propriety of their choices, either before or after the fact. In the absence of all social restraints, propriety must be judged in terms of one's own conception of self and one's long range as opposed to immediate self-goals. (See our discussion in Chapter 8.)

3. Bennett, John W., Herbert Passin, and Robert K. McKnight, *In Search of Identity:* The Japanese Overseas Scholar in America and Japan, University of Minnesota Press, Minneapolis, 1958; Cleveland, Harlan, Gerard J. Mangone, and John Clarke Adams, *The Overseas Americans*, McGraw-Hill Book Co., New York, 1960.

4. Beals, Ralph L., "The Village in an Industrial World," *The Scientific Monthly*, vol. 72, 1953, pp. 65–75.

5. See the discussion of "rites of intensification" by Eliot Dismore Chapple and Carleton Stevens Coon, *Principles of Anthropology.* Henry Holt and Co., New York, 1942, pp. 507–528.

6. For the idea of *esprit de corps* as essential to the existence of human society, see Linton, Ralph, *The Study of Man*, Appleton-Century Co., New York, 1936, pp. 92–98. For its original full development for social theory, see the writings of Emil Durkheim.

7. Grinker, Roy R., and John P. Spiegel, *Men Under Stress*, Blakiston Co., Philadelphia, 1945, Part 4. The great importance of strong primary group ties in connection with psychiatric breakdown is thoroughly documented by David G. Mandelbaum, "Psychiatry in Military Society," *Human Organization*, vol. 13, no. 3, pp. 5–15, and vol. 13, no. 4, pp. 19–25.

8. Wellin, Edward, "Water Boiling in a Peruvian Town" in Paul, Benjamin D., editor, *Health, Culture and Community:* Case Studies of Public Reaction to Health Programs. Russell Sage Foundation, New York, 1955, pp. 86–90.

9. For the definition of a status as "a collection of rights and duties," see Linton, Ralph, *op. cit.*, p. 113.

10. For an analysis of status systems as ordered allocations of combinations of rights, duties, and privileges, and for the necessity to keep them conceptually distinct from the various categories of person within a social system, see Goodenough, Ward H., *Property, Kin, and Community on Truk*, Yale University Publications in

Anthropology No. 46, Department of Anthropology, Yale University, New Haven, 1951.

11. Geertz, Clifford, "Form and Variation in Balinese Village Structure," *American Anthropologist*, vol. 61, 1959, pp. 991–1012.

12. For illustrative material see Lindgren, E. J., "An Example of Culture Contact without Conflict: Reindeer Tungus and Cossacks of Northwestern Manchuria," *American Anthropologist*, vol. 40, 1938, pp. 605–621. See also Pehrson, R. N., "Culture Contact Without Conflict in Lapland," *Man*, vol. 50, 1950, article 256.

13. Apodaca, Anacleto, "Corn and Custom: The Introduction of Hybrid Corn to Spanish American Farmers in New Mexico" in Spicer, Edward H., editor, *Human Problems in Technological Change:* A Casebook. Russell Sage Foundation, New York, 1952, pp. 35–39.

14. Opler, Morris Edward, "The Creek 'Town' and the Problem of Creek Indian Political Reorganization" in Spicer, Edward H., editor, *op. cit.*, p. 165.

15. Orlans, Harold, *Utopia Ltd.:* The Story of the English New Town of Stevenage. Yale University Press, New Haven, 1953.

16. Laxton, Paul B., "Nikumaroro," *Journal of the Polynesian Society*, vol. 60, 1951, pp. 134–160; also Maude, H. E., "The Colonization of the Phoenix Islands," *ibid.*, vol. 61, 1952, pp. 62–89.

Chapter 6

VALUES UNDER FRUSTRATION

WE HAVE OBSERVED that people's sentiments and values are complicated by the fact that some of their wants are necessarily frustrated or uncertain of gratification. To these complications we now turn. Their consideration will help us understand why people often value highly things that strike an observer as valueless. Without insight into why people want the things they do, change agents cannot easily accord their wants the respect cooperation in change requires. However much agents are prepared to deal circumspectly with the things their clients value highly when they can themselves see good reasons for doing so, they are inclined, like the rest of us, to grow impatient when their clients' refusal to give something up strikes them as "unreasonable." As we shall see, the apparently unreasonable attachment people show for things is often due to the compensations they derive from them in the face of the various frustrations and deprivations they must endure.

No one can possibly be free of frustration. Since not all wants can be gratified, the necessity to choose between them results in some frustration. Everyone has to inhibit acting on some wants in order not to close the door on gratifications he values more. Many frustrations come from the demands that the rules of our social order make upon us and from the way in which our fellows exercise the privileges the rules allow them, as when we are patients subject to hospital rules and to the privileges and powers of physicians and nurses, or workers subject to shop rules. As students, likewise, we suffer frustration from school rules and must put up with the various ways in which teachers exercise the privileges that are rightfully theirs. Highly frustrating, also, are those situations in which we are forced to choose between the public values embodied in the social order and the private sentiments by which we judge our own worth. Such dilemmas have provided the materials for high tragedy since literature began. In a minor way they are a part of the experience of many of us. The more completely we are able to incorporate public values into our sentiment system, the freer we become of such conflicts. Still other frustrations arise from circumstances outside the social order. We must suffer limitations of resources, the vagaries of weather, natural catastrophes, military conquests, and the actions of others that violate our rights and immunities as defined by the social order.

Of some of our frustrated wants we are, of course, acutely conscious. But we are not consciously aware of others, especially the frustrated infantile desires we may discover in ourselves through psychiatric depth analysis. Nevertheless, whether we are conscious of them or not and whatever their source, our frustrations are something with which we must all try to deal.

THE PROBLEM OF SELF-CONTROL

The natural immediate response to frustration appears to be anger or rage.[1] But there are many situations in which such response can avail little. When we suffer frustration because of the legitimate demands of the social order, for example, our fellows are likely either to ignore our display of temper or to frustrate us further on account of it by way of punishment. We are constrained by circumstances and other people, alike, to develop ways of coming to terms with our frustrations and deprivations. We have to learn to live with, and in spite of, them without overindulgence in temper tantrums or expressions of self-pity. Furthermore, insofar as we feel forced to inhibit expressing our natural feelings of anger and are frustrated in this respect, too, we have to learn to deal with these feelings in socially acceptable ways as well.

In the face of chronic frustration, anger gives way in time to a sense of helplessness with a turning to such other sources of gratification as may appear to be available. Thus children who have been left by their parents, as in hospitals, after their initial outcry against their loneliness are likely to become quiet and exceedingly tractable. The outrage and deep resentment they feel is vehemently expressed when they return home, however, as Bowlby's studies have so poignantly revealed.[2] The sense of deprivation carries with it not only resentment but great longing, a craving that seems insatiable when opportunities for gratification once again present themselves. Thus, after returning home from the hospital, children will cling to their parents, refusing to let them out of their sight, seeming desperately unable to get enough of them. At the same time they will take out their resentment for earlier deprivation in all sorts of ways, making themselves "impossible." In time, given sufficient parental love and patience, they settle down once more.

We use this example to illustrate in familiar terms the emotions to which frustration gives rise, especially when it persists over a period of time. Parents are so important to children, that to be deprived of their presence, especially in conditions of stress, is disturbing in the extreme. But it would be a mistake to think that chronic frustration, with the consequent mixture of empty craving and deep resentment characteristic of deprivation, is out of the ordinary in human experience. On the contrary, it marks the social maturation of every human being. We all come to attach great value to experiences we find highly gratifying only to have to give them up as we grow older. Weaning is a process to which we are subject all our lives.[3] The pleasures of infancy are taken away from us to be replaced by the pleasures of childhood. These must be abandoned for the privileges of adulthood, and they, in turn, must be surrendered in old age. We do not make these transitions without protest, and there are some of us who stubbornly refuse to "grow up." Each new step up the maturation ladder is marked by emotional storms.[4] As we win through each to the calm of a new and more mature adjustment, we gain in emotional richness and in wisdom. But we also bear the emotional scars in the form of buried resentments and old cravings, long unrequited. To see children maltreated or deprived arouses our own old hurt within us and brings to the surface our own great resentments of long ago with vindictive force. We identify ourselves completely with the abused children and regard no punishment as too severe for those whom we judge responsible.

Thus we are all confronted with complex emotional problems in which there are things we want that we cannot have, are not allowed to have, or cannot allow ourselves to have. We feel angry that this should be so, but cannot always allow ourselves to show our annoyance freely. Because the gratification of our other wants appears to depend on our ability to control ourselves in these matters, self-control over cravings and resentments alike becomes important to us. The situations that call for self-control give us anxiety when we are uncertain of our ability to exercise it. Certainly, we feel greatest trepidation on the occasions when we feel least sure of ourselves and, at the same time, have much at stake. Our feelings of anxiety are then added to the emotions we must somehow manage successfully. Our anxiety and insecurity are frustrating in themselves and incline us to be angry at ourselves and the circumstances which put us in such situations. How to cope with the desires, angers, and anxieties at odds within us in a manner that is in keeping with the public value system on the one hand and with our personal ideals for ourselves on the other is, in one context or another, an important problem in the lives of us all—so long, that is, as we value the privileges of membership in a human community sufficiently to want to abide by its rules of conduct.

The problem of control over desires and angers is largely situation bound, so that while we must keep our emotions from showing in our behavior in some settings, we are free to express them in others. If the boss has humiliated us, we will hold ourselves in check until he has left the scene and then let go when we are no longer subject to further punishment. We feel the emotion, but we restrain it. If we are anxious about our ability to restrain our emotions in situations where it is important for us to do so, we may suppress them so that we are hardly aware of their presence within us, except for a vague tension. We may make up for it by overreacting emotionally in other situations where we feel free. When we are afraid to allow ourselves the privilege of letting go at all (whether we are realistic in our fear or not), we may totally suppress all expression of the emotion in question and become through self-censorship incapable of exhibiting it even when it is expected of us. When such is the case we say we are "repressed." The clinical evidence shows that even when we are not conscious of our feelings, as when we suppress them, we still have them. The glandular processes that accompany emotional states are still going on. In more repressed individuals, these processes are likely to produce physical symptoms, giving rise to chronic bodily ailments. Asthma and stomach ulcers, for example, often have their origin in the biochemical effects of long-suppressed or repressed emotion. Such are not imaginary ailments that are "all in one's head," but genuine breakdowns that result from the bodily stresses of excessive emotional control.[5]

The frustrations, deprivations, and anxieties we individually suffer are in some ways unlike those of anyone else. No two of us have identical histories of experience. Nor do we develop identical ways of dealing with the problems of restraint and self-control. These are among the things that contribute to each personality's uniqueness. But we are concerned with personality theory only as it helps us to understand the affective meaning that people's traditional practices and customary surroundings have for them.[6]

From this standpoint, we observe that members of the same community tend to be subject to similar conditions of life, customary practices, and rules of conduct. They share similar frustrations and face similar problems of self-control insofar as the rules of their social order apply to them equally and they have similar private sentiments and personal values. We observe further that, in accordance with the way they are structured and defined, the social rules offer lines of least resistance that dispose people to develop techniques for coping with emotional problems in particular directions. Societies whose rules tolerate a good deal of physical aggression among their members in contact sports, for example, offer possibilities for draining off accumulated hostilities and resentments in acceptable ways that are not present in societies where physically violent sports are regarded as improper. Despite individual differences in innate tendencies[7] and in the strength of one's inner resources to sustain frustration, we expect that members of the same community are likely to have some emotional concerns in common and to have developed similar ways of handling them. In this way they may exhibit similar "character traits."

For this reason, we sometimes note contrasts in the kinds of personalities that people in different communities display.[8] This does not mean, to be sure, that a particular kind of personality can be attributed to all members of one community; but though they differ, the personalities of individuals in a community tend to cluster around a few prevailing modes that sometimes contrast significantly with the modes for other community populations.[9] What we referred to in the preceding chapter as prevailing styles of conduct in interpersonal relations may well reflect these modal tendencies in personality organization. Many questions about these phenomena, however, are yet to be satisfactorily answered. We need only remark, in keeping with the views expressed here, that students of personality differences between societies have concentrated their efforts to explain them by comparing the ways in which infantile wants are regularly frustrated and gratified as a result of differences in customary approaches to child-rearing and socialization.[10] Their findings to date would seem to confirm the assumption that customary patterns of frustration and gratification are an important contributing factor.[11]

TECHNIQUES OF EMOTIONAL CONTROL AND THEIR INSTITUTIONAL EXPRESSION

Everyone has to learn to live with his frustrations, deprivations, and anxieties; and everyone develops techniques for doing so. Where there are particular emotional problems that many people share, moreover, there are likely to be institutional activities that function specifically to help people manage them. Some of these activities, such as those associated with "hot-rods" in our own society, may be regarded with disfavor by a majority in the community. Some may even be classed as criminal. Among ourselves, for example, prostitution is a well-organized and established activity in spite of its being illegal. That it is unknown in some societies, as was the case until very recently, at least, in Truk,[12] suggests that its persistence among us, in spite of our laws and our public values, is a result of the kinds of problems our way of life creates for some of us. It is a paradox that in many, if not all societies, some activities which are publicly disapproved are privately condoned, so that by conducting them secretly or unobtrusively people enable themselves to abide by the social rules in the public arena and keep up proper appearances without excessive emotional strain. Some of the practices condemned by the moral code may be necessary to the continued existence of that code. On the other hand, many practices that help people keep their emotions within social bounds are looked upon with general favor and may occupy a high place within the scale of public values. The following activity on Truk provides an example.

Periodically the people of Truk expend great energy amassing quantities of food for exchange between social groups in competitive feasting. These feasts are highly valued. The emphasis is on trying to eat one's host out of his supplies, much to his shame. The guests do not expect that they will really be able to do so. The point is that this emphasis gives them license to have an orgy of eating. As one Trukese told us, "There is nothing more beautiful in this world than a great pile of food at a feast. You look at it, and you know that you can eat all you want, that everyone else can eat all he wants, and when everyone is finished there will still be a great pile of food left." At the same time, the accumulated angers over previous feelings of frustration are indulged by permitting the orgy to be expressed as a hostile act aimed at shaming one's host.

Psychological study has revealed that among Truk's people major frustrations and anxieties center around food.[13] In addition to competitive and other institutionalized feasting, religious ritual also gives expression to these concerns. The most elaborate cycle of ceremonies is aimed at ensuring by supernatural and magical means a good breadfruit harvest; and in Truk breadfruit, like bread among Europe's peasants, is the symbol of food. Although the yields of breadfruit vary sufficiently on occasion to provide reasonable basis for some concern, this variation is not sufficient to account for the anxiety people display about food in daily talk and ritual elaboration. The many little frustrations which the aforementioned study shows us that Trukese children suffer in their relations with their parents, including irregular and unpredictable (though nutritionally adequate) feeding, account more convincingly for the emotional investment in food as expressed institutionally in licensed self-indulgence and religious ritual.

We know, of course, that recreational and religious institutions function in many more ways than helping people to handle their chronic frustrations or the chronic anxieties stemming from childhood frustrations. But we need only think of the prominence given by Christian leaders to the problem of the "fleshly" desires to be reminded that those of our wants whose gratification is heavily curtailed or entirely disallowed by our public values and our rules of conduct remain a problem in our emotional or spiritual life. To make up for our inability to gratify these desires directly we have institutional ways of indulging them vicariously, as with our calendar and billboard art. And advertising regularly appeals to the young, middle-class, American housewife, driven by the many needs of husband and children and without another adult woman in the house to share her responsibilities, by appealing to her frustrated desires for time to attend to her own wants with picture displays of her imagined self in attitudes of extreme languor and narcissistic self-indulgence. If we continue in this vein of thought, we may well begin to wonder how much of what we represent to ourselves and to others as the benefits of the American way of life are institutionalized fantasies we have created in order to indulge vicariously those of our desires that are chronically frustrated for most of us in real life. If such a thought repels us as heresy, we perceive thereby how important are the fantasies and dreams in which people indulge in more acceptable manner the wants that their daily responsibilities and duties within the social order do not permit them to gratify.

Occasional licensed indulgence of normally frustrated wants or their vicarious gratification in art, literature, mythology, drama, and other forms of fantasy or play acting by no means complete the roster of techniques for dealing with the emotional problems frustration helps to generate. Psychiatrists and psychological counselors are familiar with a number of devices employed by their clients. Knowledge of these devices helps us understand the value people attach to some of their customary beliefs and practices. It will be worth our while, therefore, to discuss them further. We may illustrate them by reference to some of their major types as they have been formulated by psychoanalysts.[14] In doing so, we shall not attempt to be orthodox. Nor is our concern with emotional pathology. For us, these psychoanalytic concepts are convenient points of departure from which to illustrate the complexities and subtleties of human values.

Displacement

When a person shifts the affect he has for one object or person to another as a substitute for the first, the second acquiring the value of the first, we say that he has displaced his feelings. Both positive and negative affect may be displaced.

When we kick the door after our boss has dressed us down, we are displacing our anger at the boss onto a convenient object that cannot hurt back. Such displacement is momentary. Chronic hostility producing situations within a community, however, may result in institutional displacement of aggressive feelings onto persons from outside the community, as with the practice of cannibalism or the ritualized torture of war captives. Or hostile feelings may be displaced toward a particular subgroup within the community that provides the customary target for the others, as with the Jews in Nazi Germany or Negroes among some segments of the white population in the southern part of the United States. There is, indeed, a general principle we can observe regarding the displacement of negative affect. Since anger and hate are products of frustration, and since we are most frequently frustrated in those relationships in which we participate most regularly, the source of much if not most of our hostility is in the very relationships in which we can least afford to show it, where its immediate targets are the persons toward whom the social rules allow us the least freedom to direct it.[15] This hostility has to be displaced if it is to find expression and not remain so repressed as to lead to severe physical strain. What tends to happen, therefore, is that we show the greatest hostility in those relationships and toward those people with whom we deal frequently and who are at the same time just outside the boundaries within which we feel it necessary to restrain and suppress hostile feelings.[16] So it is that many of the people toward whom we express our greatest dislike, have a negative value for us that cannot be accounted for in terms of the actual provocation their behavior causes us. Their behavior need provoke only enough to provide legitimate excuse for making them targets upon which to displace all of our other hostilities. The provocation may be no more than the little misunderstandings that arise by virtue of minor differences in customary procedures and public values of the sort that obtain between different neighboring communities, social classes, or ethnic divisions within a plural society.

To transform traditionally hostile relationships within and between communities is not infrequently an aim of social development. Often, too, the goals of economic and political development require cooperation between groups that have been customary targets for one another's displaced hostilities. One way to deal with this problem is to try to reduce the total amount of frustration the people concerned must sustain in the normal course of living, so that less hostility is being generated in other situations to be displaced into the relationship in question. Another approach is to alter the circumstances of interraction between the traditionally hostile groups so as to bring members of each together in contexts within which, according to their own rules of conduct, expressions and even feelings of hostility are out of order. Thus Negro and white soldiers who served together in the same combat units tended to lose their conscious feelings of hostility for one another,[17] because they were members of the same group within which mutual loyalty was important in the established public value system.

It has often been asserted that if people will interact more frequently, they will lose their "prejudiced" dislike for one another. This is not necessarily true. If they interact more frequently within contexts in which their rules of conduct permit expressions of hostility, hostility may increase rather than decrease. A change of contexts as defined by their respective social orders is required. And the prospect of such change is likely to produce considerable resistance, as is evidenced by the racial segregation issue in the United States, for to end segregation is, in effect, to bring Negroes and whites into situations where they must deal with one another as schoolmates, neighbors, or fellow club members: social relationships in which the rules of the social order prohibit expressions of antagonism and hostility. The fear of those who resist integration that it will constrain them to alter their present attitudes toward Negroes is not unrealistic, though morally indefensible when judged by other values. We find this situation duplicated in India, where there is widespread popular resistance to official policies aimed at freeing untouchables from the restrictions surrounding them.[18]

Displacement of positive affect is seen when a man invests in his wife some of the feelings he formerly felt for his mother. As growing children are forced to give up infantile forms of gratification, they displace their attachment for objects that are no longer appropriate as instruments of gratification to other objects, whose value is largely derived from them. Thus an attachment for the breast or bottle is displaced to the thumb, the blanket, or some other "security symbol." Adults have their security symbols and fetishes, too, whether they be a rabbit's foot, medallion, gun, or tobacco pipe. When material objects come to stand as symbols for immaterial entities that are highly valued, as the cross stands for an event and the flag for a state, they often acquire the value of the thing for which they stand. For purposes of national recognition any agreed-upon insignia will do; but once it has been adopted, then we love or hate it every bit as much as we love or hate the country with which we associate it.

It is, of course, physically impossible to express affect directly toward many things we value highly, as with abstract ideas such as God or Country. Concrete symbols of these valued abstractions acquire corresponding value by virtue of displacement. In every society there are objects and persons to which strong affect attaches for this reason, whether it be king, idol, clan totem, home, or temple. Thus in the southern Gilbert Islands, the community meeting house is an important symbol of the local body politic. People proudly say of it that in the northern islands there may be kings, but "here the meeting house is king." The building is hedged about with taboo and ceremony, and people are expected to show it respect, dismounting from their bicycles when passing it, for example. This building is worshiped because of the many intangible and immaterial things in community relationships that are highly valued and that it represents in concrete form. It is difficult to talk about the intangibles distilled from a host of fleeting and half-forgotten experiences, but it is easy to talk about the meeting house and to show one's feelings toward it.[19]

In many instances we are well aware of the "sentimental reasons" for cherishing certain things. But when displacement results because of the necessity to deny ourselves or inhibit gratification in some other form, we may eventually be unable to give any reason at all for the value we attach to something. This is bound to be true of things that acquired value by way of displacement early in our lives before verbal facility provided a basis for developing a memory. It is also true where anxiety over self-control leads us to suppress from consciousness our feelings toward someone or something. The like or dislike that we have for something or our addiction to some fetish object will then appear inexplicable to us and irrational to anyone observing us who does not share our sentiments. We can only say that it is our "nature" to feel as we do.

There is nothing about displacement that is in itself either good or bad. Displacement from breast to thumb, to lollypops, to cigarets represents a chain of adaptive adjustments to a particular set of social realities whereby an originally infantile craving can still be gratified in an acceptably mature manner. It is only when displacement is to persons or objects that are inappropriate in view of the expectations of others and the demands of the social order that its results are personally maladaptive. The same can be said of displacement in its institutional forms. It is adaptive or maladaptive, depending on the kinds of side effects the customary displacements create and whether these side effects create more or less serious problems than they solve.

Displacement has an important bearing on what happens to people's values under conditions of change. The wider the range of objects, persons, and situations on which is displaced a particular feeling of love or hate that cannot be expressed directly, the easier it is to do without one of them as an outlet for one's feelings. As new objects for displacing affect are added to old ones, the positive or negative valuation of the old ones diminishes in intensity. The prospect of losing access to one of them triggers less resistance. Conversely, of course, with loss of access to old objects of displacement, those that remain become the targets for more displaced affect, so that they are more intensely loved or hated than before and the prospect of losing them arouses greater resistance. For this reason, we observe that as our relationship to our surroundings changes in the course of time, as our surroundings themselves undergo change, we tend to become more deeply attached to what is as yet unchanged. The remaining things and relationships become symbols of those that are gone and acquire their now displaced value. Similarly, as many contending enemies eliminate one another, the fight among those who remain becomes progressively fiercer, and the stakes seem to acquire greater value. The course of economic and social change, as it increases or diminishes the gross amount of frustration and as it adds to or subtracts from the number of displacement channels, is accompanied by corresponding fluctuations in intensity of feeling about the old, in resistance to change, and in conservative and progressive orientation.

Projection

In its widest sense, projection refers to the process by which people read into a situation things that really are not there. When people look at clouds passing overhead and see various figures represented, they are putting something into them. The origin of that something is in the thoughts, feelings, and perceptual habits of the beholders, who have projected a part of themselves into what they are looking at. In a somewhat narrower sense, projection refers more technically to the situation in which we attribute to others attitudes and feelings that they do not in fact have but that would, if they did have them, legitimize our own feelings toward them.

Paranoia, for example, usually involves an attribution of hostile intent to others as justification for giving vent to one's own angers and hates that one cannot suppress or easily restrain. It is manifest in people with well-developed consciences, who feel guilty about the feelings they have, who have tried to control their feelings, and who are suffering acute anxiety about their ability to do so. As they have increasing difficulty containing themselves, they allay their anxiety and guilt by discovering through projection that their feelings were really justified. People without conscience have no such need to project.

Hostile feelings are, perhaps, among those most commonly projected, but they are not the only ones subject to this process. A mother who has a strong desire to keep her children dependent upon her may attribute to them wants and needs by which to justify her behavior in her own eyes.

Projection often goes hand in hand with displacement. Thus people who have strong angers and hostilities toward parents or village elders, feelings they cannot legitimately feel, will be inclined to attribute hostile and aggressive motives to them. They may develop a belief that old people are powerful sorcerers and that it is, therefore, dangerous to cross them. The old people will disclaim that they are, but will agree that the allegation was true in the case of their own elders. At the same time they may exploit the belief on occasion, hinting at possible powers when they desire to control the behavior of the young. But even such inverted expression of hostility toward one's elders cannot be allowed to go too far without creating other emotional problems. One may, therefore, displace these feelings to the forest or the cemetery, attributing hostile intent to amorphous but ferocious spirits or to the ghosts of past elders. With these disembodied, symbolic substitutes for the real targets of our feelings we can freely play out the passions within us, and what we project upon them fully justifies our doing so.

Sublimation

Whereas displacement is the redirection of feelings from one target to another, whether the result is adaptive or maladaptive, sublimation refers to the rechanneling of energies mobilized by sexual or other socially taboo desires into activities that are socially approved. It is in many respects no more than a special case of displacement. We mention it because it emphasizes the rapprochement people make between their private sentiments and public values, and because it helps us understand the functional importance of some activities for a community as a whole, as well as their meaning for some individuals.

A surgeon in our society, for example, may have suppressed hostilities generated in his family relationships as a child. In his profession he can inflict bodily injury on others, thus gratifying an unconscious desire, and at the same time perform a public service which his clients value highly. The devotion he shows to his work, the hours spent in perfecting his surgical skills, may owe much to the energies his suppressed desires have mobilized. Psychologists have long postulated that people tend to be attracted to particular professions in our society because of the kinds of opportunities they offer for expressing in sublimated form important private value orientations whose more direct expression would violate the public code of conduct. A recent study of the professions gives empirical support to this deduction.[20]

Ritual not infrequently provides opportunities for people to sublimate socially disapproved desires. Among the Iroquois Indians, for example, the curing and other rites associated with the False Face Society allowed those who performed them to express their suppressed desires for passive gratification of an infantile sort in a context that was valued as socially constructive.[21] The ritual self-torture of the Plains Indians also permitted an open expression of strong masochistic tendencies as a heroic sacrifice to promote the general welfare.[22]

When a society offers its members many different roles which they may legitimately play, it maximizes the opportunities for successfully sublimating desires and urges whose expression would otherwise result in antisocial or criminal behavior. When change takes these roles away or makes them no longer respected (as with the role of local medicine man, perhaps), the resulting loss of important avenues for sublimination may lead to an increase in socially disruptive behavior. At the same time, of course, change may bring with it new opportunities. Many a former social misfit has been transformed as he found a chance to "lose himself" in a new role congenial to his personal predilections.

Sublimation calls attention to the fact that people derive from many of the customary activities in which they engage some gratifications that they cannot admit to others and may not even admit to themselves. The reasons they give for engaging in them will be acceptable to them and to their fellows because they are in line with public values and personal ideals, but they may have little or nothing to do with the true source of motive power. To an agent of change or other stranger to their community, the reasons people give in public explanation of their activities may seem entirely unconvincing. Indeed, from the observer's point of view they may reflect erroneous conceptions of reality. An agent may assume from this that once people are shown that their explanations are false they will see the lack of reason for the associated activity and be willing to abandon it. On this basis he may decide that a program of education is what is needed in order to effect a change. Such assumptions and all that follow from them, however, may be naive, concentrating on matters that are incidental rather than crucial to the real meaning of a custom and ignoring entirely its covert but important psychological functions in the fabric of community life.

Reaction Formation

When we encounter difficulty controlling impulses within us to act in ways that are socially disapproved, or that for other reasons we feel compelled to suppress, our efforts at self-control are not made easier if we are constantly confronted with temptation. If there are no opportunities to act, it is easy to refrain from acting. If we are not presented with situations in which we are afraid we may betray our suppressed desires to others and reveal ourselves as something other than what we purport to be, then we are free of anxiety. When we are confronted with such opportunities and situations, however, we not only become anxious, we also tend to resent the circumstances that try us and the persons we associate with them or hold responsible for them. As self-control becomes difficult we may seek to remove all such circumstances and persons from our lives. We may even declare war upon them, if the public value system provides a convenient rationalization for doing so, marshaling all our resources in a supreme effort to preserve a particular self-image. Such efforts are matters of vital importance to us, something to which we dedicate ourselves with passion.

Thus to turn one's secret desire for something into abhorrence of everything that one associates with it is what is technically called a reaction formation. Professional crusaders against anything suggestive of sex in our society are classic examples. And writers to the newspapers clamoring for the death sentence against people convicted or accused of murder usually express themselves in the strident and vitriolic tones of persons who can scarcely contain the murderous impulses within themselves. The overconcern of some parents for the physical safety of their children, clinical experience shows, is likely to mask a secret resentment of them. To help suppress their desire to be rid of them, they not only show concern for real dangers to their welfare but busily war against highly improbably ones as well. Excessive demonstrations of affection are also likely to represent a reaction formation in response to barely suppressed hostility. But we should not conclude from this that reaction formations are characteristic only of highly neurotic personalities or of the "lunatic fringe."

There is probably no socialized human being who does not have some antipathies or profess some affections as a result of this process. The almost universal horror that people exhibit toward cases of incest has been plausibly interpreted as a reaction formation.[23] The deep revulsion that people in our society express toward cannibalism is not improbably a reflection, in part at least, of the same process. For that matter, reaction formation undoubtedly provides the psychological foundation for emotional commitment to the sanction systems by which people seek to enforce compliance with their public code of conduct. People come to feel strongly about right and wrong as they learn to inhibit impulses within themselves. Were there no problems of self-control connected with social living, there would be no emotional feeling about the social rules. The phenomenon of morality with all the emotion with which it is laden would scarcely exist without the reaction formations a community's members share as a result of their common experiences.

So it is that people develop strong feelings about all sorts of things associated in their minds with the taboo acts that they have suppressed impulses to perform and that, in many cases, they did perform at one time in their lives with great gratification.

Children in our society, for example, have to learn not to mess in smeary things, an activity from which they seem to get genuine sensory pleasure. At first, they may displace such desires from their food at the dinner table to making mud pies outdoors, but in time they are trained to give up these pleasures as well. They are too incompatible with our standards of clean personal appearance. The end result is a strong antipathy for anything that is suggestive of the sensory experience one once enjoyed by squeezing mud between the toes or squishing pablum through the fingers. We have a pronounced aversion to all physical contact with anything that we perceive as "slimy." This aversion is not natural to the unsocialized human being, but results directly from a reaction formation shared by members of our society. In this case it does not usually lead to what we regard as pathological behavior. On the contrary it leads to a great deal of cooperation in maintaining what we agree to be proper standards of cleanliness.

As this example suggests, reaction formation is responsible not only for many private value orientations but for our commitment to many public values as well. It helps to explain the strong aversions that people in every society feel for some kinds of conduct and experience. What these aversions are, of course, differs considerably as we go from one society to another. For this reason they are among the most common stumbling blocks to cross-cultural understanding. Just as we find it difficult to understand other people's aversion to food we happen to enjoy, they find it difficult to understand our enjoyment. By all that is most firmly rooted in direct experience we make no sense to them nor they to us. So it is in other aspects of behavior. And where reaction formation is so strong as to keep people in perpetual mobilization to war upon all instances of deviation from a strict standard, they inevitably conduct themselves like fanatics when they start dealing with people who do not share this particular orientation.

Reaction formation helps to account for the fanaticism often displayed by recent converts to a new code of conduct. Not having become habituated to it, they have greater difficulty preventing themselves from "backsliding," and therefore must mobilize more strenuously and ardently against all temptations to revert to former ways. When agents of change are successful in winning a community's genuine commitment to a program that calls for changes in traditional modes of conduct, they must expect some fanaticism in their clients. They are likely to react to any deviation from the new "line" and any straying from the new "path" with a severity that may appall development agents. Many are the missionaries who have had trouble with overly zealous converts.

Before leaving the subject of reaction formation, we should take note of the way it works in conjunction with projection to foster some of the stereotypes that different ethnic, racial, and social groups develop about each other. In Nazi Germany, for example, a common accusation against Jews was that they were sexy, shady in business dealings, and in other ways lax regarding those aspects of the moral code that created the greatest problems of restraint and self-control for Germans generally. By projecting upon others the impulses we are trying to control in ourselves, we create an external enemy against which to mobilize our resources and thereby strengthen ourselves in our own inner struggle. That interethnic hostility reflects, in some measure at least, a reaction formation against our own desires, which we project upon others, is revealed by the way the accusations change, depending on the nature of our own problems. Thus a young lady of our acquaintance who is remarkable for a bustling compulsion to demonstrate herself a good and efficient worker once reported that she did not like Jews because they were "lazy." She picked a conventional target, but gave an unconventional reason for doing so, a reason, however, that expressed very neatly something she clearly fears within herself.

The common American stereotype of other peoples as "dirty" reflects a similar projection upon them of sentiments we are trying to suppress within ourselves. For, as we have already observed, we have virtually a national reaction formation regarding dirt. If the reader's immediate response is that we ought to feel that way about dirt, let him note that not a word of our discussion has said anything to the contrary. The fact remains that we tend to be fanatic on the subject and to develop stereotypes of other peoples accordingly. We need not take a stand on whether private wealth and the power it brings are morally good or bad, either; but it is obvious that Russians express an aversion to it that has all the earmarks of a reaction formation. They also make it clear that by their stereotype we are "greedy, capitalist warmongers." This projection upon us of what they are trying to restrain among themselves probably bears about the same relation to reality as does our own projection regarding dirt. Regardless of the moral rightness of the goals either of socialist peace or of aseptic cleanliness, fanaticism regarding them has not been conducive to international good will.

In such ways, then, reaction formation helps us account for strong emotional commitments to strict standards of behavior in ourselves and in others. It explains our aversions to deviations from these standards and to things we have come to associate with such deviation, which we perceive as symbols of it. Our understanding may not make it easier to empathize with the particular emotional orientations of others when they differ radically from our own; but to perceive that these orientations, however different their form, are functionally and psychologically analogous to ours helps us deal with them more wisely.

Other Processes

The several psychological processes we have reviewed all serve the purpose of helping people to deal with the emotional consequences of their frustrations without transgressing the requirements of their social order or doing violence to their own self-esteem. There are other processes that are also important in this regard.

One of them is the process of identification. We have already alluded to it in connection with the phenomenon of ethnocentrism in Chapter 2. As we identify ourselves with others and thereby make their wants our wants for them, we spare them and ourselves frustration by diminishing the possibility of a conflict of wants between us. Identification is so important in other ways of interest to us, however, that we put off its consideration until Chapter 8, when we shall consider values in relation to identity and personal worth.

Another important process operating in conjunction with all the foregoing is rationalization, by which we intellectually reconcile our emotional orientations with one another, with our personal sentiments generally and, above all, with public values. Rationalization takes us into the realm of belief generally, including people's cognitive as distinct from their value orientations. For this reason we reserve its consideration until we discuss beliefs and their functions in the next chapter.

Yet other psychological processes constitute a second line of defense, as it were, in that they tend to become operative when those we have considered fail to do their job. As long as we can successfully displace our feelings to legitimate targets, justify our actions by projections that are acceptable to our fellows, sublimate our desires by participating in publicly valued activities, and control our impulses by pursuing causes that are sanctioned by the moral code of our community, for so long we are able to be reasonably free of excessive emotional stress and to qualify as persons whose emotional adjustment is adequate to our circumstances. But when our usual displacements and projections cease to do their job, when we no longer have access to the activities through which we have successfully sublimated our suppressed desires, when our reaction formations are no longer supported by public values, and when new experience destroys our rationalizations, then we are in serious emotional trouble. In trying to use these processes in new ways, we are likely to run further afoul of public values. This easily leads to a vicious circle of greater frustration and more and more desperate and unsuccessful attempts to cope with it. The adjustments to which this may lead include regression, apathetic withdrawal, paranoia, and the espousal of social delinquencies.

Serious dislocations to our previously successful emotional adjustments are, of course, a direct consequence of change in our life circumstances. It is no accident that changes in our social position in the course of growing up are marked by emotional disturbances. And changes in a community's way of life, regardless of the forces precipitating them, are similarly accompanied by behavioral manifestations of emotional stress.[24] How to execute programs of change so as to hold such manifestations to a minimum is a major concern of change agents, their clients, and administrative authorities. What happens under the stress of change will necessarily require our close attention in Chapter 11.

For the moment we are concerned less with change than with the function and meaning of what is to be changed: people's customary ways of acting and thinking, especially as they help to solve problems of emotional control. To this end we have examined several important psychological processes. In order more fully to illustrate their workings within human institutions, let us consider the body of beliefs and practices in Truk relating to spirits, burial, and the nature of the human soul.

SPIRITS AND GHOSTS ON TRUK[25]

The people of Truk maintain that everyone has two souls: a good one and a bad one. The good soul is what one sees reflected in a mirror or on the surface of the water. The bad soul manifests itself as one's shadow. The good soul may leave one's body and wander about while one sleeps, as when one dreams. Its loss or destruction on its wanderings is an occasional cause of death. Usually, however, both good and bad souls survive the death of the body. One's character and conduct while alive have nothing whatever to do with what happens to these souls, nor does one's conduct in life reflect the nature of one's souls. A person's two souls assume importance only after he has died.

When someone dies, his body is laid out in his house for about twenty-four hours. All of his kinsmen bring gifts of cloth, perfume, and a turmeric cosmetic for which money now substitutes. They lay these gifts beside the body, to be buried with it. Wrapped in mats or, nowadays, put in a wooden coffin, the body is buried in a shallow grave on land associated with the deceased's family. There are no community cemeteries. The deceased's family and near kin watch the grave for four successive nights in order to give his good soul an opportunity to possess one of them. On the fourth day after burial, they burn his immediate personal effects, and his good soul rises in the smoke to take up its abode with the great spirits that inhabit the sky world. The soul's departure from the grave may be shown by a babylike footprint in the smoothly raked sand on top of the grave, portending a death in the household toward which it points.

If the good soul has not possessed a kinsman in the four days preceding its ascent, then no more will be heard from it. By possessing a kinsman, however, it serves notice of its intention to maintain contact with its surviving relatives. The person possessed becomes a medium for the good soul, which in turn now belongs to a special category of beneficent spirit. Symptoms of possession are moaning, violent shaking, and speaking in a special tone of voice, which signifies that a spirit rather than the medium is really doing the talking. They are easily distinguished from symptoms of possession by evil spirits.

Having found by possession that he is to be a vehicle for the spirit, or a "spirit vessel" as he (or she) is called, the medium proceeds to construct a model, double-hulled canoe, which he hangs in the meeting house with which he is affiliated. In this canoe the spirit travels between heaven and earth. When the medium stands beneath the canoe and calls to the spirit, it alights on his shoulder. Spirit and medium may then converse in a spirit-language unintelligible to others, or the spirit may enter the medium's body in order to speak to the people through his mouth. While under possession, the medium must observe a number of taboos. Refraining from ordinary food and drink, he drinks perfume, which spirits especially like. The only food he can eat is that specifically requested by the spirit. Possession may last for a few hours or for several days. During this time the spirit may demand entertainment in the form of dancing, for which purpose there are special dances.

The people ask the spirit whether they will get enough to eat, have good catches of fish, or be free from sickness. If a spirit's prophecies of sickness and health or its prognostications as to where there will be good fishing are frequently fulfilled, it may get a wide reputation and continue to serve the family, the community, or even a group of communities for several generations. The original medium may pass his office to a successor by having the younger person drink a special potion that renders him (or her) susceptible to possession. If a spirit proves unreliable, its medium can terminate relations with it by eating fermented breadfruit, whose strong, cheesy taste and smell are repugnant to spirits.

In addition to helping people obtain food and maintain health, such a spirit looks after the living in another important way. All beneficent magic connected with all special crafts and all medicines and spells for curing illness were first taught by a spirit to its medium, who in turn passed the knowledge on to his heirs. A spirit gets such knowledge from the sky deities with whom it is in direct contact. All black magic, by contrast, has its origin in the passions of men.

Failure to please the sky gods or the good souls with which people enjoy this kind of contact will result in punishment. A serious epidemic or drought or other catastrophe is a sign of a spirit's or god's displeasure. Everyone then suspends offerings of perfume and jewelry from the spirit canoe in the meeting house so as to lavish attention on the spirits in the form they most like. For those things by which men and women make themselves appealing in sight and smell, in courtship and ceremony, are the things in which spirits take the greatest delight. The idea that such gifts will favorably dispose the spirits is entirely consistent with the standard procedure for getting back into the good graces of living persons whom one has offended. By making handsome gifts to others, one can morally obligate them to grant one's requests.[26] By catering to a spirit in this way, it is possible to get it to withdraw an affliction or to intercede with the still higher powers to do so.

We may, then, summarize the relations of Trukese with the good souls of their dead as follows. A good soul may, but there is no guaranteeing it, possess someone and thereby prepare to become a spirit active in human affairs. The living must be careful to give the spirit what it asks for in the way of perfume, gifts, and pleasurable entertainment. In return, the spirit will provide the living with food, teach them new lore, and generally look after their health and welfare. Failure by the living to show proper regard for the spirit will cause it to withhold its favors until atoned for by a presentation of gifts and show of regard sufficiently extraordinary to compel a benevolent attitude again.

As for the bad soul, after death it becomes a malevolent ghost. When visible, it appears as a ball of light or a glow in the darkness, and by day it may assume the shape of a plover bird, revealing itself by its distortion of the bird's usual call. Many Trukese have seen ghosts, and all go in terror of them at night. No one, for example, would think of walking into the bush at night without a companion. At night ghosts are especially active. They frequent the bush and the vicinity of graves; sometimes they even invade people's houses. One informant told of returning home at night to find the members of his family huddled together on the sleeping platform of the house. They were terrified by the ghost of his wife's sister's recently deceased husband, which was flitting about the house, making whistling noises. While the man sat with his family trying to persuade the ghost to leave, it jumped up on the mosquito netting above the platform and, leaning down, kept plucking at his hair. For this man, ghosts were all too terrifyingly real.

But what is there about ghosts that makes them so frightening? They feed on the good souls of the living and on human bodies, living or dead. By "biting" or "devouring" people, they cause sickness and death. Most illnesses are diagnosed as due to the "bite" of malevolent spirits, among which the ghosts of the dead are prominently numbered. Whether all evil spirits were originally ghosts of the dead is not clearly formulated one way or the other—just as the heavenly deities are not clearly separated conceptually from good souls of the dead. According to one man, all ghosts eventually sink into the earth, becoming a particular class of malevolent spirit, called "earth spirits" whose bite causes elephantiasis.

Ghosts are of special importance, moreover, in sorcery, all forms of which are based on the same principle. The body of a once living thing is prepared with medicine, such that when the appropriate spell is recited over it and it is placed in proper orientation toward its victim, the ghost of the corpse will devour the victim, causing his sickness and death. It appears to be the good soul of the victim that is the object of such cannibalistic attack. The body of a fish is usually used in such sorcery, but the most effective kind makes direct use of the human body. In war, the body of an enemy taken in a night raid used to be set up facing his home territory with mouth propped open. On one occasion of record, the body of a murdered chief was used by his own kinsmen as the vehicle for such sorcery against his murderer's family.

To sum up, the bad soul of every individual survives as a ghost whose identity in the course of time becomes merged with that of evil spirits generally. Ghosts, along with the evil spirits, are cannibals, causing sickness and death by "eating" people.

Interpretation

In accordance with the interpretation of custom that we have been developing, we assume that the beliefs and practices just described have proved useful in helping at least a great many Trukese to cope with recurring problems in their lives. These beliefs were firmly held by every Trukese with whom we had dealings, despite the fact that Christianity had been important in native life for half a century and most Trukese of our acquaintance were active participants in church affairs. Spirit mediums were no longer practicing openly, because of the personal embarrassment which they felt as a result of missionary disapproval. But nothing else that we have described showed any signs of weakening. No Trukese questioned the truth of these beliefs. The funeral we observed followed all the steps we have outlined, including the watch on the grave.[27] Ghosts were a subject of everyday conversation and were often given as a reason for avoiding certain places or not going out at night alone. We suspect, therefore, that these beliefs and practices help Truk's people deal with some problem in their lives that has not been significantly modified by the social and technological change accompanying European and Japanese political control. Whatever this problem is, moreover, we suspect that it is less adequately handled by Christian beliefs concerning the nature and survival of the soul, because other aspects of Christian belief and practice have been widely accepted. Where, then, are we to look for the source of a need that is likely to be served by these traditional Trukese beliefs and practices?

Our own conventions incline us to say that people believe in some kind of survival or afterlife because they are afraid to die. Death is easier to face, we say, if there is something to look forward to.[28] While such may be responsible for the Trukese belief that good souls of the dead go to live with the heavenly gods, it does not account for the belief in two souls, a good and a bad, nor in the belief that some good souls may unpredictably become active watchdogs of human welfare, while all bad souls become cannibalistic ghosts. We must also reiterate that what happens after death has nothing to do with one's conduct during life, one's sex, or one's age at death—in theory, at least. These beliefs have no explicit social function as a rationale for sanctions supporting the Trukese moral code. In contrast with Christian beliefs, which are concerned with one's own hereafter, Trukese beliefs are not concerned with the self. Interest is in the already dead as something with which the living must reckon.

When we ask who the already dead are and why they should be reckoned with, it seems obvious that they are one's elders, especially those of one's elders with whom one had to reckon when they were living: one's parents in particular and senior kinsmen in general. Indeed, we can see the good soul of the dead that has possessed a surviving kinsman as playing what is essentially the parental role in relation to the living, helping to provide food, imparting knowledge, and protecting people from sickness and misfortune. But to make this rather obvious identification raises more questions than it answers. Why should only some good souls, and those unpredictably and without regard to their conduct when alive, assume parental responsibility in relation to the living? Why should all of one's elders at the same time turn upon the living as man-eating ghosts once they have died? How does this fit into the parental role? Or, since it is the living who hold these beliefs about the souls of the already dead, what in the relationship between junior and senior kinsmen or between children and parents creates such problems or needs in the children that they derive satisfaction from believing the things they do about the parental souls?

The answer to this question is contained in the conclusions of Gladwin and Sarason regarding the major problem areas in the personalities of most Trukese.[29] Their data from various psychological tests, life histories, and direct observation of child care all point consistently to certain severe frustrations in dependency relations in childhood and to certain widely shared anxieties as their consequence in later life. First, there is early oral frustration due to capricious feeding rather than to serious food shortages, a matter to which we referred in describing Trukese feasting customs. Nursing is at the mother's convenience, and frustration continues after weaning. Food is prepared in bulk for several days at a time, and it usually happens that the larder is empty before people get around to preparing it again. The result is that small children are frequently compelled to go for several hours at a time without food after they have already become hungry. Mothers also withhold food as a method of punishment. Because of their own anxieties and concerns, moreover, adults tend to be preoccupied with indulging their own wants. Accordingly, they feed and care for the children attentively one minute and neglect or reject them the next, all rather unpredictably from the child's point of view. The result is that children are heavily frustrated by their elders with respect to precisely the same wants for which their elders are also the principal agents of gratification. Considerable hostility toward the elders is to be expected, and was much in evidence in the psychological test materials. But children are still dependent on their senior kinsmen for the gratification of their major wants and needs: for food, the knowledge and skills needed to be successful adults, care and doctoring when sick, and protection against the hostility of nonkin. Since one's only support and refuge are these same frustrating older kin, one must suppress one's hostility. This situation remains in force in adult life, as well. Within Trukese family groups, authority is based strictly on age, the eldest male having ultimate authority over everyone else. It is impossible to live independent of one's kinsmen without loss of almost all one's rights, privileges, and immunities within the social order. For most of his life every Trukese must continue to depend for his own welfare on the good will of his senior kinsmen, whose authority he must accept unconditionally, and against whose caprices and whims he has little better recourse than to threaten suicide. Honor and morality require that elders assume their responsibilities faithfully, to be sure, but their own long history of frustration and emotional deprivation render them unable to do so consistently. Since the undependability of elders is manifested to children from the beginning in relation to food, the Trukese tend to be orally fixated and to make food the symbol *par excellence* of all that is the object of their frustrated dependency cravings. Earlier in this chapter we noted their use of food as a medium of orgiastic self-indulgence. We should not be surprised if food and eating are also media for expressing both dependency and hostility in Trukese fantasy.

There are other important facets of Trukese personality described by Gladwin and Sarason, but they relate more directly to other customs than the ones we are considering. We are ready, therefore, to appraise the meaning of Truk's customs and beliefs concerning the human soul and to explain the high value the Trukese people attach to them.

Salvation seems to consist largely in realizing one's childhood aspirations by finding a perfectly reliable, feeding and nurturing, parental figure. Always, therefore, when someone dies, his kinsmen hope against hope that maybe his good soul will provide the support they so much desire: feeding, teaching, and curing his living juniors, so long as they cater to his own desires for self-gratification. At the same time, the suppressed hatred of the living for their elders finds release and expression in their belief about the bad soul. Because it has been necessary to suppress this hostility, we should expect even its displaced expression to be accompanied by guilt, anxiety, and fear. Thus the bad soul becomes something to be hated and feared as a ghost with an avid determination to gratify its own oral cravings at the expense of its junior kinsmen. "Given an insecure, jealous, dependent man who doubts his own masculinity, and a self-centered, highly sexed, and rejecting woman," to use Sarason's words,[30] both of whom as parents are often more preoccupied with their own needs than those of their children, it is perhaps fitting that their feeding of their own emotional hungers at their children's expense should lead the latter unconsciously to picture them as cannibalistic ogres.

It would appear, then, that their beliefs about the soul and their associated practices provide an institutional means of externalizing a major conflict between desire and hate in the psyches of most Trukese. Family solidarity, along with the whole complex system of social relationships and the sanctions that support them, would be impossible if existing cravings and hostilities were allowed expression toward their true targets. By displacing their feelings onto those of their kinsmen who are safely dead, by giving separate targets to their positive and negative orientations, and by projecting upon each of them characteristics that justify their behaving toward them as they do, they are able to act out their emotions and at the same time to live productive and constructive lives. As long as their way of life, however much changed by outside influences, continues to generate these emotional conflicts in Truk's people, we may expect this belief in the dual nature of the soul to persist, along with such of the associated practices as missionaries and governmental authorities will tolerate.[31]

There is no society whose social order does not produce emotional conflicts of some kind. It would be a mistake to regard the people of Truk as pathological simply because their problems and symbols for dealing with them are not the same as our own. Every community has customs and beliefs that are analogous in function and meaning to those we have just described.[32] Understanding their function and meaning makes it easier to estimate where the emotional source of resistance to change lies and to discern what are the customs and beliefs that are likely to prove most persistent in the face of an agent's efforts to get them changed.

VALUES AND CHANGE

We should not close this chapter with the implication that customs and beliefs of the sort we have been discussing do not change. As circumstances alter the intensity of people's wants, change the nature of their emotional conflicts, or provide new channels for dealing with them, the meaning and value of their established customs and beliefs also change. Community development, insofar as it changes the conditions of life, necessarily has an effect on the meaning of traditional customs. If development provides acceptable means for gratifying wants that were formerly frustrated, then any compensating beliefs and practices will lose value—much as a bachelor's interest in pin-up girl art tends to disappear after marriage, and an impecunious young intellectual loses his interest in radical political movements as greater affluence, a growing family, and fuller participation in community affairs give him a sense of increasing self-fulfillment. We reasonably infer that as community development removes existing frustrations, it undermines such institutions as helped to compensate for them. Thus changes in one set of customary practices may deprive other customs of the meaning and value they formerly had for people, leading to their eventual disappearance.

On the other hand, changes resulting from development efforts may have the effect of intensifying existing frustration and even add new frustrations to them. In the Gilbert Islands, those who adopted Christianity and who, as Christians, refused to teach their children and grandchildren protective spells against sorcery and natural disasters, rendered their descendants more dependent upon professional magicians. Grimble quotes a Gilbertese elder's response to governmental disapproval of magical practitioners.

> . . . if you punish those who are willing to sell *tabunea* [spells] for good luck, what must the Christians do then? Where will they go to find magic for good eating and good sleeping, for excellent fishing and success in love, for being favoured by their masters or their friends, for happiness in their dwellings and their work, for blessings upon their canoes and land and cooking ovens, for finding out their lucky days and their unlucky days, for making their wives fruitful and their children strong, for all the comforts between dawn and dawn that the magic of kindness brings them? . . . If the government or missionaries could give them something to keep their hearts alive night and day even as the magic of kindness does, perhaps they could be happy. . . . But if you cannot give them an equal thing in return, you will kill their hearts by robbing them of their loved wizards.[*33]

Agents of change sometimes seek support for their proposals by trying to arouse new wants in their clients. In this way change agents try to develop the motive power needed to get action started. If too successful, they may create wants that cannot

* Reprinted with permission of the publisher from *We Chose the Islands:* A Six-Year Adventure in the Gilberts by Sir Arthur Grimble. William Morrow and Company, Inc., New York, pp. 205–206. © 1952 by Sir Arthur Grimble.

readily be gratified. Overselling by a development agent can leave a community better off in the light of its members' old wants, but more frustrated than ever in the light of their new ones. There is, moreover, a possibility that the successful removal of some frustrations may make the remaining ones harder rather than easier to bear. Everyone has many unfulfilled wants that he dismisses as idle day-dreams. When changing conditions begin to render a few of these capable of gratification, it becomes much more difficult to dismiss the others as unrealistic or unreasonable. In our own society, the housewife who has cheerfully put up with all sorts of makeshift and shabby furnishings in her home through her husband's early years of low income becomes suddenly impatient to junk everything and start anew when her husband's income takes a turn for the better. It is, moreover, a truism that some success often has the effect of increasing rather than diminishing the expectation of still more success. The feeling that they are making progress, that they cannot be stopped, is of great value in helping people to generate the effort needed to carry something through to completion in spite of the difficulties involved. But it also makes them terribly impatient with whatever obstacles they encounter. Historians have observed that political revolutions tend to occur when conditions are actually improving but not at a rate commensurate with the expectations and desires that past improvements have stimulated.

Finally, we should observe that the meaning and value of established customs may be so altered under some conditions as to lead people to reject them as vehemently as they once embraced them. When this happens to many customs at once, revolutionary movements appear that are totalitarian in scope. But we reserve such developments for Chapter 11.

SUGGESTED READING

Hallowell, A. Irving, *Culture and Experience*. University of Pennsylvania Press, Philadelphia, 1955.

Honigmann, John, *Culture and Personality*. Harper and Bros., New York, 1954.

Opler, Marvin K., editor, *Culture and Mental Health*. Macmillan Co., New York, 1959.

Opler, Morris E., "An Interpretation of Ambivalence of Two American Indian Tribes," *Journal of Social Psychiatry*, vol. 7, 1936, pp. 82–115, reprinted in Lessa, William A. and Evon Z. Vogt, editors, *Reader in Comparative Religion*, Row, Peterson and Co., Evanston, Ill., 1958, pp. 375–389.

Powdermaker, Hortense, "The Channeling of Negro Aggression by the Cultural Process" in Kluckhohn, Clyde, Henry A. Murray, and David M. Schneider, editors, *Personality in Nature, Society, and Culture*, 2d. ed., revised and enlarged. Alfred A. Knopf, Inc., New York, 1953, pp. 597–608.

Whiting, John W. M., and Irving L. Child, *Child Training and Personality: A Cross-cultural Study*. Yale University Press, New Haven, 1953.

NOTES TO CHAPTER 6

1. Dollard, John, and others, *Frustration and Aggression*. Yale University Press, New Haven, 1939.

2. Bowlby, John, *Child Care and the Growth of Love*. Penguin Books, Baltimore, Md., 1953.

3. This is true not only in our own lives but in the lives of people in other societies as well, no matter now "primitive," as is clearly brought out by John W. M. Whiting, in *Becoming a Kwoma:* Teaching and Learning in a New Guinea Tribe, Yale University Press, New Haven, 1938; by O. F. Raum, in *Chaga Childhood: A Description of Indigenous Education in an East African Tribe*, Oxford University Press, London, 1940; and in the biographies and autobiographies of people from other exotic societies, for example, Ford, Clellan S., *Smoke from Their Fires: The Life of a Kwakiutl Chief*, Yale University Press, New Haven, 1941.

4. Erikson, Erik Homburger, "Growth and Crises of the 'Healthy Personality' " in Kluckhohn, Clyde, Henry A. Murray, and David M. Schneider, editors, *Personality in Nature, Society and Culture*. 2d ed., rev. and enl., Alfred A. Knopf, Inc., New York, 1953, pp. 185–225.

5. For an extensive review of the relations between emotional stress and disease, see Simmons, Leo W., and Harold G. Wolff, *Social Science in Medicine*, Russell Sage Foundation, New York, 1954, pp. 109–169.

6. We should note, however, the reasoning that has led Spiro to conclude, "In the absence of human personality there could be no human culture." Spiro, Melford, "Human Nature in Its Psychological Dimensions," *American Anthropologist*, vol. 56, 1954, p. 29.

7. The fact that it is possible to breed dogs for either low or high attack thresholds, for example, suggests that people, too, may differ genetically in their readiness to make aggressive responses to frustration. This would make the control of aggression a greater problem for some individuals than for others. We are indebted to Benson E. Ginsburg for calling our attention to this.

8. See, for example, the contrast between Sioux and Yurok described by Erik Homburger Erikson, in "Childhood and Tradition in Two American Indian Tribes," *The Psychoanalytic Study of the Child*, vol. 1, 1945, pp. 319–350. See also the contrasts between Irish and Italians, even in schizophrenia, described by Marvin K. Opler, "Cultural Differences in Mental Disorders: An Italian and Irish Contrast" in Opler, Marvin K., editor, *Culture and Mental Health*, Macmillan Co., New York, 1959, pp. 425–442.

9. See, for example, the studies by DuBois, Cora, *The People of Alor*, University of Minnesota Press, Minneapolis, 1944; Gladwin, Thomas, and Seymour B.

Sarason, *Truk: Man in Paradise*, Viking Fund Publications in Anthropology, no. 20, Wenner-Gren Foundation for Anthropological Research, New York, 1953; Hallowell, A. Irving, *Culture and Experience*, University of Pennsylvania Press, Philadelphia, 1955; Leighton, Dorothea, and Clyde Kluckhohn, *Children of the People:* The Navaho Individual and His Development, Harvard University Press, Cambridge, Mass, 1947; Spindler, George, *Sociocultural and Psychological Processes in Menomini Acculturation*, University of California Publications in Culture and Society, University of California Press, Berkeley, 1955; and Wallace, Anthony F. C., *The Modal Personality Structure of the Tuscarora Indians as Revealed by the Rorschach Test*, Bureau of American Ethnology, Bulletin 150, United States Government Printing Office, Washington, 1952.

10. For example, Whiting, John W. M., and Irving L. Child, *Child Training and Personality:* A Cross-cultural Study. Yale University Press, 1953.

11. For an interesting attempt to view social change and economic growth in relation to shifts in personality orientation, see Hagen, Everett E., *On the Theory of Social Change:* How Economic Growth Begins, The Dorsey Press, Inc., Homewood, Ill., 1962.

12. For sexual customs in Truk, see Goodenough, Ward H., "Premarital Freedom in Truk: Theory and Practice," *American Anthropologist*, vol. 51, 1949, pp. 615–620; Gladwin, Thomas, and Seymour B. Sarason, *Truk: Man in Paradise*, Viking Fund Publications in Anthropology, no. 20, Wenner-Gren Foundation for Anthropological Research, New York, 1953, pp. 100–117; and Swartz, Marc J., "Sexuality and Aggression on Romonum, Truk," *American Anthropologist*, vol. 60, 1958, pp. 467–486.

13. Gladwin, Thomas, and Seymour B. Sarason, *op. cit.*

14. The reader will find them discussed in almost any exposition of psychoanalytic theory; for example, Munroe, Ruth L., *Schools of Psychoanalytic Thought:* An Exposition, Critique, and Attempt at Integration, Dryden Press, New York, 1955. See especially Chapter 6.

15. Spoehr observes, "It is possible that the very existence of the family makes conflict and tension in certain relationships, such as those between siblings, or between parent and child, an ever-present, potentially disruptive force." (Spoehr, Alexander, "Observations on the Study of Kinship," *American Anthropologist*, vol. 52, 1950, p. 12.) For a specific example, see Sayres, William C., "Ritual Kinship and Negative Affect," *American Sociological Review*, vol. 21, 1956, pp. 348–352.

16. This observation was stimulated by discussion with Ronald Berndt.

17. Stouffer, Samuel A., and others, *The American Soldier: Adjustment During Army Life*, Studies in Social Psychology in World War II, vol. 1, Princeton University Press, Princeton, N. J., 1949, pp. 586–595.

18. Abel, Elie, "India's Untouchables—Still the 'Black Sin,' " *The New York Times Magazine*, March 1, 1959, p. 21.

19. For an example of a parallel in our own society, see the account of the symbolic significance of the rainbow to members of the "Rainbow" Division in World War I by Ralph Linton, in *The Study of Man*, D. Appleton-Century Co., New York, 1936, pp. 424–425.

20. Roe, Anne, "A Psychologist Examines 64 Eminent Scientists," *Scientific American*, vol. 187, November, 1952, pp. 21–25.

21. Wallace, Anthony F. C., "The Institutionalization of Cathartic and Control Strategies in Iroquois Religious Psychotherapy" in Opler, Marvin K., editor, *op. cit.*, pp. 63–96.

22. Erikson, Erik Homburger, *Observations on the Yurok:* Childhood and World Image. University of California Publications in American Archaeology and Ethnology, vol. 35, no. 10, 1943, p. 291.

23. Freud, Sigmund, *A General Introduction to Psychoanalysis*, Garden City Publishing Co., Garden City, N.Y., 1938, pp. 186–187, 291–296. For a more up-to-date treatment of incest, see Murdock, G. P., *Social Structure*, Macmillan Co., New York, 1949, pp. 284–313; and Slater, Miriam Kreiselman, "Ecological Factors in the Origin of Incest," *American Anthropologist*, vol. 61, 1959, pp. 1042–1059.

24. Leighton, Alexander H., "Mental Illness and Acculturation" in Galdston, Iago, editor, *Medicine and Anthropology:* Lectures to the Laity, no. 21, New York Academy of Sciences. International Universities Press, New York, 1959, pp. 108–128.

25. This account is adapted from a paper entitled "Survival of the Soul on Truk," read at the Fifty-Fourth Annual Meeting of the American Anthropological Association, November 19, 1955. For the psychological problems dealt with by belief in spirits and ghosts in a related society, see Spiro, Melford, "Cultural Heritage, Personal Tensions, and Mental Illness," in Opler, Marvin K., editor, *op. cit.*, pp. 141–171.

26. For a fuller discussion of the morally compelling nature of gifts and favors in Truk, see Goodenough, Ward H., *Property, Kin, and Community on Truk*, Yale University Publications in Anthropology, no. 46, Department of Anthropology, Yale University, New Haven, 1951.

27. This funeral is described in detail in Gladwin, Thomas, and Seymour B. Sarason, *op. cit.*, pp. 160–167.

28. On this point Thomas Gladwin and Seymour B. Sarason (*op. cit.*, p. 289) state: "Their life goals . . . place primary emphasis on just being an obscure Trukese. With no unachieved goals beckoning toward the future, they have little interest in what happens tomorrow; they do not speculate or worry unduly over the prospect of their deaths, nor do even those who have most firmly embraced the Christian faith show much interest in a life after death, whether good or bad."

29. *Ibid.*, pp. 247–289.

30. *Ibid.*, pp. 234–235.

31. By way of a parallel, several observers of Navaho Indian society have commented that Navahos who are most acculturated to White ways, including those who no longer believe in the efficacy of Navaho medicine, still retain their fear of witches. See Sasaki, Tom T., *Fruitland, New Mecixo:* A Navaho Community in Transition, Cornell University Press, Ithaca, N.Y., 1960, p. 24; Vogt, Evon Z., *Navaho Veterans:* A Study of Changing Values, Papers of the Peabody Museum of American Archaeology and Ethnology, vol. 41, no. 1, Cambridge, Mass., 1951, p. 114; Kluckhohn, Clyde, *Navaho Witchcraft, ibid.*, vol. 22, no. 2, 1944, p. 48.

32. For a comparative study demonstrating a connection between beliefs about the malevolence and benevolence of supernatural beings and established patterns of parent-child relationships, see Lambert, William W., Leigh Minturn Triandis, and Margery Wolf, "Some Correlates of Beliefs in the Malevolence and Benevolence of Supernatural Beings: A Cross-Societal Study," *The Journal of Abnormal and Social Psychology*, vol. 58, no. 2, 1959, pp. 162–169.

33. Grimble, Sir Arthur, *We Chose the Islands:* A Six-Year Adventure in the Gilberts. William Morrow and Co., New York, 1952, pp. 205–206.

Chapter 7

BELIEFS

OUR EXAMINATION of some of the reasons people value their customs has implied a good deal about beliefs. As we saw with Trukese ideas about the soul, beliefs provide a rational framework for emotionally important customs. But there is more to understanding the role of belief in human affairs than this, particularly in the relation of belief to emotional orientations.

Development agents themselves can get rather emotional about beliefs, especially the beliefs of their clients that seem bizarre and senseless. The apparent irrationality of others tends to baffle and infuriate all of us. No obstacle seems more frustrating than a patently irrational belief that we do not understand and before which we feel helpless.

It is not easy to see the reason in beliefs that differ from our own. Our own beliefs necessarily appear reasonable to us, and this, of course, renders contrary ones unreasonable. The public values of western society, moreover, with their great stress on scientific truth and objective realism, make it difficult for us sometimes to appreciate the force of beliefs that rest upon other imperatives, particularly moral or psychological ones. In order to be able to deal sympathetically with strange beliefs, it is important for us to understand both their cognitive background and their functions in everyday life.

COGNITION AND BELIEF

In Chapter 4, we outlined the universally needed conditions for purposive human action. We gave first place to the need for a coherent cognitive organization of experience. Not only is such an

146

organization a necessity if people are to act with purpose on their surroundings, it seems to be something people are constitutionally impelled to try to create for themselves. Certainly, we are all familiar with the sense of panic that comes from the knowledge that we are acting blindly in a situation. What happens to our sense of well-being, for example, when we discover that we are completely lost in the woods or have lost all sense of direction in a storm? Nor is this distress limited to disorientation in a physical sense only. It can be fully as distressing to be lost socially, as when a small child is separated from his family or an adult suffers from amnesia. We have to know who we are, where we are, what we are doing, and why we are doing it. These are fundamental preconditions of mental health.

Perception

Each person's cognitive organization of experience includes a catalogue of phenomena that he has discerned directly with his senses. Every experience is like or unlike a previous one. A small child is beset by new experiences, but as he grows, increasingly fewer things occur that he cannot perceive as similar to events with which he is already familiar. So we come to perceive things in terms of classes or categories of phenomena. We operate with sets of color categories, shape categories, taste categories, and so on, whose combinations provide the basis for a perceptual taxonomy of our world.[1] Cognitive organization also includes the ways in which the phenomena we discern appear to us to be mutually associated or arranged, and it includes the transformations from one to another perceptual category that phenomena appear to undergo as their mutual associations change. These discernments of phenomena and process are our *percepts*, as psychologists have called them.

The percepts with which different people operate are inevitably somewhat dissimilar. Our own classification of colors, for example, is a rather arbitrary division of the spectrum which could be just as easily divided into different categories. In our society men tend to work with a more limited color taxonomy than do women; and what some Pacific Islanders regard as shades of a single color includes what we regard as shades of the two colors blue and green. These differences do not necessarily represent physiological differences, as with color blindness; they are simply different ways of reducing to finite proportions the infinite variety of external reality.[2]

Since each of us necessarily perceives reality in terms of his own percepts, he is inclined to regard different perceptions as distortions of reality. Many observers of Pacific Island peoples have commented on their "inability" to see the difference between blue and green. The point, of course, is that every percept system, including one's own, is inevitably a distortion in that it is an arbitrary simplification of reality. Without simplification we cannot learn to deal effectively with reality at all.

If, for this reason, the perceptions of others strike us as odd, the belief systems they construct out of them may seem strange to us, indeed.

Concepts and Propositions

Our language provides us with a set of behavioral percepts that serves as a code for our other percepts. It enables us to reduce the rest of experience to a set of coded items and propositions about them. By substituting one item of the code for another in various propositions, we can symbolically create new arrangements of phenomena by analogy with old ones, new arrangements that we have not experienced directly at all. Thus by substituting one coded item for another we move from the experience of purple flowers and purple hats to the vicarious experience of purple cows. Such analogies bring us to new discernments that we have not perceived in direct experience but have conceived as products of the manipulation of coded experience. These products, our *concepts*, may be perceivable in sensory experience or may remain, like one's more remote ancestors or like the ether of nineteenth-century physics, things whose existence can be postulated but never directly observed. Our concepts, once coded as part of our language, can be manipulated along with our percepts to produce even more concepts.

Another important product of the linguistic manipulation of percepts and concepts is a body of propositions. We perceive the condition of a piece of paper, let us say, before and after it has been rained on. A repetition of this observation leads us to infer a consistent relationship between water and the condition of paper. This inferred relationship is a proposition. As generalizations, propositions organize past experience; at the same time, they express expectations for the future. They are, therefore, indispensable to purposive action, predictively relating means to ends. To anticipate the future, of course, is to describe events that have not yet occurred, events that belong to the realm of fantasy. The intellectual processes essential to defining and accomplishing human purposes also lead people to infuse their world with products of their imagination.

Reasoning and Logic

The body of percepts, concepts, and propositions with which we operate enables us to cope with situations that have never confronted us before. When an unusual situation arises, we make an inventory of its properties in terms of our existing percepts. What makes the situation appear novel is not so much the things we see or their arrangements as the total combination of things and arrangements, such as a familiar shape and a familiar color never before seen together or two acquaintances known to be enemies now acting like friends.[3] Because novelty so often has this character, it is usually possible for us to describe what we have newly perceived in terms of the existing linguistic code by simply bringing already available words together in a new (though still grammatical) arrangement. Having taken inventory of a new situation and determined its properties, we can take the propositions with which we are already familiar, make analogical substitutions within them according to what we have just discerned, and thereby arrive at a conception of what actions in the situation will lead to what results. Thus we arrive at new propositions conceptually or theoretically appropriate to the situation at hand and providing a rational, as opposed to a trial-and-error, basis for deciding how to accomplish our wants within it. If the actions prove gratifying in the way anticipated, we regard the new propositions as valid and resort to them again when a closely similar situation arises. This eliminates the necessity of thinking through a course of action all over again. With language, moreover, we are able to communicate the actions we have found suitable for particular situations, thereby relieving others of having to think things through for themselves.

The process described above obviously involves reasoning and logic. Reasoning is, after all, a matter of subjecting one's observations to some kind of orderly manipulation that results in a proposition. Language, or some other symbolic system such as mathematics, is the instrument by which we manipulate our observations, and as already indicated, the process involved is largely one of substitution. There are a limited series of proposition frames—like a simple declarative sentence. By substituting one word for another in the same frame we arrive at new inferences. Thus, given a frequent pairing of propositions to the effect that "X is big and X is strong," the observation that "George is big" quickly leads to the inference that "George is strong." Our direct observation that George can substitute for X in one proposition leads us to substitute George for X in other propositions as well. This is one of the ways in which inference is drawn.

This book is not the place to elaborate on the reasoning process or the various ways of inferring things. Some mention must be made of them, however, in relation to logic, since the comment is so frequently made that other people's beliefs are illogical.

Logic is in a formal sense a codification of the reasoning process, a set of rules of inference. In the ancient syllogism "All men are mortal; Socrates is a man; therefore Socrates is mortal," the correctness of the inference rests upon the proposition that any proposition that is valid for a class is also valid for any member of the class. This says in effect that one can always substitute something less inclusive for something more inclusive and the new proposition will be as valid as the former one. The rules of logic are rules governing the kinds of substitutions that can be made and the kinds of inference one can draw from them. Logic, in other words, is a set of propositions about the manipulation of propositions. Whether or not a person's reasoning is logical has nothing to do with the ultimate validity of these propositions; it is a matter of how well his reasoning conforms with them. In all societies, people not only reason, they judge one another's reasoning as correct or incorrect. This means that in all societies there are generally accepted propositions about the manipulation of propositions. There is no society without a logic. The extent to which propositions about the manipulation of propositions differ among different societies has not as yet been ascertained. The author's own experience with so-called primitive people suggests that in most respects the differences are slight. Once he had learned the local language and could use it with some facility, and once he had learned what were the propositions people accepted as axiomatic, then their procedures for manipulating these propositions to arrive at new ones and the points at which they caught one another out in argument seemed entirely reasonable to him.

Beliefs

We have said that cognitive organization of experience consists of (a) percepts and concepts of phenomena; (b) a code or language for manipulating them; and (c) sets of propositions about their properties, about their modes of arrangement, and about the transformations that accompany their rearrangements, in other words a body of knowledge. When we speak of people's beliefs we usually have reference to the last, to the propositions they accept as true. That the earth is flat, that men are inherently wicked, or that the presence of germs causes disease are beliefs or not, depending on the extent to which they are accepted as guides for assessing the future, are cited in support of decisions, or are referred to in passing judgment on the behavior of others. This is the sense in which we refer to beliefs throughout this book.

BELIEF SYSTEMS

When our experience leads us to propositions that are inconsistent with other propositions we already believe to be true, we are disturbed. Whatever the reasons for it may ultimately be, human beings are bothered by contradictions in which two things appear to be true but according to their reasoning cannot both be true.[4] We are not much disturbed, of course, when the propositions in question seem to pertain to different domains of our experience, having no immediate relevance for one another. Then we can answer the query "How do you square what you said about A with what you now say about B?" with the reply, "Oh, that has to do with something entirely different." It is when contradictory propositions appear to us to be relevant to one another, to belong to the same domain, that we are most uncomfortable.

Faced with such inconsistent propositions, we seek to find some way of construing things so as to resolve the inconsistency. We do this by postulating some other proposition which, if true, would account for the apparent contradiction; and we accept the fact that it resolves the contradiction as *prima facie* evidence that the postulate is true. It *has* to be true, or nothing makes sense. Thus, if someone reports something to us that is contrary to other things we already believe, we tend to assume that he is lying or that he is misinformed. When we see things ourselves that according to our beliefs cannot occur, as when a stage magician performs some incredible magic, we postulate the existence of some hidden mechanism. By assuming that what we see is an illusion, we reconcile our present observations with the beliefs they contradict. Or, again, we postulate that the contradictory propositions really pertain to different domains, as the Trukese have postulated that there are two kinds of sickness, a general kind for which European medicine is effective and a purely Trukese kind that requires traditional native treatment.[5]

To have too many separate domains, however, poses a problem of another kind. Whatever our beliefs may be, they provide the basis for the strategies by which we seek to gratify our wants in everyday life. The wider the range of situations in which the same strategy is applicable, the simpler our problems seem to become. A postulate is appealing when it joins what would otherwise be independent domains of experience so that each set of observations now follows logically from the same proposition. Thus we may observe that unpleasant things happen to us when our actions have offended our fellows. And we may observe that a proper display of contrition and atonement predisposes them favorably toward us once more. From this we develop a strategy for mitigating the punishments we might otherwise have to endure. We suffer many other unpleasantnesses as well, sometimes for no apparent reason at all. If we postulate the existence of unseen beings who are easily offended, we can then account for all misfortune as punishment for our own misconduct. Furthermore, our strategy of contrition and atonement now becomes applicable as a way of mitigating misfortune generally.

This process of making further assumptions to reconcile an inconsistency or to bring together otherwise separate domains of experience is what we mean by *rationalization*. This definition is broader than popular use of the term, where it refers only to postulates that enable someone, even in the face of controverting evidence, to cling to a belief that we regard as false. As we have defined it, rationalization may lead to true as well as to false propositions. Popular usage overlaps the psychiatric, where rationalization refers to a person's attempts to hide his real motives by elaborate self-justification. As we have defined it here, however, rationalization is an intellectual process independent of one's motives for employing it. People may rationalize purely for the esthetic pleasure of bringing a little more order into their cognitive system, or they may do so to link disapproved with approved domains of behavior, thus justifying their actions to themselves and their fellows. The intellectual process is the same in both events.

The same process goes on, moreover, in the construction of scientific theory. Scientists regularly assume the existence of things to reconcile apparent contradictions in what they observe. Among other things, such rationalizations have led to the discovery of new particles in the nucleus of the atom, a particle's existence having been postulated to account for some discrepancy between prior theory and newly observed fact and a subsequent search for it having led to its discovery.

Rationalization is a normal consequence of the fact that human beings are impelled to relate their various percepts and concepts to one another in a systematic and orderly way. It is essential for complex learning that they do so. People are freed from having to remember many isolated facts when they can construe them as all following from one principle.[6] As soon as we discover "the principle of the thing," we become master of a whole body of material and are able to deal with any problem that arises regarding it. We are also free to turn our attention to the learning of new things. The organizing and unifying principle is, of course, what rationalizes the hitherto unrelated facts.

This ability to relate things systematically to one another also enables us to explain things we do not want to believe and to reconcile apparently contradictory evidence with the organized body of beliefs that we already hold. Much of the rationalizing that people do, both in science and in everyday experience, is intended to save as truths the propositions they already believe to be true and to save the whole system of truths arising from their particular way of looking at things.

In every society, then, there is a body of propositions accepted as true by its members. Some of these propositions are rooted in everyday experience and appear to be self-evident truths. Others are inferences drawn from them and logically consistent with them. Still other propositions are postulates that integrate the various self-evident truths and inferred truths, in that they all seem to follow logically from the postulates. Any other propositions that appear to follow logically from these unifying postulates are themselves plausible truths.

Unifying postulates appear to be true because they make so many other things clear. We are reluctant to question their truth because of the cognitive chaos into which disbelief might plunge us. When people's beliefs are well integrated into coherent systems, a change in any specific belief may have the same effect of destroying the whole system. If something that follows from the master definition proves false, then the master definition becomes suspect, and the whole edifice may start to crumble.

Revision of our belief systems need not be too painful a process if it is all at the level of an intellectual game. Difficulty arises when the beliefs affected by change are not in the realm of academic theory alone but justify habitual modes of action. Our master definitions, especially, provide us with basic strategies for coping with the countless day-to-day situations in which we must act in order to accomplish our purposes. Disillusion with them leaves us without policy, having to grope our way painfully through situations in which we formerly moved with confidence. Thus we are reminded that people have reasons for *wanting* to believe that their beliefs are true.

CREDENCE AND TRUTH

Because beliefs are propositions that people accept as true, the question necessarily arises why people have beliefs that are patently false. Does not this imply that their reasoning powers are deficient? Are there primitive ways of thinking that are "pre-logical," as the French theorist Lévy-Brühl once argued?[7] Anthropological experience compels us to answer these questions negatively.[8] As far as we can determine, mental processes are pretty much the same in all populations. But if that is so, then why don't people believe the same things and why do they insist on believing things that are untrue?

Popularly, we think of beliefs as being either true or false. The truth, we aver, is ascertained by our senses. The entities we perceive are what we perceive them to be, and those propositions about their mutual arrangements and transformations that we are able to verify by direct observation are true. Other propositions that follow logically from these are presumably also true. The whole body of propositions consistent with what we perceive reality to be provides a measure by which we judge other propositions to be true or false. But with such a measure, what is true and what is false is a function of our percepts, the categories in terms of which we habitually perceive things; and these, we have observed, are themselves abstractions from experience and, as such, selective and arbitrary.

It is obvious that in any real situation confronting us there are many more features capable of discernment than we in fact discern. Perception, the decision as to what is there, is itself a selective act involving the use of stereotypes. Different people, using different stereotypes, perceive the same situation differently. Every language, for example, consists of a set of sound categories in terms of which its speakers hear the utterances of their fellows. These categories differ widely from language to language. The result is that an Englishman and an Italian listening to French for the first time do not hear the same sounds; the one hears in terms of English and the other in terms of Italian sound stereotypes. The same is true of other perceptions as well. An American tourist watching a Hopi snake dance does not see it as a Chinese tourist would, and neither will see it as a Hopi does.

Another source of selectivity in perception has to do with the emotional orientations of the perceiver. Two persons with essentially the same system of percepts will perceive the same situation differently because of different hopes, fears, and expectations they have brought into the situation with them. Each is on the lookout for different things.[9] Consistent tendencies to perceive in certain ways are, of course, among the more important criteria by which we discern personality differences among our fellows. Assuming that their percepts are the same as ours, we infer their emotional orientations from their selective use of them in sizing up situations to which we are also a party. This makes assessment of emotional orientations in other societies very tricky, indeed, because there is less likelihood that people are selecting from among percepts similar to our own.

As for the problem of truth, differences in perceptual categories together with differences in how people are inclined to apply the same categories mean that almost any event is capable of verifying different, inconsistent, and even downright contradictory propositions. A friend tells of discovering that he was color blind when he got into an argument with a military examiner as to what numbers were shown on a page of different colored dots. Neither could see what the other saw, and yet what both saw was there to be seen. In this case there were physiological differences at work, but different cognitive systems and different interests have a similar effect. Try to get witnesses to agree on an event!

But what about science as a measure of truth? We increasingly resort to science as the measure of truth in our society, although there remain subjects that many people prefer to hold apart from scientific appraisal. But at any point in time, science is only one of many percept-concept systems with which to record experience. The scientific approach, moreover, demands that every scientific theory be subject to systematic question and attack, so that what is scientific truth today is often a mistaken idea tomorrow. Science is concerned with multiplying our ways of looking at things and broadening our perspectives. For this reason it may well be the best measure of truth man has so far devised, but one of the truths it teaches us is that whatever we believe to be true is probably true only within the limitations of our experience as we are currently in the habit of recording it.[10]

BELIEFS AS VALUES

The question of what is true has little relevance for understanding our fellow men as believers, compared to the reasons why people accept propositions as true. This brings us back to values, for to accept a proposition as true is to value it in some way. We may say that people believe because it gratifies them to do so. It is fitting, then, that we examine the kinds of gratification people get from their beliefs.

Ultimately all beliefs have some connection with behavior. As we have been at some pains to note, they provide the means whereby people orient themselves to their surroundings in ways they find gratifying. Propositions are valued as true when they rationalize the strategies and the tactics by which people anticipate the future successfully enough to realize their objectives. So also do people value the propositions that account for their failures and those that justify the demands they make on others. If willingness to accept a belief as true depends on the way it serves wants and felt needs, then we should expect to find the explanation of beliefs, in part at least, through an examination of wants and the kinds of gratifications that people seek. We should be careful not to confine ourselves to practical considerations alone, however. We must not overlook the fact that people have social, emotional, and intellectual concerns as well. A belief that provides social or emotional rewards acquires value as readily as one that consistently leads to the accomplishment of material goals. Let us, then, consider some examples of how beliefs function in relation to human purposes from these several points of view.

BELIEF AS A BASIS OF ACTION

One of the most important reasons for accepting a proposition as true is that it seems to fit the facts as they have been perceived. Even a scientifically false belief does not necessarily lack predictive value. The belief that the world will end tomorrow is quickly found wanting; but a theory and practice of farming that has long-range deleterious effects on the soil does not year after year result in crop failure. Normally, the beliefs that people have, however false from an outsider's point of view, show at least a rough fit with those aspects of empirical reality most intimately connected with their immediate concerns.

For a closely reasoned and empirically tested belief, consider the following comment by a Pacific Island navigator, who was defending his belief that the sun goes around the earth.

> I am well aware of the foreigner's claim that the earth moves and the sun stands still, as someone once told us; but this we cannot believe, for how else could it happen that in the morning and evening the sun burns less hot than in the day? It must be because the sun has been cooled when it emerges from the water and when toward setting it again approaches the water. And furthermore, how can it be possible that the sun remains still when we are yet able to observe that in the course of the year it changes its position in relation to the stars?[11]

This man's confidence in his theory and in the system of celestial navigation based upon it is understandable. Using it, island navigators have for centuries successfully sailed in the Pacific, coming accurately upon their destinations, tiny islands sometimes hundreds of miles distant over the open sea. However wrong from our point of view, his belief was well considered and quite adequate to his needs. We can understand in the light of his reasoning and experience why he considered it foolish to accept a foreigner's belief that seemed so thoroughly contradicted by the facts.

Another example of a belief whose practical utility we can assess is the Trukese conviction that elephantiasis is caused by malevolent spirits. These spirits frequent the muddy ground in the swampy area where taro is grown. They are especially active at dawn and dusk, when they are said to rise from the ground and bite human beings, thereby making them ill. People are warned not to go to work in their taro patches before the sun is well up and to stop working before the sun gets too low. From a scientific point of view the belief is false, but the advice predicated on it is sound. Empirically, it would seem, the ancestors of these people have learned to associate elephantiasis with swampy ground, especially at dawn and dusk, when mosquitoes, which actually carry filaria, the responsible parasite, are especially active. By staying away from such places at these times people minimize their exposure to filarial infection, thus lowering their chances of developing the more extreme symptoms to which repeated infection makes one liable.

Because several different propositions may have fairly good predictive value, people are free to choose those that are consistent with their other beliefs, as we have already had occasion to note in discussing belief systems. The Trukese belief about elephantiasis provides an explanation of the causes of the disease consistent with their general theory that disease is normally caused by the "bite" of a ghost or evil spirit. This is consistent in turn with a host of other beliefs, such as those having to do with the survival of the soul, which we saw had important emotional value for Truk's people. Our own ancestors, suffering from the ague, which we now know to have been malarial seizures, came up with an entirely different kind of belief to account for it. There was nothing of "bites" in their theory, although, of course, a mosquito was responsible for their chills and fever. They believed it was the nocturnal effluvium arising from swamps and marshy ground, a miasma, that caused their ills. This belief was consistent with their view of the importance of "bad air" in sickness generally. Although for the one group it was bad air and for the other bad spirits, the result was that both, on the grounds of their beliefs, sought to avoid swamps when the mosquitoes were active.

Maintaining consistency sometimes leads people into positions that strike an observer as absurd. A poor fit between the observed facts and a belief that is consistent with a larger belief system puts pressure on people to alter their beliefs. Yet, like the fundamentalist who rejects evolution as inconsistent with his belief in the literal truth of the Bible, people may cling to consistency in the face of absurdity so as not to deprive themselves of the other gratifications their beliefs give them. See, for example, the Trobriand Islands belief about procreation described on page 165.

Belief and Authority

To a very large extent people are dependent on the experience of others for the beliefs that guide their actions. Sometimes their acceptance of what others say is justified by future events; sometimes it is not. People feel a need, therefore, to know the source of a belief and the qualifications of the source as a reliable authority. In all societies some activities are the primary concern of specialists. The beliefs they express about their specialties are accepted by others in the society in recognition of their greater experience. Trust in those with experience more often than not helps people accomplish their purposes.

The Pacific Island navigator already cited illustrates the point. It was his business to observe the heavenly bodies and the regularities of their apparent movements, to formulate theory about them, and to apply his theory to the solution of navigation problems. His experience was far greater than that of most persons in his society, and because of this his beliefs carried weight. On the strength of them, he could take people where they wanted to go. As a man of experience he had confidence in his beliefs and could be expected to alter them only when personally convinced that European beliefs were based on even greater experience. Was the foreigner who told him he was wrong also a specialist in these matters?

With this question in mind, it is revealing to look at the field personnel of governmental and social service agencies trying to persuade people to change their beliefs and the practices they justify. They are often young, which in itself suggests inexperience. Much of what they seek to persuade their clients to accept as true, they are themselves accepting on faith with little or no experience of their own to support it. They are repeating what the authorities to whom they look tell them. Medical practice, social work, teaching, and administration alike are characterized by the adoption of new gospels, accepted on faith as the latest truth until replaced by newer scientific or scholarly revelations. This would seem to be inevitable in the clinical and applied professions, whose busy practitioners must look to others for their theoretical orientations. No problem arises in their relations with their clients, so long as the clients also accept the same authorities. But in community development, the field agent's authorities for his beliefs may have no standing with his clients. An agent who cannot represent himself as a qualified authority in accordance with his clients' views of accreditation cannot expect to enjoy much confidence.

In any community where the conditions of life are relatively stable, experience demonstrates over and over again that one's elders know better. To go against their advice is to court failure. Yet agents of change so often ask people to do just this and become impatient with them when they hesitate. Under conditions of rapid change, when people are confronted with new circumstances and problems that their elders and other specialists have never faced, people find themselves in the unhappy position of the child who discovers he can no longer trust his parents. Lacking dependable authorities, people now feel the need to find them. Under these conditions they may be eager to believe what aliens tell them and attribute to their opinions an authority they do not deserve. Missionaries, government administrators, and other agents of change are sometimes dismayed to find some casual, spur-of-the-moment comment picked up by their clients as gospel and acted upon with unhappy results. Depending upon the degree of trust his clients repose in their traditional authorities, then, an agent may find himself either without authority at all for what he has to say or with too much.

Self-Validating Beliefs

Some beliefs fit the facts of experience because they lead people to act upon their world in such a way as to make future experience consistent with their beliefs. The paranoid, to take a familiar example, believes that others are hostile to him. Assuming this to be true, he treats them as his enemies and thereby maneuvers them into making hostile responses. These reactions seem to demonstrate that his original suspicions were well founded. The child who goes around pouting and complaining that everyone picks on him invites others to pick on him by this behavior and makes it very difficult for others to show whatever positive feelings they may have toward him. In this way belief and experience become a closed system, each reinforcing the other, even though the belief may at first have had little basis in fact, being largely a projection of the believer's own feelings. We are, unfortunately, all too keenly aware these days how international tensions can be perpetuated in just this fashion.

Beliefs about human character and motives are especially likely to become self-validating in this way. As people grow up, they tend to acquire a view of themselves consistent with prevailing beliefs and to act accordingly. The Trukese assume that young men in their twenties are irresponsible, and therefore they do not give them responsibility. This invites the young men to be irresponsible, and they often tend to be so. Similarly, in a society where people believe that everyone will steal whenever he has an opportunity, the chances are good that nearly everyone will.

The mutual reinforcement of behavior and belief may occur in other institutional contexts as well. Belief in sorcery as a cause of death is one that development agents frequently encounter. Where the belief exists, people who learn they have been hexed often seem to develop a hysteria or melancholia that leads to their death unless they have access to remedial steps in whose efficacy they also believe. Because of the belief, sorcery can be a real cause of death.[12]

Whenever men have the power to create or modify the conditions in which they live, they tend to do so in such ways that their expectations, stemming from their beliefs, are actually realized. Belief is molded by experience, to be sure, but experience is at the same time molded by belief, each acting on the other to create a closed world of empirically validated truth.

BELIEFS AS INSTRUMENTS OF SOCIAL PURPOSES

When agents of change ask their clients to accept a new body of propositions and abandon their former beliefs, they are often asking them to make a social as well as an intellectual decision. As we have already noted, they are asking them to repudiate the traditional authorities for established beliefs, the recognized specialists and the elders from whom people have learned, including their own parents. This means taking from a kinsman, neighbor, or fellow tribesman some portion of his standing—his rights, privileges, and immunities—and conferring it upon an alien.

In a large and complex society like our own, we tend to forget just how closely involved with their experts people are likely to be in simpler communities. We may reject this or that physician in an urban setting without its affecting our social relations; but in a small community of which the specialist is himself a member, his former clients must go on living and dealing with him as a neighbor and kinsman even though they reject him as a specialist. This is not easy to do. We are reminded of how important for their social relationships are the things people believe—even more what they profess to believe.

Some beliefs serve as symbols of a person's social position. There are right ways to think in order to be accepted as a member of a particular social class, of a particular religious congregation, or even of a community as such. An American is not likely to find favor in the eyes of his fellows these days if he expresses the belief that the socialization of heavy industry will have a beneficial effect on his country's economy. Most Americans appear to believe that such a course would be catastrophic, the end of everything they value. Few of them have seriously tried to inform themselves on the matter; but they frequently express their belief, thereby reconfirming their commitment to membership in the society as it now stands and ensuring their acceptance as a fellow member by others.

Among religious beliefs, likewise, profession of the Nicene Creed is necessary for acceptance as a member in some church denominations. Reciting this or the Apostles' Creed is an integral part of morning and evening prayer. Few who recite it, however, are aware of the doctrinal controversies and political struggles the early Church Fathers intended the Creed officially to resolve.[13] People profess the Creed because they want to belong to the Church; few wish to belong to the Church because they already believe in the content of the Creed. The more intense a person's desire to be identified with the Church, moreover, the more jealously he guards against efforts to tamper with its established doctrines.[14]

Because professing articles of faith is the price of admission and continued membership in social and religious groups, people say that they want to belong because they already believe. They rarely admit that they want to belong because they fear they will lose their friends if they do not or because they want to please their parents, improve their social standing, or gain a sense of moral advantage in dealing with others. Nevertheless, their profession of belief may prove highly rewarding in such ways.

It is often difficult, however, to profess one thing while believing something else in private. We are usually at some pains to rationalize the dogmas we feel called upon to profess so that they square reasonably well with our private beliefs. It is not simply to avoid judging ourselves as hypocrites, but because we are called upon to act on our beliefs. When the beliefs we profess are at variance with our personal convictions, we have to be constantly on guard lest we betray our lack of faith in what we profess. When the consequences of such betrayal may prove costly, we have good reason for finding a rational basis for believing what we say we believe. Thus it is very difficult, today, for a white man from the deep south in the United States not to believe in the superiority of the white race and still maintain cordial relations with other white men. For they insist not only on his profession of belief in white supremacy but on his behaving in a manner consistent with it.

Development agents often find themselves apparently persuading people to particular points of view only to find them failing to act accordingly and even denying what they formerly seemed to accept. For example, a young expectant mother comes regularly to a maternity clinic for instruction in child care and expresses apparent interest in learning what the nurse or health worker has to teach her; she then proceeds to care for her child strictly in the traditional way after it is born. Sometimes she does so because she cannot accommodate the new practices to existing domestic routines. Often, however, she does not herself have the power to make the necessary decisions about the kind of care the child will receive, this being the prerogative of her husband, mother, or mother-in-law. Since her fellows require her to continue to act in ways consistent with traditional beliefs, it is more comforting to her to return to her old beliefs once again and accept them as valid. As a rule, new beliefs, even if privately accepted, are not likely to lead to economic or social change, as long as people feel that doing something about them may seriously jeopardize existing good relations with their fellows.

BELIEFS AS MEANS OF EMOTIONAL GRATIFICATION

We have seen how Trukese beliefs in the nature of the human soul provide emotional gratification. These beliefs give objective structure to a subjective problem, thereby permitting people to act in ways they find answering to their needs. Where emotions and feelings are the source of people's problems, they must project their feelings into something outside of themselves, objectivize them, and thereby render them capable of analysis and resolution through symbolic manipulation. Many beliefs that people express are products of this process of objectivizing subjective states.

The problem that the good and bad souls of Truk help to solve is peculiar to Truk; at any rate, it is far from universal. There are some general categories of problem, however, with which most people have to deal and for which beliefs are the only suitable instruments. Let us examine some representative examples.

Rationalizing the Inevitable

People are often required to do things against their wishes. Few men in our society, for example, want to go to war and run the risk of being killed. They insist that there be good reasons that they should do so, before they will accept their participation in war as an unpleasant obligation. Many beliefs serve the purpose of rationalizing the inevitable or of making more palatable some burdensome duty. Sometimes, their relation to the end they serve is fairly obvious; at other times, not. By way of illustration, let us look at an apparently bizarre belief held by the inhabitants of the Trobriand Islands in Melanesia.[15]

The Trobriand people assert that sexual intercourse does not produce children. Children are conceived when a clan spirit enters the mother's womb. They insist on clinging to this belief in spite of the amusement it occasions their Melanesian neighbors and the efforts of others to argue them out of it. Their belief has been interpreted as evidence of primitive ignorance, but they hold to it as an active dogma, and at the same time espouse other beliefs and values that are not entirely consistent with this one. If we examine some of the demands Trobriand society places on its individuals, we can see how this particular belief may answer their felt needs.

Membership in the Trobriand clans is based on matrilineal descent—people belong to their mother's and not their father's clan group. Each clan owns a village or portion of one, which is the only place where its adult men have a legal right to live. They can live in other villages only on sufferance of the clans that own it. Thus, a young man, growing up in his father's village has no right to live in that village except as a dependent of his father. Upon marriage he must leave the community in which he grew up and in which he formed his close ties and move to the one associated with his own clan, where his senior maternal uncles already reside. Furthermore, his relations with his father have been warm and indulgent, while his maternal uncles, his clan seniors, have always been disciplining, authoritarian figures, toward whom he has much suppressed hostility. The move is one that many young men would rather not make. And their indulgent fathers would also like to keep them with them. But in each case, house sites in the father's village are claimed by the father's junior clansmen, moving in from the villages where they grew up. Willy-nilly, a man must eventually move to his own clan village. But why must he? Why can't he be a member of his father's clan as well as his mother's?

The Trobriand answer is simple. It is in the order of nature that people belong to their mother's clan. Anything else is unnatural.

> Totemic nature is conceived to be as deeply ingrained in the substance of the individual as sex, color, and stature. It can never be changed, and it transcends individual life, for it can be carried over into the next world, and brought back into this one when the spirit returns by reincarnation.[16]

The bond between a father and his son is one of nurture only and depends on the kind of nurture given; but that between a man and his fellow clansmen, including his maternal uncles, is one of nature. The preeminence we give in our society to biological parentage, as is so poignantly revealed in custody cases, is given by the Trobrianders to clan affiliation. This affiliation is rendered more absolute and unquestionable by the belief that one's very existence is owed to one's own clan alone. Only clan mates are of "one body."

Their social system makes a sometimes difficult demand of Trobriand men, but they see no reasonable alternative to accepting it, just as our justices see no alternative to removing a happy foster child from the only parents he has ever known when the biological parent invokes the mystic bond of blood.[17] In each society decisions have to be made as to where a person's rightful place is. Whatever the criteria used, some people are going to dislike the results of their application. Rationalizations that make these decisions seem inescapable, logical, or just are something people can ill afford to be without. They value highly the beliefs from which such justifications credibly follow.

Relieving the Individual of Responsibility

People not only have to put up with their own frustrations, they have to deal with the consequences of the frustrations they inflict on others. Parents, for example, have on occasion to punish their children and yet be able to continue to live in general amity with them. In many other relationships also people are the immediate agents of their fellows' discomfiture. When we suffer injury or frustration at the hands of others, we resent it most if we suspect that they have acted for private reasons of their own. If, on the other hand, they are simply performing their duty as defined by the social and moral order, then whatever resentment we may feel is displaced from them to more remote authorities. Thus we regularly do things that others are likely to resent not in our own name but in the name of such higher authorities as God, the Law, or Public Opinion. When we are told "Sorry, it's contrary to regulations," we are less likely to blame our frustration on the fellow who told us this and more likely to curse the regulations. If we have an abiding respect for the regulations, we may even apologize for having raised the question, guiltily turning the blame back on ourselves.

In every society there are congeries of beliefs that support the idea of higher authority and that attribute to that authority more than ordinary powers. "This is taboo"; "the ancestors will be angry"; "witches will get you"; "it is written"; "God ordained"; "what will people think?" and many like expressions stem from beliefs that give them force and validity. Armed with such beliefs, we depersonalize the enforcement of rights and duties by making their enforcement a duty rather than a privilege, or a friendly, for-your-own-good kind of action rather than a hostile or indifferent one. The beliefs through which people are able to handle the problem of personal responsibility for frustrating behavior are inevitably highly valued.

There are also many occasions, of course, when people feel a strong need to disclaim responsibility in those contexts where they are normally held responsible by their fellows. Each society, for example, offers a set of approved life goals for the individual. Their achievement provides the basis for prestige ratings and the measure by which people judge one another and themselves as successes or failures. Achievement is rationalized as due to the presence of various personal virtues, being those attributes that the society's members most value in their fellows. The trouble is that there are always some people who succeed where they are expected to fail, and some who fail when their virtue should entitle them to succeed. Few people, moreover, are able to achieve the personal goals for themselves to which they aspire or to live up to the expectations of others on all occasions. Most of us feel a need to save face and to salvage our self-esteem. This is accomplished by displacing the responsibility for failure to some external cause. Thus, in our society, we believe in luck as a capricious and unpredictable force and seek magical ways of controlling it in our favor. The Polynesian has an analogous belief in a force he calls *mana*. In other societies it is fate.

When we displace responsibility from ourselves to other people rather than to impersonal forces, we necessarily attribute our difficulties to secret action by others who wish us ill, that is, to sorcery, or to contact with persons who by their nature bring disaster and misfortune to others, to witches. Why some people tend to rationalize failures in terms of the counteraction of impersonal forces, why others emphasize the displeasure of fellow human beings or anthropomorphic gods, and why still others resort to a belief in witches are questions we are not yet able satisfactorily to answer, though the degree to which aggressive and hostile feelings are permitted expression in ordinary social relationships seems to be an important factor.[18] The fact remains that responsibility for our actions raises important emotional problems. Beliefs and practices that we find repugnant, such as those associated with sorcery, may be valued by others because they meet these problems in the same way that our different beliefs meet them for us.

Mitigating Feelings of Guilt

In no society is the code of conduct toward one's fellows uniform. Behavior that is outlawed in one relationship is condoned or even encouraged in another. This means that people have to square their consciences with the fact that they treat some people in ways they have been taught to regard as bad when dealing with others. They do this, of course, by believing that those whom they treat badly deserve such treatment. It is not necessary to be nice to some people because they are "low class." People of other races are "scarcely human," anyway, so it is all right to treat them more or less as animals. To change the beliefs that rationalize our behavior is to make ourselves guilty where we have not been before. We tend therefore to resist such change and to regard counter-doctrines as subversive of the social order, which indeed they are, for we could not in conscience continue to structure our social relationships as we do if we allowed ourselves to believe them. In our society we have for some time justified our treatment of those who violate the law, for example, by beliefs about the nature of human character, many of which social science is discovering to be false; but popular resistance to new ideas about the causes of delinquency and ways of dealing with it remain strong. There are few of us without guilt if they are true. Public treatment of the mentally ill is similarly based on a set of beliefs about insanity that medical science has demonstrated to be largely false. An effort seriously to educate the public about mental health in a Canadian community met with determined resistance and popular outrage, largely, it would seem, because of the guilt to which it exposed too many people. The rationalizations by which they justified to themselves their past treatment of mentally ill relatives, friends, or employees could not be questioned except at heavy emotional cost.[19]

How quickly people can develop beliefs to justify behavior that would be unconscionable without them is illustrated by Klineberg's résumé of changing beliefs about Chinese immigrants held by California's white population.

When the Chinese were needed in California—when the white migrants from other parts of the United States were so anxious to get rich quickly that they had no patience with domestic labor or with work in the cigar factories—the Chinese were welcome. During that period newspapers and journals referred to them as among "the most worthy of our newly-adopted citizens," "the best immigrants in California"; they were spoken of as thrifty, sober, tractable, inoffensive, law-abiding. They showed an "all-round ability" and an "adaptability beyond praise." This flattering picture prevailed during a considerable period. Then around the 1860's, when the economic situation had changed and other groups were competing with the Chinese for the positions which they were occupying, there was a corresponding change in the stereotype of the Chinese. In the elections of 1867 both political parties introduced into their platforms legislation "protecting" Californians against Mongolian competition. The phrases now applied to the Chinese included: "a distinct people," "unassimilable," "their presence lowered the plane of living," "they shut out white labor." They were spoken of as clannish, criminal, debased and servile, deceitful and vicious; they smuggled opium; Chinatowns were full of prostitution and gambling; the Chinese were filthy and loathsome in their habits, undesirable as workers and residents in the country.

This startling change in the "characteristics" of the Chinese can hardly be accounted for by any change in the nature of the Chinese population of California. The only acceptable explanation is that the change in economic conditions there made it advantageous for the whites to eliminate the Chinese from economic competition as far as possible, and the stereotype was altered in a direction which would help to justify such action.*[20]

* Reprinted by permission from Otto Klineberg, *Tensions Affecting International Understanding:* A Survey of Research. Bulletin 62, Social Science Research Council, New York, 1950, pp. 114–115. Copyright by Social Science Research Council.

When beliefs serve to protect us from a sense of guilt, we are not merely unresponsive to the efforts of others to get us to change them, we actively resent and resist them. We also may resist expanding our acquaintance with relevant facts for fear that such experience will compel us to change our present beliefs.[21]

There are other emotionally charged problems that people resolve through their beliefs. Many of them, as the foregoing examples suggest, have to do with how people feel about themselves as persons. They relate, that is, to questions of identity and personal worth. How people see themselves and how others see them, the esteem in which they hold themselves and in which others hold them, these considerations lie at the heart of so much that goes on in the conduct of human affairs that it will repay us to devote the next two chapters to them. We need not, therefore, continue detailing specific types of emotional problems. We have seen enough to observe how beliefs acquire value for people and to glimpse the reasons that people want them to be true.

SHARED BELIEFS AND SOCIAL COOPERATION

Few of us would think seriously to question the truism that common understandings and common values are essential to social life. Yet, we have been emphasizing the lack of consensus among people, even among members of the same community. We have said that no two individuals have exactly the same cognitive system or accept all the same propositions as true. There is evidence, moreover, that where people profess the same beliefs, they differ in their motives for doing so.[22] Some individuals, furthermore, may have no emotional concerns that make a particular belief important to them, though it is valued highly by their fellows. Certainly, under pressures to change a belief, some people respond more readily than do others. Even within a single community, the same beliefs cannot possibly serve everyone equally well. It is evident that social living does not depend on common understandings in the sense that everyone actually believes the same things or has the same cognitive view of their circumstances. But, we may ask, is not the smoothness of social living enhanced in proportion as people share the same beliefs?

Don't people get along better with one another the more they see eye to eye? It is true that if people have beliefs that lead them to act in conflicting ways, social life is disrupted; but the same beliefs can lead people to compete for possession of a limited number of valued objects with disastrous effects upon their common welfare. Convincing arguments have been advanced, moreover, to show that it is unnecessary for the participants in a social system to have the same conceptual picture of it or to believe the same things about matters of common interest for social relations to proceed harmoniously and for the social system to work smoothly.[23]

For example, there are a number of relationship systems in our society that can be satisfactorily maintained only if the parties to them believe different things about the relationship and the circumstances in which it is operative. Certainly, physicians feel that their patients must be ignorant of at least some of the realities as they, the physicians, see them, if a satisfactory doctor-patient relationship is to obtain. Military men have long assumed that an army can operate as a social system only so long as enlisted men are kept ignorant of the off-duty conduct of commissioned officers. And every business executive feels a need to conceal from his employees some things about the business of which he is aware for the work of the business to get done. What is required is not that people's views be the same but that their views lead to actions that are mutually supporting.[24]

In any social system, to be sure, there are rules of the game that all participants must be willing to follow, but often enough, these rules function to ensure that people will have different understandings of what is going on. We may ask, indeed, whether any relationship system calling for the playing of different roles can be maintained to everyone's satisfaction if all participants have the same beliefs and values. Men have to be willing to be men and to play men's roles, and women have to be willing to be women and to play women's roles. This is not likely to happen if men and women hold exactly the same views of manhood and womanhood.

In community development, it often seems necessary to try to get people to change their beliefs. As they see themselves and their circumstances in the light of new beliefs and understandings, they become more strongly motivated to change and willing to accept new methods of doing things. But what is likely to happen if a development agent successfully educates his clients to view their community as he does and to believe what he believes about them and about the rest of the world? If his beliefs would not let him be content to live in their community, even after considerable development, their acceptance by his clients will lead to a desire to emigrate. We can hardly consider such a result to represent successful development. Development usually requires that a community's members be able to feel good about themselves as members of their community. For this, they may have to believe different things about themselves and their world from what the agent believes. In development as in other social situations, the achievement of mutually gratifying conditions is likely to require that the interested parties have somewhat different beliefs about them.

SUGGESTED READING

Boulding, Kenneth, *The Image:* Knowledge in Life and Society. University of Michigan Press, Ann Arbor, 1956.

Erasmus, Charles John, "Changing Folk Beliefs and the Relativity of Empirical Knowledge," *Southwestern Journal of Anthropology*, vol. 8, 1952, pp. 411–428.

Evans-Pritchard, E. E., *Witchcraft, Oracles, and Magic Among the Azande.* Clarendon Press, Oxford, 1937.

Festinger, Leon, *A Theory of Cognitive Dissonance.* Row, Peterson and Co., Evanston, Ill., 1957.

Firth, Raymond, *Human Types:* An Introduction to Social Anthropology. Rev. ed., Mentor Books, New York, 1958, chap. 6.

Hallowell, A. Irving, *Culture and Experience.* University of Pennsylvania Press, Philadelphia, 1955, chap. 9.

Leighton, Alexander H., *The Governing of Men.* Princeton University Press, Princeton, N. J., 1945, chap. 17.

Nadel, S. F., "Witchcraft in Four African Societies," *American Anthropologist*, vol. 54, 1952, pp. 18–29.

Wallace, Anthony F. C., *Culture and Personality.* Random House, New York, 1961.

NOTES TO CHAPTER 7

1. Lenneberg, Eric H., and John M. Roberts, *The Language of Experience.* Indiana University Publications in Anthropology and Linguistics, no. 13, Department of Anthropology, Indiana University, Bloomington, 1956.

2. Ray, Verne, "Techniques and Problems in the Study of Human Color Perception," *Southwestern Journal of Anthropology,* vol. 8, 1952, pp. 251–259.

3. Barnett, Homer G., *Innovation: The Basis of Cultural Change.* McGraw-Hill Book Co., New York, 1953.

4. Festinger, Leon, *A Theory of Cognitive Dissonance.* Row, Peterson and Co., Evanston, Ill., 1957.

5. For a similar compartmentalization of local and European medicine in northern India, see Gould, Harold A., "The Implications of Technological Change for Folk and Scientific Medicine," *American Anthropologist,* vol. 59, 1957, pp. 507–516.

6. Miller, George, "The Magical Number Seven, Plus-or-Minus Two: Some Limits on Our Capacity for Processing Information," *Psychological Review,* vol. 63, 1956, pp. 81–97.

7. Lévy-Brühl, Lucien, *How Natives Think: Primitive Mentality.* George Allen and Unwin, Ltd., London, 1926.

8. Hallowell, A. Irving, *Culture and Experience.* University of Pennsylvania Press, Philadelphia, 1955, pp. 14–31.

9. See, for example, the perception experiments described by W. H. Ittelson and F. P. Kilpatrick, "Experiments in Perception," *Scientific American,* vol. 185, August, 1951, pp. 50–55.

10. On this point, see Hallowell, A. Irving, "Psychic Stresses and Culture Patterns" in Opler, Marvin K., editor, *Culture and Mental Health: Cross-Cultural Studies,* Macmillan Co., New York, 1959, pp. 24–25.

11. Girschner, M., "Die Karolineninsel Namoluk und ihre Bewohner," *Baessler-Archiv,* vol. 2, 1913, p. 173. (Our translation.)

12. For example, see the discussion by Leo W. Simmons and Harold G. Wolff in *Social Science in Medicine,* Russell Sage Foundation, New York, 1954, pp. 92–96. See also Cannon, W. B., " 'Voodoo' Death," *American Anthropologist,* vol. 44, 1942, pp. 169–181.

13. Goodenough, Erwin R., *The Church in the Roman Empire.* Henry Holt and Co., New York, 1931, pp. 46–52.

14. Along these lines, a study of the attitudes and opinions of college students reveals that "students rated as religious believers tend to be reluctant to countenance any kind of deviation or nonconformity . . . they are more likely than others to indicate attitudes and opinions that conform to their social roles . . . they are likewise readier to express intolerance of minority racial and religious groups." This holds for Catholics, Protestants, and Jews alike. See Goldsen, Rose K., Morris Rosenberg, Robin M. Williams, Jr., and Edward A. Suchman, *What College Students Think,* D. Van Nostrand Co., Princeton, N.J., 1960, p. 183.

15. Malinowski, B., *The Sexual Life of Savages,* Liveright Publishing Co., New York; G. Routledge and Sons Ltd., London, 3d ed., 1932 (first published 1929). See also Austen, Leo, "Procreation Among the Trobriand Islanders," *Oceania,* vol. 5, 1934, pp. 102–113.

16. Malinowski, B., *op. cit.,* p. 416.

17. It is interesting to observe that the Albanian mountain tribes, with a strong patrilineal organization, express beliefs about reproduction that are the exact opposite of those in the Trobriand Islands. Biological continuity is, as in Europe generally, believed to be based on blood, but an Albanian gets his blood entirely from his father and has biological kinship with his patrilineal kinsmen alone. His mother serves only as a nurturing vehicle within which the seed implanted by his father has an opportunity to grow. He and his mother have no blood in common. Ties to one's maternal kin are the result of human action and sentiment alone; what men have made they can unmake. But ties with one's paternal kin are a part of the cosmic order, and men are powerless to change them. See Durham, M. E., *Some Tribal Origins, Laws and Customs of the Balkans*, G. Allen and Unwin Ltd., London, 1928, pp. 15, 147 ff.

18. See, for example, Spiro, Melford E., "Ghosts, Ifaluk, and Teleological Functionalism," *American Anthropologist*, vol. 54, 1952, pp. 497–503. For an extensive list of hypotheses regarding the relationship between religious beliefs and psychological forces, see Spiro, Melford E., and Roy O. D'Andrade, "A Cross-Cultural Study of Some Supernatural Beliefs," *American Anthropologist*, vol. 60, 1958, pp. 456–466.

19. Cumming, John, and Elaine Cumming, "Mental Health Education in a Canadian Community" in Paul, Benjamin D., editor, *Health, Culture, and Community: Case Studies of Public Reactions to Health Programs*. Russell Sage Foundation, New York, 1955, pp. 43–69.

20. Klineberg, Otto, *Tensions Affecting International Understanding: A Survey of Research*. Bulletin 62, Social Science Research Council, New York, 1950, pp. 114–115. The author summarizes the findings of B. Shrieke, *Alien Americans*, The Viking Press, New York, 1936.

21. See, for example, the reluctance in our own society to believe what scientific study has revealed about alcohol, as described by Berton Roueché, "Annals of Medicine: Alcohol, II—The Shortest Way Out of Manchester," *The New Yorker*, January 16, 1960, pp. 39–81.

22. Harper, Edward B., "Hoylu: A Belief Relating to Justice and the Supernatural," *American Anthropologist*, vol. 59, 1957, pp. 801–816.

23. Wallace, Anthony F. C., *Culture and Personality*. Random House, New York, 1961, pp. 39–41.

24. On this point, see Boulding, Kenneth, *The Image: Knowledge in Life and Society*, University of Michigan Press, Ann Arbor, 1956, p. 57.

Chapter 8

IDENTITY AND PERSONAL WORTH

HUMAN BEINGS are anchored to reality and purpose by a firm sense of who they are. There are few human conditions more frightening than amnesia, where the individual, cut off from such a sense, drifts aimlessly, his actions without meaning or purpose to himself. When an amnesia victim goes to some authority in his plight, it is to get help in finding out *who* he is. And it is always striking to see how zealously other people set to work to hook him back onto the identity from which he has come loose. Whatever his problems may be, there seems to be no way to get at them until he recommits himself to a particular identity in a world of other identities, until he becomes a specific person again.

Concern with identity pervades human existence. Parents spend much time with their toddlers coaching them on their infant identities within the social order, thereby giving them a grip on social reality. And other people continually test them on their knowledge. What's your name? Are you a girl or a boy? How old are you? Whose girl or boy are you? These are among the first identity questions to which a child must have answers. Later on we ask him what school he goes to, what grade he is in, whether or not he is a Scout, what sports he likes best, and so on. The kinds of things adults say and the questions they ask help the child acquire an ever more deeply focused image of self.

Social living makes people the instruments or agents of one another's gratifications and frustrations. Depending on our conduct, we acquire positive or negative value as persons for our fellows. Our dependence on others makes it essential that we be valued and accepted by them. The social isolate, rejected by all, is an unhappy creature, indeed. Only the emotionally ill court ostracism. Because of their extreme dependence, children have an especially great need to be accepted by others. An infant is valued without effort on his part; but as he gets older he finds that his continued acceptance and the gratification of his wants are increasingly contingent on his conducting himself in accordance with the desires of others. It becomes important to be the kind of person that others want him to be. Because their own happiness depends upon it, people commit themselves to developing their identities in socially approved ways, to trying to achieve publicly valued identity goals. In the eyes of his fellows, moreover, how a person ought to conduct himself is contingent upon his place in the social order, as is the kind of treatment he can expect in return. His own social fate is linked with the fate of whatever group or category of person he happens to belong to.

Identity is thus rooted in the social order. This is true both in the cognitive or substantive sense of who and what a person is and in the evaluative sense of how he is affectively regarded by his fellows and how he feels about himself. These things derive from his place in the social order and from his ability to conduct himself according to the role relationships attaching thereto. Any change that affects the existing social order or a person's ability to conduct himself in accordance with it must also affect his identity and sense of worth. Social change is likely to involve the very core of being, affecting things that help to shape even the "innermost self."

Identity, finally, is not even normally static. A person's identity changes all through his life as his abilities change and as he accumulates a record of achievements and failures. Since community development aims at helping people achieve a new sense of identity and worth, both individually and collectively, what we understand of the process of identity change will help us understand community development as a process also.

A consideration of identity and personal worth, then, appears crucial to the central problem of this book. In this chapter we shall explore identity in relation to the social order, to values and sentiments, and to customary practices and beliefs. In the next chapter we shall consider the process of identity change and its implications for community development.

THE NATURE OF IDENTITY

Identity is so complex a phenomenon that it will help us if we sort out its more important components before we discuss it in detail.

First of all, we must distinguish between our perception or recognition of someone's identity for what it is and our evaluation of it. To recognize that this is Mr. Jones and that he is a policeman involves considerations different from those involved in deciding whether we think well or ill of him, or what we think of policemen generally. In considering identity, therefore, we have to consider both the combinations of attributes or features by which we discern particular identities and the esteem these attributes differentially enjoy.

Secondly, we must bear in mind that a person's identity as he perceives it, his self-image, does not necessarily coincide with his identity as perceived by others, his public image. We must similarly distinguish the estimation in which a person holds himself from that in which others hold him, his self-esteem from his prestige. A person may enjoy different public images and different prestige ratings, according to the nature of his relations with different individuals and groups of individuals in his social world, and yet maintain a fairly constant image and estimation of self.

We must also distinguish the features or attributes that define identities from those that are merely associated with them and that serve as symbols or badges of identity. A woman is married by virtue of the occurrence of a particular ritual event, not because she wears a wedding ring. By wearing a ring she may masquerade as married. The ring does not define her identity but is a symbol of it, communicating her identity to others. Badges of identity are obviously of great importance in social relationships. With the badges they select people present themselves to others as having particular identities, promote particular public images for themselves.

In thinking of ourselves and others, moreover, we usually regard some features of identity as personal and independent of one's social or occupational station in life, whereas we see other features as social, in that they derive from membership in a group or category of persons. Thus a man may be honest and industrious regardless of whether he is a free man or a slave. Of course, in some societies it may be axiomatic that no slave is honest. Features of personal and social identity are often assumed to be correlated. Personal characteristics, moreover, are important determinants of eligibility for membership in some social groups and categories. Being a bank president as part of one's social identity in our society requires personal as well as other qualifications. Indeed, the value people place on particular social identities depends in part, at least, on the personal qualities they assume to be correlated or associated with them. Nevertheless, there are many occasions when we sharply differentiate between personal and social aspects of identity. In military service, for example, recruits are told that they must salute all officers regardless of whether or not they conduct themselves properly as officers, for one "salutes the uniform and not the man," that is, the social and not the personal identity.

Finally, we shall have to distinguish between the features of identity that people regard as inescapable, as a part of one's inherent nature, from those that they see as products of human action and subject to change by human action. As we shall see, features of both social and personal identity can be of either type. This distinction has obvious relevance for community development.

IDENTITY FEATURES

Identity features are the things about a person by which others see him or he sees himself as like or unlike other persons. There are, of course, a great many dimensions in terms of which such perceptual and conceptual discriminations can be made. Such things as physical appearance, age, sex, skills and talents, ethnic and social group affiliations, past performances, social rank, and style of conduct come readily to mind. Separately and in combination, such dimensions provide the basis for a set of percepts and concepts without which we can hardly think of ourselves or of others at all.[1] To be sure, each of us has a kinesthetic sense of self as a physical entity apart from his environment and, of course, we perceive other persons as physically unique individuals;[2] but the substance of our own self and of the other selves around us, what we and they are, depends on the cognitive system we use for classifying and ordering our social experience. I am a *boy;* John is *honest;* George is *taller* than I am; Bill tends to be *introverted;* James is *married;* Joseph is an *engineer;* Ivan is a *Russian;* and Edward *has class.* Each of these categorizations implies other complementary categories of sex, morality, physical appearance and build, personality orientation, marital status, occupation, ethnic affiliation, and style of behavior. Each set of complementary categories comprises an identity system.[3] It is with whatever repertoire of such systems we happen to possess that we necessarily see and think about ourselves and others. Although anyone is like someone else with respect to any one identity feature, his identity is unique in the total combination of features that characterizes him.

The identity systems with which people work vary, of course, from society to society. Some American Indian societies allow for a third sex, for example, known to anthropologists as *berdaches:* men who have elected women's dress and specialize in women's occupations. Truk's age categories are somewhat different from ours, and a person is not regarded as a fully responsible adult until he reaches middle age. The Nakanai classify people from the standpoint of personality as "men of anger" or "men of shame." The man of anger has a quick and violent temper, a propensity for practical joking and disruptive behavior in youth, and shows readiness of speech, wit, audacity, initiative, and energy. The man of shame is more serious, sensitive, introverted, quiet in speech and manner, inclined to be inventive, and prone to skilled craftsmanship. Both of these personality types are regarded as normal and desirable, provided one is not lazy and undertakes to make something of oneself. Men readily classify themselves and their fellows as one or the other.[4]

The members of a community largely share the same systems of categories for perceiving their own and others' identities. If they did not, they would lack the means for maintaining a social order. The identity discriminations which they make in common are reflected in the vocabulary of their language and in the various identity badges they display. Children are constantly being defined to themselves by others, explicitly in words and implicitly in the different kinds of treatment they receive. Thus they learn to respond to themselves in terms of the identity systems by which their elders are already responding to them. The identities of other people are similarly defined to children. People are held up as good or bad examples; and children seek to cultivate their own identities by using others as models. It is axiomatic among students of personality that a person's self-image is largely derived from the social relationships in which he regularly finds himself.[5]

Although a system for categorizing identity features is shared by a community's members, this does not guarantee that they will agree as to what any particular person's identity is in all of its aspects. Thus we may agree that someone is mayor of the city and upon the qualifications for being a mayor and yet disagree as to whether the incumbent possesses these qualifications. How we use our system of perceptual categories in relation to ourselves and others necessarily varies according to our emotional predispositions. We do not ordinarily perceive all the relevant features of a situation but jump to conclusions on the basis of those that first come to our attention. What they are depends very much on what are our dominant concerns, what we are looking for. We may even project identity features upon others or imagine them in ourselves. Thus agreement as to what are the criteria by which to judge a person as lazy or industrious, good or bad, friendly or hostile does not guarantee agreement as to how these criteria are manifested in concrete situations. Wants, hopes, frustrations, anxieties, and fears lead us to distort our images of ourselves and others in accordance with the various psychological processes described in Chapter 6. And we frequently cling to these images with elaborate rationalizations in the face of all kinds of evidence to the contrary.

Features of Social and Personal Identity

We have observed that quite apart from the distinctions between cognitive and evaluative aspects of identity and between a person's self-image and public image we must also distinguish between social identity and personal identity. Identity features to which rights and duties attach and with respect to which people have well-defined expectations regarding the boundaries within which they are to contain behavior are all features of social identity. In any situation a person's social role comprises the rights and duties attaching to his social identity in relation to the social identities of the others with whom he is dealing.[6] The social role of a *father* in relation to his *son* in our society, for example, is specified by the duties he owes his son and the things he can demand of him. Within the boundaries of conduct delimited by rights and duties, as we noted in Chapter 5, is the domain of privilege. How one conducts oneself with reference to these boundaries is a matter of personal style. Discriminations of style provide the features, along with others to which no rights and duties attach, by which we discern personal identity. Thus we assess the father as a person on the basis of how he exercises his privileges, his style of play as a stern or indulgent parent, for instance, and on the degree to which he oversteps the boundaries of his social role with brutal behavior or economic neglect.[7]

Different social identities enjoy differential prestige. An executive enjoys more prestige than a laborer. Yet it is easy to divorce the evaluative from the cognitive aspects of these two social identities. It is less easy to do so with personal identity because we are used to using stylistic differences as a means of evaluating people as to their competence and morality. Much of the vocabulary we employ in talking about personal identity is value-loaded. Somebody is nice, mean, lazy, responsible, direct, or untrustworthy. This does not mean that cognitive and valuative aspects of identity correspond with social and personal aspects. Such differences in personal style as are signified by the words "strict" and "easy-going," for example, have quite different value connotations depending upon circumstances. There are times when we value a strict style of play more than we do an easy-going one, and there are times when we value it less. Features of personal identity, then, are not to be confused with esteem or prestige, but they are obviously of great importance in personal evaluations. Indeed, a person may be said to have social prestige insofar as his prestige derives from the value people attach to his social identity, but to have personal prestige in accordance with the value attaching to the features of personal identity that others see in him.

People find different social identities more or less congenial, depending on how compatible the associated rights and duties are with their established styles of conduct. This is undoubtedly a factor in the selection of occupations in our own society. The fit between personal style and social identity can be a serious problem in connection with changes in social identity. As one moves from being a child to being an adolescent, for example, or from being a bachelor to being a husband, the consequent changes in one's social roles, with new duties, rights, and privileges, provide new bases for assessing one's personal capacity to "measure up" and new opportunities for developing one's behavioral style. Such change may give freer scope to one's established style so that the person making it seems to "blossom out." On the other hand, personal styles that had privileged play before may be disallowed by the duties attaching to a new social identity, so that the change brings with it the necessity of developing a new style. In either event, a change in social identity may have a profound effect upon the personal prestige and regard a person enjoys and upon his contentment with himself. People in our own society frequently find themselves in a dilemma when they are offered job promotions. The new social identity will enhance their social prestige, a thoroughly attractive prospect. At the same time it may require alterations in their style of play which they fear they will be unable to make successfully. In this way the new identity poses a threat to their personal prestige. We shall have much more to say about these matters in the next chapter.

Identity Features That Do Not Change

Some features of one's identity, of course, do not change. They are automatically ascribed by one's fellows in accordance with the rules of the social order, as with lifelong membership in a family, or in accordance with what is regarded as inherent, as with a person's sex or temperament.[8] Though a woman may wish she were a man, she cannot change her sex. If she tries to masquerade as a man, she still cannot conceive of herself as really a man; she knows that she is only masquerading. Her womanhood remains a part of her self-image even though her masquerade may make it no longer a part of her public image.[9]

Every community regards some features of social identity as immutable. Among ourselves, for example, one's identity as a white or a Negro is as profound and theoretically unalterable as is one's identity as a man or woman, although there are other societies in which differences in skin color are not relevant for social identity at all. One's identity as noble or serf was equally fixed and theoretically inescapable in parts of medieval Europe. So is one's identity as a member of a matrilineal clan in the Trobriand Islands, as we saw in the preceding chapter.

Features of personal identity may be believed to be equally inescapable and immutable. This is what we tend to believe in our society about the identity features we refer to as temperament and character. Parents watch for signs of a child's developing style and arrive at conclusions regarding him as one who is inherently lazy, rebellious, cheerful, or the like. Once his image of self in these terms has formed, he is likely to regard it as incapable of alteration. Another society, however, may believe that such features of identity are susceptible of change. In our own at the present time, there is conflicting opinion about the mutability of features of personal identity, our traditional views regarding "human nature" being in the process of revision.

As the foregoing implies, societies differ markedly in the extent to which they regard features of social and personal identity as inherent. Characteristics believed to be immutable in one community may be regarded as alterable in another. In England one's social class position is far more inescapably a part of one's permanent identity, and accepted as such, than it is in the United States.

These differences have serious implication for programs aimed at political and social development. People may be unhappy with their lot as members of some ascribed social category and wish that theirs were a different fate. Yet they may not try to avail themselves of proffered opportunities to change their lot because they accept the view that it is their nature to be as they are, that their present identity is something that is beyond human power to change. If trying to be something different can, at best, be only a skillfully executed masquerade, then it offers little promise of accomplishing a change in one's self-image. A change in one's public image will, to be sure, result in different treatment by others, and this will in turn provide the basis for developing a new self-image. The fact remains that when people see a proposal as one in which they are pretending to be something they know they are not, they may appreciate its intentions and yet be unable to commit themselves to it.

This problem is illustrated by MacMillan and Leighton in their account of a depressed North American community, a rural slum they call "The Road." They conclude that the chief obstacle to any improvement in its circumstances "is the widespread conviction of the constitutional inferiority of the people of The Road—and the most fatal aspect of this belief is that they themselves share it. They resent it and they regret it, but they believe it."[10] The authors go on to indicate that there are some things that could still be profitably undertaken by way of community development. The major problem remains, however, that under such circumstances the people involved must become convinced, really convinced, that the unwanted features of their identity are not necessarily theirs by fate or nature.

Similar problems of self-image are reported for the former inhabitants of Bikini in the Marshall Islands, who have been resettled on the island of Kili. Their new home offers resources that differ markedly from those of much drier Bikini. At the same time they are now in closer contact with other Marshallese to whom they have traditionally felt a little inferior, like "country cousins." Mason observes, "If they can learn to think of themselves as Marshallese, not as ex-Bikinians, they should find it easier to dispel some of their present anxieties and to seek more objectively the solutions to those problems which remain from a decade of having to adapt a traditional way of life to a strange physical and social environment."[11]

As the example of The Road further suggests, while it is essential for people to believe that undesirable features of their identity are capable of alteration if they are to commit themselves to doing something about them, the success of their efforts depends ultimately on the attitude of others in the larger social world around them. The West African who has sought a European education and who dresses and lives in accordance with European conventions is obviously seriously endeavoring to alter his former identity. His efforts avail him little, however, if Europeans insist on continuing to treat him exactly as if he had never done any of these things, choosing to regard him as engaging in an impertinent masquerade rather than as having significantly changed his identity. One of the major obstacles to successful development is the public image the client community itself has among other communities in the larger society, especially when that image is composed of features that the others refuse to regard as capable of alteration.

In the Bikini example, moreover, we see how the idea that certain features of identity are immutable and fixed in the established order of things may become anachronistic when outside forces change a community's circumstances. To overcome a lifelong view of oneself so as to be free to make new adjustments is exceedingly difficult. The frequent disintegration of men after retirement in our society, where occupation is so important a feature of identity, is a familiar case in point. The demoralization of the Sioux Indians as warriors and hunters deprived first of their weapons and later of their cattle is a matter of record.[12] To help people become free of a view of themselves that they regard as unalterable requires much patience. The new self-image may come only as a gradual awakening. Probably more often, however, final abandonment of the old and formulation of the new occurs suddenly in what strikes the person experiencing it as a genuine revelation. Of this we shall say more in Chapter 11.

IDENTITY CONSIDERATIONS IN SOCIAL RELATIONS

Whenever a person interacts with another he bases his actions on what he construes to be his own and the other's personal and social identities. He also takes into account how he believes the other person construes their respective identities. To avoid misunderstanding and to facilitate adherence to the rules of the social order, every society needs conventions governing comportment that serve to communicate identity, as when in our society we introduce people to one another or expect them to wear special articles of clothing as badges of their identity. We also take care to teach our children "good manners" because their display expresses features of identity important in our prestige system.

Although societies vary in their conventions regarding identity symbols and the communication of identity features, they emphasize the communication of things that people are most concerned to have known. These include the things people want to know about their fellows in order to place them in the system of social categories. Beyond this, there are the things about themselves that people would like others to know. Much human effort is spent in cultivating desired public images. Finally, there are things people perceive about another's identity that they want him to know—features of his public image that people want him to incorporate in his private image, as when we seek to teach our children the effect of their conduct upon others.

Things People Want to Know About Others

What people most want to know about a person would appear to be the things they inquire about. But this does not take into consideration the things they already know. Some of these, if not known, may be regarded as much more important. We assume, therefore, that the things people regard as most essential to know about their fellows are revealed by those symbols of identity that they require one another to display and those things about the self that they regard as one's duty to reveal upon demand.

When a society is divided into subgroups, for example, and relations between them are an important determinant of the roles their respective members play in dealing with one another, everyone may be required to display his group affiliation by observing certain food taboos, speaking in a particular dialect or style, wearing some identifying item of clothing, or displaying his passport or identity card. In Truk people regularly identify themselves to others as "so-and-so of such-and-such a matrilineal clan and such-and-such a locality" when these aspects of his identity are not already known. It is essential for Truk's people to know these things in order to be able to orient themselves socially to one another. From this information they can deduce many other things they feel it important to know. To middle-class members of our own society, on the other hand, an important feature of anyone's identity is the kind of work in which he is regularly engaged. When getting acquainted, people quickly inquire of each other the nature of their employment as crucial information regarding their respective identities. There are other divisions in our society, however, in which such inquiry is improper and in which one's occupation is irrelevant for orienting social relationships. For middle-class people, however, occupation is regarded as the principal means of social mobility. It is so important to one's identity that parents express much concern over the occupation or profession their children will elect because of what this choice means for the kind of public image they will enjoy as adults.

Things About Himself a Person Wants Others to Know

A shady past is, of course, something a person may wish to conceal. On the other hand, there are things about himself that he may be eager to have others know. A child whose achievement in school or in sports has done positive things to his self-image is likely to burst into the house shouting to his parents, "Do you know what I did?" Or he may eagerly display some new accomplishment with an insistent "Look at me!" Adults, likewise, have their techniques for inviting attention to themselves. Important among them is the display of identity symbols.

If we want our fellows to know that we are rich, for example, we wear expensively styled clothes, ride in an expensive car, live in a large and luxuriously appointed house, and take up an obviously costly hobby or sport.[13] People who are "upward mobile" in our system of social rank are likely to seize upon every opportunity to be seen in the right places, displaying all of the right symbols, in an effort to establish a public image commensurate with their self-goals. Those who disclaim any ambitions for recognition in this direction just as assiduously display symbols of whatever other things about their identity they want firmly established in their public image. The arty bohemian of our society makes himself known as such in a number of conventional ways; and even those rebels against convention known as the "beat generation" display their identity in a manner that is sufficiently conventional to communicate at once the image they want others to have of them.

Sometimes we display certain symbols that are aimed at promoting a more desired public image. A poor man may sink everything he has into a big flashy car or into expensive clothes in order to create for himself an illusion that his identity is other than it really is, or in order to make a calculated impression on others. Indeed, people are constantly using identity symbols to put up false fronts. They may do so because they would feel ashamed if the truth about themselves were known; or else they may wish to gain some advantage they otherwise lack the means to achieve. Such use of identity symbols is by no means confined to relations between individuals within the same society. It obviously characterizes much that goes on in the guessing game of international relations. Agents of development will certainly find it entering into their relations with their clients.

The fewer the contexts in which people have direct dealings with one another, the easier and the more tempting it is to present oneself as something one is not. A housewife cannot fool members of her own family regarding the condition in which she normally leaves her home, nor those of her friends with whom she is so intimate that they feel free to drop in for a visit without warning. But her acquaintances with whom she is on less intimate terms can gain the impression that she is an immaculate housekeeper, everything having been put in order for their benefit on the few occasions when they are guests in her home. The rooms reserved for family use and not to be seen by guests may present quite a contrast. We regard it as good manners not to call upon our acquaintances without warning, in order to allow them the opportunity to erect the facades necessary to maintain "face."

What we call "face" is, in fact, the goodness of fit between the public image we try to present to others and the one we actually enjoy. When something about ourselves is revealed that is inconsistent with the image we are trying to foster, whether as a result of our own behavioral lapse or the betrayal of a confidence by someone else, we suffer loss of face. The attendant emotion, the feeling of humiliation and shame, is one of the most important motivating forces in human action.

As members of groups, people are concerned with their group identity in the same way. The members of a university faculty, for example, know that there are some things about their university inconsistent with the public image that university officials try to promote and that the university may, in fact, enjoy. To preserve this image, they avoid washing their dirty linen in public, preserving not only the public image of the university but also the reputation they individually enjoy as members of its faculty. There are, similarly, parts of one's home town to which one proudly takes visitors and parts one does not willingly show them at all. Every nation is busily engaged in fostering an image abroad that closer scrutiny would impair.

Members of the community in which a development agent works are going to be similarly sensitive about the image of their community held by outsiders.[14] Proposals that will help to remove whatever bad name the community's members already knowingly suffer are likely to be received cordially. Not so proposals that appear to threaten those things in which they have always taken pride.

Things Others Want a Person to Know About Himself

People are just as concerned to make sure that others have a self-image of the sort they want them to have as they are that they should be seen by others in a favorable light.[15] To the extent that we want others to see social situations and relationships as we see them, their image of themselves as well as their image of us must correspond with ours. We spend a great deal of time educating our children and newcomers to our social groups in the identity implications of their behavior. Once they learn the meaning to others of their actions, the desire to avoid presenting an identity that will incur censure becomes a strong internal monitor of their behavior. But even when a person has been thoroughly socialized, he still needs information as to how others perceive his identity in order to avoid inadvertently misdiagnosing the role he is expected to play in a given situation.

Every community has a set of conventions by which this information is communicated, especially in connection with the way people approach one another. We convey important information about another's identity, for example, when we slap him on the back, rise when he enters the room, or remain silent until spoken to.

Prominent among conventions of this sort are the names and titles people use in address. We often assume that differences in these conventions reflect different value orientations regarding social relationships, as when we say that one society is very "formal" because of its emphasis on the use of titles while another is "informal" because of its lack of such emphasis. Certainly, the kinds of titles and names that people give to one another, and the way in which they regularly use them in address would seem to have the effect of selecting particular things about people's identities for special emphasis. By briefly comparing naming customs and modes of address in Truk and Nakanai we can glimpse their importance in emphasizing identity characteristics.

Before the introduction of Christian and Japanese names in Truk, no two persons ever had the same given name. Each individual's name set him apart from every other, no one ever being named after anyone else. Genealogies listing hundreds of people over six to eight generations show no duplication of native names and hardly any duplication of newly introduced ones.[16] The Nakanai, by contrast, use a limited number of personal names. There is hardly anyone who does not share his name with someone in his own village, often with several people. Each name, moreover, carries with it the obligation to give one's firstborn a specific other name, as if everyone named John had to name his first child James, every James had to name his first child Joseph, and every Joseph had to name his first child John, thus completing the cycle. Subsequent children are regularly named after older relatives, and there are special rights and duties that accompany the namesake relationship. A name does not give expression to a person's separate identity as a distinct person, therefore, but emphasizes his place in a genealogical chain. This contrast carries over into nicknames, as well. In Truk a nickname is descriptive of some feature of the personal identity of the person to whom it is given. Nakanai nicknames are also descriptive, but are passed on to namesakes along with regular names, so that such a nickname as "Crooked Mouth" implies nothing personal at all. There may be a half-dozen people with this nickname in one village, all of them sharing the same given name as well, nickname and given name having become inseparable sometime in the past.

In Truk, moreover, everyone is addressed by name, even within the immediate family, very rarely by title or other reference to social categories of rank, occupation, or kinship. On the other hand, the Nakanai rarely address each other by name. Furthermore, unlike the Trukese, they taboo the use of personal names in a wide range of contexts and relationships. The most frequent mode of address is either by terms that signify kin relationships and ritual partnerships or teknonymously as the father or mother of one's first born. Thus James would be addressed from childhood on as the "father of Joseph." Customs of address seem to emphasize one's individuality and uniqueness in Truk and to stress one's membership in a network of kin relations or a procreative chain in Nakanai. Naming and mode of address ignore one's place in the social order in one society and call attention to it in the other.

To assume from this that Trukese society is more individualistic in its patterns of organization than Nakanai society would be a grave mistake. The fact is that corporate groups are highly elaborated in Truk, that authority is based on relative age, that there is relatively little a person can do on his own independent of the groups into which he is born. The structure of social relationships in Truk heavily deemphasizes personal independence or individuality. The system of naming and mode of address stress something that tends to be submerged by the rest of the social system. No one needs to be reminded of his kin obligations or of his membership in a continuing corporate group. He rarely has a chance to forget it, anyway. In Nakanai, on the other hand, corporate groups are weakly developed; the individual has a much wider range of choice in his social relationships; and authority and prestige are something to be earned by one's own efforts. In this more competitive society, names and modes of address serve constantly to remind people that they are, after all, part of a social order, something of which the Trukese need no reminding.

In each instance, then, conventions regarding names and address function as constant reminders to people of things about their identity. In the Trukese case, they are probably things about their identity most people want to be reminded of. In the Nakanai case, they appear to be things about which most people want to remind others. This fits their tendency to taboo the use of names when any special relationship is established between two persons and to require the use, instead, of titles that remind them of the relationship in which they now stand.

It would be dangerous to infer that names and modes of address are always used to help counterbalance the emphasis a social order otherwise gives to people's images of themselves and of one another. Anthropologists have yet to make the necessary comparative study. The contrast between Truk and Nakanai, however, reveals that different social orders tend to structure people's identities, both their self-images and public images in quite different ways. It also suggests that existing conventions regarding the use of names and titles may have important psychological as well as social functions.

Etiquette

Because of its obvious importance in social relationships, etiquette deserves a further word. In view of our own tendency to be impatient with codes of courtesy and social rituals we encounter in alien societies,[17] we may profitably note some of the more important ways in which etiquette functions in relation to identity.

First of all, etiquette requires us to reveal some things about ourselves to others. At the same time it sets limits and protects us from having to expose ourselves in ways that may be detrimental to our public image. Etiquette systems are often elaborated so that the ability to observe their niceties becomes itself a mark of one's identity—for example, as a member of a social elite. For this reason, those of us who are ideologically opposed to snobbery are inclined to take an iconoclastic attitude toward elaborate systems of etiquette. But we should not let this one aspect of the formalities of social intercourse blind us to its other functions.

When we fail to respect a people's etiquette system, we run the serious risk of subjecting them to shame and embarrassment. For we are likely to expose to public view things about themselves that they had assumed would be safe from such exposure, and we are likely to fail to communicate our recognition of those things about their identity that they value, where lack of recognition constitutes a public humiliation. Useem describes a so-called labor expert who tousled the heads of the Palauans in a show of good fellowship, inadvertently taking what they regarded as extremely embarrassing liberties with their persons, liberties from which they assumed they were immune.[18] A system of etiquette defines a set of boundaries within which people presume they can trust that their public images will enjoy certain immunities. A guest thanks his hostess in our society for the excellence of her meal, thereby assuring her that in exposing herself to his appraisal of her style as a housewife and hostess she has not suffered any loss of face.

We are normally interested in protecting the public images only of those persons for whom we have some positive feeling. We show our dislike of others by refusing to accord them the usual courtesies and amenities, by "cutting" them or otherwise ignoring the usual forms of respect for their identities. A system of etiquette is thus a two-edged sword. It protects people from shame under normal conditions and, at the same time, supplies those who wish them ill with weapons of attack. When an agent of development treats lightly his clients' rules of etiquette, he gives evidence of a lack of regard for their persons and presents himself as one who does not wish them well.

Any program of change inevitably affects some aspects of a people's self-image and public image. An agent of change is well advised, therefore, to minimize whatever his clients are likely to perceive as threats to their identities by according them all the respect he can in his personal dealings with them. As an experienced British colonial administrator has aptly said:

. . . what most men need or expect from their neighbours in any environment is not a diurnal gush of sympathetic emotion over the hedge, but just a silent respect for their private occasions. Romans are ultimately convinced of the stranger's goodwill towards them, not by the extent to which he does as Romans do, but by the extent to which he avoids treading upon their innocent grass-plots. Workaday sympathy for neighbours is, in fact, most commonly expressed through a number of civilized avoidances, which are usually drilled into one during childhood by a series of fundamental DON'Ts. The very least that ethnology and history have to teach any colonial administrative service is a list of such local DON'Ts.*[19]

The least that an agent of community development can do is to learn and respect them.

PERSONAL WORTH

A person's style of play and his ability to keep within the boundaries of duty and obligation, we have said, are the bases for discerning the nature of his personal as distinct from his social identity. These discernments also involve personal evaluations that contribute to one's worth as a person in the judgment of others. Also contributing to a person's worth are the social categories he occupies, for the various categories of a social system are differentially esteemed, both in the public value system and privately in the sentiment systems of individuals. People normally seek to improve their standing in the eyes of their fellows by handling themselves in their present social identities in an exemplary manner and by achieving new social identities to which more prestige attaches in the values of those whose esteem is being cultivated.

People also constantly judge their own worth, in accordance both with their own sentiments and with the values they attribute to others. These self-judgments have their emotional accompaniments, ranging from pride to shame. Provided their other interests and concerns do not interfere, people regularly seek to achieve social and personal identities that they and their fellows esteem. Indeed, it is next to impossible for a person to engage in any activity or social interchange without his own sense of worth and his worth to others being reaffirmed or altered. We all learn to pay close attention to how any situation in which we find ourselves may affect our public esteem and self-esteem and seek to orient ourselves in it so as to protect or improve them both.

* Reprinted by permission from Sir Arthur Grimble, *Return to the Islands*. John Murray, Ltd., London, 1957, pp. 212–213.

An important consideration in personal and social evaluations is the mutual compatibility of the identity features a person exhibits. In the workings of any social order, certain identity features tend to be associated statistically, so that people come to expect certain combinations and not others. More important still is the feeling that some identity features are logically or morally inconsistent with others. Indeed, the cognitive organization of social relationships requires that people systematize their categories of personal and social identity and the features by which they discern them. There are, consequently, plausible and implausible or reasonable and unreasonable ways in which they may conduct themselves. For the same reason symbols of identity may be used in a congruous or incongruous manner. Thus it is incongruous for an adult to act in a way characteristic of a child, or for a priest to speak in the language of the gutter.

Such incongruities provide plenty of humor, as in the Gilbertese poem:

> That man came shouting, "I am a chief."
> Certainly he looks lazy enough for the title;
> He also has the appetite of a king's son,
> And a very royal waddle.
> But he shouts, "I am a chief";
> Therefore I know he is not one. *[20]

Some incongruities are also regarded as signs of mental derangement, especially those that have to do with ordinary everyday patterns of conduct. It has been observed that observance of the conventional social amenities in a congruous manner is a major criterion for judging the recovery of patients in our mental hospitals.[21]

When the incongruities relate to valued features of personal identity, what we call integrity comes into question. Two things in combination are essential for us to have a sense of personal integrity. There must be some features of our identity, especially our personal identity, that we value highly, and we must be able to operate so that the remaining social and personal identity features we exhibit are consistent with them. If there is nothing

* Reprinted by permission from Sir Arthur Grimble, *Return to the Islands*. John Murray, Ltd., London, 1957, p. 206.

in our identity that we value, there is no focus around which a sense of integrity can develop. If we cannot be consistent with the things we value in ourselves, our integrity is compromised; we have not been "true to ourselves."

Changing circumstances often have the effect of making it difficult or impossible for people to maintain their sense of integrity. Efforts at directed change can generate embarrassment and resistance for this reason. To try to introduce into a community new activities for men that involve features of a sort traditionally associated with women is an obvious example. In such a case, men are asked to do things that violate their masculinity, their identity as men.

We have observed a problem of this sort in connection with political changes in Truk. Traditionally the proper role of a district chief was one in which he made no direct show of authority over others. It was bad form for him to express his displeasure directly, or personally to exert his authority. In those activities in which he had authority, he was expected to wield it indirectly through members of his family, who informed the people of the chief's desires. It was then up to the people to take the necessary steps to meet his wishes, which they did out of respect for the chief's office and in the knowledge that what he wished of them was within his rights as chief. When colonial government was established in Truk, chiefs found themselves given new responsibilities by the administration. These were duties they owed the administrators rather than their own people, and in order to carry them out the administrators expected them to exert their authority, openly and forcefully if necessary. To meet the approval of the administrators, chiefs were required to act like "bad" chiefs by local standards and to do so, moreover, in relation to matters where they traditionally had no authority or other claim on the people at all. Some chiefs were unable to perform in their new role because it violated their sense of personal integrity as chiefs. Finding them ineffectual, the administration deposed them in favor of "more forceful" personalities who could "get results." Those who tried to operate within the new role, violated the people's conception of themselves as citizens in the community. Not only did they feel their rights as persons to have been infringed, they considered the behavior of the new chiefs an affront to their own dignity as free men and to the dignity of the chiefly office as well. Similar problems of role conflict are reported for chiefs in Africa.[22]

Because people's identities are so thoroughly embedded in the structure of the existing social order, any change in that order is almost certain to produce problems of the sort just described. Because social change so directly affects people's sense of personal worth and integrity, they tend to be highly resistant to changing their social system, except when that system already operates so as to leave them compromised and humiliated. Then, of course, the same emotional forces promoting resistance to change can create an intense desire for it, a matter we shall consider in Chapters 10 and 11. In the meantime, we observe that when new roles incompatible with the existing identity system are introduced into a community, for whatever reason, its members are faced with the necessity of revising their mutual expectations, their system of social identities, and their sense of the congruous accordingly. This means their arriving at a new consensus regarding the content and structure of their social order. Until they manage to do so, misunderstanding and bitterness are inevitable.

IDENTITY IDEALS

Everybody has notions about a state of being in which he will find contentment or realize his aspirations for himself. For one person it may be to have complete control over his social and material environment, for another it may be to feel fully and completely loved. Some of these desired states may be widely shared by a community's members, while others have appeal only to a few individuals. The achievement of some will be entirely consistent with public values, may even bring their achiever wide public acclaim. But some self-goals that are privately aspired to are likely to be such that their achievement guarantees public opprobrium, as with a man who feels he can find personal contentment only by murdering, preferably by inches, a bullying and mean-spirited neighbor. Most of us feel some degree of conflict between our private aspirations for ourselves and the effect their achievement will have on our public identities and public esteem. Conflicts of this sort can take place within the individual, too, so that he is a house divided, one part of him seeing salvation only by means whose identity implications lead to self-condemnation by the other part—the classic picture of neurosis. If such conflict becomes severe enough, its resolution may become the dominating goal for the self. Most of us have not one but a number of self-goals, which may be more or less compatible with one another. But whatever they may be, escape from inner conflict, release from unhappy physical and social circumstances, or winning public recognition as a successful man, their achievement involves or is felt to involve an identity change.

A particular identity change may be the goal desired, as with winning public recognition as a great artist. At the same time some sort of identity change is also seen as a necessary means to achieving one's goal. To be recognized as a great artist, it is necessary to develop artistic skills and to create fine works of art. As skills develop and works appear, the artist's public image and self-image both change. The resolution of inner emotional conflict also seems to require winning a new identity, though it is difficult to say whether the new identity comes as a result of the resolution or the resolution as a result of the new identity. Ideal states of being are so intertwined with the evaluations people place on particular identities and with their assessments of personal worth that it is difficult to disentangle them.

Because achieving self-goals so often requires changes in social and personal identity, we are reminded that everyone's identity is, in fact, an ever changing thing. It changes imperceptibly, day by day, as a person's experience and knowledge of himself and his society's experience and knowledge of him accumulate and change. It may also change in dramatic leaps, as when Miss Nobody-In-Particular is crowned Miss America, a student graduates from college, a man performs some feat of which he had not believed himself capable, or an emotionally disturbed person gets a flash of healing insight. The process of identity change will be considered in the next chapter. Here we are interested in idealized states of being that are widely shared by a community's members, and in their relation to the community's institutional structure. We are especially interested in the effect of widely desired states of being on the kinds of identities that people value.

Some Institutional Examples

In every community there are clearly defined identity ideals. Some are so defined as to be theoretically attainable by everyone, as with the religious state of grace. Others involve competition, as in the case of positions of leadership. What social and personal identities are idealized as worth pursuing, however, vary considerably from community to community, as do the routes by which people can legitimately and successfully pursue them. Let us consider some examples.

We have already observed the Trukese concern with achieving what might be called a perfect dependency relationship with a responsible, supporting, and nurturing figure. This goal derives from widely shared personal sentiments resulting from common frustrations. Needless to say, this particular self-goal does not promote high individual achievement aspirations, and Trukese society is one whose social order allows little room for independent individual action. The socially destructive effects of a frank and open pursuit of this goal require that the Trukese sublimate this desire by acting it out in relation to the spirits of the dead, as we have seen. Among the ideals for the self on which public values lay stress, being a good "organization man" is prominent. The good Trukese man or woman should subordinate personal interests to the welfare of his lineage as a whole. As he gets older, he should master the knowledge and skills on which the welfare of his junior kinsmen depends. The more such knowledge and skill he can acquire, the more important a person he becomes. Those in control of the most complex bodies of knowledge and magical skill are at the top of the prestige ladder. Until recently, at least, individuals who were sufficiently free of pressing dependency needs devoted considerable effort to developing proficiency as fighters, craftsmen, healers, and magicians. It was from this that much of their worth in terms of the public value system derived. The achievement of satisfactory dependency relations requires that others be the sort of people on whom one can depend. The public value system, therefore, extols virtues that individual Trukese have difficulty living up to but value highly in others.

Any consideration of Trukese goals for the self would be incomplete without reference to illicit love affairs, which are a major preoccupation. The strong emphasis in the public values on being good organization men and women tends to give people little opportunity to feel that they count for anything purely as individuals, especially in their youth. To be valued for oneself alone one must cultivate relationships that are not sanctioned by the rules of the social order. The illicit, secret, adulterous, love relationship is perfectly suited to this purpose, for one's own value as an individual is enhanced by the risks that one's lover is willing to take in achieving an assignation. The frustrations people endure in the pursuit of illicit love are considerable; nevertheless, the very effort itself provides one of the most important avenues to self-fulfillment according to the sentiments of most Trukese. It is obvious from the boasting of young men and from the subject matter of stories that success as a lover is an important ego ideal.[23]

Observers of Truk's people have commented that their self-ideals do not provide them with strong motivations to make the sacrifices and sustain the effort needed for long-range betterment programs. They are more interested in immediate gratifications. Their dependency needs make them unwilling to take action independent of their lineage groups or contrary to the wishes of their lineage mates. This has seriously affected efforts to get the Trukese to raise capital for their economic development or to invest in local enterprise. The most successful effort so far was one that emphasized lineage solidarity rather than individual initiative and put the raising of money in the context of traditional group festivities and rituals.[24]

As we go to other parts of the world, emphases change markedly. Whoever aspires to be a big man among the Nakanai must give repeated demonstrations of his industriousness, courage, superior knowledge, and generosity. By becoming an outstanding warrior and by assuming responsibility for others over and above his minimum obligations he develops a following among his junior kin. Symbolic of his energy, diligence, and social responsibility are certain traditional wealth tokens, the exchange of which accompanies all important social transactions. The scope of his activities as big man in the community are limited by the degree to which he commands these tokens of wealth. It is essential that he be able to sponsor large-scale festivals and play host to several villages at once, successfully discharging all his responsibilities in doing so, if he is to achieve success within the framework of the public values.

To some American Indians, on the other hand, the road to self-realization was through the acquisition of power from spirits. This power was materially represented in a medicine bundle, without which one could not be successful as a hunter, warrior, or shaman. Only by personal suffering in fasting and self-torture could one induce the spirits to provide "medicine." The men whose medicine was strongest, who had achieved the highest degree of personal potency, enjoyed the greatest prestige. The test of one's potency was one's success in difficult undertakings. The more dangerously one could live and get away with it, the more effective one's medicine must be. Shamans were even reputed to engage on occasion in contests to the death to see who had the greater spiritual powers, much as rival moguls in our own society used to engage in tests of financial power.[25]

Identity Ideals and Community Development

These differences in what people value as the ideal states of being, whether they derive from public values or from private sentiments, have obvious relevance for community development. If a development proposal accords with people's self-goals and appears to them to offer wider opportunities for self-realization, it is likely to meet with a positive reception. The same proposal in another community, however, may be met with indifference or even with hostility if it appears to hinder rather than help the achievement of the self-goals they value. People who have a warrior tradition, who pride themselves on their ability to terrorize their neighbors, and who value most highly features of identity that can be achieved only in warlike activity, are likely to greet with disdain any proposals aimed at taming them, unless they offer opportunities to live dangerously in activities that are less immediately disturbing to their neighbors. Some American Indians who have for years resisted efforts to make them over in the image of the peaceful, cautious, conservative American farmer, tied to a strict daily and seasonal routine, are finally discovering occupations in industry and construction that fit their identity values much better. The reputation that the Iroquois have earned for themselves as workers in high steel construction is especially noteworthy. Hiring out together in crews far from home on jobs that involve much physical danger, they have managed to attach to this work many of the values they formerly associated with war expeditions.[26]

There are times, of course, when the goals of development include accomplishing change in a community's self-ideals. The extent to which it is possible for development agents to bring about such changes is far from clear. Changes of this sort obviously require radical alterations of the social order and the public values it expresses. In the history of European societies such ideological reformations have almost invariably been accompanied by social and political revolutions. And they have occurred in the wake of other changes, social and economic, which rendered adherence to older values increasingly frustrating for more and more people, as with the Puritan revolution under Cromwell in England. We shall give closer attention to this aspect of change in Chapter 11. In the meantime we have to consider the processes by which people build their identities, especially the process of identification and the use of others as models in the pursuit of identity goals.

IDENTIFICATION AND IDENTITY MODELS

Identity in the sense of both public image and self-image is rooted, we have seen, in social interaction. A person's image of others and image of self take shape at the same time. A very young child begins to acquire these images unselfconsciously, but it is not long before a consciousness of self emerges and a consciousness of his identity as something to be cultivated. This involves a lot of learning. He must learn the system of identity categories with which others work. He must also learn how identity symbols, role expectations, and styles of performance relate to these categories and then master the use of these symbols and develop the skills to perform the roles in the appropriate styles. In addition to this kind of learning, identity formation involves a relating of self to people and things in one's environment in several ways, to which we ordinarily refer under the blanket label "identification." We turn now to look at these several modes of relating the self to others and their role in identity building.

We have observed, first of all, that the perception of identity, whether another's or one's own, requires some system of categorization. When we categorize anything, of course, we *identify* it with all those other things that already make up the membership of that category. The building of identity through the process of categorization and recategorization, therefore, inevitably gives to our self-image features that are common to images we have of others. Thus we identify with others, and thus others become extensions of ourselves and can serve as symbols of our own identity or of features of it, can even become our alter egos. We need not, of course, confine our identifications to other persons. We can perceive men and animals as having common identity features, real or imagined; and we can identify ourselves with imaginary beings as well as with living ones.

Identifications of this kind provide the basis for collective liability, as when one member of a group is liable to punishment for the actions of other members of his group; they are both Joneses. Such identifications also contribute to many of the resentments and jealousies in human relations. Why should so-and-so, whom I perceive as the same kind of person as myself, for example, be accorded more respect by others than I receive? Our elders are constantly presenting us to ourselves in terms of such identifications also, telling us that we look just like our parents or that we act just like Uncle George.

The social groups to which a person belongs are among the features of his identity. To the extent that he makes membership in them an important part of his self-image and derives his sense of self-esteem from the esteem in which they are held, we say that he identifies himself with these groups. Here, identification means incorporating in our self-image features of social identity that others ascribe to us.

There is still another sense in which the term "identification" is commonly used. Here it refers to the process in which a person commits himself to trying to achieve an identity like that of someone else, which may include trying to achieve membership in the particular groups to which he belongs. It is not so much the other's being what we also are that counts, but the other's already being what our fellows expect us to be or what we would like to become. Taking another as our ego-ideal in this way, we try to modify or develop our own identity features so as to enable us to identify or be identified with him. To this end we encourage our children "to grow up to be like Mommy and Daddy." Using parents and other adults as their models is, indeed, one of the most important means by which children eventually transform themselves into responsible adults.

To be effective as a guide for the development of one's own identity, there should be some features of the model's identity that are already like one's own. The already similar features of a biological nature in their respective identities, for example, help a boy identify with his father. Parents emphasize these common features to their children and artificially provide them with a great many other common features of dress, style of haircut, and the like in order to influence the models their children will select for themselves.

When we identify ourselves closely with someone else (or with a group) or feel ourselves to be closely identified with him by others, we necessarily become emotionally concerned about his personal fortunes. His failures and his humiliations are damaging to our esteem. His successes contribute to our self-esteem and prestige. Necessarily, we become acutely sensitive to any actions of our own that may adversely affect him. Through our identifications, indeed, we come to evaluate our wants as against the wants of others and to see the effect of our actions upon others as affecting ourselves. So we incorporate the interests of others into our own scale of preferences, giving them a place in our sentiment system.[27]

As this suggests, identification is an important source of emotional conflict; and at the same time it helps people deal effectively with such conflict. By removing the conflict of wants between oneself and others from the arena of social relationships to a new one within oneself or one's psyche, identification transforms social conflicts into psychological conflicts. Incorporating the wants of others into our own sentiment system not only provides the basis for a conscience, it can also give rise to acutely ambivalent feelings. On the other hand, it is a common practice for us to take as our ego-ideals persons who seem to be free of the conflicts that plague us. A major feature of some established religions, for example, is the figure of the "savior" who has himself achieved a state of being that is apparently without conflict and who therefore recommends himself as an object of identification for others. By seeking to identify with the savior, others may themselves be saved.[28]

People give behavioral expression to their efforts at such identification in various ways. A person may try to adopt another's mannerisms of speech and posture, wear similar clothing, or engage in the same occupation, or he may try to accomplish the merging of identity by attaching himself to his ideal or hero like a "man Friday." We may look to our hero to take an active part himself, asking him to teach us what we must know and to train us to be more like him. If he is a god, we may seek his help through revelation or possession. Instead of trying to identify ourselves with him, we may endeavor to extract his desirable attributes from him and incorporate them into ourselves. Thus we may even seek literally to ingest him into our own body so as to absorb him within ourselves. All of these techniques are evident in religious ritual. Dressed like their gods or wearing masks that represent them, people lose their separate identities for a while in that of the spirit or divinity they impersonate; and incorporating the Saviour into one's own body is exemplified by the Christian rite of Holy Communion.

To identify with people as the incarnations of our own identity ideals is not the only way in which we use others as models. Instead of trying to identify with another, for example, we may do the very opposite and try to dissociate ourselves from him by acquiring as few features of identity in common with him as possible. Our emotional involvement with such negative models can be as profound as with those in whom we see our ideal selves. People take their Satans and their Antichrists seriously.

There are for all of us many other models that we take more casually, using them as guides when convenient, but without seeing in them the embodiment of all we aspire to be or not to be. Our fellows, moreover, present us with hosts of examples. "Why can't you be like Bill?" and "You don't want to grow up to be like George!" are everyday parental utterances. Every society has its traditional models of both good and bad conduct, stock characters of story and legend whose deeds provide the case materials for helping its younger members develop identities in keeping with public values.[29] We do not identify with them all, and we identify but briefly and casually with many. But they are an important resource. The truthful George Washington, the little boy who held his finger in the dike, John Paul Jones, the saints and martyrs and heroes, all are there for us to identify with according to our circumstances. With their example we increase our ability to exercise restraint and self-control in the face of pain and frustration and are better able to meet difficult situations with courage and moral strength, better able, in short, to be the kinds of persons we would like to be, even when the going gets rough.

As we try to achieve our goals for ourselves, there are two ways in which we measure our success. One is with reference to the state of being that we feel within ourselves, such as the sense of our own power or of our own inner tranquility. The other measure is less subjective, being our acceptance by others as the kind of person we aspire to be. All of us seek continually in the deference others show us and in the things they say about us for evidence of how we are getting on. It is hard to maintain an image of ourselves that is not reinforced by the view others have of us. Depending upon our goals for ourselves, of course, we select different persons or groups as the ones whose judgment we consider critical in these matters. Sometimes they are the very persons or groups who embody our ego ideals and with whom we seek to identify. We are familiar enough with the role that parents, teachers, and age-mates play both as judges and models.

People do not confine their judges and models to members of their own social class, community, or even nation. If someone of middle-class background wishes to acquire an upper-class identity, then members of that class necessarily become both his models and his judges at the same time. He will try to make himself as much like them as he can and will be constantly on the lookout for any signs that they are prepared to accept him as a social equal. International relations are characterized by much the same sort of thing, the people of one country often aping the manners of another that currently enjoys international prestige. And people who have been treated by Europeans as their inferiors and who are unwilling to regard themselves as such are everywhere striving to model themselves after these same resented Europeans in order thereby to force their acceptance as equals.

MODELS AND DEVELOPMENT

How the members of an underdeveloped community look upon an agent of change and the community he represents as possible models and judges for themselves is obviously crucial to achieving cooperation in any development program. If they look upon the agent's community as the antithesis of what they themselves want to become, the chances that the agent will gain a friendly hearing are obviously minimal. It then becomes necessary for him to try to dissociate himself and his activities from whatever stereotypes they may have about him and his community of origin. He may discover, however, that his clients have a positive view of him and his community and are eager to model themselves upon them, but in order to achieve goals for themselves that the agent has difficulty endorsing.

The latter situation is illustrated in many parts of Melanesia today. Here the important symbols of personal worth have been largely material in nature. Like money among ourselves, native shell "currencies" served as tokens of a man's ability to work hard, his enterprise in trade, and his ability to lead others and command their labor. The more tokens a man controlled, as we have already observed in the case of the Nakanai, the more he presumably measured up to the ego-ideal in the public value system of his community. The ultimate validation of his worth was to distribute food and material goods to others as the sponsor of public festivals. Men who had proved their worth in these terms were held up as models to young people and as objects with which properly to identify. Those of no worth, who commanded no one's labor, who lacked enterprise and were lazy, provided negative models, being despised as "rubbish men." When Melanesians encountered European explorers, traders, and labor recruiters, they were greatly impressed by the material wealth these men controlled and by their willingness to give it away. The European's gifts as tokens of friendship where he was uncertain of his reception and his payment of goods in return for services rendered were frequently seen as the distribution of highly valuable commodities in keeping with the role of an important man. Europeans not only controlled and distributed fabulous wealth, they obviously commanded the labor of many natives on their plantations. Their operations were on a far grander scale than anything the biggest of Melanesian "big men" had ever dreamed. In terms of their own traditional measures of achievement Melanesians were compelled to see Europeans as bigger men than themselves and to see themselves, indeed, as "rubbish men" by comparison. In this judgment Europeans aggressively concurred.[30]

The result has been widespread adoption of the European as a model, on the assumption that if one can conduct oneself in accordance with European modes of conduct, this will prove to be the right "way" to recapture the lost sense of worth in accordance with Melanesian ego-ideals. Europeans have provided verbal encouragement in this direction. Missionaries held out the promise of the "way" and found ready converts. At the same time, of course, Europeans threw discriminatory roadblocks in the way of natives' acquiring their objective. Symbolic in this regard, for example, was the prohibition against natives wearing trousers in Australian New Guinea prior to World War II, a prohibition that is still privately, though illegally, enforced by a few Europeans. They were required by law to wear a cloth kilt, instead. Such barriers to their aspirations have further convinced Melanesians that in the European way of life is to be found the secret of their own lost worth; for otherwise Europeans would not be so eager to guard their monopoly of the symbols of worth or to reserve for themselves the knowledge and the opportunities to apply it from which possession of these symbols somehow follows. Thus great resentment of Europeans is coupled with an intense desire to identify with them, as is clearly manifested in the various politico-religious movements known as Cargo Cults, which are flourishing in Melanesia today.[31] There is a widespread hope that some European will appear as their savior and teacher; but no European has yet felt able to try to fill the role they would give him without being a traitor to his fellows or compromising some of his own most cherished beliefs and values.

In these movements, we should note, there tends to be a regular pattern in the selection of positive and negative symbols of ambivalent feelings toward Europeans. The people express strong dislike of the governing or power wielding authorities and the nation they represent, while adulating a more distant nation of equal or greater power with which they have few dealings. Thus the Nakanai channel their negative feelings against the Australians and look hopefully and wistfully to the United States. We see the same thing in Castro's Cuba, where an under-developed and long-exploited people is focusing its resentments against the wielders of power in the modern industrial world upon the United States, for obvious reasons, and at the same time implementing its desire to participate in that world on more equal terms by developing the Soviet Union as a positive image with which to identify. Despite these complications resulting from ambivalence, there are many ways in which the Nakanai want to be more like Australians and the Cubans more like North Americans, even though they may use other nations toward which they have no hostile feelings as their symbolic equivalent for conscious identification purposes. Though they might meet with hostile receptions, American agents of development in Cuba and Australian agents in New Guinea represent a way of life that the people there value highly and with which they would like to be identified.

The very different situation, in which a community is prepared to see nothing of value in the agent and what he represents and is predisposed to look upon him as a negative model in virtually everything, is described by Erikson as characterizing the relations between Sioux Indians and Indian Agency personnel.

The roaming trappers and fur traders seemed acceptable enough to the nomadic Sioux. They shared the Indians' determination to keep the game intact; they brought knives and guns, beads and kettles; and they married Indian women and became devoted to them. Some American generals, too, were entirely acceptable, and in fact were almost deified for the very reason that they had fought well. Even the Negro cavalry fitted into Sioux values. Because of their impressive charges on horseback, they were given the precious name of "Black Buffaloes." Neither did the consecrated belief in man demonstrated by the Quakers and early missionaries fail to impress the dignified and religious leaders of the Sioux. But as they looked for fitting images to connect the past with the future, the Sioux found least acceptable the class of white man who was destined to teach them the blessings of civilization—namely, the government employee. *[32]

Now the point has been reached where Sioux and agency personnel each regard the other as the antithesis of almost everything they value.[33]

Intelligent planning for community development must obviously concern itself with where its clients' identifications currently lie, the nature of the values they see embodied in their important reference figures, and where the development agents and their values are likely to fit into them.

SUGGESTED READING

Bennett, John W., Herbert Passin, and Robert K. McKnight, *In Search of Identity:* The Japanese Overseas Scholar in America and Japan. University of Minnesota Press, Minneapolis, 1958.

Berreman, Gerald D., *Behind Many Masks:* Ethnography and Impression Management in a Himalayan Village. Monograph no. 4, Society for Applied Anthropology, Ithaca, N. Y., 1962.

Foote, Nelson, and Leonard S. Cottrell, Jr., *Identity and Interpersonal Competence:* A New Direction in Family Research, University of Chicago Press, Chicago, 1955.

Goffman, Erving, *The Presentation of Self in Everyday Life*. Doubleday Anchor Books, Garden City, N. Y., 1959.

Hallowell, A. Irving, *Culture and Experience*. University of Pennsylvania Press, Philadelphia, 1955, chaps. 4 and 8.

Lynd, Helen Merrell, *On Shame and the Search for Identity*. Harcourt, Brace and Co., New York, 1958.

Merton, Robert K., *Social Theory and Social Structure*. The Free Press, Glencoe, Ill., 1957, chaps. 8 and 9.

Strauss, Anselm L., *Mirrors and Masks:* The Search for Identity. The Free Press, Glencoe, Ill., 1959.

Tagiuri, Renato, and Luigi Petrullo, editors, *Person Perception and Interpersonal Behavior*. Stanford University Press, Stanford, 1958.

NOTES TO CHAPTER 8

1. For an analysis of a social taxonomy into its conceptual components, see Goodenough, Ward H., "Componential Analysis and the Study of Meaning," *Language*, vol. 32, 1956, pp. 195–216.

2. That even such perceptions are in terms of categories of physiognomic features is revealed by the fact that when we have dealings with people of other races whose physiognomic variations are not easily sorted out by the taxonomic system with which we are used to working, we find that they "all look alike" to us.

3. How this works is illustrated by Ward H. Goodenough, in "Componential Analysis and the Study of Meaning," *op. cit.*

4. I am indebted to C. A. Valentine and Ann Chowning for information regarding the Nakanai example.

5. For an important early statement of this position see Mead, G. H., *Mind, Self, and Society*, University of Chicago Press, Chicago, 1934. For more recent discussions, see Foote, Nelson, and Leonard S. Cottrell, Jr., *Identity and Interper onal Competence: A New Direction in Family Research*, University of Chicago Press, Chicago, 1955, and Strauss, Anselm L., *Mirrors and Masks*, The Search for Identity. The Free Press, Glencoe, Ill., 1959.

6. Ralph Linton in *The Study of Man* (D. Appleton-Century Co., New York, 1936, pp. 113–114) defines a status as "a collection of rights and duties," and a role as "the dynamic aspect of a status." For further development of these concepts, see Goodenough, Ward H., *Property, Kin and Community on Truk*, Yale University Publications in Anthropology, New Haven, 1951, pp. 111–119. See also Gross, Neal, Ward S. Mason, and Alexander W. McEachern, *Explorations in Role Analysis:* Studies of the School Superintendency Role, John Wiley and Sons, New York, 1958; and for a highly theoretical discussion, see Nadel, S. F., *The Theory of Social Structure*, The Free Press, Glencoe, Ill., 1957.

7. As thus defined, personal identity has an obviously close relationship with what is generally meant by personality. Whatever an individual's personality really comprises, neither he nor anyone else can perceive its manifestations except in terms of some categorical system or systems. The things about himself that are thus perceived as distinct from the rights and duties defining his social roles, constitute the features of his personal identity.

8. See the distinction between "ascribed" and "achieved status" by Ralph Linton, *op. cit.*, pp. 115–116.

9. We might be inclined to think of the woman in this case as having a social identity as a man but a personal identity as a woman; but this would be to confuse social identity with public image and personal identity with self-image. We might also think of someone's sex as being a part of his personal identity because it is inherent in his biological nature. Sex categories are features of social identity, however, in that different rights and duties characterize the relations between persons of the same or opposite sex. We do not judge someone as a person from his sex alone (except where we assume certain styles of conduct to be correlated with it), but rather on the way in which he conducts himself as a man or as a woman.

10. Macmillan, Allister, and Alexander H. Leighton, "People of the Hinterland: Community Interrelations in a Maritime Province of Canada" in Spicer, Edward H., editor, *Human Problems in Technological Change:* A Casebook. Russell Sage Foundation, New York, 1952, p. 242.

11. Mason, Leonard, "Kili Community in Transition," *South Pacific Commission Quarterly Bulletin*, vol. 8, April, 1958, p. 46.

12. See MacGregor, Gordon, *Warriors Without Weapons:* A Study of the Society and Personality of the Pine Ridge Sioux, University of Chicago Press, Chicago, 1946; also, Erikson, Erik H., *Childhood and Society*, W. W. Norton Co., New York, 1950, pp. 98–140.

13. In our society, of course, there are different conventions for displaying one's identity as a rich man, depending on one's class background, occupation, and other subgroup affiliation.

14. For a vivid account of this and how it affected his relations with the people of an Indian village in ethnographic study, see Berreman, Gerald D., *Behind Many Masks:* Ethnography and Impression Management in a Himalayan Village, Monograph no. 4, Society for Applied Anthropology, Ithaca, N.Y., 1962.

15. Indeed, one's perception of others is not unrelated to one's perception of self, so that our desire for others to perceive things about us is necessarily also a desire for them to perceive things about themselves. See Foote, Nelson, and Leonard S. Cottrell, Jr., *op. cit.*

16. Goodenough, Ward H., *op. cit.*, Charts 3–22.

17. The reader should consult the excellent analysis of Samoan etiquette and protocol and its effect on the pattern of European-Samoan relations by Felix M. Keesing and Marie M. Keesing, *Elite Communication in Samoa:* A Study of Leadership, Stanford University Press, Stanford, 1956.

18. Useem, John, "South Sea Island Strike" in Spicer, Edward H., editor, *op. cit.*, p. 157.

19. Grimble, Sir Arthur, *Return to the Islands.* John Murray, Ltd., London, 1957, pp. 212–213.

20. *Ibid.*, p. 206.

21. Goffman, Erving, "The Nature of Deference and Demeanor," *American Anthropologist*, vol. 58, 1956, pp. 473–502.

22. See Fallers, Lloyd, "The Predicament of the Modern African Chief," *American Anthropologist*, vol. 57, 1955, pp. 290–305; also, Beattie, John, *Bunyoro, An African Kingdom*, Henry Holt and Co., New York, 1960, pp. 45–46.

23. Goodenough, Ward H., "Premarital Freedom on Truk: Theory and Practice," *American Anthropologist*, vol. 51, 1949, pp. 615–620; Gladwin, Thomas, and Seymour B. Sarason, *Truk: Man in Paradise*, Viking Fund Publications in Anthropology, no. 20, Wenner-Gren Foundation for Anthropological Research, New York, 1953, pp. 100–117; Swartz, Marc J., "Sexuality and Aggression on Romonum, Truk," *American Anthropologist*, vol. 60, 1958, pp. 467–486.

24. Mahoney, Frank J., "The Innovation of a Savings System in Truk," *American Anthropologist*, vol. 62, 1960, pp. 465–482.

25. See the summation by Ruth Benedict in *Patterns of Culture*, Mentor Books, New York, 1946, pp. 47–50, and the account of Crow religion by Robert H. Lowie in *Primitive Religion*, The Universal Library, Grosset and Dunlap, New York, 1952, pp. 3–32.

26. Mitchell, Joseph, "The Mohawks in High Steel," *The New Yorker*, September 17, 1949, pp. 38–52.

27. In this regard, see Foote, Nelson N., "Identification as the Basis for a Theory of Motivation," *American Sociological Review*, vol. 16, 1951, pp. 14–21.

28. Goodenough, Erwin R., "Religion and Psychology." Unpublished manuscript.

29. Klapp, Orin E., "Heroes, Villains and Fools, as Agents of Social Control," *American Sociological Review*, vol. 19, 1949, pp. 56–62.

30. Melanesians in this example experienced what Hagen has termed "withdrawal of status respect," something he regards as a significant step in the process by which traditionally oriented people become more innovative. See Hagen, Everett E., *On the Theory of Social Change: How Economic Growth Begins*, The Dorsey Press, Homewood, Ill., 1962, pp. 185 ff.

31. Worsley, Peter, *The Trumpet Shall Sound: A Study of "Cargo" Cults in Melanesia*. MacGibbon and Kee, London, 1957.

32. Erikson, Erik H., *Childhood and Society*. W. W. Norton and Co., New York, 1950, p. 101.

33. See the analysis by Erik H. Erikson, *op. cit.*, and "Observations on Sioux Education," *Journal of Psychology*, vol. 7, 1939, pp. 101–156. For an analysis of the greater ease with which Samoans have identified with American as compared with New Zealand administrators, see Keesing, Felix M., and Marie M. Keesing, *op. cit.*, pp. 191–197.

Chapter 9

IDENTITY CHANGE*

THE LIFE HISTORY of every individual is marked by a succession of identity changes in both his public image and self-image. As he gets older, his fellows insist on his assuming more responsibility and seek to redefine their mutual rights and duties. They promote him to new social categories and ascribe to him new features of identity. Since some social categories allow for rights and privileges that make them more attractive than others, people continually seek to change their own as well as their fellows' social identities in directions they deem desirable. The same is true of personal identity. Past performance in his social roles may bear on a person's eligibility for a desired change in social identity. He has to have shown himself to be industrious, resourceful, brave, and so on. Doing something about one's own and other people's identities is, in fact, a major concern everywhere. We have already considered the role of identification and the use of others as models. We now examine the procedures by which people in all societies seek to motivate and facilitate identity changes.

These procedures necessarily interest us, because community development is itself aimed at accomplishing change in some feature or features of a people's identity. Changes in their material and social circumstances that have little effect on their public image and self-image can scarcely be regarded as contributing to development. How people arrive at changes in their identity, therefore, is a matter of crucial importance for understanding the

* Portions of this chapter appear in a paper by the author entitled "Education and Identity" in Gruber, Frederick C., editor, *Anthropology and Education*, University of Pennsylvania Press, Philadelphia, 1961, pp. 84–102. Grateful acknowledgment is herewith made to the Trustees of the University of Pennsylvania for permission to incorporate the bulk of that paper into this chapter.

215

psychology of community development. Knowledge of the steps by which identity changes normally take place will help us appraise the possibility of stimulating and guiding their occurrence in the development situation.

THE REQUISITES FOR IDENTITY CHANGE

When we stop to think of the more important identity changes people must undergo in their lifetime in our own society, it is evident that we frequently celebrate them with some kind of ceremony, festivity, or other special mark of recognition. We have graduation, marriage, and inaugural ceremonies, for example. We celebrate impending marriages and impending motherhood with "showers." There are "coming out" parties, "house warmings," funeral rites, and mourning observances. In less dramatic fashion we accompany the celebration of birthdays with formal redefinitions of their identity to our children. It is at the new birthday that new privileges are extended: staying up a half-hour later at night, acquiring a driver's license, drinking the first cocktail, perhaps, or becoming a voter. In other societies, also, we find social formalities associated with identity changes. Dramatic among them are the rites that in many societies attend transition from childhood to young adulthood. Elaborate initiations into new social identities are by no means confined to primitive or underdeveloped societies, however. They are matched in our own with the acquisition of one's occupational identity. The apprentice in a trade, the rookie in military service, the graduate student working for his Ph.D. degree, all are subjected to institutionalized physical and mental ordeals, tests of competence, and organized hazing. At the same time they receive instruction in the performance of their future occupational roles, are let in on professional secrets, and are indoctrinated with a code of "professional ethics." The main difference between our own and simpler societies is that there are many very different adult identities into which one may be initiated in the former and few in the latter.

These transition rites,[1] as anthropologists call them, represent solutions people have found for dealing with the problems accompanying identity change. The specific solutions vary, as we might expect, depending on the way these problems present themselves in different social settings, for when we get down to cases there is considerable variation in the degree to which the necessary conditions for initiating and executing identity change seem to require implementation. But what are the necessary conditions? If community development is a form of identity change, we must know what they are. First, there must be desire for identity change. There must also be a commitment to making a change. What needs to be changed must be understood. People must know what are the roles, symbols, and styles of performance appropriate to their new identities; and they must be physically and emotionally able to perform these roles, use these symbols correctly, and accomplish the necessary changes in style. Their new identities must be recognized and accepted by others. Finally, those making the change must come to conceive of themselves as actually having new identities. We shall now look at these requisites for identity change more closely and examine their implications for community development.

ACHIEVING A DESIRE FOR CHANGE

It often happens that people are contented with themselves as they are, but their fellows are not. The self-image appears good, but not the public image. A child may be contented to act as he did when he was two years younger, while in the eyes of his playmates he ought to be more grown up and "act his age." Or a man is satisfied with his identity as a skilled laborer, but his fiancée wants him to be "respectable" in some kind of white collar job or in a business of his own. Similarly, we want the criminal to become law-abiding, the insane to become sane, the boor to become a gentleman, and the intemperate to become temperate. The change we desire may be in his social identity or it may be in some feature of his personal identity, his style of play. Whichever it is, there are various techniques by which we seek to create in others a desire to alter their identities.

The first thing we do is to acquaint them with their public image, on the assumption that if they see themselves as others do, they will want to change. If this does not produce results, we undertake to make their present conduct no longer gratifying. When a child asks for something in baby talk, for example, we may refuse to give it to him. We may go further and actively punish him whenever he fails to act in accordance with the public image that we desire him to present to us. Another technique often linked with this one is to permit the indulgence of some hitherto frustrated want as an inducement for change. Parents offer new privileges to induce their children to assume more adult responsibilities or to do well in school. Behavior that is ordinarily disapproved may be temporarily licensed. We are willing to tolerate in the college freshman and sophomore conduct we would not tolerate for a minute from anyone else—or, at least, we have been until recently. Inducements have also played a prominent role in identity changes of the kind involved in community development. Missionaries have offered the opportunity to acquire much coveted objects of European manufacture as inducements to conversion; and, more recently, some missions are using the desire for European schooling as an attraction. The dictum that development agents should try to link their development objectives with the wants and felt needs of their clients is a less barefaced way of saying that there must be inducements to cooperation in change.

These techniques are primarily aimed at inducing outward conformity with the desires of others. They may be effective in getting people to change the public image they present to others, but they do not necessarily have much effect on their private view of themselves. Yet there are occasions when what we desire of others is that they *want* to change their identity. We are not satisfied that they present themselves in the guise we desire just because we desire it, but insist that this guise reflect the way they truly want to feel about themselves. We do not want our children to foster a public impression of their honesty alone; we insist that honesty be an ego-ideal they hold for themselves. Only then can we trust them to be honest even though there is no apparent way anyone else will be the wiser if they are not. No missionary, to take another example, feels that he has succeeded if his converts conduct themselves in accordance with his teachings only when in his presence or only because of his material inducements or threats of punishment. Religious conversion involves, by definition, a change in a person's conception of self and in how he feels about himself as a person, so that he can no longer be satisfied with his identity as it was, but feels compelled to repudiate it in favor of a new one more in keeping with his ego-ideals.

Much of the literature on community development envisions it as trying to accomplish just this sort of change. Development, we are told, is not successful unless the changes are accepted by the community's members as something they want for themselves. Development, it is argued, must come from within; the agent of change is only a catalyst. The community must in the end be able to maintain the changes that have occurred without outside help. The changes must be fully incorporated and integrated into its way of life. And, ideally, development aims at stimulating change not only in material well-being but in the feeling the people have about themselves, so that their capacity for self-improvement and further self-development is increased. What is pictured is a change in which people have a new hope for the future and a new confidence in their ability to realize that hope.[2] This, of course, is the message of many religious missionaries. They may differ from agents of community development in the content of their programs and the doctrines by which they rationalize them, but not in their psychological objective, which is a new image of self and world and a new sense of purpose and accomplishment. Development would be a sorry thing indeed, if it were not aimed at helping people feel that life is more worthwhile. But we must face up to what this implies. The psychology of identity change does not vary according to the god or message in whose name such change is undertaken.

The problem that faces development agents, then, is to find ways of stimulating in others a desire for change in such a way that the desire is theirs independent of further prompting from outside. Restated, the problem is one of creating in another a sufficient dissatisfaction with his present condition of self so that he wants to change it. This calls for some kind of experience that leads him to reappraise his self-image and reevaluate his self-esteem.

Revising One's View of Self

Self-reappraisal may be essentially evaluative, as when a person continues to see himself as the same kind of person he has always been but revises his estimation of himself as such for better or worse. Reappraisal may also be cognitive, as when he sees himself as a different kind of person with features of either personal or social identity that differ significantly from those he formerly thought he had. Such reappraisal also has its evaluative aspects, of course. The kind of person one is, whatever it may be, has more or less value in relation to other kinds that one might be instead. While changes in self-esteem and self-image are linked, they represent distinctly different dimensions in terms of which people reappraise themselves.

Either kind of reappraisal comes about following some kind of new experience. It may or may not be wanted; it may be deliberately courted or result from circumstances beyond one's control. The experience may be traditional within the community, as with marriage and initiation rites, or it may be entirely without precedent. A change in the categories by which we perceive things, in our criteria for evaluating what we perceive, or in our habits of using these categories and criteria will necessarily lead to new experiences of our own selves, even when objectively there has been no change in our circumstances. But such change is not necessary for a new view of self. When the dark-skinned Nakanai first saw Europeans, they were already familiar enough with light color and with human beings, but not in combination. There was question as to whether Europeans were spirits of the dead or not, because of their light color, but this was soon settled. Here was a new kind of human being, but it required no change in habits of perception to see that this was so. In fact, it was their established habits of perception that made the experience striking.[3] It meant, of course, that dark-skinned people were not the only kind of people in the world, and the Nakanai found at least one feature of their self-image changed as a result. We saw in the preceding chapter how their contact with Europeans also led them to revise their estimation of themselves in accordance with their traditional criteria for self-evaluation.

Change of this sort requires little or no effort. Some effort may be required, however, to start using our established perceptual categories or value criteria in new ways, but when the effort is made, radical reappraisals of identity may result. The criteria we regularly use for evaluating behavior in church contexts, for example, are not necessarily those we use in business contexts. If, for some reason, we begin evaluating our business behavior in terms of our church values, the result may be a considerable revision of our sense of worth. Since people tend, moreover, to perceive themselves as well as others in terms of those categories about which they are especially concerned emotionally, there is usually considerable room for them to revise their perceptions in terms of other categories that are also applicable. The situation is not unlike that represented in the line drawing of the box.

Whether one is looking up at the box or down on it depends on how one happens to see it. People's perception and evaluation of self are likely to be similarly capable of alteration within the framework of categories and values already available to them. Because of emotional investments in looking at themselves as they do, people often have difficulty making such perspective changes.

We stimulate such shifts in the perceptions of our fellows by inviting them to consider themselves in the light of other considerations. Thus we may ask the man who sees his large convertible as a symbol of his worth and importance whether it is not also an expression of his vanity and evidence of his selfishness, since he could have spent less money on equally adequate transportation and have used the balance in the interest of others. This seems to be an important technique in psychological counseling. By letting the client talk and exhibit his categories for perceiving himself and others and the values he attaches to these categories, especially as they relate to experiences about which he feels strongly, a counselor begins to be able to confront his client with himself in the way just illustrated. The client will seek to evade looking at things as the counselor suggests. His rationalization is not disputed by the counselor, who, instead, uses it to confront the client with himself in relation to something he said earlier in a different context. A counselor can thus confine himself to occasional questions, "Do you mean, then, that . . .?" or "Does that strike you as . . .?" or "Is that what you meant when you said . . .?" Some therapists try to limit themselves simply to repeating and echoing the important categorizing words the client uses, thereby underlining them and inviting the client's attention to the fuller implications of what he is saying.[4] In time, these confrontations, which seem to follow inexorably from the very things on which the client tries to erect his defenses against having to change his view of himself, have an accumulative effect. He is progressively stripped of whatever rationalizations he can himself accept as reasonable. Feeling more and more pushed to the wall, he suffers acutely. Then, suddenly, he has an insight; that is, he allows himself to see his actions and the actions of others in the light of other categories than those he has habitually used. His wants and felt needs change accordingly, leading him to behave in new ways, which provide tangible evidence that he no longer regards himself as he did.

The preliminary study of a community's conditions by a development agent before drawing up proposals for change can have this effect of confronting people with themselves. In the Moturiki project in Fiji, for example, investigations by the development team led the people to be more acutely aware of the public image they presented, which in turn increased their desire for development.[5] In this case, all of the members of the development team were fellow Fijians. In making their survey they were confronting their clients with themselves in their own language, that is, in terms of categories of perception with which they were already familiar. This calls attention to an important point. A psychological counselor is able to confront his client with himself in the manner just described because he and his client share the same general criteria for both perceiving and evaluating identity features, although they are in the habit of using them differently from context to context. If a counselor asked questions using words that did not have the identity implications for his client that they had for him, he would have no way of confronting his client with himself. This may help account for the observation that psychological counselors in our society have a greater rate of success with clients from their own social class than with those outside it.

With good reason, then, experienced development workers stress the necessity of defining a community's problems to its members in terms that are meaningful to them according to their established categories for perceiving and evaluating things. Efforts to "educate" people to feel a need for change where none has been felt before must follow the confrontation approach of psychological counseling. To try to teach an entirely new perceptual framework or new values regarding the existing one may seem tempting, but this approach quickly degenerates into meaningless lecturing and scolding, because unless people can perceive a good reason to learn something new, they are not going to make the effort and will regard exhortations by others as an impertinent nuisance. An agent of change cannot reasonably expect his clients to see things in terms of his own alien and strange perceptual criteria derived from a host of experiences they have never had. Nor can he expect them to evaluate what they see in accordance with his own sentiment system or the public values of his alien society. He must try to help them gain insight into their circumstances and the possibilities for altering them by using their own perceptual frame in ways they are not in the habit of using. To do this, of course, he must learn their system of categories and the values they attach to the things they discern with it. The intensive learning the establishment of a common frame requires is primarily the agent's responsibility. Some learning of this sort by the community's members may also appear necessary, however, which brings us to consider the most difficult way people acquire new views of themselves.

Learning New Criteria of Self-appraisal

People can and do learn to make new perceptual discriminations and to develop new evaluative criteria. One is forced to do this when exposed to a new language or to the customs of a different society. One's own habits for discerning speech and events don't make sense out of what is going on. To escape from confusion one is forced to make the effort to learn new discriminations. And if what is going on is a reflection of someone else's criteria for perceiving and evaluating, then those are the criteria to be learned if one's experience is to make sense.

People teach others to see things as they want them to by subjecting them to experiences they have never had before in situations that are sharply delineated and highlighted with reference to the new discernments to be learned. We do this in educating our children, having considerable power to control the experiences they will have. When industrial or plantation labor is recruited from underdeveloped areas, the workers are subjected to new experiences that are structured by their foremen in strange ways. Necessarily they learn new ways of seeing and evaluating things, including themselves. Once learned in these new contexts, of course, there exists the possibility of applying the new perceptual frame to other contexts as well. The young man who gets a new conception of self in the radically different environment offered by military service may later bring it home with him. The Army, indeed, just may have "made a man of him." All over the world, the industrial revolution and the expansion of colonial power has had this effect of forcing people to learn new ways of looking at themselves.

In educational practice, demonstrations are a technique for providing others with the necessary kinds of new experience needed to learn a particular way of perceiving something. Development agents properly exploit this technique, as with demonstration farms. Its success or failure depends, of course, largely on the degree to which the demonstration actually subjects people to new and confusing experiences and the degree to which they feel compelled to make sense out of those experiences. A demonstration farm is going to have much more effect on the perceptions of the people hired to work on it than it is on those who are taken on short tours through it. Industrialization affects the perceptions of those who go to work in the new industrial towns much more profoundly than it does the perceptions of their kinsmen who remain on the land.

Although new, confusing experiences provide opportunities to give people new ways of looking at things, and although these new ways, when extended to other contexts, may lead to considerable alterations in their view of themselves, there are practical limitations on the extent to which agents of change can subject their clients to such experiences. The ethics of development provide that a client community's participation be voluntary. An agent cannot, therefore, require his clients to undergo radically new experiences until they have become willing to do so, which is likely to require some alteration in their conception of self in the first place. As development progresses, the new experiences that come out of it provide a basis for further revision of their view of themselves and a consequent development of new wants. But when changes in a people's self-image are necessary to provide the motivation to participate in a development program at the outset, these changes must be accomplished mainly through the use of perceptual frames already available to them. The teaching of new ones can only come later.

Once acquired, moreover, people must continue to have experiences to which their new perceptual and evaluative systems are applicable. When these fail to make sense of what is going on, they will necessarily be abandoned once more. We notice this especially in those situations where young people have been taken out of their home communities and sent away to be educated in alien ones. Of necessity they acquire the perceptual categories and evaluative criteria of the community in which they are educated. Then they are sent to their home communities once more to educate their fellows. Here they are likely to find themselves in a world whose events make no sense in terms of what they have learned outside of it. They must learn the local categories and values or resort back to them in order to interact meaningfully with their own people. In doing so, they may reject what they have learned on the outside, exhibiting the so-called "reversion to type" which has been so frequently observed and almost as frequently misunderstood. In the Gilbert Islands, we were told, native medical practitioners stationed on islands where they have little direct contact with other practitioners or English physicians tend in time to get caught up in the usual grooves of native community life and to lose the view of themselves and their work that effective medical practice requires. The problem was being solved by bringing practitioners back at regular intervals for tours of duty at the colony hospital in a community of fellow professionals.

As this example shows, to maintain a capacity to operate effectively in two different social identity systems, a person must continue to have experiences that are uniquely relevant to each. If daily experience is meaningful in terms of one system alone, then the other is superfluous and will become inoperative. It is much the same with languages. To be effectively bilingual we must have to deal with some people who speak only one of our two languages and with other people who speak only the other. As soon as we can get along with one language alone, the other falls into disuse and our ability to speak it gradually disappears. If, moreover, a person is to operate exclusively in terms of a new system of categories and values, then he must not be put in situations where it is of no use to him. It is a waste of effort to teach people a new way of looking at things unless one can be certain it will give meaning to the circumstances in which they will normally find themselves. The new view of themselves that motivated the people of Moturiki to get out and work was sustained largely by their dealings with the development team. When the team left their community, they no longer experienced the social relations in which this view was fostered, and their motivation to continue self-development on their own grew weaker.[6]

Discontent with Self in Underdeveloped Societies

Our interest in the problem of stimulating a desire for development in people who otherwise lack it has led us to concentrate on change in people's self-images as a preliminary step in the development process. Having become dissatisfied with themselves as newly perceived and evaluated, their problem becomes one of altering their customary behavior, their circumstances, or both, so as to achieve an identity with which they can again be comfortable.

Actually, many of the communities in which development agents are called upon to work have already reached this stage.

Their members have been subjected to many new experiences resulting from industrialization, working as plantation labor, pacification by colonial authorities, the construction of large-scale hydroelectric projects, or other changes in their circumstances that have been thrust upon them and to which they have had to try to accommodate themselves. From their dealings with labor foremen, colonial police officers, and other persons who have influenced their view of these experiences, they have acquired new perceptual criteria and begun to appraise themselves in terms of them. They are also appraising themselves in their altered circumstances in terms of their old criteria. From both vantage points they have already acquired new and less gratifying views of themselves. They are eager to devise means of changing their circumstances or themselves so as to achieve a self-image with which they can be reasonably content. Here, the agent's task is not to stimulate motivation for change by getting people to take a new look at themselves, but rather to fit himself into a situation where new looks have already been taken and where people already want to make further changes in their identity of a sort they regard as desirable.

As we shall see, the reaction to such situations by responsible authorities, including development agents, are rarely based on a clear understanding of the forces with which they are trying to deal. And even in those situations where it has been necessary for agents to stimulate a desire for change, if they are successful they must then relate themselves realistically to these very same forces they have helped to set in motion. Let us go on, then, to see how people normally do change those features of their identity with which they are discontented.

COMMITMENT TO CHANGE

People often feel anxious and have second thoughts even about changes they want very much to make. The new roles that a new social identity requires us to play are likely to call for important modifications of our previous personal style. Ways in which we have habitually displaced and sublimated emotional problems may no longer be suitable, adding to the uncertainty about our ability to bring off the change successfully. Because of these implications for our personal identity, changes in our social identity are often major crises. Indeed, social scientists speak of the more important ones as "life crises."

Changes in social identity are a source of anxiety for another reason. It takes time to learn new roles and to become habituated to a new conception of self. The period of transition is likely to be characterized by confusion as to just what one's identity is. The teenager in our society acts like an adult one minute and a child the next. Anyone in the process of identity change frequently finds himself acting or being treated in ways that are inconsistent with the new public image and self-image he is trying to cultivate. He is constantly being surprised about himself, often unpleasantly, with the result that these transitions make him terribly self-conscious, rob him of his confidence and leave him with a heightened sense of shame.[7] We are understandably anxious, therefore, about entering college, starting our first job, getting married, or becoming a parent for the first time, even though we want to do all of these things.

One way of helping our fellows prepare for changes in their social identity is to anticipate their new status, starting to direct toward them the roles appropriate to the new identity we want them to accept. Thus we help them get the feel of their new social identity before they have formally entered upon it and start playing in earnest. And after a person has formally assumed his new identity, we order our relations with him so consistently and insistently in terms of it that we leave him little alternative to trying to play his new roles except open defiance.

When an identity change is impending, moreover, we often prepare people for it by congratulating them or involving them in obligations that make retreat from the change difficult. In our society "showers" before a young woman's wedding or before she has her first baby help to facilitate the change in a material sense, but more importantly they help to commit her to the idea of becoming a wife or mother; and by means of the gifts given, they reinforce her moral obligation to carry through what she has started. Although marriage and motherhood are among the life goals for women on which we place highest value, there have been many brides and mothers who were rendered less reluctant by the congratulatory and envious attentions of their friends.

Such ways of stimulating commitment to change can be highly effective with changes in social identity, especially those changes that are part of the normal life process. They help to overcome reluctance generated by anxiety and shame about changes that are at the same time valued and desired. They can only stimulate and reinforce, however. The actual act of commitment can be made only by the person making the change.

This act is a turning from things associated with one's former self with a sense of finality—with a feeling that whatever happens, one's bridges have been burned. Commitment is often expressed by an action that eliminates or destroys something symbolic of one's former identity. On a humble scale is the little ceremony in which mother and child throw the last baby bottle in the trash or a man throws out all of his tobacco. To destroy old symbols with which one has been identified is in a very real sense to destroy one's former identity, to make it very difficult to be the same again, especially if the symbols are not easily come by, as when religious converts destroy the temples and idols it took generations of effort to create.

A famous episode on a mass scale is the one in which King Kamehameha II (Liholiho) of Hawaii in 1819 deliberately and publicly broke the taboo against men eating with women, precipitating a mass repudiation of the whole Hawaiian taboo system and the religious institutions that supported it. People not only broke the taboo, they set out to destroy all their formerly sacred places and the images of their gods. A generation of dealings with Europeans had poised them on the brink of having to develop a new collective identity, and thus they committed themselves to a changed future irrevocably.[8]

Physical destruction is not the only way to express commitment, of course. A person may exhibit a sudden new rudeness or a radical change in dress and mannerisms and thus force others to regard and treat him differently from the way they did before. By thus ridding himself of the kinds of treatment he received in the past, he destroys something of his old identity. The effect may be to lower his estimation in his fellows' eyes, but it will have changed it from what it was, at least, breaking his identity out of its old mold. Whatever his new behaviors are, to be effective they must be dramatic enough in their impact to make it impossible for others to go on viewing him as they did before. Antisocial actions are, therefore, a tempting way to commit one-self to identity change; they are dramatic and effective. Whatever their consequences, one cannot be the same person afterward. Extreme action of this kind occurs when a person sees the problem of change mainly as one of forsaking his former identity and has only minor concern with what the new identity will be, as with many of our delinquent teenagers in depressed neighborhoods. When he has sharply in focus the new identity he desires, the act of commitment is more likely to be one that leads in the direction of its achievement and less likely to be indiscriminately destructive of his past. Nevertheless, because identity change necessarily involves the replacement of former identity features by new ones, it almost inevitably appears to require the eradication of some part of one's former self. The act of eradication, therefore, is the one by which we commonly take the plunge. And the more anxiety people feel about change, the more convulsive and violent the act of commitment is likely to be. Social revolutions, especially in their earlier stages, are almost inevitably punctuated by violent acts of commitment in which both human and material symbols of the old order suffer destruction.

UNDERSTANDING WHAT NEEDS TO BE CHANGED

No matter how dissatisfied a person may be with his present identity, in order to change it he must have some credible explanation of what is wrong and what needs to be done to correct it. Lacking such explanation, he can only seek escape from his present identity by destructive revolt, refusing to conduct himself properly in accordance with its roles and by negatively doing the opposite of what he is supposed to do. The only change he can make is to an identity as a social delinquent. For a positive change to occur, he must have clearly in mind what are the features of identity that he now lacks and must acquire, and also what identity features he now possesses of which he must be rid, in order that others may see him and he may see himself as the sort of person he wishes to become.

In all societies, therefore, people are at pains to make clear to their fellows the qualifications of those social identities that everyone is supposed to try to achieve. Each social system, in fact, contains one or more identity sequences, with value placed on the successive achievement of each identity in them. However discontented a person may be with his present identity, there is another one to work for that will presumably be more gratifying. The definition of what must be altered for each step in the series gives an overall purpose to life, culminating in the practically unattainable ego-ideal that incorporates simultaneously all the identity features enjoying maximum prestige in the public value system. In this way the discontent that on occasion all people feel with themselves is expressed in socially constructive rather than destructive behavior—constructive in that it does not disrupt the conduct of normal activities and possibly even contributes to their orderly prosecution. Mythological and historical figures, as we have seen, serve as models concretely illustrating identity objectives. A person can compare himself with them in order to see more clearly in just what ways he must alter his present self.

A problem arises when people find themselves blocked by changing circumstances from following the progression of identity changes and self-development that their social order allows them and that they find meaningful in terms of their values. After being deprived of their hunting grounds and the opportunity to engage in war, for example, many American Indians found themselves unable to pursue the activities that were essential to the normal development of their identities in the direction of their ego-ideals. Offered other kinds of activity that did not fit their identity values, blocked from those that did, they could only escape their present identities by resort to alcoholism, coupled with sporadic efforts to break the impasse by outbursts of violence, or, as we shall have to consider later, by participation in new religious movements.

A similar problem arises when the progression of identity changes available in their social order loses its appeal for people, as when new experiences lead them to reappraise the worth of their traditional models as ego-ideals. This is the situation we have seen for the Nakanai. It appears to have been common in many parts of Melanesia following contact with Europeans. Margaret Mead's account of the Manus in 1928 shows them already unhappy with the channels open to them in their social order. This condition could scarcely have been true in precontact times, and by 1953 it had led them to revolutionize their social order.[9]

This brings us to consider what people can do when they find themselves either blocked from achieving their self-goals by new circumstances or no longer enamored of traditional self-goals because of wants arising from new experiences.

As our remarks have implied, so long as the social order offers people new identities which they perceive as desirable, whatever their present dissatisfaction with self, they are free to accept the social order as it is and to work to achieve new identities within it. But if a person finds himself blocked by circumstances that prevent his fulfilling himself within the social order, he must either try to restore prior circumstances and get back to the "good old days," or he must seek a new social order.

In connection with the second alternative there are several possibilities. If a person feels unable to change features of his identity that lack prestige or that bar him in the eyes of others from achieving an identity to which he aspires, he may try to persuade his fellows to change their valuation of his present identity and accord it the same privileges and esteem that more desirable identities in the social order enjoy. Negroes in the United States are presently concerned to have their identity as Negroes reevaluated by whites. This approach seeks to accomplish a change in the scale of values and in the allocation of rights and duties to existing social categories, but does not seek directly to change the categories as such. Failing in this approach, people may seek membership in a new community with a different system of social categories. There, other things serve as significant identity features, and it may become possible to achieve a new and more satisfactory identity as a result. Thus a slave may try to escape to another society where slavery does not exist. Some societies provide special communities where people who feel a need to escape from the standard social order may fulfill themselves in a parallel but different identity system, as with monasticism. When none of the foregoing is possible, people may try to persuade their fellows to adopt an entirely new social system; or, if they feel they have the power to do so, they may seek to impose one by force.

A delightful case has been reported of a Papuan headman who eloped with a kinswoman who was within the degree of relationship for which marriage was prohibited as incestuous. He succeeded in having his behavior reappraised as "good" rather than "bad," at least by many, and his social identity reclassified from that of "criminal" to that of "reformer." To accomplish this he first maneuvered his and his wife's kinsmen into ratifying his marriage as legal. The community was now in the position of having to live with a morally wrong marriage that it had, however reluctantly, legalized. Its members were willing to listen to rationalizations that would render the situation more palatable. The husband in the case, moreover, had undermined his moral authority as a headman who judged legal infractions and needed to do something to restore it. By presenting himself as a social reformer, he saved everybody's face, preserved people's feelings of integrity, and left everybody with no alternative but to accept the marriage reforms that he now formally promulgated, including a new definition of incest.[10]

This example shows how a skillful individual was able to solve an identity problem that was peculiarly his own. We are more concerned with what happens when the problem that seems to call for reform of the social order is shared by many people or is felt to be a collective problem. For when people feel a need to revise their social order, they are presumably in precisely that frame of mind without which community development is difficult or impossible.

Under these conditions, people act according to one or another of the possibilities just indicated. If there are ample opportunities for them to escape into a different social environment, they will seek to do this, individually migrating from the country to the city, for example. If people perceive no opportunities of this sort that seem attractive, they tend to develop organized movements.

The direction these movements take depends on how they perceive their problem.

If people still value traditional goals for the self but feel blocked by circumstances from doing the things that are traditionally required to achieve them, they will aim to remove the apparent obstacles. There is, of course, a wide range of possibilities as to what the apparent obstacles are likely to be. Landlords may become the focus of attention, in which case their dispossession and the free distribution of land will appear as the action that will free people once more to pursue the good life. Colonial governments are almost inevitable targets, and the apparent solution is to achieve nationalistic self-government. On other occasions the obstacle to self-realization appears to be the failure by one's fellows to observe the proper rules of conduct of former times, a situation calling for some kind of moral reawakening.

If the traditional means of self-realization no longer have value, then it appears that what one must do is to revise one's social order and reform one's way of life. Revolutionary movements are the normal consequence. To get rid of the old way of life, of course, one needs to have some vision of a new one. Some model of what is being aimed at is necessary. If no other models are available, then the old order serves as a negative one, what is to be achieved being seen as the antithesis of the old. This is indeed likely to be a component of any revolutionary movement. Thus if divorce used to be easy, it must now be made difficult; or if it used to be difficult, it must now be made easy, to take a familiar modern example. Whatever institutions were most symbolic of the old order and its values are the very ones that must be most vigorously assaulted: family, church, and property in the case of European societies; the whole taboo system, as we have seen, in the case of Hawaii. There may also be more positive models to compensate for the nihilistic features of such movements. Such a model may be entirely Utopian, in that it is not based on the way of life of any one other society but compounded of elements drawn from many sources. Or the model may be some specific other society with which people have had some kind of contact. Their image of European society, for example, is the model the Nakanai have for themselves. This is also the case with the Paliau movement in the Admiralty Islands.[11]

Because they aim at reforming one's whole way of life, revolutionary movements of this sort are inevitably totalitarian in scope. And because they have as their ultimate objective the achievement of a state of being approximating the ideal, a state, that is to say, of individual and collective salvation, they are also religious movements. Given such aims, they are bound to be unrealistic in many of their undertakings. Nor are their leaders usually aware of the nature of social processes or of all the more important functions of the institutions they wish to reform. When outside societies serve as points of reference, moreover, the resulting models are likely to be caricatures of their originals, all sorts of misinformation and wishful thinking being projected into them. How to help people who are engaged in such movements to develop realistic and rewarding models for themselves and how to deal effectively with the associated emotional forces are major problems in community development.

KNOWING THE CONTENT OF NEW ROLES

Successful identity change requires adequate information concerning the roles one is to play in one's identity. A person may know what he has to do in order to qualify for membership in some new social category; but if he is then unable to play the part successfully, the change will not be gratifying. To get to be appointed president of a company, for example, is not the same as doing the president's job properly. We must know what are the appropriate symbols of our new identity and how they are supposed to be displayed. And we must know what our specific duties and responsibilities in the new identity are. If the change is one that others also desire us to make, they will, of course, try to inform us as to our new roles. Schooling of this sort is usually an important part of formally organized transition rites, as with the period of "basic training" on entering military service.

Because it is so essential to be informed, people making identity changes want clearly defined standards with which to conform and examples and models that bear the stamp of public approval.

Psychologically, their orientation is one that is highly "other-directed," to use Riesman's expression.[12] We see this among many people in our own society today where extensive social mobility makes people want to have what is expected of them clearly indicated so that they can play the roles and exhibit the symbols that go with the identities toward which they aspire, and do so with a sense of certainty. This orientation is much less evident among people who are contented with their identities as they are. Already secure in the knowledge of their roles, people without social aspirations, including members of well-established, upper-class families, exhibit less concern with problems of conformity.

When the whole system of social identities is the object of change, people have a special problem. The visions they have for themselves are likely to be vague. They want to change, but lack a clear conception of the identities they might try to cultivate. In their discontent with themselves as they are, they are likely to be shopping around for models and for clarifying definitions. Anyone who presents himself as speaking with authority on the matter is likely to enjoy a receptive audience. Insofar as the leaders of social reform or other development movements feel it necessary to alter the system of social identities in their society, they have to be specific as to just how people are to conduct themselves. They must specify the rights and duties in social relationships, explicitly redefine the categories of person, and indicate what styles of performance will carry prestige. Once committed to the idea of change, their followers, far from resisting such dictation, welcome it.

A problem here, however, is the leader's source of information. What is the guarantee that his information is correct, that he really knows, and that the social order he is trying to create will effectively solve the identity needs people feel? He must offer acceptable credentials as proof of his superior knowledge regarding the problems they all share. If some outside society is serving as model, then the leader must have had more intimate acquaintance with that society. Otherwise, his authority must rest on inspiration, and he must present himself according to whatever are the accepted beliefs as to sources of inspiration. The leaders of Cargo Cults and other reform movements in Melanesia are either men who can claim special knowledge of the white man's world, such as former members of the Territorial Police, or men who claim to be in contact with the spirit world or some other source of presumably infallible information.

This brings us to an important problem in community development: the authority with which the agent speaks. For regardless of the soundness of his knowledge, he is not likely to enjoy an audience unless he presents credentials that are meaningful to the people with whom he is dealing.

As we saw in connection with the credibility of beliefs in Chapter 7, every society has recognized authorities on matters of local concern. The Pacific Islands have authorities whom they follow on gardening, fishing, curing, and astronomy and navigation, for example. These experts were educated by experts and have had experience in applying their special knowledge— experience that other people lack. When a technician enters a community to suggest that changes be made in medical and gardening procedures, he is almost inevitably challenging the validity of the knowledge and experience of locally recognized authorities. If his credentials do not match theirs in local eyes, he cannot expect to have a serious hearing, any more than we in our own society are prepared to accept a new cure that is not endorsed by our medical profession.

What constitutes satisfactory credentials depends on local traditions and local orientations. Some workers in underdeveloped areas seem to think that being a European or coming from the big city constitutes all the credentials they need in order to make pronouncements on virtually everything. If their clients are burning with desire to make themselves over in the European or urban image, such agents will very likely be deemed appropriate authorities. But if their clients are interested mainly in getting better crop yields, then they will look to whomever they regard as proper agricultural authorities. The outside agent is at the usual disadvantage here, in that he obviously is less familiar with local conditions than local authorities are. A study of the factors governing acceptance by Iowa farmers of new varieties of seed corn has revealed that what the extension agent said was of little importance to most farmers. They followed the lead of those among themselves who had the reputation of being successful farmers. If one or two of these men, after experimenting with the new seed, decided to use it, then the others would follow suit.[13] Agents are likely to encounter similar reactions in other parts of the world.

MASTERY OF ONE'S NEW ROLES

It goes without saying that knowledge of one's new role requirements does not make for successful identity change unless one is also actually able to turn in a satisfactory performance. It is essential for people to have opportunities to develop skill in the application of their knowledge. Such skill can be developed only by doing.

Officials in underdeveloped areas often say that local people are not yet ready to assume responsibility for the conduct of this or that enterprise. There are times when this is undoubtedly true. Lack of experience, however, is not a valid excuse for preventing people from having a chance to acquire experience. We let our children drive the family car, knowing very well that they are not yet competent drivers and that some damage to the car is likely to result. We do not, of course, start them out in heavy traffic. But we cannot forever deny them the opportunity of learning to deal with traffic on the grounds that never having done so they are not yet ready to try.

The problem, of course, is that successful management of a community's enterprises is something development agencies often feel to be more important than the actual development of the community's people. For one thing, they want the community's members to be spared the consequences of their mistakes. But they also are faced with the possibility of serious criticism from onlookers for whatever inefficiency and bumbling may occur in the learning process. Many people seem to feel that it is better for a community to have its affairs handled efficiently than for its members to try to handle them themselves. When people are committed to changing their ways, however, they necessarily insist on having the chance to do for themselves those things without which they cannot get the new feeling about themselves that they desire.

As people gain confidence in their ability to play their new roles, their sense of mastery helps to make them pleased with their new identity and with the whole identity system of which it is a part. For a while they may play their new roles to the utmost. They are, indeed, likely to overplay them. The sophomore is the most ardent defender of college and fraternity custom, glorying in his ability to conform to it and insisting on its sanctity lest the new self-image he has painfully acquired as a freshman become a mockery.

This is something we should note well for community development. The very process of mastery serves to heighten people's commitment to and acceptance of new ways. Where change is radical, people are less likely to become discouraged if they can enjoy the feeling of mastery at frequent enough intervals. A development program that can be broken down into a succession of small triumphs is more likely to succeed than one that requires prolonged effort without any new sense of accomplishment along the way.

ACCEPTANCE BY OTHERS

A few years ago a student of our acquaintance came to one of his professors baffled and desperate. He needed a fellowship badly in order to finance his studies. He had an almost straight "A" record for two years of course work, but had been turned down twice for financial aid in favor of other students whose record was not as good as his own. What were his professors' objections to him? In his case, it turned out, a stereotyped conception of him as a mediocre student had arisen when he first started his studies, based mainly on his previous educational background. Decisions regarding him had been made in terms of this stereotype rather than in terms of his subsequent good, but quiet accomplishments. His plea woke his teachers up, and he then received the recognition he rightly felt he had earned. He wanted an identity as one of the better students and the benefits to which such an identity entitled him; but although he fulfilled all the requirements for that identity, he could not achieve it until others were willing to confer it upon him. Without such recognition, the best of efforts at identity change fail.

In most cases of identity change there are key persons whose recognition is essential. Often they are the people with whom we interact most frequently and intensively. It is far more important that a growing child's changes in identity be recognized and accepted by his family and playmates, for example, than by the corner grocer or anyone else with whom he has only occasional dealings. It frequently happens, however, that certain persons— for example, teachers, employers, voters, and members of social clubs—have or are given power to pass on the qualifications of others. General acceptance hinges on their acceptance. Just who these key persons are depends on the identity being sought and the allotment of rights, privileges, and powers among the various categories of person and group within one's social order. Such persons or groups necessarily play an important role in the process of identity change, whether or not they are also the models that those making a change seek to emulate.

Recognition and acceptance is vital to successful identity change because it is impossible to play the roles appropriate to one's new identity in a social vacuum. Thus when a man is promoted to a higher position in his business firm he may continue to play much the same range of roles in his dealings with others that he played before; but those whom he treats as equals, superiors, and inferiors will now be different, and those who treat him as an equal, superior, or inferior will also change. If all continue to treat him as they did before, the effect is to nullify the promotion, and his efforts to reallocate his roles will meet with constant frustration.

Nonrecognition does not present itself as a problem when a person's identity change is one his fellows want him to make. Parents eagerly watch for signs of their children's further maturity and begin treating them in accordance with their new identities to encourage the change. Nonrecognition becomes a serious problem, however, when a person seeks to make a change that his fellows do not want. In many colonial areas, there are Europeans who deliberately refuse to treat well-dressed and well-educated natives in any way but as menials, thereby successfully frustrating their achieving the new public image and self-image to which they aspire.

It is, of course, an infuriating experience to present oneself as having a certain identity with what one understands to be the proper credentials, only to have the credentials ignored and to be treated as if one's identity were of another kind. People do this deliberately, of course, in order to wound others toward whom they harbor feelings of hostility or aversion. But a real hazard of any identity change is the possibility that one may suffer such humiliation from the thoughtlessness or ignorance of others. Badges of identity, prominently displayed, help to serve as reminders to one's fellows. Public announcement of more important identity changes, as with weddings and graduations, helps to minimize ignorance and to prepare others for the presentation of new self to follow. Involving the community in ritual or festivity upon the occasion of an identity change also helps to put others in an appropriate frame of mind. They are more likely to accept the change if they have participated in the events by which the change was formally accomplished.

Community Development and Outside Recognition

To regard community development as a process of collective identity change, in which a community's members come to look upon themselves as a different kind of people and on their community as a different kind of place, calls attention to the importance of recognition by others—in this case by outsiders. As development progresses, the community's members are eager for words of praise and approval from outsiders, especially those outsiders who have been their severest critics. Such comment reassures them that their efforts are being recognized by others and that they are on the way to a collective identity of which they can be proud within the larger world community. Acquisition of each new symbol of the identity to which they aspire is a noteworthy event. They want everyone to know it and proudly put it on display. In doing so, of course, they make themselves exceedingly vulnerable to humiliation. It is a crushing blow to their new self-image and self-esteem if others respond with indifference. If, as so often happens, others respond with disparagement or disdain, they invariably earn the undying hatred of the community's members. For just this reason, the United States has acquired not simply the political enmity but the venomous hatred of Chinese communists. European colonials all over the world have sneeringly thwarted the efforts of local people to better themselves by adopting what they regard as the symbols of European status. They are now reaping the harvest of hate. There is virtually no one toward whom people direct greater spite than those from whom they have suffered humiliation of this kind. The trouble is that even well-intentioned people thoughtlessly inflict such shame and then are baffled by the hatred they discover they have incurred, but for which they can see no reason. How this can come about is illustrated by recent developments among the Nakanai.

An important symbol of the European way of life as the Nakanai know it is corrugated iron roofing. In their desire to achieve a pattern of life more like that of Europeans they established what they called a "company." All those who joined the company contributed to it whatever copra they produced. The copra was traded for corrugated iron, which was then distributed to the company's members in accordance with a system of priorities so that they could build "new style" houses. Delivery of the first sheets of iron roofing was a momentous occasion, calling for a big public celebration and much self-congratulation. Here was a token of what they could do with their company and tangible evidence of an important step in the realization of their identity goals. To most local Europeans the venture was thoroughly impractical. The uninsulated houses were impossibly hot during the day, as the Nakanai themselves admitted. In European eyes possession of corrugated iron did not affect the identity of the Nakanai in the least bit, but served mainly to reinforce the existing European image of the native as improvident and impractical. Some who were interested in their welfare, instead of congratulating the company's leaders on their achievement, bent their efforts to dissuade them from buying corrugated iron at all, urging them to use their income for things the Europeans felt they needed instead. By thus showing themselves not to be with the Nakanai in this matter in which their ego aspirations were so heavily involved, these Europeans found themselves regarded with suspicion.

Here we see illustrated one of the most difficult problems in community development. Once a community's members have clearly in mind the identity they wish to achieve for themselves, they are as eager to acquire the symbols of the new identity as to obtain its substance, if not more so, for without the symbols they cannot properly present themselves to others and gain their recognition and acceptance. This concern with symbols has been a frequent annoyance to development agents. We are often baffled, for example, by the insistence of heads of client governments that a steel mill must have top priority or that the acquisition of modern weapons must take precedence over agricultural improvement. What these clients want are the things that symbolize to them the prestigious identity of western powers in the community of nations. Without these symbols, they cannot present themselves as the others' social equals any more than the Nakanai feel they can show themselves to be as good as Europeans without corrugated iron roofs. Nor can government heads present themselves favorably to those from whom they derive political support as leaders without taking positive steps to meet the people's aspirations for their nation. It is not so important that the steel mill produce steel efficiently, or at all, or that the weapons really alter their military position in any appreciable way. What matters is the nation's ability to present itself in proper attire. Refusal to help in these "impractical" projects, as experience has shown us, serves only to earn the ill will of our clients. It does not incline them to follow our advice and engage in what we regard as practical or worthwhile projects instead. In an earlier chapter we remarked that what a community *needs* in the development situation is not so much a matter of fact as a matter to be negotiated. Here we see one of the reasons.

Once committed to changing their identities, people often have not one but several possible models from which to choose, any one of which they perceive as possessing identity features of the sort they deem desirable. To become recognized as an equal among the leading nations of the world, the younger nations emerging from colonial status have among others the United States, France, Great Britain, and the Soviet Union as possible judges and models. As they try to develop their new national

identities, the degree of acceptance and recognition they anticipate receiving from each of these nations may be a more important consideration in their selection of models among them than
the amount of material aid received from them. On a smaller
scale we observe how acceptance as equals by one group of whites
and nonacceptance by another is affecting the choices of Sioux
Indians who are seeking assimilation in the larger American
society.

The tradespeople, well-to-do farmers, and government employees, who form the middle class of South Dakota and Nebraska, look
upon most Indians as socially and economically inferior. The Indians
who are acceptable to this white group are those whose education,
employment, and social behavior are like their own.

There is, however, another group of whites in the area to whom
the Indians, especially the mixed-bloods, are more acceptable and
with whom there is some intermarriage. This group is largely composed of the poorer farmers and townspeople, often those who live on
the "wrong side of the track." Because of the greater freedom of social
relationships with these white people, the Indians are adopting their
pattern of living and their social attitudes and values. In other
words, the Indians are merging to a greater degree with the lower
than with the middle class of South Dakota whites.*[14]

We conclude that a program that undertakes seriously to alter
the collective self-image of its clients must attend to the problem
of outside recognition. In presenting the client community with
models for its new identity, agents must consider whether those
who serve as models will be willing to play their part in the development process. Whatever models seem most suitable, agents
must also plan to give high priority to their clients' desire to
acquire the symbols of their new identity, disregarding any other
practical value they may have. As agents we have too often
thought mainly of the substance of change, while our clients were
thinking largely of the symbols. The fact is that both are essential
to identity change.

* Reprinted by permission from Gordon MacGregor, *Warriors Without Weapons:
A Study of the Society and Personality of the Pine Ridge Sioux.* University of
Chicago Press, Chicago, p. 84. Copyright 1946 by The University of Chicago.

THE SENSE OF NEW IDENTITY

The ultimate requisite of identity change is a consolidated sense of self as the new kind of person one hoped to become. Alterations in self-image of a sort with which people are unhappy may be needed to stimulate a desire for change, as we have seen. And alterations of self-image, at least of a destructive nature, are normally involved in the act of commitment to identity change, as we have also observed. Now we are concerned with a new sense of self of a more positive sort, that which, for the time at least, marks the end of the entire process, which is the fruition of the requisites for identity change already discussed. Indeed, the act of commitment, the acquisition of new skills, and treatment by others in accordance with one's new identity are among the things that help a person *feel* that he has changed and changed in a certain way. As this feeling increases, it in turn provides the self-confidence needed to complete and consolidate the identity change.

The device of self-confrontation, which we have already discussed, is one of several by which people try to help their fellows get this feeling of change. Another technique is to subject a person to a new and extremely trying experience, so that once he has been through it he can never feel the same about himself again. This is a standard feature of initiation procedures. Still another effective measure is permanently to alter a person's physical appearance. The sense of new identity conveyed by the plastic surgeon's art is a well-known phenomenon. Similar effects are accomplished among nonwestern peoples by such practices as circumcision, scarification, tattooing, and the knocking out of teeth. Their association with rites initiating boys and girls into young adulthood is far too common to be coincidental. The explanation that such physical cruelties reflect the jealousies or other resentments of elders at encroachments on what had been their exclusive preserves is unconvincing. That such rites do allow people to indulge any sadistic tendencies they may have and to work off the hostilities they feel, whatever their origin, is obvious enough, and jealousy may be a contributing factor. The consistent association of such practices with identity change, however, requires us to examine more fully the role they play in such change.

From this point of view, circumcision obviously subjects a youth to a new and trying experience. Physically and experientially his former identity is dead. At the same time he has been dramatically provided with the means of identifying himself with other adult men, who have all had the same experience and bear the same mark of it. Sharing such experience contributes to the common sentiments without which there can be no we-feeling or mutual identification and empathy among past initiates. It is noteworthy that death and rebirth are common themes explicitly associated with the various ordeals and mysteries characterizing the more elaborate transition rites. We also observe that anthropologists reporting on initiation ceremonies among nonwestern peoples frequently receive the impression from their older informants that the ordeals were much more severe in former times. Drill sergeants likewise impress on military trainees how much tougher basic training was in their day. While sometimes true, we suspect that this is a standard part of the mythology by which those who already possess the identity that the initiates are expected to acquire render themselves more impressive as models to be emulated.

Visions and hallucinations provide another form of intense experience leading to an altered view of self. Many American Indian tribes cultivated such experiences as essential to identity changes in the direction of traditional ego-ideals. Not the physical ordeals by which to induce such visions, but the visions themselves provided the critical experiences, as is revealed in the autobiography of a Winnebago. Finding himself unable to have a vision, he faked one to qualify for manhood, only to be pursued by self-doubt for the rest of his life.[15] Intense mystical experiences are not uncommon among members of our own society, but those who have them have difficulty persuading their fellows to recognize and accept the new identity they feel themselves to have, unless the whole experience conforms to the pattern prescribed by the religious sect with which they and their families and friends are affiliated.

As we shall see, new self-development movements often get their start because of a profound experience in which many people share, so that they feel their identities to be affected not only as individuals but also as groups. Thus, presumably, were the despondent disciples collectively transformed by the vision of the risen Jesus. So, too, were all those who were seized by religious ecstasy in the Admiralty Islands on hearing that the "cargo" ship had been sighted and would arrive momentarily.[16] All the villages that underwent this experience joined together to build themselves a new identity in the white man's image. That the ship did not arrive, was beside the point. It is significant that individuals in these villages who for various reasons had missed this experience were the ones who were seized by similar ecstasy several years later. Though residing in the new communities established in the wake of the first mass experience and presumably dedicated participants in the movement that followed, it seems that they could not feel themselves to be *bona fide* in their new identities until they, too, had had the same mystical experience.[17] Similarly, it was Paul's later vision of Christ that justified his regarding himself as one of the apostles.

Whether or not it is mystical, somewhere in the course of development a community's members must have an experience that dramatizes their new selves to themselves, such as success in an undertaking in which they could not have thought of themselves as successful before. "Look what I can do!" is the child's way of expressing it. Once they have had such an experience, moreover, people seek to repeat it, which brings us to a final point.

As people come to feel themselves as having a new, desired identity, they court for a while every opportunity to experience themselves in it, thereby to consolidate it. They display the badges of their new identity whenever they can find an excuse. They demand that others treat them in accordance with whatever new rights their new identity gives them, insisting on every prerogative. They display whatever new powers they may have acquired, flexing their muscles and exerting their new found power at the slightest provocation. They strut their stuff before mirrors and seek to convert the world into one large mirror of their new selves. We are familiar enough with such behavior in our children, also in ourselves. One of the difficult things we have to learn as we grow older is how to contain it within the bounds of good taste. We are familiar with it, too, in connection with national movements, as when the Nazis, full of their new selves, sought to make the world a reflection of their self-image. Unfortunately, it appears that one of the facts of life is this tendency for people who have experienced identity change to make themselves obnoxious to their fellows. This tendency may be expressed only in a mild bumptiousness, or it may produce more aggressive and, at times, even horrendous behavior. How it is manifested depends on the nature of the new identity and the role it plays as an outlet for pent-up frustrations of the past. Thus people who have been waiting for a chance to push others around will revel in whatever powers their new identity gives them, while others, with different emotional orientations, may act pompously.

With changes in individual identity, the community has effective means of control that keep the attendant behavior within tolerable limits. Since the changes are routine for the members of the society, the whole process becomes standardized, and people know that their fellows go through stages when they tend to be a bit difficult and make allowances for them. The new identities being tested and consolidated, moreover, are ones that have a recognized place in the social order and to which those assuming them are entitled. These controls tend to weaken and disappear entirely when identity change is experienced collectively. Indeed, when a whole community undergoes change, acquisition of its new collective identity is likely to be marked by the creation of a new social order. The very conception of the new order is a projection of hitherto constrained emotional forces, and its structure is designed to give these forces free play. Emergent nationhood brings a new identity that allows people to repay their former masters for past humiliations of second-class citizenship. The least the new nations can do to demonstrate to others and to themselves that they are indeed nations and no longer colonies is to proclaim themselves neutral in the international quarrels of their former colonial masters. To support them is to be in no different a position from their previous one. They have to prove to themselves and to others that they are free not to support them. Only afterward can they render support and have it appear as a voluntary decision by free men. It has taken us Americans almost two hundred years to get over having to prove to the English that we are as good as they are. In development, as in other identity change, our clients need to get the feel of themselves in their new identities, to confirm to themselves that they now are what they have hoped to become. So the Soviet Union must demonstrate achievement of first rank as a world power by humbling those who were reluctant to accord her recognition; and as of this writing, Cuba's government leaves no stone unturned to impress upon us that there is a new Cuba that is no longer the economic servant of the United States, while at the same time damning us for discontinuing her wages. Even when our clients' aspirations are most laudable and we have been most exemplary in our role as development agents, we cannot realistically expect them to refrain from feeling their oats. If we are prepared for the fact that our development efforts, if successful, are likely to be rewarded by bumptious and aggressive behavior with strong narcissistic overtones, we will be able to respond to it with greater tolerance as a trying but normal phase of the development process.

SUGGESTED READING

Chapple, Eliot Dismore, and Carleton Stevens Coon, *Principles of Anthropology*. Henry Holt and Co., New York, 1942, chap. 20.

Cottrell, Leonard S., "The Adjustment of the Individual to His Age and Sex Roles," *American Sociological Review*, vol. 7, 1942, pp. 617–620.

Eisenstadt, S. M., "Reference Group Behavior and Social Integration: An Exploratory Study," *American Sociological Review*, vol. 19, 1954, pp. 175–185.

Erikson, Erik H., *Identity and the Life Cycle*. Psychological Issues Monograph 1, International Universities Press, New York, 1959.

Hagen, Everett E., *On the Theory of Social Change:* How Economic Growth Begins. The Dorsey Press, Homewood, Ill., 1962.

Van Gennep, Arnold, *The Rites of Passage*. University of Chicago Press, Chicago, 1960.

Whiting, John W. M., Richard Kluckhohn, and Albert Anthony, "The Function of Male Initiation Ceremonies at Puberty" in Maccoby, Eleanor E., Theodore M. Newcomb, and Eugene L. Hartley, editors, *Readings in Social Psychology*. 3d ed., Henry Holt and Co., New York, 1958, pp. 359–370.

NOTES TO CHAPTER 9

1. Also known as "rites of passage," following the pioneering work by Arnold van Gennep, *Les Rites de Passage: Études Systématiques des Rites*, Emile Nourry, Paris, 1909 (recently issued in English translation as *The Rites of Passage*, University of Chicago Press, Chicago, 1960). Among these rites van Gennep distinguishes "rites of separation," "transition rites," and "rites of incorporation," seeing the process of identity change as having three major phases. One or another of these phases may receive special ritual emphasis, depending on the nature of the problems associated with a change. See also Chapple, Eliot Dismore, and Carleton Stevens Coon, *Principles of Anthropology*, Henry Holt and Co., New York, 1942, pp. 484–506.

2. This position is expounded at length, for example, by T. R. Batten in *Communities and Their Development: An Introductory Study with Special Reference to the Tropics*, Oxford University Press, London, 1957. It is the explicit goal in terms of which the Moturiki project in Fiji was conceived, as reported by Howard Hayden in *Moturiki: A Pilot Project in Community Development*, Oxford University Press, New York, 1954.

3. All of my children, on encountering their first Negro some time after they began to respond to people as individuals, showed unmistakable signs that they immediately perceived him as strangely and disturbingly different from other people, to my embarrassment. They did not have to be taught that there was a difference; what they had to be taught was to ignore that difference. If, however, Negroes and whites had both been a part of their daily environment from birth on, they would have seen this difference in the same light as other differences in physical appearance among individuals and, if they lived where social discriminations were based on skin color, they would have had to be taught to make something special of this particular difference.

4. Rogers, Carl R., *Client Centered Therapy*, Houghton Mifflin Co., Boston, 1951. See also the excellent discussion of the therapeutic process by John Dollard and Neal E. Miller, *Personality and Psychotherapy: An Analysis in Terms of Learning, Thinking, and Culture*, McGraw-Hill Co., New York, 1950.

5. Hayden, Howard, *op. cit.*, p. 43, implies this when he says that "the general stock taking . . . had made the people of Moturiki very conscious of their problems."

6. *Ibid.*, pp. 115–126.

7. Lynd, Helen Merrell, *On Shame and the Search for Identity*. Harcourt, Brace and Co., New York, 1958.

8. See Kuykendall, Ralph S., *The Hawaiian Kingdom, 1778–1854:* Foundation and Transformation, University of Hawaii Press, Honolulu, 1947, pp. 65–70. See also the interpretation of this event by A. L. Kroeber, *Anthropology*, rev. ed., Harcourt, Brace and Co., New York, 1948, pp. 403–405.

9. Mead, Margaret, *Growing Up in New Guinea:* A Comparative Study in Primitive Education, Willlam Morrow and Co., New York, 1930, reissued as a Mentor Book, New York, 1953; and by the same author, *New Lives for Old:* Cultural Transformation—Manus 1928–1953, William Morrow and Co., New York, 1956.

10. Pospisil, Leopold, "Social Change and Primitive Law: Consequences of a Papuan Legal Case," *American Anthropologist*, vol. 60, 1958, pp. 832–837.

11. Mead, Margaret, *New Lives for Old:* Cultural Transformation—Manus 1928–1953.

12. Riesman, David, Nathan Glazier, and Reuel Denny, *The Lonely Crowd:* A Study of Changing American Character. Doubleday Anchor Books, Garden City, N.Y., 1954, pp. 32–40. Our thesis as to the conditions that produce "other-directedness" obviously differs from Riesman's.

13. Gross, Neal, Eugene A. Wilkening, and others, *Sociological Research on the Diffusion and Adoption of New Farm Practices:* Report of the Sub-Committee on the Diffusion and Adoption of Farm Practices. Rural Sociological Society, Kentucky Agricultural Experiment Station, University of Kentucky, June, 1952. See also Katz, Elihu, "The Social Itinerary of Technical Change: Two Studies on the Diffusion of Innovation," *Human Organization*, vol. 20, no. 2, 1961, pp. 70–82.

14. MacGregor, Gordon, *Warriors Without Weapons:* A Study of the Society and Personality of the Pine Ridge Sioux. University of Chicago Press, Chicago, 1946, p. 84.

15. Radin, Paul, editor, *Crashing Thunder:* The autobiography of an American Indian. D. Appleton-Century Co., New York, 1926.

16. Mead, Margaret, *op. cit.*

17. Schwartz, Theodore, *The Paliau Movement in the Admiralty Islands—1946 to 1954.* Anthropological Papers of the American Museum of Natural History, vol. 49, part 2, New York, 1962.

Chapter 10

DIMENSIONS OF COMMUNITY
CHANGE

OUR REVIEW of what happens in identity change has prepared us
to understand the emotional accompaniments of change in a
people's way of life. But before we consider them further, we must
turn our attention to the ways in which communities themselves
change. If our discussion is to lead to understandings of practical
value, it will be necessary to introduce some concepts with which
most readers are likely to be unfamiliar. These concepts, moreover, will require a shift in the reader's established habits of
thought. This chapter, therefore, will demand close attention.
What we have to say, however, is essential for understanding
change processes. The reader will have to resign himself to a
slower pace. In the next chapter the pace will pick up again.

REAL AND PHENOMENAL CHANGE

When we talk about change, we often have reference to a community's conditions as they, presumably, really are—the way
they appear to us as natural scientists. The community is a part
of the real world, as distinct from the way men see it, and this real
world is presumably infinitely variable and continuously changing. Nor can any part of it change without some other part being
affected.

There is a sense, of course, in which the real world, or parts of
it, may achieve relative stability for periods of time. Stability
arises when mutual causes and effects in change counterbalance
one another so that the flow of change tends to remain within

narrow limits. As the real world approaches such equilibrium, the course of change comes closer and closer to repeating itself in time. The flow of events becomes confined to narrower bands of variability, retracing much the same routes over and over again, as in the annual round of the seasons and the recurring sequence of birth, growth, decay, and death. The limits within which variation is confined may also change without affecting the relative stability of a system in equilibrium. And the changes in limits may themselves tend to be cyclical, as with shifts from warmer to colder to warmer winters. All of nature, indeed, can be conceived as containing more or less internally stable systems which are the components of larger and yet larger ones, from atoms to stellar galaxies, from individual cells to complex organisms, and from single species to ecological systems. No part of the real world, of course, is perfectly stable, though it may appear to hang in a state of balance for some time, especially when viewed macroscopically. But the repetition of events within it is never exact, merely a modal clustering of tracks. These modal clusterings, however, are essential to human cognition, for in their absence people would be unable to discern discontinuities in their surroundings by which to discriminate categories of phenomena and thus build the percepts and concepts with which they discern the real world, cognitively organize it, and orient themselves in it.

Any human community presents itself to us as a distinct entity because it is a relatively stable system, a sort of galaxy of people and things whose mutual attractions and repulsions keep them continuously rearranging themselves over roughly similar tracks, the several tracks changing the mutual arrangement of their course spirally through time, the pathways sometimes narrowing to make statistically tighter patterns and sometimes widening, perhaps to the point where equilibrium is so far lost that the galaxy dissolves. We can think of contact between communities as like the collision of galaxies in space, the modal patterns of arrangements and rearrangements in each being modified as a result of their mutual intrusion. When we investigate a community from this detached perspective, our concern is to record everything that is really happening, on the assumption that we are all-seeing observers and that, as scientists, we are interested only in observable facts. Not knowing what the facts that we observe mean, we count them and sort them statistically, and invent theories to rationalize the results. When we talk from this naturalistic viewpoint about the ways in which customary practices (the modal tracks of behavioral events) relate to one another and to other modally recurring events, we have reference to their functions (as distinct from their meanings) as discussed in Chapter 4. When we want to understand how a community's customs change in their function, we try to see how the community is changing as a relatively stable system in the real world.

But customary practices can be viewed as something other than the modal tracks of behavioral events; they can be seen as sequences of behavioral forms, whose order of occurrence makes sense in terms of the systems of cognition and belief of the performers. This brings us to another way in which we may consider community change: change in a community's conditions, not as they really are, but as they appear to its members (or anyone else) in terms of their criteria for perceiving them. Here we are thinking of the community as a part of someone's phenomenal world and are concerned with how that phenomenal world appears to be changing.

The world as people see it and understand it, as they have it cognitively organized, is composed of discerned forms, forms of things and forms of relationships. Like the real world, it is constantly changing, but here change appears as discrete, qualitative shifts from one combination of percepts to another, from one form of thing or arrangement to another. Since the number of forms discernible with a given set of percepts is finite, change is more narrowly confined than in the real world, so that the phenomenal world is capable of achieving a higher degree of apparent stability. To be meaningful to others, human behavior must conform to a shared system of forms; and to accomplish their purposes, people must try to maintain their phenomenal world in certain arrangements and confine events within it to particular recurring sequences of forms. Therefore, people actively work to stabilize their phenomenal world and to make the course of change within it more narrowly repetitive. As the same categories of event repeat themselves in recurring sequences and associations, people can formulate propositions about them that have empirical validity and from which they can predict future events in their phenomenal world with considerable accuracy. The recurring association of particular forms with their own feelings of gratification lead people to value the forms in their phenomenal world—and this, in turn, allows people to have purposes. The propositions they formulate permit them to devise tactics for acting on their phenomenal world so as to accomplish their purposes. Indeed, all meaningful behavior is aimed at maintaining or changing arrangements within a phenomenal world and can be understood only in relation to the perceptual and other cognitive criteria that give it form and structure.

Phenomenal Novelty

Because people can perceive the changes that are taking place in the real world only when they are of sufficient magnitude to be noted by their percepts—thus producing a change in their phenomenal world—they often become aware of change in one place before they notice concomitant change in another. They frequently perceive a change that results from another earlier change before they perceive the change that caused it. To some degree, therefore, events in the phenomenal world appear mysterious and unpredictable, as the inevitable limitations of people's perceptual categories (to say nothing of their senses themselves) lead them to observe effects without observing their causes. Such mysterious and unpredictable changes as occur undermine people's beliefs about the nature of things, demanding ever new rationalizations, and invite them to develop new percepts or new combinations of percepts and thus cognitively to reorganize their phenomenal world. Thus the phenomenal world is subject to change both as the real world changes and also as people change the cognitive criteria by which they see it.

A great deal of novelty can occur within the phenomenal world, however, without seriously affecting one's criteria for cognitively organizing experience. If we think of phenomena as composed of elementary forms (minimal percept combinations), arranged and combined into more complex forms, then most observed change will be in the structure of the more complex forms, at the higher levels of conceptual organization. This can be seen most clearly in the case of linguistic forms, whose structure has been more fully analyzed, thanks to alphabetic writing, than that of any other system of cognitively organized forms. Each elementary speech form, a *phoneme*, is itself composed of a combination of percepts, each percept being what distinguishes it from some other phoneme in the same language. Thus in English the phoneme we represent with the letter "t" is distinguished from "p," "k," and "ch" by position of articulation in the mouth, from "d" by lack of voicing, and from "n" by both lack of voicing and lack of nasalization. The percepts whose combinations comprise each phoneme are the discriminations we make along the acoustical dimensions we call articulation, voicing, and nasalization (describing the effect on the hearer's ear by referring to what happens in the speaker's mouth to produce the effect). The phonemes, in turn, are combined into the more complex forms we call words, and the words into phrases, the phrases into sentences, and the sentences into messages. The messages we hear are often new, even after we have mastered English, but the words we hear are seldom new, and the phonemes we hear are never new.

The degree to which a change appears novel, moreover, depends on the level of complexity at which it takes place. A new combination of already familiar complex forms will appear less strange than a new combination of already familiar elementary forms. The coined word *shild* (to rhyme with *child*) is a new combination of already familiar lesser combinations of elementary English sound forms (*shi-*, *-ild*) as witness the words *shy, shire, shined, mild, child, riled*. For this reason, it appears less strange than such coinages as *ngild* or *shchild*, for there is no precedent in English for a word to begin with the *ng* sound, nor for the juxtaposition of the elementary sound forms *sh* and *ch* within the same word. The fact that *ng, sh,* and *ch,* are elementary sound forms in English, however, and that we are already used to their occurring in such expressions as *wrong aisle* and *rash child*, makes these more novel coinages present fewer problems cognitively than we experience when we try to follow someone who speaks English with a marked foreign accent. In this case, the speaker is trying to produce the more complex combinations of forms that comprise English words and sentences by combining elementary sound forms from his native language, which are novel to English and which force the English hearer to make new perceptual discriminations and to work out equations between these new (to him) sound forms and those to which he is already accustomed. Much more disruptive cognitively is a situation where we need to orient ourselves in a German or French speaking community. Many of the discriminations we have developed for bringing maximum order to a world in which English is spoken are rendered useless. All we can discern from a babble of confused noise are a few tones of voice. The job of developing a new set of discriminations so as to bring order out of this apparent chaos is a long and arduous one.

Turning to other examples, consider the invention of radio, television, airplanes, and now space vehicles, and the extensive changes they have wrought in our phenomenal world. While they have required us to modify our beliefs and have led us to develop new propositions about things, they have not left most of us with a sense of utter confusion or even with a feeling of moderate cognitive disorientation. The system of elementary forms with which we work was not rendered unusable by these developments. Things still stand in the same kinds of spatial arrangements, have the same colors, are subject to the law of gravity, and so on. Change was mostly at the level of highly complex combinations of forms. It was as if we were having to listen to new poems with rhyme schemes we had never heard before and using the English language in ways that had never occurred to us, but poems put together out of familiar English words in accordance with the familiar principles of English grammar so that they were at once meaningful despite all of their novelty.

CULTURE*

It should be evident from what we have said so far that we may examine economic and social change in a community as changes

* Much in this section appears in substantially the same form in Goodenough, Ward H., "Comments on Cultural Evolution," *Daedalus*, vol. 90, 1961, pp. 521–528. Grateful acknowledgment is herewith made to the American Academy of Arts and Sciences for permission to use this material.

in the real world (the phenomenal world of the scientist) or as changes in the phenomenal world of its members. Most analyses of change follow one or the other approach, or mix up the two without clearly distinguishing between them. A great deal of what is called "cultural" change in social scientific literature also amounts to no more than change in a community's real or phenomenal conditions, only incidentally including changes in the criteria by which people discern things, their beliefs about things, their purposes in relation to them, or their principles for dealing with them. These are among the things, however, that most anthropologists seem to have in mind, some precisely and some more vaguely, when they speak of a community's culture—the things we attribute to its members' heads and hearts in order to make sense out of what they do.

With this in mind, anthropologists frequently define culture as the shared products of human learning.[2] More precisely these may be said to comprise:

1. The ways in which people have organized their experience of the real world so as to give it structure as a phenomenal world of forms, that is, their percepts and concepts.

2. The ways in which people have organized their experience of their phenomenal world so as to give it structure as a system of cause and effect relationships, that is, the propositions and beliefs by which they explain events and design tactics for accomplishing their purposes.

3. The ways in which people have organized their experience of their phenomenal world so as to structure its various arrangements in hierarchies of preferences, that is, their value or sentiment systems. These provide the principles for selecting and establishing purposes and for keeping oneself purposefully oriented in a changing phenomenal world.

4. The ways in which people have organized their experience of their past efforts to accomplish recurring purposes into operational procedures for accomplishing these purposes in the future, that is, a set of "grammatical" principles of action and a series of recipes for accomplishing particular ends. They include operational procedures for dealing with people as well as for dealing with material things.

Culture, then, consists of standards for deciding what is, standards for deciding what can be, standards for deciding how one feels

about it, standards for deciding what to do about it, and standards for deciding how to go about doing it.

A community's culture in this sense should never be confused
with its culture in the sense of the patterns of recurring events
and arrangements that characterize the community as a relatively stable system. The relationship that the former bears to the
latter is crudely analogous to the biological relationship that
genes bear to the phenotypic characteristics of a population. In
order to understand community change we must be able to see
how changes in its culture in the one sense relate to changes in its
culture in the other, which we cannot do if we fail to hold them
apart in our thinking. In order to avoid confusion, therefore, we
shall hereafter refer to change in the patterns characterizing a
community as a system in equilibrium from a scientist's viewpoint as change in the community as a *real system*. We shall refer
to change in these patterns from the viewpoint of the community's members as change in the community as a *phenomenal
system*. And we shall refer to changes in its member's organization
of experience, their standards for perceiving, predicting, judging,
and acting, as changes in their *culture*.

To illustrate the distinction, there are a whole series of changes
in the patterns of relations among people in the United States
that have followed the invention of the automobile. All of them,
whether we are aware of them or not, are changes in our national
community as a real system. The changes that we perceive, in
the form that we perceive them, are changes in our national
community as a phenomenal system. The changes in our ideas
about things and in our principles of conduct, as for example in
courtship, are changes in our culture.

As we have defined culture, no two persons can be said to have
exactly the same. How, then, can we speak of a community's culture? In what way can we consider culture as we are defining it
to be shared? These questions require us to clarify further what
it is we are talking about.

Culture and the Individual

A part of every man's personal organization of experience is
his conception of how his fellows have organized *their* experience,

his conception of the standards by which they perceive, predict, judge, and act. With it he predicts their reactions to events, especially the ways in which they will perceive, judge, and react to his own behavior. He discovers, moreover, that he can control the reactions of his fellows and accomplish his purposes involving them only insofar as he gains a reasonably valid conception of what their standards are and uses them as a guide for his own actions, makes them in effect his own, at least in the contexts in which he has dealings with them. Thus a child learns to deal with his schoolteachers according to what he believes to be their standards. He also finds that he can much more readily accomplish his purposes by discovering with his fellows' help their standards for dealing with his social and material surroundings than he can by trying to develop standards independently through trial and error. For these reasons, his efforts to arrive at an image of his fellows' standards are heavily reinforced as an efficient means for developing his own.

Each of us is aware of individual differences in our fellows and takes them into account when dealing with people we know intimately. But we also find modal tendencies among what we presume to be our fellows' individual sets of standards as they reveal them to us in their behavior and in the things they tell us. We discover that our conception of A's standards is a fairly valid guide not only to A's behavior but to B's as well, especially if B resembles A in many features of his identity and belongs to the same network of interactions and social participations as A does. Thus we develop a generalized image of the standards of others corresponding to what G. H. Mead called the "generalized other."[3] We discover, moreover, that there are limits beyond which we cannot safely generalize, that our experience of some people requires us to attribute different sets of standards to them, at least with respect to some contexts. So we learn that our teachers' standards in school are not always the same as our parents', and that the neighborhood gang of boys has still different standards.

In this way each individual's private culture, if we may call it that, includes his conception of several wholly or partially distinct cultures (some well elaborated and others only crudely developed in his mind) which he attributes to others individually and collectively, both within and without his community. A person's private culture is likely to include knowledge of more than one language, more than one system of etiquette, more than one set of beliefs, more than one hierarchy of choices, and more than one set of principles for getting things done.[4]

These other cultures have differential value for several reasons. From a practical standpoint, some are more useful as guides to a person's behavior in some contexts, and others are more useful in others. He is not likely to accomplish his ends using the culture he attributes to his tavern mates when engaging in social pleasantries with his boss's wife. A person shifts from one to another of the cultures in his repertoire as social contexts and his own purposes within them change, using this one as his guide here and another one as his guide there. The particular other culture he selects is for the time being his *operating culture*.

In the normal course of living, a person finds one or two of his several operating cultures most appropriate for his purposes most of the time. He develops considerable skill in operating according to their standards and is confident of himself when using them as his guide. When he resorts to other cultures that he uses rarely or not at all, he is clumsy, unsure of himself, and more vulnerable to embarrassment. Other things being equal, people obviously have a predilection for using as operating cultures the cultures in which they are already skilled. As others try to accommodate their behavior to fit what they believe to be his culture, moreover, a person discovers that he has some freedom of choice regarding the standards he will use to guide his behavior in dealing with them. There are limits, to be sure, beyond which they make it clear that they do not want him to go, but within those limits they are willing to accommodate him. He has some freedom, therefore, to modify his several operating cultures to fit his own private standards for himself, his physical capacities, his temperament, and whatever skills he has already developed. Thus he adapts them to fit his personal style. Some of the several other cultures of which he learns are more readily adaptable to his personal style than others. He prefers them as guides to his behavior in all contexts where their use is tolerated. He may even combine features of several different other cultures, synthesizing an operating culture that does not match any of the cultures he attributes to his fellows. In this way he is able to establish an identity peculiarly his own, one that defies ready classification by his fellows. Also governing a person's selection of other cultures as guides to his behavior are the identifications he makes. He prefers to use as his guide the culture he attributes to the individuals and groups with which he wishes to identify himself and with which he wishes to be identified by others, as when a parvenu tries to make his behavior conform to what he believes to be the standards of upper-class culture or a spy seeks to hide his foreign identity by conforming in every respect to the standards of speech, dress, and conduct he attributes to those with whom he wants his dupes to identify him. For such reasons as these, then, a person selects from among the various other cultures within his private culture—with some modification and recombination—those that serve as his several operating cultures.

The larger and more complex the society in which a person lives, the wider the range of other cultures of which he is likely to have knowledge and from which he can select. The individual who has lived extensively among alien peoples will likewise have acquired a variety of other cultures in his private culture. People, on the other hand, who have spent all of their lives having very limited contacts with any but their family and immediate neighbors will know of few other cultures from which they can select. An important consequence of increased interethnic contact is the increase in the number of other cultures in the private cultures of the individuals involved. Change in a person's phenomenal world and in the contexts in which he regularly finds himself, change in his purposes, and change in his identifications independently affect what culture among those available to him he will select as his operating culture.

Clearly, the selections people make, the considerations governing them, and the content of the cultures available for selection are major factors affecting the course of community change.

Culture and the Community

To come back to the question of the sense in which we can speak of a community as having a culture, it is obvious that the

generalized culture a person attributes to the aggregate membership of any social group is for him the culture of that group. For
any member of a community, its culture is the generalized culture
he attributes to all of its other members. For the outsider, such as
an anthropological observer, it is the generalized culture of all of
its members (who are all "others" to him).

Thus viewed, of course, the generalized culture of a community
is always a part of someone's private culture and, as such, cannot
be quite the same for any two individuals. Strictly speaking,
therefore, there is no one "true" description of a community's
culture possible. Presumably there are as many somewhat different working models of a community's generalized culture as there
are members of the community. All that an anthropologist can do
is to construct another model of his own. If it makes the behavior
of the community's members as predictable and understandable
to him as it is to them, and if used as a guide for his own behavior
it makes his conduct as intelligible to each of them in terms of
their models of their community's culture as is the behavior of
most of their fellows, then the model the anthropologist has constructed and which he describes to us as *the culture* of the community is a valid one, although he might have constructed another,
equally valid one.

But there is a sense in which a community may be said to have
a culture apart from its members' or an anthropologist's individual conceptions of it.

Regardless of the differences between their own private standards for themselves and those they attribute to their fellows,
people are usually at some pains not to reveal these differences in
their overt behavior. Insofar as a person tries to conduct himself
according to the standards he attributes to others, others are
likely to attribute to him a private culture that is in reality a reflection of his generalized culture for them. And it is their generalized cultures for others that people usually use as their operating cultures when their behavior is subject to others' scrutiny. As
people who have regular dealings with one another try to conform
to the generalized cultures they individually attribute to their
mutual fellowship and as they modify their individual conceptions of these cultures in order to increase their predictive value,

these conceptions will increasingly converge. Thus a high degree of consensus can develop both regarding the content of the generalized cultures they individually attribute to each other and consequently regarding the content of the operating cultures which they individually use to guide their interactions with one another. To the extent that there is close agreement of this sort among its members, a group may be said to have a *public culture*, a culture that its members share and that belongs to all of them as a group. The public culture of a community, together with the public cultures of its several subgroups, is what many anthropologists seem to have in mind when they speak of a community's culture;[5] and it is in this sense that we shall speak of a community's culture in this book. Corresponding to the four major aspects of culture outlined on page 258, a community's public culture consists of the perceptual and conceptual features embedded in the meanings of the vocabulary of its language and other public symbols,[6] a public body of knowledge and beliefs, a public value system, and a set of public conventions, rules, and recipes with regard to behavior and operational procedure.

In a simple, small community, there is likely to be a single public culture for all its members governing many activities in which they engage, with existing differences in operating cultures, such as they are, confined largely to different sex and age categories. Large, socially complex societies with many economic specialties have a common public culture that covers relatively few activities and situations. For other contexts of living each of the many subgroups has its separate public culture; and the several cultures may differ considerably. We have already touched on these differences and the problems they raise for social harmony in complex societies in our discussion of public values in Chapter 5.

As we shall see, the processes affecting change in a community's public culture are not the same as those affecting change in an individual's private culture or his selection of an operating culture. Considerable change in the private cultures of a community's members can occur, moreover, without corresponding changes in the public culture they all share. But before we turn to culture change, we must consider the relation of a culture to its artifacts and clarify what it is we have meant by "custom" in our previous discussions.

CULTURAL ARTIFACTS AND CUSTOMARY ROUTINES

All that we can see of a culture is its products or artifacts, the things people make, do, and say. Because we are able to make inferences about a culture's content only through the study of its artifacts, we rather easily confuse it with them; but failure to keep the two conceptually distinct blurs our understanding of change.

In one sense, a culture's artifacts include whatever its bearers observe in their phenomenal world, whose forms are artifacts of their percepts and concepts. This includes not only the things they observe in nature, but also the material things they make and the social arrangements and groupings they discern and create in their relations with one another. Indeed, we can say that a person's entire phenomenal world is an artifact of his culture. Thus what is for us an unidentified glow in the dark is a ghost for a Trukese. His culture makes the same event a different phenomenon for him from the one our culture makes it for us.

In another sense, and the one to be pursued more fully here, a culture's artifacts include all the states of affairs, whether in the phenomenal world of its bearers or of an outside observer, that have resulted from its bearers' actions. We may think of them, of course, as artifacts of behavior rather than of culture, but they can also be said to be artifacts of the operating cultures that guided the behavior producing them. Some artifacts in this sense are intended, as with the things people have manufactured, the rites and activities they have performed, and the social groups they have organized. For example, the idea of steel companies, the standards by which men organize them, by which they govern what they do in them, and to which they seek to make their products conform, these are a part of the culture of steel production in our society. But the various steel companies that actually exist in the United States, the things men actually do in them, and the things they make there are all artifacts of that culture. Other artifacts are unintended, such as the erosion of soil or the pollution of streams resulting from past farming and industrial practices.

Whether intended or unintended, once it has been produced and provided it has come to someone's attention, any cultural artifact can be used as a model. The idea of it becomes a standard for the construction of future artifacts. In this way, the relation of a culture to its artifacts is much like that of a language to the things its speakers say. The language is a set of models and standards for perceiving and constructing utterances, and the linguistic constructions people actually make—their sentences, essays, speeches, and poems—are artifacts of the language. Any of these linguistic constructions may become a model, however, for making future constructions. Included among them are what we call the clichés of speech, the standardized utterances we habitually employ to deal with recurring situations and problems. Similarly, cultural artifacts that prove to be particularly efficacious in handling recurring situations become the models for dealing with similar situations in the future. Thus the standards by which people get things done come to include a host of recipes and segments of recipes whose habitual use produces the standardized routines comprising their procedural clichés.

This brings us to customs, the routines by which people habitually deal with recurring situations. Of course, there are routines of which a person is aware but to which he does not habitually resort. Such routines are a part of his private culture but not a part of his operating culture. They have been tried and found less effective than others for accomplishing purposes under existing conditions, or their use would have an undesirable effect on the public image the user wishes to cultivate. Routines that are habitual at one period in a person's or a society's lifetime may cease to be so later. As long as people know of them, however, the recipes for these routines are no less a part of their culture and may be brought back into use in the future. A culture includes many more routines than those that are currently customary.

For any set of conditions, then, if there is a habitual routine by which people deal with it to accomplish a particular purpose, that is their custom for that purpose in those conditions.[7] Customs are the complex combinations of standards for action and social organization that provide prefabricated solutions to recurring problems and to which people regularly resort when faced with these problems. They are derived from those of a culture's past artifacts that have come to serve as models for the production of future artifacts, being the recipes by which people habitually make things, go about doing things, and organize their dealings with one another. As such they are an important part of a people's operating and public cultures. But they are a special part of these cultures. For in any situation that does not seem to permit the ready use of a customary routine, their cultures are a resource with which people improvise suitable courses of action. In the same way, although we conduct the ordinary business of life largely in terms of verbal clichés, combining and recombining the same old prefabricated phrases with a minimum of effort, when we want to be very precise in communicating an idea that is out of the ordinary, our language is a resource from which we create new word combinations to accomplish our purpose. Such creative use of one's language and culture, however, is hard work, and it may involve considerable trial and error before a combination is found that will accomplish one's ends. A handy kit of clichés and customs makes life less exciting and a lot more secure.

Customs and the Phenomenal System

Every recipe requires certain states of affairs in the phenomenal world for people to be able to act in accordance with it. A recipe may call for the use of certain raw or fabricated materials, all of which must be available. It may require a number of synchronized acts by several individuals, necessitating a minimum personnel. It also may call for certain kinds of skills for the design to be properly executed. Much human energy goes to maintain the phenomenal world in a state of readinesss so that the materiel, personnel, and skills required by customary recipes and routines are available. A community's store of manufactured goods and their distribution, its standing organizations of personnel, and the existing distribution and level of skills are not only features of the phenomenal world of its members; they are also artifacts of their culture. From their past experience of them, as of other artifacts, people develop standards that guide their efforts to maintain their world in a state of readiness affording optimal opportunity for conducting their affairs according to customary designs and routines. These standards for materiel, skills, and social organization become a part of their culture, guidelines for future action. But the skills people have actually mastered, the materiel they have stockpiled, the standing organizations of personnel they have created, these are artifactual features of their phenomenal world, and are maintained, like houses, roads, bridges, and fields, as requisite conditions for the operation of customary routines.

As features of the phenomenal world cultural artifacts may undergo all kinds of change that do not reflect changes in the cultural standards that produced them. Thus an organized group for hunting may be maintained under conditions when game is plentiful and be allowed to lapse when game becomes scarce, without any change in the cultural principles for organizing and maintaining such a group or for deciding when to organize one and when to let it lapse. In Truk, to take another example, when young people marry they expect to reside in an extended family household. Residence with the household with which the wife was affiliated before marriage is preferred, provided certain conditions obtain, but under other circumstances residence with the household with which the husband was affiliated is regarded as more appropriate. In a Trukese community some couples are living in one way and others in the other, depending on their circumstances, but all in accordance with the same cultural principles of household affiliation.[8] The percentages may vary considerably for different Trukese communities and change radically in time within the same community without there being a corresponding change in the cultural principles governing residence decisions. Such changes in the composition of households are of the same order as changes in the kind of clothing people put on in response to changes in the weather. Yet observers commonly make the mistake of assuming that observed changes in material, behavioral or social artifacts and their arrangements in a community necessarily reflect a change in its members' culture: in their values, principles of action, and standards for getting things done.

This highly fallacious assumption is constantly leading foreign and colonial officers, missionaries and development agents of all kinds to misinterpret events and to commit both strategic and tactical errors in executing policy. A common problem in community development, for example, is the reversion to past practices by a community's members once the agency removes itself from the scene. We have already noted how identity considerations relate to this problem. Even more important, probably, is the presence of the agency itself as a significant alteration of local circumstances, which makes changes of behavior and social organization appropriate within the framework of the community's culture. As long as the agency is present and affecting conditions consistently in a given direction, social and behavioral arrangements and routines may follow a pattern different from the one that used to obtain, not because the culture has changed but because circumstances have changed. When the agency withdraws and circumstances return to their former condition, the social arrangements and procedural routines by which people get things done return to previous patterns, also.[9] For a change to endure, either circumstances must continue to remain altered even after the agency withdraws, as when new roads have been built or new lands brought under cultivation, or the people's culture must have changed so that they no longer see or value old circumstances in the same way or employ the same principles for dealing with them. This is why achievement of an agency's development goals so often seems to require changes in people's cognition and beliefs, their values, and their principles for getting things done, to require, that is, extensive cultural change and intensive educational efforts to bring it about.

The concern people have for maintaining their world in a state of readiness so that their customary routines may be effectively put into operation as needed is matched by another concern. It is to keep their routines and recipes for action such that the skills they have mastered, the materiel they have stockpiled, and the standing organizations of personnel they have developed can all readily implement them. Changes in custom that do not require new skills, different materiel, or new organizational arrangements, but only the employment of existing ones in different combinations can be accomplished relatively easily, provided there are no special emotional attachments rendering their present mode of combination sacrosanct. But as soon as new skills, materiel, or standing organizations of personnel are involved, people find it harder to change their customary routines. It takes time and effort to develop them, and in the meantime life must go on. Such changes, therefore, present more serious logistical problems. As long as old activities can be continued while new ones are being experimented with and the necessary means for conducting them developed, this kind of more radical change remains feasible. But when development of the new can take place only after abandoning the old, as with new forms of community government or as with new methods of tillage where all the land available for cultivation is needed for subsistence, change appears to involve great risk.

It often happens that people perceive existing routines to be ineffective means to desired ends, but at the same time feel that they cannot risk the consequences of possibly unsuccessful experiments with new ones or of temporarily decreased effectiveness while mastering new skills. The resulting sense of being trapped, of wanting to change but fearing to risk it, is emotionally stressful. Proposed solutions that involve no apparent risk are especially welcome, such as those provided by rites, prayers, and other kinds of symbol manipulation. The adoption of less "safe" solutions is likely to be a convulsive act of the sort we have already discussed in connection with problems of commitment to identity change.

SOCIAL SYSTEMS AS CULTURAL ARTIFACTS

In Chapter 7 we noted that mutually satisfactory relations can be maintained between people who believe different things about the subject matter of their relationship. It is similarly possible for groups with different public cultures—and for individuals with different operating cultures—to interact in mutually gratifying ways without their having to develop an overall public culture that they all share. So long as their respective cultures are such as to lead them to behave in mutually predictable ways with results that are positively valued (though it may be for very different reasons), individuals and groups with different cultures can develop social systems in which they all participate but for which they have little or no culture in common. A social system, at least as viewed by an outside observer, is not necessarily, therefore, a part of the culture of any society.[10]

We see this clearly with complex economic or political systems. In the United States, for example, people with many different public and private cultures are daily making economic decisions that affect the conditions in which they will make future decisions. A consequence of all these decisions is a complicated series of productive, distributive and consummative acts whose mutual effects produce the fairly stable state of affairs we call our economic system. But the cultural features of which this system is an artifact, including the models of the system in people's minds, are by no means common to all who participate in it. It is obvious, moreover, that the shapes of international economic systems are largely determined by the actions of people who are culturally oblivious to these systems' existence. For those anthropologists who choose to equate culture with such systems in the phenomenal world of the scientific observer, people do not *have* cultures but *participate* in them.[11] As we have defined culture, however, its ultimate locus is within individuals. The economic and social systems we observe in operation are created and maintained as products or by-products of culturally guided human action and, as such, are artifacts of culture. Some systems are artifacts largely of one public culture, others are artifacts of the simultaneous operation of a number of cultures. There are economic and social systems, therefore, that may be properly characterized as multicultural, such as those in many colonial areas. But in labeling things cultural because they are the products of cultures, we must remember not to confuse things that are cultural with culture.

Community development is obviously much more directly concerned with change in economic and social systems and in cultural artifacts generally than it is with change in culture *per se*. Changes in artifactual systems depend primarily on changes in the content of customary routines. Some such changes can be made without any cultural change, resulting simply from the receipt of information that according to existing principles calls for reliance on well-understood, but hitherto little used, alternative modes of action. Changes of this kind can often be achieved in a fairly orderly manner. To make other changes in their phenomenal world, of course, people have to have changed their culture first; and changes in artifacts may in time lead to change in culture with far-reaching effects on the course of future events. Indeed, a cycle of change in a community may start with changes in customary activities and modifications in the artifacts people seek to maintain, or it may start with changes in culture, in the perceptions, values, and beliefs of members of the society. Once started, of course, either kind of change tends to stimulate the other kind as well, both then going along together and each feeding back on the other. To understand community change, therefore, and to forecast its consequences, it is necessary to consider both culture and its material, social, behavioral, and emotional artifacts together.

CULTURE CHANGE

We have now isolated the major variables to be considered in analyzing community change: the private cultures of a community's members; their operating cultures; the community's public culture and the public culture of its subgroups; the material, social, and behavioral conditions which the community's members, guided by their cultural resources, try to maintain in their phenomenal world and which are their cultural artifacts; and the customary routines by which they seek to produce and maintain the conditions they desire. We are ready, therefore, to consider how cultures change.

Change in Private Culture

Change may be in any of the four major aspects of culture delineated above: percepts and concepts, propositions and beliefs, values and sentiments, and principles of action and operational recipes. It may be in the form of additions to or refinements of existing organizations of experience, or it may involve the acquisition of completely new organizations of experience parallel to those already developed, as with the learning of a new language. Change may also be a reorganization of past organizations of experience. Whatever form change takes, its results represent additions to one's private culture, not replacements within it. Replacement is an aspect of change in operating culture but not in private culture. Any percept, proposition, sentiment, or principle of action, once learned, remains a part of an individual's personal cultural repertoire, whether or not he operates in terms of it.

Changes in private culture necessarily arise in connection with a person's efforts to organize new experience or relate himself purposefully to conditions that he cannot handle successfully with his existing culture. The things he expects to happen don't happen, and he is baffled and confused. Under such conditions, people feel a need either to expand and develop further their private cultures or to insulate themselves in some way from any further experiences for which their existing culture is inadequate. Thus some immigrants to a new country make strenuous efforts to learn all the things they must know in order to orient themselves properly in their new social milieu, while others try to have dealings only with fellow immigrants from their homeland so as to avoid the necessity of expanding their private cultures. In connection with the latter reaction, the writer and his fellow research workers in the War Department in World War II discovered that those soldiers who complained and were uncooperative when they were asked to fill out attitude and opinion survey questionnaires were also invariably men of low Army General Classification Test score, that is, men whose private cultures for whatever reason were not up to dealing with the survey situation. Feeling painfully inadequate, they rejected the situation in which they found themselves. They became thoroughly cooperative, however, when they were not asked to read and fill out the questionnaire but were interviewed orally by trained interviewers instead. Whether people will try to meet the challenge of a new situation by expanding their private cultures or will respond to it negatively and seek to withdraw depends not only on how important it seems to them, but on such things as their ability to learn, their confidence in their ability, and the degree to which they see themselves as having an adequate opportunity to learn.

The conditions that cause people to feel a need to expand their private cultures may themselves be artifacts of an alien culture or they may simply result from the operation of impersonal forces in the real world. When there is another culture available to be learned and when there are people willing to help one learn it, expansions in private culture are easier to make than when no other culture has yet evolved that will make experience meaningful. In the latter case, people are in the position of the natural scientist, who is having to create a new culture to bring order to the phenomena he studies, a slow process indeed. However much effort it may take, it is quicker to add to one's private culture by trying to learn a different other culture, using the behavior of others as a guide. It is a lot easier to learn to speak and act like a Frenchman or a Samoan, especially while living with Frenchmen and Samoans, than it is to invent a language and culture that has no precedent. For this reason major additions to people's private cultures (after they have achieved adulthood) are almost invariably stimulated by their contact with people in other societies (or subgroups in their own society) and by the intrusion into their phenomenal world of the strange artifacts of alien cultures.

Private cultures, we have observed, change not only through the addition of new generalized other cultures but also through the reorganization of their existing content. These reorganizations also represent an addition to previous organizations of experience, which are lost from a person's private culture only very slowly over long periods of disuse, as with a language that he has not spoken for a long time. But the novelty is now essentially in the recombination of basic elements already present in a person's private culture. The reordering may be confined to one of the several other cultures comprising his private culture, or it may involve bringing together in a single systematic arrangement elements that were compartmentalized in different other cultures, as when a person incorporates a meaning he has discovered in one language into the system of meanings in another and coins an appropriate word to represent it. This process is familiar to us in religious syncretism. We shall have more to say about it in a moment when we consider changes in customary routines.

Change in Operating Culture

As we have seen, any individual's private culture normally includes not one but several generalized cultures which he attributes to different social groups. He has had direct dealings with some of these groups; others he has heard or read about. Through books, motion pictures, radio, and television in our own society, people of all social classes and geographic regions acquire conceptions of the accepted modes of conduct and styles of living of other classes and regions. As we have seen, moreover, people select one or another of these other cultures as the guide for their own behavior according to their purposes and identifications, making it their operating culture. As a person changes his identifications he is likely to change his operating culture accordingly, selecting the standards of new sets of others as the guide for his behavior. Such a change does not necessarily represent any modification of his private culture, except that his conception of the other culture which he has selected as his new operating culture is likely to undergo modification and refinement as he seeks to conform to its standards and develops his skill in using it. Changes in a person's operating culture, however, are dramatically obvious to other people, who are likely to be unaware of changes in his private culture unless these changes are manifested in his operating culture. Indeed, efforts at inducing culture change in other people are regularly aimed at changing their operating culture, usually with the object of getting people to adopt as their new operating culture the standards that those seeking the change have in mind for them. Changes in an operating culture may also result from the reorganization of its components or from the syncretistic incorporation within it of elements from a different other culture within one's private culture.

A common reason for change in a person's operating culture is that he is identified with individuals and groups whose own operating cultures are undergoing change, with the result that their standards for him are changing. He modifies his generalized culture for them, therefore, as his experience of their changing ways seems to require, and he adjusts his own behavior to meet what he now understands their expectations of him to be. In this way a community is able to maintain the consensus necessary for a public culture while the operating cultures of its members are undergoing change.

Important features of any operating culture are the prefabricated and time-tested formulas, the recipes, to which people habitually resort to accomplish their recurring purposes. Situations are constantly arising, however, for which existing customary routines appear or prove to be inadequate. Whether they reflect a change in wants or a change in conditions, the rest of a person's operating culture and also the other generalized cultures in his private culture constitute a resource on which he may draw in order to accomplish his ends.

Learning experiments with animals indicate that there is a marked tendency to revert to former response habits in situations where the latest habits to be established cease to achieve their anticipated results.[12] We may assume that human beings also show a tendency to "regress" to formerly customary recipes that have been replaced by others. When customary procedures appropriate to adults fail to accomplish their purposes, people may resort to recipes they found gratifying in their youth and exhibit more "childish" behavior, as when a young man who is "on his own" runs out of money and calls on his parents for a 'handout." Similarly, people may turn to the no longer customary recipes of former generations—provided they are still known—as when a farmer whose car breaks down resorts to the horse and buggy, if he still has them available, or a camper who has lost his matches may seek to make fire by rubbing sticks. Though we would not classify it as regressive behavior, people often resort to a recipe that they customarily use for another purpose, if it seems feasible for the problem at hand. Indeed, it would appear that as conditions change, people have recourse first to other recipes known to them but not customarily used for the purpose of moment. Such recourse strikes us as regressive if the recipe used to be used for this purpose.

If no other existing recipe seems suitable, the next step is to think one up. This amounts to breaking existing recipes down into their component parts and reassembling them. The result may simply be a reordering of steps in the former recipe, or it may combine elements from several different recipes used for different purposes. So people resort to the tools they normally use to accomplish other ends, substitute an organization of personnel that they normally use in other activities, or look for substitute raw materials.[13]

When such substitutions and rearrangements appear to be of no avail, people begin to look farther afield. They become interested in the recipes that people in other societies have worked out. In borrowing them, however, they usually try to use as much of their own materiel, skills, and social organization as appears compatible with these alien recipes. When they take over foreign recipes indiscriminately, it is because they are identifying themselves with the alien society rather than looking for leads to solving a specific problem.

These approaches to the development of new recipes for handling changing circumstances may all fail. In every society people live with a certain number of problems for which they feel they have yet to find a solution. They seem to have no alternative but to break everything in their private cultures back to their elementary cognitive and operational components and try recombining them in completely novel ways. Breakdown and recombination of more complex components is something people do consciously with relative ease, especially at the levels of organization at which they are used to doing it, as in the regrouping of phrases and words to make new sentences. But the closer to elementary percepts and concepts people come, the more difficult it is to make radical recombinations that appear to add up to something useful. People play with this kind of breakdown and recombination as a form of mental doodling, accidentally discovering new and useful combinations, but solutions to pressing problems do not come easily this way. People discover them only after prolonged mulling in what appear to be sudden flashes of insight, sometimes in dreams and hallucinatory visions.

Change in Public Culture

Changes in a community's public culture arise in three different ways. In the first, they result from modifications in the generalized culture that the community's members mutually attribute to one another and that they use as their operating culture. In the second, the number of contexts for which there is a public culture may increase or decrease, as also may the frequency with which these contexts arise. Finally, change results from an agreement to select a different generalized culture as the model and guide for all, as the one everyone will use as his operating culture. The first kind of change is analogous to a modification of rules for playing football. The second is analogous to changes in the aspects of football for which there are no rules at all, increasing or decreasing the freedom of each team to act as it will. The third is analogous to a decision by the several football teams in the same league to play rugby instead.

Contributing to the first kind of change is the necessity for every individual to work out for himself, no matter how much help he receives from his fellows, what the generalized culture of his fellows (the public culture of his community as he understands it) is. The experiences of each generation are not exactly alike, and the interaction rates among age mates, except in early childhood, are usually greater than among people of disparate ages. Each generation tends, therefore, to arrive at a slightly different consensus, and even this consensus undergoes continual modification as individuals introduce small changes into their operating cultures from other parts of their private cultures, forcing their fellows to take account of them. The small increments of change in a society's public culture resulting from the operation of these processes can add up to considerable change in time without anyone being aware of much change at all.

Changes of the second type frequently arise in response to changing conditions in the phenomenal world of a community's members. Lands once fertile become unproductive, populations grow or decline, peaceful isolation gives way to chronic attack by warlike neighbors. People deal with these changes according to the provisions of their public culture, but with resulting changes in the frequency with which they engage in various activities, in the frequency with which they interact with one another, in the rhythm of their lives, and in the emotional climate in which they live. All of these changes may lead to the formation in time of new expectations and new values in people's private cultures, which with subsequent modifications of their operating cultures eventually set the stage for further changes in the public culture.

Among the effects on the public culture is an erosion of previous consensus because changed circumstances no longer permit people to participate in those activities in which the common and mutual learning necessary to maintain a consensus takes place. The result may be a diminution of the scope of a community's overall public culture and the emergence of multiple lesser public cultures in different subgroups within the community. At the same time, more frequent participation in other activities may develop consensus or strengthen it where it was lacking or weak before. In this way shifts in the overall budgeting of people's time in the activities in which they engage may radically affect the conditions under which consensus can be maintained.

Ralph Beals describes how changing economic activities have affected consensus in the village of Nayon in Ecuador.[14] Formerly a self-sufficient agricultural community, Nayon has become integrally tied to the larger economy centering on the capital city, Quito. The village now produces primarily for export to the Quito market, and the villagers have become increasingly involved as middlemen in the expanding trade economy. To market their produce and engage in other trade, which has led to a significant rise in their material standard of living, the men and women of Nayon are having to spend a lot of time away from the village and from their homes. Many men are away from home more than half the time. As Beals describes the effect:

> Not only do women take some part in trade, with long absences from home, but they also are carrying on an increasing amount of agricultural work. Today, it is not uncommon to see women plowing—a sight very rare, if not unknown, ten or fifteen years ago. Small children are commonly relegated to the care of older siblings, who at early ages may be in complete charge of the home for large parts of the day. More and more the school is a major factor in the training of the young, and it is inculcating the values of the city rather than of the village. Even in child training, the church now occupies only a minor role in the community.[15]

He goes on to point out how the shift to a money economy and increasing importance of activities away from the village have caused the old systems of mutual aid in the village to fall into complete disuse. No longer is Nayon organized as a village community with close cooperation among neighbors and kinsmen; relations among the villagers have taken on much of the impersonality characteristic of urban neighborhoods. That there has been a reduction in the scope of the public culture of Nayon is evident.

Changing conditions often have a marked effect on people's private cultures without resulting in any immediate corresponding changes in public culture. People continue to conduct themselves in accordance with the public culture of their group because they assume that others expect them to do so, although there have been a number of additions and changes in their private cultures. Such is the case when people become aware of new ways of thinking, believing and acting, following contact with members of other communities, and are privately attracted by some of them. At the same time, they continue to conduct themselves in public according to their community's established public culture, to which they believe their fellows still subscribe. There is, therefore, an inevitable lag between change in the private cultures of a community's members and change in its public culture. And for the same reason, there can be considerable differences among the private cultures of a community's members while at the same time they all share a public culture.

As time goes on, more extensive changes in the private cultures of a community's members lead to new wants that cannot be gratified within the framework of the established public culture. For a time people continue to try to operate in terms of the public culture, assuming that others expect them to do so, but as they become aware that others are also disinclined to continue to follow the public culture, they become less scrupulous about living up to its standards. Consensus as to its content may continue, but the common commitment to it is weakened. With decreasing commitment to abide by the old public culture, there is an increase in behavior that is delinquent by its standards. Social problems tend to multiply as personal commitment to the old consensus weakens. To combat these problems people make strong appeals to one another to continue to comply with the provisions of the public culture. People are thus caught between the pull of new wants and felt needs arising from their changed private cultures and their desire to live in an orderly society. Furthermore, only by continuing to do the right thing as defined by their old public culture can they continue to earn public approval and develop prestigious identities. But at the same time, the lack of commitment by a person's fellows to the old culture makes the prestige to which he is entitled less valuable. Others don't envy him as they used to, nor do they take him as seriously. As a result, people become increasingly frustrated, increasingly prone to irresponsible and delinquent behavior, increasingly concerned with the acquisition of real power (regardless of its legitimacy) in order to enforce compliance with their own wants from their fellows. At the same time they are increasingly burdened with feelings of guilt and personal inadequacy, as they judge themselves by the old public culture from which they are not yet completely disengaged. Under such psychologically stressful conditions there develops a growing felt need to reform the old public culture or replace it with a new one; but in either case, the result must be a culture about whose content there is general consensus and which everyone is willing personally to commit himself to follow as the guide for his behavior and the avenue for his self-fulfillment. There is simultaneous need for both a new consensus and a new commitment, for what amounts to the third kind of change in public culture listed above; the deliberate selection of a new one.

Finding a New Consensus

Achieving a new common understanding as to beliefs and propositions, values, and rules of conduct is not easy. In every society there are legislative procedures, however simple in form, by which people customarily arrive at mutually binding agreements as to how to apply their public culture to the task of modifying customary practices to accommodate to changing conditions. Changes in the public culture are not so much at issue as changes in its application so as to alter the structure of the phenomenal world. Whenever possible, people also use their legislative procedures to implement change in their public culture itself. But the possibilities for doing so would appear to be limited. When people already have a feeling that they are approaching a new consensus, the legislative process helps to consolidate it. But when the discrepancies between personal and public cultures are such that minor modifications of the public culture are insufficient to resolve the stresses people feel, or when the discrepancies differ so much from individual to individual as to preclude general commitment to any new formulations, traditional legislative procedures prove inadequate and may become themselves an aspect of the old public culture with which people are increasingly disaffected.

Because a new consensus is so hard to achieve, we can appreciate why it often happens that people take what they understand to be the public culture of another society with which they have had dealings as the model for their own new public culture. It is already one of the generalized cultures present in the private cultures of most members of the community. If contact with this other society has been responsible for new wants and for present dissatisfaction with the old public culture, the image people have of this society and its culture may prove highly attractive as the model for a new public culture. The fact that there is already some degree of consensus as to its content makes it all the more inviting. In the absence of such an alternative culture to which to turn, the old public culture may serve as a negative model for the new; consensus regarding the new can be achieved by utilizing the existing consensus concerning the old as a point of common reference. We have already seen how the old can be used as a negative model in connection with identity change in Chapter 9.

Regardless of the basis for a new consensus, the content of the new public culture must be carefully delineated and promulgated. As we shall see, such new consensuses are regularly achieved through the doctrines and formulas for living preached by someone as ideological leader and adopted by a following of converts. Each individual's conversion is his commitment to the formula for a new public culture and is also his commitment to the leader personally as the one to clarify misunderstandings and settle disagreements as to its content, a commitment to him as the arbiter of consensus. Since it is rare that everyone in a community is willing to accept such a leader, and since it often happens that there are rival leaders competing for followings, the achievement of a new consensus and common commitment is often limited to a segment of the former community, which may now try to establish itself as a community apart. Communitywide acceptance is likely to be achieved only after one of the rival groups succeeds in gaining control of the sources of power in the community.

Indeed, the twin objectives of consensus and commitment are almost invariably achieved through social movements that are often totalitarian in scope and mood, especially where large-scale revisions or substitutions in the public culture are involved. To the extent that they are concerned with the problem of defining a new public culture and gaining the commitment of people to it as a set of standards and principles for ordering their affairs and personal conduct, these movements are ideological and largely religious in emphasis. To the extent that they are simultaneously concerned to reorganize the phenomenal world into new stable arrangements more in keeping with the change in people's sentiments and the newly defined public values, such movements become concerned with economic and social reform. Because of their need for power to accomplish reforms, they become political movements as well.

Insofar as community development aims at accomplishing widespread changes in the private cultures of a client community's members, it seeks to create those conditions under which people are most likely to want to make deliberate substitutive changes in their public culture. In other words, development often tends to foster the conditions that give rise to movements of the kind just mentioned. Equally often, community development is aimed at helping already disorganized societies to arrive at a new and gratifying public culture. Often, too, as with many of the new nations emerging from colonial status, development is aimed at helping people already caught up in these movements to implement the changes in their phenomenal world which their new values render imperative to their sense of well-being. The social-psychological process that these movements express is necessarily a matter of paramount concern to planners and development agents. We consider it in detail in the next chapter.

SUGGESTED READING

Barnett, H. G., *Innovation:* The Basis of Cultural Change. McGraw-Hill Book Co., New York, 1953.

Barnett, H. G., "The Innovative Process" in *Alfred L. Kroeber: A Memorial.* Kroeber Anthropological Society Papers, no. 25, Berkeley, 1961, pp. 25-42.

Geertz, Clifford, "Ritual and Social Change: A Javanese Example," *American Anthropologist*, vol. 59, 1957, pp. 32–54.

Hallowell, A. Irving, *Culture and Experience*. University of Pennsylvania Press, Philadelphia, 1955.

Kluckhohn, Clyde, and William H. Kelly, "The Concept of Culture" in Linton, Ralph, editor, *The Science of Man in the World Crisis*. Columbia University Press, New York, 1945, pp. 78–106.

Kroeber, A. L., *The Nature of Culture*. University of Chicago Press, Chicago, 1952, especially pp. 22–51, 152–166.

Mandelbaum, David G., editor, *Selected Writings of Edward Sapir*. University of California Press, Berkeley, 1951, especially pp. 305–385, 544–559.

Merton, Robert K., *Social Theory and Social Structure*. Rev. and enl. ed., Free Press, Glencoe, Ill., 1957, chaps. 4 and 5.

Wallace, Anthony F. C., *Culture and Personality*. Random House, New York, 1961, chap. 1.

White, Leslie A., *The Science of Culture*. Farrar, Straus, and Cudahy, New York, 1949. Paperback edition, Grove Press, New York, 1958.

NOTES TO CHAPTER 10

1. Much in this section appears in substantially the same form in Goodenough, Ward H., "Comments on Cultural Evolution," *Daedalus*, vol. 90, 1961, pp. 521–528.

2. For a review of various definitions of culture, see Kroeber, A. L., and Clyde Kluckhohn, *Culture: A Critical Review of Concepts and Definitions*. Papers of the Peabody Museum of Archaeology and Ethnology, vol. 47, no. 1, Cambridge, Mass., 1952.

3. Mead, G. H., *Mind, Self, and Society*. University of Chicago Press, Chicago, 1937.

4. Anthony F. C. Wallace employs the term "mazeway" for the more comprehensive private culture. See his "Mazeway Resynthesis: A Biocultural Theory of Religious Inspiration," *Transactions of the New York Academy of Sciences*, Ser. II, vol. 18, 1956, pp. 264–281.

5. In this sense a community's culture differs from the generalized culture which an anthropologist attributes to it as an aggregate of others, but an anthropologist aims to arrive at a conception that does not exceed the range of variation delimiting the area of consensus among its members and that is therefore as close an approximation as is possible to its public culture. To do this, he must have experiences that are comparable to those that the community's members have had and through which they have individually modified their conceptions of the generalized cultures of the groups in which they participate to a point where a high degree of mutual understanding and predictability is achieved. Ethnographic method in anthropology is necessarily concerned with developing techniques for allowing an anthropologist to have the range and kinds of experience needed for constructing a valid model of a public culture within the constraints imposed by time and by his not having been born and reared a member of the community under study.

6. For an example of the semantic analysis of cognitive categories, see Goodenough, Ward H., "Componential Analysis and the Study of Meaning," *Language*, vol. 32, 1956, pp. 195–216. See also the discussion by Anthony F. C. Wallace and John Atkins, "The Meaning of Kinship Terms," *American Anthropologist*, vol. 62, 1960, pp. 58–80.

7. There is, of course, another way in which we may define custom, alluded to earlier. Looking at a community without reference to its culture, simply as a relatively stable system in the real world, we can label as customs those modal tracks over which behavioral events seem to pass most frequently. This is a purely statistical definition of custom. It is more useful for our purposes to consider a custom as a routine or recipe regularly used in a particular combination of culturally defined circumstances.

8. Goodenough, Ward H., "Residence Rules," *Southwestern Journal of Anthropology*, vol. 12, 1956, pp. 22–37.

9. Such, for example, is the situation for stream clearance as a means of controlling sleeping sickness in the Anchau Scheme in Nigeria, as reported by Horace Miner, "Culture Change Under Pressure: A Hausa Case," *Human Organization*, vol. 19, 1960, pp. 164–167.

10. Contrast with the equation of "social system" and "society" in Parsons, Talcott, and Edward A. Shils, editors, *Toward a General Theory of Action*, Harvard University Press, Cambridge, Mass., 1959, p. 196.

11. See Aberle, David, "The Influence of Linguistics on Early Culture and Personality Theory" in Dole, Gertrude E., and Robert L. Carneiro, editors, *Essays in the Science of Culture in Honor of Leslie A. White*, Thomas Y. Crowell Co., New York, 1960, p. 14.

12. Mowrer, O. H., "An Experimental Analogue of 'Regression' with Incidental Observations on 'Reaction Formation,'" *Journal of Abnormal and Social Psychology*, vol. 35, 1940, pp. 56–87.

13. For examples of this kind of change, see Barnett, H. G., "The Innovative Process" in *Alfred L. Kroeber: A Memorial*, Kroeber Anthropological Society Papers, no. 25, Berkeley, 1961, pp. 21–42.

14. Beals, Ralph L., "The Village in an Industrial World," *Scientific Monthly*, vol. 77, 1953, pp. 65–75.

15. *Ibid.*, p. 73.

Chapter 11

REVITALIZATION MOVEMENTS
AND COMMUNITY DEVELOPMENT

REVOLUTIONARY MOVEMENTS have dominated the world scene in the twentieth century. Some, like many of Melanesia's cargo cults, have had peaceful objectives; others, like the Nazi movement, considered military conquest essential to their aims. It is clear, moreover, that revolutions will continue to dominate the scene for some time. We must expect that revolution will provide the context in which much community development will be undertaken and accomplished.

Because revolution is disruptive of the existing social order, we tend to regard it with consternation as an undesirable and somehow unnatural phenomenon. If we looked upon physical illness as unnatural, however, we would not have the kind of understanding on which modern medical science is based. Revolutions recur so regularly in the history of human societies as to be obviously a part of the natural process in which social systems and public cultures undergo change. If we are to deal with them intelligently, we must understand them as a part of this process. Community development, for that matter, is a kind of revolutionary undertaking aimed at redesigning the pattern of community life, if need be by radical alterations of public culture, and thereby transforming the way people feel about themselves. This is clearly the objective of many revolutionary movements, too. We shall call them *revitalization* movements, using Wallace's term.[1] In this way we can distinguish them from revolutions that lack these objectives, such as those aimed at capturing political control by extra-legal means in order to enjoy the perquisites of power rather than for the purpose of economic, social, or spiritual reform. A close examination of revitalization movements may tell us something instructive about the development process itself.

THE BACKGROUND OF REVITALIZATION MOVEMENTS

It is commonly assumed that economically depressed peoples are ripe for revolution. But economic depression is not the only promoter of revolutions, nor does it invariably produce them. It would be more accurate to say that revolutionary movements have their roots in human frustration, in the feeling that one's major wants for oneself, whatever they may be, are unfulfilled and without any prospect of fulfillment under existing circumstances. Whether the frustrated desire is for food, power, or dignity does not matter. Frustration of self-goals having to do with physical comfort and material welfare is frequently an important factor in the background of revitalization movements. But there are many other kinds of self-goals. The frustrations arising out of compromised integrity or that accompany feelings of personal worthlessness also carry great revolutionary potential.

Opportunities for self-realization in some form or other, to achieve a sense of moral or other worth, are essential to the viability of a social order. Either there must be sufficient opportunity for self-realization according to existing values for a significant majority of the society's membership, so that the overall level of frustration remains within bounds, or the minority that is not severely frustrated must enjoy so much real power over the frustrated majority as to leave the latter feeling that however bad things may be, any effort to change them will only make them worse. But in the latter event, a new vision of hope will transform a passive society into a restless one; and either a sudden increase in the amount of frustration felt or a new sense of power to alter existing conditions may precipitate revolutionary action. After years of passive acceptance of frustration under Trujillo, for example, the Dominican Republic was transformed into a scene of revolutionary action following his death. In Cuba, moreover, it seems that Castro's ability to survive Batista's early efforts to defeat him increased for many Cubans the feeling of their own power and led to heightened revolutionary activity. The repressive measures of Batista's police against this activity heightened frustration, thereby increasing determination to use the developing sense of power in further revolutionary activity. The tremendous sense of collective power following the successful overthrow of Batista's regime gave many Cubans a feeling that they could now do something about many other frustrations that had not been immediately at issue before. The success of the first revolution set off the beginning of another.

Change and Frustration

Many things contribute to individual feelings of frustration. At the moment, we are especially interested in the processes that produce frustration on a mass scale. These are the processes of community change, considered in the preceding chapter: change in the community as a phenomenal system and widespread change in the private cultures of its members.

Change in the phenomenal system, in the pattern of physical and social conditions in which people see themselves as living, may on occasion have the effect of increasing opportunities to gratify traditional wants and to realize traditional self-goals in accordance with customary procedures for doing so. Indeed, an aim of community development is to create changes that will have this kind of effect. More often, probably, change in the phenomenal system has the opposite effect, providing fewer opportunities for self-fulfillment in ways that meet with public acceptance and approval. This is evident in the case of many American Indian societies after they were cut off from hunting and warfare. Here the heightened sense of frustration and non-fulfillment appeared to result from the intrusion of white men upon the scene of community operations, to emanate from forces outside the society. In the case of our own great depression during Hoover's Presidency, changed conditions seemed to stem from the effects of customary practice upon the system; mass engagement in practices that promised to be individually rewarding altered the conditions that had enabled them to be rewarding in the past. In both instances the reaction was similar. The Indians dreamed of a restoration of conditions that would allow customary practices to be resumed, and the New Deal program set out to change existing conditions so that traditional economic practices could be carried on again, with minor alterations to prevent their producing another depression of such severity.

By contrast with this, people may still be free to pursue traditional goals in traditional ways, but contact with alien peoples or other changes in their circumstances have produced alterations in their private cultures resulting in new wants and new self-goals that they cannot gratify or achieve within the framework of customary activities or their established social order. The social order still allows the pursuit of traditional goals valued in the established public culture, but these goals have lost their value in the private sentiment systems of the community's members. The contact experiences of the Nakanai with Europeans, we saw, produced this kind of situation. In such case, frustration and nonfulfillment appear to result from the public culture and customary practices of one's community and from one's identity as a member of it. The problem may be solved by emigration from one's community to find new opportunity by identifying with another, or if people do not wish to or cannot dissociate themselves from their community, they may solve their problem by a deliberate effort to change its public culture.

Even where opportunity to follow traditional practices appears to be blocked by changed circumstances, efforts to deal with them are likely to set in motion a chain of functional dislocations that end up making changes in the public culture appear desirable. By one route or another, the course of community change usually leads to functional dislocations that can be resolved only by modifications of public values and the principles for structuring social relationships, by changes, that is, in the public culture itself. But as we have seen, deliberate change in public culture, especially of a constructive nature, is not easy to achieve. The result is that changing circumstances frequently lead in time to a situation where people feel effectively blocked from adaptive action, where they find small-scale reforms more frustrating than rewarding, an impasse from which only a tremendous mobilization of concerted effort and total reorganization of custom, or a miracle, can deliver them.

Increasing Emotional and Social Distress

The behavioral, emotional, and social effects of this kind of impasse are far reaching.

One effect that we have already noted is an increase in the amount of socially disapproved behavior. Rising frustration leads to the displacement of ungratified wants onto whatever objects of gratification are still available. People are increasingly likely to indulge in excesses of rage, alcoholism, sexual promiscuity, or indolent irresponsibility. These excesses lead to public and self-condemnation, with serious damage to the individual's feelings of personal worth. Mounting delinquency is thus accompanied by an increase in emotional conflict, as people are torn between leaving increasingly pressing wants ungratified and suffering the shame of fractured self-esteem and/or the guilt of compromised integrity. Increase in delinquent behavior impairs people's capacity to get the normal business of living done as efficiently as before. Work that needs to be done remains undone. Material resources are less well maintained. These developments are followed by further loss of pride in self and by an increase in general dissatisfaction; and these promote in a vicious circle further delinquent and irresponsible behavior. As people become more discontented with their traditional social order, they tend to detach their own identities from the system of identities which it provides. Traditional models lose their appeal, and there is little to replace them. This produces increasing uncertainty about one's identity and loss of a sense of direction and purpose in life. Failure by others to operate in accordance with normal expectations also has the effect of providing less reinforcement of one's own sense of identity. The increasing emotional distress occasioned by these developments results in a higher incidence of both mental and physical disorders.[2] These exacerbate further the breakdown of mutually gratifying relations in the conduct of daily affairs.

As the process continues, neighboring communities progressively downgrade the community so affected, according its members less and less prestige, judging them to be unstable, lazy, brutish, immoral, and the like. Similarly, the ideologically more coherent and morally outraged conservative faction within the community seeks to gain or consolidate a position of power from which it can coerce conformity with the rules of the traditional social order. At the same time it seeks to insulate itself from the rest of the community by geographic, political, or social barriers, and to make the rest of the erstwhile community a community apart. If the conservative faction is successful in this and if neighboring communities similarly insulate themselves from the disturbed population, the level of frustration of its members is greatly increased and their ability to take remedial action is even further curtailed. Ultimately it will emerge as a depressed, outcaste group like the people of the rural slum called the Road, of whom we spoke in Chapter 8.[3]

The Quest for Salvation

Before this state of true social pathology is reached, however, people make repeated efforts to break out of the vicious circle, with varying degrees of success. Their problem is essentially one of achieving a new identity (or romanticized former one) that will provide maximum opportunities for the gratification of wants, freedom from present wants considered immoral or unworthy, the restoration of dignity and of public and self-esteem, and a sense of purpose in life and of accomplishment in relation thereto. Solution to the problem requires that all the conditions for successful identity change be met. The features of one's present identity that must be given up, the new identity features that must be acquired, the means of acquiring them, how one is to conduct oneself in one's new identity, these must all be envisioned. There must be commitment to the change, and others must accord it recognition and do all the things needed to reinforce and consolidate it so that a sense of new identity can actually be attained.

Efforts in this direction necessarily start when some individual tries to do something about his own identity problem. The conditions of success, however, require him to enlist his fellows' cooperation. They must look upon him in a new light, and to do so they must be converted to a new way of looking at things generally, especially if the light in which they are to see him is without precedent in the traditional social order or does not befit the place he would be traditionally assigned within it. Often, too, a person will see a change in the identity features of the entire group or community with which he identifies himself as the only means by which his personal identity problem can be solved. This makes the cooperation of his fellows and their conversion to his definition of things all the more essential. If his fellows are to respond sympathetically, they must be convinced that he speaks with knowledge and must see advantage to themselves in joining with him to implement the changes he proposes. Different individuals will inevitably see different kinds of advantage for themselves. But if the person initiating the change is to find widespread sympathy, he must appear to offer hope to many others for escape from their own identity problems. The means by which he proposes to find his salvation must spell salvation for others, too. For this to happen, there must be many other people who are also distressed with their present identities. If these conditions obtain, a revitalization movement is likely to get under way. Through it people expect to find release from their present disturbed emotional state by adopting a new public culture, by radically restructuring their phenomenal world, or by a combination of the two. Concern with personal and collective salvation inevitably gives such a movement many of the psychological characteristics of a new religion or cult, even when, as with the communist movement today, it explicitly disavows a belief in supernatural agencies. Intense involvement in the movement subsides as it leads to new conditions in which people find themselves approaching an emotional "steady state."[4]

Because they represent a process in which people seek collectively to change their identities, revitalization movements must meet the conditions for identity change in order to be successful. These conditions, as we discussed them in Chapter 9, explain much of the common pattern that, according to Wallace's comparative study, characterizes the course of revitalization movements. Let us consider this pattern, as he has formulated it, in greater detail.[5]

THE REVITALIZATION PROCESS

Six major phases or steps mark the course of a successful revitalization movement, one that restores its participants to a new emotional equilibrium.

Inspiration

The first step is the initial reformulation of a new social order. This new formulation usually comes to some individual in a flash of insight that strikes him with amazing force. It is frequently interpreted, therefore, depending on existing beliefs about the nature of such experiences, as a divinely inspired revelation. Cognitively the sudden conception of a new order or "key" to all existing problems is no different from that which scholars and scientists experience when they suddenly perceive a new pattern in their data or get the insight by which everything with which they are working at last makes sense. Emotionally, however, there is a difference, in that the problems of the scientist are not likely to involve his relations to other people or questions of what is morally right and wrong. The insight into social and moral problems has soul-saving value, because it offers relief from guilt and anxiety and promises to resolve inner emotional conflicts. The person who gets such insight finds himself with a mission and message. Indeed, his "vision" can have value for him only as he proceeds to try to act on its implications, and this requires that he win the cooperation of others.

Often the insight is obtained in the course of an hallucinatory experience. The likelihood of such experience is greatly increased under conditions of physical stress and exhaustion. Wallace observes that in the great majority of revitalization movements examined by him, the initial revelation came to one individual in the course of an hallucinatory vision or a series of such visions, and that in most of these cases the vision experience was preceded by some form of severe physical stress. He suggests, moreover, that the vision experience is not in itself psychopathological; on the contrary, it often has genuine therapeutic value enabling already sick individuals to resynthesize experience, reorder their values, and achieve thereby a new coherent view of self and world which resolves former emotional conflicts.

The revelation regularly expresses the individual's desire for a supporting, reliable authority. It is often represented as stemming from a supernatural power or spirit or from a much revered figure in mythology or history, which appeared in a vision. A traditional sacred text whose true interpretation provides the key to present problems, the utterances of a former prophet, which have hitherto been misunderstood, or a new "scientific" discovery may also be the source of revelation. The vision often gives expression to ideas of world destruction, with apocalyptic or millennial content, reflecting the demise of the visionary's old unsatisfactory identity through which he is freed to achieve a new one. Ideas of death and rebirth, reflecting the same thing, are also common. The vision also expresses feelings of guilt and anxiety, clearly defining what is moral in a series of rules or enunciating some basic moral principle that is to supersede all the old conflict-producing rules. It frequently defines certain things as having been responsible for past difficulties and enjoins the visionary to put them out of his life. These flaws in his former identity may be particular habits of behavior, some newly adopted customs or long-established ones, the worship of a "false" god, or association with certain individuals, including social or racial groups (for example, the Jews in Nazi Germany). Finally, the vision expresses the longing for a new satisfactory pattern of life by presenting the possibility of a utopian existence and prescribing certain rituals or other actions that will serve to bring the utopian order into being.

Communication

In the second or communication phase of the revitalization process, the visionary reveals his vision to others and seeks their cooperation. There are generally two fundamental motifs in his message: that those who accept the truth of his vision will, like himself, find the comfort and security to be derived from their unquestioning faith in the infallible authority behind it, and that by identifying themselves with him and performing the acts his vision prescribes, they will bring into being a new order from which they will all derive both spiritual and material benefit.

In order to win converts, the prophet embellishes his vision. He attributes it to whatever authorities he feels will be most respected by others. The inspiration cannot simply have been his, but must have authoritative backing. Thus the elderly visionary who gave impetus to the latest revitalization movement among the Nakanai of New Britain, presented his message in the form of an elaborate origin myth, which he maintained was told to him in his own youth by a senior relative, now long deceased, who had come by it from more remote ancestors—a carefully guarded account handed down, like many other items of lore, within his family from generation to generation—in spite of the fact that it spoke of jeeps, military landing craft, and other things that had never existed before World War II. Authoritative support for the vision may also be attributed to science, to the writings of past scholars, or to an apparent miracle.

Organization of Converts

Accompanying the communication phase of the budding movement is the third or organization phase. If the prophet finds an audience whose emotional needs have made it responsive to his message, he makes converts. In emotional turmoil themselves, highly suggestible in their sense of oneness with the prophet and his followers, new converts are likely to have hysterical seizures. Some may have ecstatic visions of their own in which the prophet's message is confirmed to them. Still others may be swayed by more rational arguments. There are always some "converts," of course, who join the movement for purely opportunistic reasons. A small inner circle of disciples or lieutenants soon develops around the prophet, forming an embryonic executive organization. As more followers are won, the lieutenants take over more and more executive functions and may actually take control of the movement, the prophet functioning only as its inspirational leader. If the prophet dies early in the course of the movement, inspirational leadership may also be taken over by a former lieutenant, as by Brigham Young, but in the name of the original prophet.

For his converts, the prophet is himself an infallible authority. The sense of security and well-being that accompanies dependent faith in him gives to the convert a foretaste of the final state of being that is the salvation promised in the prophet's message. The ultimate promise is thereby rendered all the more real. Even when people become disillusioned with the prophet later on, their hope for salvation and their faith in the idea that a true prophet may come are reinforced, and they are all the readier to listen to the next one. The infallibility his followers project upon him and the other expectations they have of him soon come to shape the role of the prophet as much, if not more, than his own desires in the matter. Although he has tremendous power to control the actions of his followers in many ways, he is also impelled by them to say and do things, some of which in his own judgment may not be in the best interests of the movement. Because his followers regard his pronouncements as sacrosanct, moreover, it is very difficult for him to change his ideas without recourse to new revelation. However genuine his first revelatory experience may have been, he may have to pretend to subsequent ones in order to adapt his message to the exigencies of circumstance.

Adaptation to Resistance

This brings us to Wallace's fourth or adaptation phase in the development of revitalization movements. As he describes it,

> The movement is a revolutionary organization and almost inevitably will encounter some resistance. Resistance may in some cases be slight and fleeting but more commonly is determined and resourceful, and is held either by a powerful faction within the society or by agents of a dominant foreign society. The movement may, therefore, have to use various strategies of adaptation: doctrinal modification; political and diplomatic maneuver; and force. These strategies are not mutually exclusive nor, once chosen, are they necessarily maintained throughout the life of the movement. In most instances the original doctrine is continuously modified by the prophet, who responds to various criticisms and affirmations by adding to, emphasizing, playing down, and eliminating selected elements of the original visions. This reworking makes the new doctrine more acceptable to special interest groups, may give it a better "fit" to the population's cultural and personality patterns, and may take account of the changes occurring in the general milieu. In instances where organized hostility to the movement develops, a crystallization of

counter-hostility against unbelievers frequently occurs, and emphasis shifts from cultivation of the ideal to combat against the unbeliever.[6]

As the last point suggests, the unbeliever poses a serious threat to the success of a revitalization movement, and not simply because of his antagonism to it. Even in the absence of antagonism, his unbelief raises doubts for the believers, who having committed themselves to the prophet and his promise can no longer tolerate that their commitment be questioned. They want their commitment reinforced on all sides. The unbeliever quickly becomes a scapegoat for any disappointments the prophet and his followers suffer. It is his unbelief that stands in the way of salvation. His refusal to recognize the new identities of the converts for what they believe and hope them to be does, of course, deprive them of the very thing they are striving for. For such reasons, converting the unbeliever, by force if necessary, becomes a major part of the program of many revitalization movements. When there is active resistance to the movement and its program, the agents of resistance are understandably viewed as maliciously and malevolently trying to prevent the prophet and his followers from achieving their identity goals. But even mild disapproval or lack of enthusiasm is likely to be interpreted as evidence of hostility toward the movement and its aims.

This often presents governmental authorities with a serious dilemma, because frequently a part of the program of action preached by the prophet is that a supreme act of faith is necessary in order to bring about the new order, this act regularly involving the destruction of something vitally important in the old order. His followers must give away all their belongings or destroy their gardens (they won't need them anymore); they must refuse to pledge allegiance to the flag or must do things in violation of existing law (thereby dissociating themselves from the old order). Efforts by governmental authorities to enforce existing law or to prevent the disastrous consequences of the destruction of gardens seem to the movement's followers to be aimed at preventing the millennium's arrival. These authorities now find themselves defined as implacable foes of the movement. They can get little cooperation and find that their own removal from office has become a major objective in the movement's program. The lines of hostility can emerge with tremendous rapidity. Often they are thoroughly solidified before authorities have had a chance to discover what they are all about.

Enacting a Program

As the prophet makes converts and an organized following begins to emerge, a new spirit begins to pervade their society. Former delinquencies and behavioral excesses become greatly reduced. People feel good about themselves; they feel emotionally revitalized and are prepared to embark with enthusiasm on an active program that will help to realize their hoped-for future. With such a program the movement enters Wallace's fifth phase, that of social and cultural transformation, in which concrete steps are taken systematically to alter the conditions of life and to forge a new order. There is no guarantee, however, that the program will be realistic or adaptive. The program of the American Indian movement known as the Ghost Dance was highly unrealistic in the form it took among the Sioux, who believed that a special shirt would render them invulnerable to the bullets of the United States Army.[7] But other programs have been sufficiently realistic so that successful projects of social and economic reform have resulted, as with the communist revolution in Russia.

Realistic or not, so much is felt to hang on the success of the program that the movement's participants are highly intolerant of any deviation from strict adherence to the letter of its prescriptions. Because the program is a blueprint for a new collective identity in which people are as yet unsure of themselves, the prophet's followers are eager to be told just what to think and do about every new problem that arises in their efforts to carry it through. The programmatic phase of a revitalization movement almost inevitably acquires a totalitarian flavor. In a Nakanai village, for example, whose members were fully caught up in the movement that was widespread there in the years following World War II, all the major activities of the day began and ended at the sound of a bell. People got up in the morning to the bell, sat down to breakfast to the bell, prayed to the bell, began eating to the bell, finished eating to the bell, fell out in squads in the village street to the bell to be assigned work details for the day, had evening prayer to the bell, sat down to supper to the bell, finished supper to the bell, and went to bed to the bell. This practice clearly was taken from their experience of life in mission schools and in the New Guinea Territorial Police. It helped ensure that everyone would conform to the proper formula for living prescribed by the movement's leaders.

The program's objective may be to revive the traditional way of life, to turn the clock back to the "good old days," as was the expectation among Sioux adherents of the Ghost Dance, when it was held that the White Man would disappear and the herds of buffalo would miraculously return.[8] The program may, however, be aimed at importing and establishing an alien way of life, as is the emphasis with the Cargo Cults of Melanesia.[9] It may conceive of a new kind of order for which there is no precedent in the past or among contemporary societies but which represents a utopia to be realized now for the first time. Such was the conception of the socialist and communist movements. Most movements of record show varying combinations of all three orientations: the revival-istic, the importing, and the utopian. The current movement among the Nakanai, for example, justifies its effort to import European ways on the ground that these were originally the ways of their own ancestors in a former golden age. Having fallen from grace, they lost these ways and the material benefits that derive from them. By following the right formula for living, which the Europeans have preserved, they will win back to their original state and true heritage.[10]

We cannot say for certain what factors promote revivalistic as against importing orientations in revitalization movements. Wallace suggests that people heavily dominated by outsiders tend to identify with them (even though hating them) and hence to be importing in orientation, while people less subject to direct domination will tend to be more revivalistic.[11] This does not accord with the observation by Reina[12] that peasant communities in the vicinity of Guatemala City are much more conservatively oriented than are the villages in remote areas that are much less heavily dominated by the central government. In our own view, revivalistic orientations tend to occur when traditional self-goals continue to be valued but people feel themselves blocked from achieving them as a result of outside circumstances. The objective of a revitalization movement will then be to remove the obstacles or to circumvent them so that traditional means of self-realization will be available once more. Importing orientations, on the other hand, develop where traditional means to self-goals are still largely available but have lost their value, as under colonial conditions of indirect rule where people are still free to operate in accordance with their former way of life but cannot overcome within it the indignity of inferior social status or achieve within it any longer a sense of self-respect.

Whatever its orientation, the programmatic phase reminds us that community development of some kind is a normal part of the revitalization process. That some programs lead only to disaster, as when people set out to destroy all their crops or possessions preparatory to being swept up into heaven, does not alter their character as self-development projects in the eyes of those participating in them.

Routinization

If the action program and the new conditions of living resulting from it are successful in reducing emotional stress, in gratifying wants, and in giving people a sense of purpose and accomplishment, a revitalization movement moves into its final phase in which the new pattern of living becomes a matter of routine. The totalitarian character of the movement lessens as people become accustomed to their new identities and feel secure in them. Many aspects of life over which the movement's leaders exerted direct authority become secularized and the leadership more and more restricts its function to doctrinal and ritual matters, to concern with the preservation of the morals of the new order, popular commitment to it, and popular morale within it.

Success and Failure

Revitalization movements succeed or fail in varying degree. If a movement progresses to the point of routinization and the achievement of an emotional steady state among its followers, it may be regarded as completely successful (as a movement). Many movements, of course, are abortive; some, indeed, never get beyond the first phase. Some would-be prophets in modern urban American society, for example, are simply hospitalized as insane by their fellows. Others may be jailed as subversive of the established order. Some movements, once started, fail to make the necessary adaptations to attract a wide following and either peter out or achieve success with a narrow segment of the larger society, becoming established as minor religious sects, splinter political parties, or esoteric cults.

As to success or failure in the later stages, Wallace observes:

> Two major but not unrelated variables seem to be very important in determining the fate of any given movement: the relative "realism" of the doctrine; and the amount of force exerted against the organization by its opponents. "Realism" is a difficult concept to define without invoking the concept of success or failure, and unless it can be so defined, is of no use as a variable explanatory of success or failure. Nor can one use the criterion of conventionality of perception, since revitalization movements are by definition unconventional. While a great deal of doctrine in every movement . . . is extremely unrealistic in that predictions of events made on the basis of its assumptions will prove more or less in error, there is only one sphere of behavior in which such error is fatal to the success of a revitalization movement: prediction of the outcome of conflict situations. If the organization cannot predict successfully the consequences of its own moves and of its opponents' moves in a power struggle, its demise is very likely. If, on the other hand, it is canny about conflict, or if the amount of resistance is low, it can be extremely "unrealistic" and extremely unconventional in other matters without running much risk of early collapse.[13]

Indeed, as long as a movement can successfully overcome resistance to it, the chances that it will achieve the routinization phase are good. How long the new order will remain viable thereafter, however, depends on whether it can function to keep emotional stress within tolerable limits.

COMMUNITY DEVELOPMENT AND THE REVITALIZATION PROCESS

A revitalization movement is obviously a spontaneous development project, arising within a community in response to the felt needs of its members. Indeed, the phases of a revitalization movement are fundamentally the same as those of successful development: (1) perception of a solution to an existing problem by the development agent or prophet; (2) communication of the solution to others and their conversion to, or acceptance of, it and the point of view from which it stems; (3) organization of the following, with the community's converted leaders acting in the role of disciples or lieutenants; (4) adaptation of the proposed solution and its accompanying doctrine to adjust to unforeseen problems and to meet objections by prospective converts and supporters; (5) transformation of the community as it mobilizes to put the proposed solution into effect; and (6) routinization of the changes wrought as objectives are met, new and old ways are integrated, and satisfactory routines for perpetuating the new doctrines (for example, the germ theory of disease) become institutionalized. As with revitalization movements, the success of a development project depends in the short run on the ability of its proponents to cope with opposition mobilized against it and in the long run on the workability of its solution. But it does not depend on the scientific accuracy of the doctrine used to justify the solution and make it acceptable to the community's members.

It is difficult, moreover, to see how a development project that plans for any major reorganization of a people's way of life can succeed without acquiring some of the religious and totalitarian overtones of spontaneous revitalization movements. Commitment to the major identity changes involved and the zeal needed to effect the changes planned guarantee considerable emotional intensity, intolerance of deviation, and dependence on charismatic leadership. It is not invocation of supernatural power, but emotional involvement, that imparts a religious character to an undertaking. At the same time, like revitalization movements, a development project is necessarily political in that leadership, organization of people, exercise of authority, regulation of conduct, and decisions of strategy and tactics are all required. The greater the effort needed and the broader the scope of the envisaged program, the more fully religious and political at once— the more fully totalitarian—the project must be if it is to succeed. If this conclusion is correct, development agents and planners working with communities where people are demoralized and stress-ridden must take account of the emotional forces that development efforts are likely to mobilize.

It is also evident that where economic or other development is undertaken in communities whose members find their way of life satisfying, the resulting changes are likely to promote conditions of the sort from which revitalization movements spontaneously arise. For example, it is a recognized principle of community development that people will participate in a program only insofar as they expect it to meet felt needs. For this reason, development agents often feel called upon to create a sense of need where none exists at present, as when they wish to introduce better public health practices. As we observed in connection with identity change, educational efforts to stimulate a sense of need are in effect aimed at making people no longer satisfied with their present identities and their present ways; they aim to leave people with a feeling that they cannot fulfill themselves except by changing their customary practices and reordering their social relationships. Education plays on the dire consequences of present practice with the object of increasing emotional stress by heightening anxiety about crop failure or guilt about one's children's health; at the same time it raises doubts about the truth of existing beliefs and the adequacy of traditional practices. To induce felt needs is to promote an emotional state that, carried far enough, is the precondition of revitalization movements.

The Reactions of Government Authorities

The foregoing considerations bring us to one of the remarkable paradoxes of planned change. All over the world, agencies that seek to introduce change, whether for selfish or altruistic reasons, frequently come to resist the results of their handiwork as represented by community effort to do something about existing problems and achieve a new steady state. It is remarkable that as soon as communities start taking charge of their own development in the revitalization process, they often have to fight the agents who got them started. Religious teachers who encourage people to think more seriously about their relations with God are, if successful, faced with what they regard as heresies. Colonial governments that seek to broaden the extent of self-government among their subjects find themselves fighting nationalistic movements. Plantation owners who justify their employment of local labor on the ground that they are teaching new economic techniques find themselves resisting attempts by those they have employed to apply these techniques for their own economic advantage.

There is no part of the world in which revitalization movements are not a common consequence of the work of the various kinds of change agent. Occasionally they take a form that is congenial to these agents, who use the forces thus mobilized to promote what they consider further constructive change, as when a prophet preaches that adoption of Christianity or some other established religion is the solution to a community's problems, and its elders, converted to his proposal, invite a missionary to come among them. More often, however, revitalization movements take forms which agents of change and others who have some responsible connection with the community find disturbing and which they resist. Even the Kremlin, it appears, is not entirely happy with the results of its former proselyting in China.

Sometimes change agents resist the revitalization movements they have stimulated because they feel they cannot give up control over its affairs to the community's members, as when colonial officials sabotage attempts by local populations to take over governmental functions for themselves. Yet the leadership of any revitalization movement must attempt to regulate the conduct of its followers if the movement is to achieve the discipline necessary to carry out its objectives. Thus the Manus set up village courts analogous to magistrates' courts in order to handle organizational problems arising within the Paliau Movement. There was no provision for such courts, however, in the administrative code for the Territory of Papua and New Guinea. They represented, therefore, a usurpation of governmental powers and a breach of territorial law.[14] Because in some respects, at least, they are revolutionary, revitalization movements inevitably prescribe practices that are in violation of existing law and therefore to be resisted by those whose duty it is to uphold the law. Seeing these practices as unlawful, government officials tend to regard them as bad, something to be punished or at least stopped. Rarely do they seem to consider the possibility of readjusting the law to fit existing needs until after attempts to enforce existing law have failed. By that time, what was at the beginning a legal and administrative problem in need of resolution has become an occasion for a contest of wills and struggle for power.

Sometimes also change agents and other responsible authorities resist revitalization movements because they fear that if they do not, they will be adversely judged by those to whom they are administratively responsible, or because they anticipate loss of privilege if the movement is successful. Frequently, however, agents resist the results of their handiwork because they include forms of behavior and expressions of belief and value at variance with the agents' own values and sense of what is proper.

For example, government officials and change agents are used to working within a framework of orderly procedure. They are likely to be disturbed, if not repelled, by anything that is not in accord with what they regard as a rational approach to human affairs and problems. They regard themselves as reasonable men and condemn views and values that strike them as irrational and unreasonable. In their work with representatives of other societies, they are attracted to those persons who seem to appreciate the reasonableness of what they have to say. These are the "reliable" men in the local community, the people "you can work with." As reasonable men, agents and other officials profoundly mistrust those persons who attribute things to supernatural causes, who talk of miracles, or who rave and rant in fanatical devotion to any cause, even that of their own self-improvement. They are often suspicious of leaders of local revitalization movements for just these reasons and try to undermine them rather than to work with them. Indeed, officialdom tends to reject as irrational, mystical, and misguided the very forces whose mobilization is essential to successful radical reform and development.

Agents whose own background is occidental, moreover, have been brought up to regard any kind of visionary or hallucinatory experience as abnormal and as possible evidence of insanity. People who "see things" should hardly be given social responsibility or handed the mantle of community leadership. (Of course, even in western society it depends on what one sees and how one describes the vision.) Their own cultural bias, therefore, leads development agents to regard as evidence of psychological degeneration what is, as Wallace points out, evidence of psychological revitalization.[15]

Beyond this, revitalization movements often repel change agents because of their uncompromising and totalitarian character. As we have seen, revitalization movements almost inevitably acquire such a character. Those in Anglo-American tradition, such as the Puritan movement, were as totalitarian and uncompromising in their day as modern communism in ours. Early Christianity was no less so, nor are the missionary efforts of the more militant Christian denominations today. We must frankly ask ourselves to what extent economic and medical missionary efforts can be otherwise, if their object is to do more than get people to build privies. Important economic or social changes, because of the functional links between customary activities, often require a reorganization of many if not all aspects of living. Even such a simple thing as boiling drinking water, analysis has shown, would have disrupted the whole pattern of daily living for many people in a Peruvian town if they had adopted it.[16] Almost any change of the sort contemplated in community development projects has such wide implications that once it gets started it is likely to promote within the community need for a revitalization movement to enable its members to achieve emotional equilibrium again.

An example of negative reaction to revitalization movements by responsible authorities concerned with economic and political development for the above reasons is afforded by the early response of lower level government officials in the Territory of Papua and New Guinea to the Paliau Movement among the Manus people. Mead describes their reaction to Paliau, the movement leader, thus:

> He was called, even in the notes made by officers on patrol, "The Emperor," whose attempted reign was illuminated with comparisons to Hitler and the Emperor of Japan. He was said to have maps of his proposed empire which would include not only the Admiralty Islands but New Ireland and New Britain as well! He was said to

maintain a huge harem of women, to have his food served to him by a line of kneeling servitors—Japanese style—to have established a totalitarian régime which flouted every canon of free government and used such loathsome devices as drilling, bells, curfews, passes. He was said to have claimed to have been given a key to Heaven by God, with whom he was in personal communication, so that he could "drop in any time." [*][17]

It is true that school boys were given close order drill as part of the program of education in the unofficial schools that Paliau's followers established in the hopes of westernizing the education of their children. It is true that village people were summoned to meetings, to church, and to line up for the detailing of community work projects by the ringing of a village bell—following established practice on European plantations and mission stations. It is true that the people revered Paliau as superhuman. Undoubtedly many of them believed that he was in direct contact with God, and said so. The fact remains that Paliau was leader of a movement that wanted increased responsibility for its affairs through the village council system of local government (whose extension was established government policy), that desired better education for its children along western lines in accordance with established governmental hopes, that wished to develop its economic resources in order to improve its material standard of living, and that hoped to reorder its way of life in accordance with European models. The movement's program was to try to accomplish the very things that it was government policy to help New Guinea natives accomplish, and Paliau, after a visit to the territorial capital wisely arranged by top governmental authorities, expressed a willingness to achieve these goals by means the government was already providing for some other New Guinea communities. But because government officers mistrusted a revitalization movement, they seem to have been reluctant to take advantage of the situation. For a time they resisted requests for councils, schools, and cooperatives, and tried to sabotage the movement by establishing a truncated council designed to be unworkable, at least from Paliau's point of view.

* Reprinted with the permission of the author and publisher from *New Lives for Old:* Cultural Transformation—Manus, 1928–1953. William Morrow and Company, Inc., New York, pp. 190–191. © 1956 by Margaret Mead.

In fairness to New Guinea's officers, who are handling a difficult job with considerable credit to themselves, we should add that their dislike of Paliau was also due to his having worked with the Japanese in World War II. By contrast, they supported the war hero Peter Simogun in his efforts at community development in the Sepik River District. Furthermore, they eventually adopted a policy of greater cooperation with Paliau. This change of attitude, however, came after the movement, despite opposition, had survived its early phases. Its leadership was now emphasizing less the miraculous and more the organization of projects and the routinization of changes already accomplished. The movement now presented a more rational and sensible facade to authorities than when it underwent the spiritual seizures and ecstasies through which, as Schwartz has shown, it originally gained a dedicated group of adherents with the will to organize and build for the future.[18]

The paradox in this instance from New Guinea went even further. While government officials were hesitating to provide local government councils for the followers of Paliau, who wanted them, they were simultaneously trying to introduce them to the closely knit Raluana group near Rabaul, which did not want them. In government eyes, it seems, the Raluana were a progressive group who were "ready" for a council and ought to have been willing to develop themselves further as the government provided opportunity. The Manus, on the other hand, were caught up in something ideologically repellent, which suggested that they were "not ready" for councils. From our point of view, it appears that the community that was in a steady state was presumed to be ready to have that state disturbed, whereas the community that was not in a steady state was not ready to have help in its effort to restore it.

In this, officials were reacting in a way characteristic of all reasonably well-adjusted human beings. People prefer to deal with those of their fellows who are emotionally well balanced. Those who are in the process of winning through to a new identity and restoring a lost emotional balance are, as we have already observed, a trial to their fellows. Officials, likewise, find that among the communities with which they deal, those that are in a relatively steady state have much greater appeal to them than do those that are not, especially when the latter are in the throes of trying to do something to restore it. In the former, people are reasonable, steady, and pleasant. Surely they should be better able to absorb and adjust to development projects that envision considerable change in their present social order. Communities that are not in a steady state appear unable to sustain any serious change; they seem "not ready" for development, especially if they are producing crazy prophets preaching "a lot of nonsense" and inciting people to do things that make trouble for administrators.[19]

So it was that officials to whom we talked about the Raluana presented a picture of a group that had succeeded in sustaining a number of changes in the past without serious impairment of its members' emotional stability. They were said to be the "most intelligent" and "most energetic" of the several groups in the Rabaul area, if not in all New Guinea. They were described as having a strong sense of their own importance and worth. What was said of them fitted a population that was taking care of itself and its problems within the framework of its present institutions quite successfully, at least in its own eyes. This was why the Raluana were well regarded and respected by responsible Europeans. Their adamant refusal of councils, their insistence that the government's attempt to introduce them was an unwarranted interference in their affairs, and most of all their united show of intention to resist by force, if necessary, was baffling to those to whom we talked. "What's come over the Raluana?" was the incredulous question. It is just possible that the Raluana were contented as they were and could see no reason that they should be subjected to an overhaul for their own good. It was not the Raluana who needed a council, but the government that needed them to have it.[20]

So we are back to one of our basic principles; the best customers for community development are those with a need they are themselves aware of. If the proposed program reflects the felt needs of the community, it has a chance of acceptance; if it reflects only the needs of the developing agency, it will be rejected out of hand. It is difficult to follow this principle, however, because we like to do things for the people we like and with whom we have been able to get along well in the past, and we don't like to do things for those who make trouble for us. We may be prone, therefore, to select communities whose members feel little need for development projects and to eliminate from consideration those whose felt need is great as being too difficult to work with or in a condition that requires giving official recognition and administrative support to "dangerous" prophets and "subversive" movements.[21]

Revitalization movements are not easy to deal with, however. Because they so frequently have an anti-American or anti-European orientation, American and European development agents are in a difficult if not impossible position *vis-à-vis* the leaders of communities caught up in such movements. The best chances for cooperation would appear to be with communities where there is a strong felt need and where the revitalization process has not yet got under way spontaneously. Development can then serve to trigger a kind of revitalization movement in which the community and development agent are allies rather than enemies. The trouble is that failure to help people with their felt needs early enough may leave authorities unacceptable as development agents later on. Interested in "preserving order," they tend to block incipient efforts at self-development, only to find themselves cast in the role of monsters to be eliminated in the programs of subsequent, more intensive efforts at self-development. How this comes about is clearly revealed in the following report of an investigation into the background and meaning of a strike by public utility workers on the island of "Agria" (a pseudonym) in the United States Trust Territory of the Pacific.*[22]

> The Agrians were an anxious and an insecure people when they came under American control. We have heightened their feeling of insecurity because, regardless of the reasons for our acts, we have succeeded in frustrating rather than in freeing them from their fears and repressions. To them the administration has come to symbolize an almost completely negativistic influence upon their ambitions.

* Reprinted with permission from *Anthropology in Administration* by H. G. Barnett. Harper and Row, Publishers, Incorporated, New York, 1956, pp. 163–165.

Each added rejection of a request for help or permission further sensitizes them to this aspect of our trusteeship responsibility. The danger is, of course, that the latent hostility which is being generated by their frustration will manifest itself in calculated resistance to government controls.

It takes two ingredients to create frustration: one is the urgent hope or expectation of getting something, and the other is the consistent failure to get it. The Agrians have experienced this sort of exasperating impasse repeatedly in several important areas of their lives. In particular, they have felt that they are being denied their proper expectations with respect to equalitarian rights and economic development. These are the reasons:

a) *Equalitarian rights.* Americans have understandably attempted to indoctrinate the Agrians with our ideal of democracy. This would be well enough except that the attempt has succeeded only in creating the desire without the means. There are three obvious reasons for this predicament. One is that the principle of democratic choice runs directly counter to the traditional authoritative system of the Agrians —and we play it both ways as convenience indicates. Secondly, in Agria, as in the United States, there is an obvious discrepancy between theory and practice in the functioning of our system of opportunities and privileges, and the Agrians are beginning to doubt our sincerity in advocating it. On the one hand we encourage them to act as our equals and on the other we set barriers in the way of their doing so. Thirdly, our most outspoken champions of the democratic way of life have fallen into the typical American error—now being committed the world over—of presenting only one side of the system. They emphasize the rights and privileges of the individual to the almost total neglect of a definition of the responsibilities which must go with these freedoms. As might be expected from the nature of their assignments, the educators, the justices, and the public defender are most vulnerable to this criticism. But regardless of the source of their indoctrination, the great majority of the Agrians—and other Trust Territory natives—who have learned about their Bill of Rights have no conception whatever of the price on the freedoms which that document guarantees them. Because they do not realize that every right entails a compensatory obligation they take the freedom that we urge upon them as a gift—and feel that the administration is obstructing their desires when it cannot pay for them with the money, time, power, intelligence, or skill at its disposal.

b) *Economic development.* There is no doubt that the Agrians are suffering from an economic depression to which they are acutely sensitive. That they are aware of the gap between their material wants and the means of satisfying them is, in fact, the explanation and the measure of their depression. In other words, their cash income does not meet their physical needs because they expect greater satisfactions than their and our resources will permit. On this score they are therefore frustrated and demanding.

Agrians have scaled their economic demands by reference to standards in other times and places. One reference point has been our own idea of what they should have. Their impoverished condition has been the object of concern for interested Americans ever since the war, and by now the Agrians are as convinced as we are that something should be done about their plight—but it has not been. In addition, the Agrians have the examples of Guam and Saipan before them as models to copy, yet they are thwarted in this ambition. Finally, the Agrians, out of their disappointment with the present, have turned to the past for a standard. They tend more and more to contrast their prosperity under the Japanese with their poverty under the Americans. The economic well-being that they experienced before the war is becoming standardized as an ideal to be achieved once again. All these goals are currently beyond their reach. Yet they feel that they are entitled to aspire to them.

From an administrative standpoint the Agrians have, until quite recently, presented few problems because of the high value that they place upon submitting to authority and because they have accepted the Americans as their superiors. Their docility has continued in spite of multiple aggravations on the part of inconsiderate Americans ever since the war. The inertia of American prestige still protects us from direct hostility, and will probably continue to do so; but the accumulation of repressed and oblique resentments over the past six years is a development which cannot be passed over lightly. The strike gives particular emphasis to this warning. Some of the retorts made by employees to the District Administrator during the mass meeting in March left the Agrians themselves awe-struck with their own audacity: but they could set a precedent. . . .

Here we see how resentment against authorities develops in conjunction with a situation productive of mounting stress. The same report points out elsewhere that the only means the Agrians could see of alleviating this stress was to emigrate to Guam or Saipan, something they were very eager to do; but they were prohibited by the Administration from doing so—for their own good, of course. It is evident, moreover, that the Agrians are approaching a point where they are likely to begin to generate revitalization movements with a strong anti-American bias. If this should happen, it is safe to predict that authorities will use the powers at their disposal to suppress these movements, employing the techniques to which colonial and other authorities regularly resort—arresting their leaders, imposing curfews, and withdrawing existing privileges—thereby preparing for an even more bitter and desperate revitalization effort later.

If the foregoing considerations indicate that authorities are advised to treat revitalization movements and other efforts at self-development with respect, no matter how absurd or ideologically repellent they may on occasion appear, we must also recognize that authorities often have no practical recourse but to resist popular movements which, if allowed to run their course, would clearly result in widespread suffering. In their early stages, when they tend to stress the miraculous, and when they are seeking converts, revitalization movements frequently advocate destruction of symbols of their past or of the source of their frustration, these acts serving to commit the converts irrevocably to the movement and its future fortunes. The objects of destruction may be such relatively innocuous things as traditional forms of wealth, as in the Manus instance, or they may be traditional offices, which are abolished, as in political revolutions. They may, however, be individuals or categories of individual, such as landlords; or, again, they may be the traditional sources of production and livelihood. Authorities cannot but seek to prevent acts that lead to famine or that incite to mob violence. But they must also reckon carefully with the consequences. By such interference they become liable to blame for the failure of the miracles; they lay themselves open to the charge of being the one great obstacle standing between the people and their aspirations.

We conclude, then, that when development agents or other authorities find themselves reacting to a movement as something terrible that is to be stopped by all means, they are advised to examine their reasons for so reacting with great care. If their reactions have no overriding practical basis but stem largely from considerations of ideology, convenience, and personal distaste, they may do better in the long run to conceal their distaste and try to ride with the movement, rather than resist it.[23]

Adapting Development to the Revitalization Process

If a movement is unrealistic, its adherents will soon start wondering what they have done wrong to prevent their hopes from being realized. When they begin to question unrealistic means, as they will if authorities will let them go ahead and learn for themselves that they are unrealistic, they may be ready to listen to a development agent's suggestion as to how they can more realistically meet their felt needs.

In our own experience, we have encountered a missionary in New Guinea who seems to have followed this course with considerable success from the standpoint of his objectives. There had been a strong cargo cult in his area just before the outbreak of war in the Pacific. The missionary's predecessor had openly resisted it and preached sternly against it. For his pains, he was seized and tortured by the cult's leaders following the departure of Australian authorities in the face of the advancing Japanese, who ultimately rescued him. The movement momentarily collapsed when the Japanese failed to fulfill the role prophesied for them and the prophet himself became disillusioned, but the forces it had mobilized coalesced again under the disciples of the old movement following the presentation to them of a new myth which provided the charter for a new movement. Loss of the original prophet and disillusion with him personally did not mean the demise of their aspirations or of their movement, but led to the search for a new leader. The disciples came to the present missionary when he reopened the mission station, showed him the new myth, which they had written down, and asked him what he thought of it. He did not sneer, but expressed approval of its obvious Biblical content, of the aspirations it revealed, and what it was they were trying to conceptualize within the outwardly fantastic myth. Finding that he was not hostile, they asked him if he could show them the road by which they might achieve their aspirations. By agreeing to teach them the way, he came to occupy the position of "prophet" for the revitalization movement, at least in the people's eyes. In this way he acquired considerable control over its adaptation and transformation phases. He succeeded, accordingly, in getting the several villages in the movement to revise a number of their marriage and family customs in the direction endorsed by his religious denomination. The movement, of course, still had and would continue to have many features incompatible with Christianity in any form. Had the missionary denounced it for this reason, however, he would, like his predecessor, have lost his influence. There were certain overtones in the way he played his role which we found personally distasteful, but it was clear that through the movement and its organization he had succeeded in introducing many changes in the pattern of village life fully in keeping with the aims of the mission he represented, and that he held a position in which he could exert a maximum of influence on the future direction of the movement, though even he could not hope to determine that direction entirely.[24]

We are not recommending that agents of community development try to make themselves prophets of revitalization movements. But this missionary's experience demonstrates that sometimes, at least, it is possible for development agents to take advantage of such a movement's existence. During its adaptation phases, especially, an agent who enjoys the confidence of its leaders can recommend modifications of doctrine and policy that help to solve emerging problems; and in the phase of social transformation, he can give advice and possible material help in planning and executing specific projects. With this in mind, we can appreciate the following excerpt from a report on a project to build a community center in a mushrooming Palauan community showing many of the symptoms of social disorganization attendant upon urbanization. Under the heading of "Timing" it states,

It was considered most important to get the clubhouse building under way early in the fall of 1952 in order to take advantage of a surge of interest in rejuvenating traditional fellowship groups of age mates among both men and women. Aboriginally every village had several organizations of this nature, but in recent times they have ceased to function as real social units. In the summer of 1952 one such association of women stirred itself and put on a vigorous campaign to build a clubhouse for its members. Other dormant associations were inspired—and piqued—by this precedent, and soon all Koror was affected by the movement. The planners . . . concluded that the opportunity of taking advantage of this creative excitement should not be lost. In retrospect it appears that the decision to act on this reasoning was sound; for there was, it seems, a carry-over of enthusiasm from the one situation to the other with scarcely a break in the work rhythm as first the women's clubhouse and then the Center's clubhouse were erected.*[25]

As this case indicates, revivalistic as well as importing movements may be effectively utilized by development agents. There remain two problems, however, that accompany attempts to use the forces for collective action which revitalization movements generate.

The first problem stems from people's tendency to attach unrealistic hopes to any proposed solutions or programs they are prepared to accept, particularly when their sense of need is fully aroused and they have been repeatedly frustrated in doing something about it. The greater the stress or sense of need, the more likely they are to look for miracles. It is out of the impatience born of stress that credence in miracles comes. Exaggerated expectations of a development agent are equivalent to looked-for miracles in revitalization movements. Disillusion with the agent is likely to follow failure of these miracles to appear, so it seems advisable that agents should try to discourage exaggerated hopes at the outset. But this raises another problem. Under conditions of stress, belief in an imminent miracle helps to sustain a population's morale. By seeing a project as leading to their immediate salvation rather than as one step in a long, hard road to expanded opportunity or improved welfare, people work up their enthusiasm to get something done at all. In warfare, similarly, as a nation begins to suffer one defeat after another, its leaders may talk increasingly of new secret weapons about to be unveiled that will save the day if only everyone will work a little bit harder in the meantime. This talk is temporarily successful because it says precisely what everyone wants to hear. Indeed, many a battle has been won or project successfully completed because of the boost to morale that rumor of a miracle gave to a discouraged populace at a critical moment. False hopes are the prelude to

* Reprinted with permission from *Anthropology in Administration* by H. G. Barnett. Harper and Row, Publishers, Incorporated, New York, 1956, p. 148.

disillusion, but they may also be the stimulus for winning through. Development agents may have to be as careful in discouraging as in encouraging them.

As for the second problem, if belief in miracles increases with stress, we may presume that there is also an increasing likelihood that anyone proposing a solution that receives a positive reaction will be regarded as a prophet, savior, or charismatic leader—will find that he has evoked a religious response to his own person. The more pressing the felt needs, in other words, the more likely it is that a development agent who succeeds in rallying support for his proposals will find himself, willy-nilly, in the position of leader of a revitalization movement. While such a role may have definite appeal to some individuals, many development agents will hesitate to follow through in this way with what they have started. For them to assume such a role is also likely to produce misunderstandings between them and other local Europeans (in colonial or trusteeship areas), between them and other agency personnel to whom they may be responsible, and between them and local government officials who are responsible for maintaining peaceful good order. In spite of these problems, an agent should think carefully before he refuses the role at the outset, if going along with it seems to be the only way he can gain the community's cooperation.

Indeed, the community is in this respect behaving very much like a psychoanalytic client who seeks to impose upon his therapist in so-called "transference" a relationship expressive of his own emotional hungers. Psychoanalytic technique exploits transference, in that it helps to reveal to the therapist the nature of his client's problem and provides a basis for confronting the client with himself and the unsuitability of his projections, whence he gains the insights that are essential in the therapeutic process.[26] A development agent can likewise exploit the prophet role, representing the dependency transference of his clients, to help his clients do things from which they derive therapeutic value. Like the psychiatrist, moreover, he must avoid trying to exploit the role in which his clients cast him for his own emotional gratification. This means that he must be emotionally stable and secure himself. His acceptance of the role then does not imply that he wants personally to play prophet but expresses his acceptance of his clients and their needs and his willingness to work with them in the context of their need. Like a psychiatrist, moreover, he is concerned to use their relationship as a means for helping his clients find solutions to their problems that will free them from feelings of dependence upon him. This is a major difference between development agents and natural prophets, whose own needs are fed by the transference of their followers and who tend to exploit it as much for their own as for their followers' benefit. This tendency, indeed, is one of the reasons that agents are likely to find the role of prophet repugnant; it evokes within themselves well-suppressed desires whose emergence in consciousness is threatening to their self-image and self-esteem, so they fear that playing the role will compromise their integrity. For this reason, they assume that anyone else who plays it will also be corrupted by it. Yet there is no reason that a secure individual who is aware of the processes at work cannot successfully utilize his clients' transference in the development situation to help them solve their problems and do so in such a way that he weans them from their dependence upon him, leading them to reject their former dependence.

Our look at the revitalization process has led us to draw inferences about agent-community relations that may strike many readers as repugnant. We confess that our own values do not make us entirely comfortable with these inferences, either. But we are not concerned to cater to the biases of our rationalistic ethic in examining the phenomena of change. It is rather our job to try to see how present knowledge of human behavior and social process can clarify the problems which beset community development efforts. To find that a major difficulty in dealing effectively with certain recurring situations arises from our own beliefs and values should not be too surprising. Should we be surprised, then, if solutions to the difficulty require us to act in ways that make us uncomfortable?

SUGGESTED READING

Blumer, Herbert, "Social Movements" in Lee, Afred McClung, editor, *Principles of Sociology*. College Outline Series, Barnes and Noble, Inc., New York, 1959.

Burridge, Kenelm, *Mambu:* A Melanesian Millenium. Methuen and Co., Ltd., London, 1960.

Cantril, Hadley, *The Psychology of Social Movements.* John Wiley and Sons, New York, 1941.

Festinger, Leon, Henry W. Riecken, and Stanley Schachter, *When Prophecy Fails.* University of Minnesota Press, Minneapolis, 1956.

Gruenberg, Ernest M., "Socially Shared Psychopathology" in Leighton, Alexander H., John A. Clausen, and Robert N. Wilson, editors, *Explorations in Social Psychiatry.* Basic Books, New York, 1957, pp. 201–229.

Leighton, Alexander H., *Human Relations in a Changing World.* E. P. Dutton and Co., New York, 1949, especially pp. 228–289.

Leighton, Alexander H., and Robert J. Smith, "A Comparative Study of Social and Cultural Change," *Proceedings of the American Philosophical Society,* vol. 99, April, 1955, pp. 79–88.

Linton, Ralph, "Nativistic Movements," *American Anthropologist,* vol. 45, 1943, pp. 230–240.

Mead, Margaret, *New Lives for Old:* Cultural Transformation—Manus, 1928–1953. William Morrow and Co., New York, 1956.

Schwartz, Theodore, *The Paliau Movement in the Admiralty Islands, 1946–1954.* Anthropological Papers of the American Museum of Natural History, vol. 49, part 2, New York, 1962.

Turner, Ralph H., and Lewis M. Killian, *Collective Behavior.* Prentice Hall, Inc., Englewood, N. J., 1957. See especially pp. 307–529.

Wallace, Anthony F. C., "Revitalization Movements," *American Anthropologist,* vol. 58, 1956, pp. 264–281.

Worsely, Peter, *The Trumpet Shall Sound:* A Study of "Cargo" Cults in Melanesia. MacGibbon and Kee, London, 1957.

NOTES TO CHAPTER 11

1. Wallace, Anthony F. C., "Revitalization Movements," *American Anthropologist,* Vol. 58, 1956, pp. 264–281.

2. Leighton, Alexander H., "Mental Illness and Acculturation" in Galdston, Iago, editor, *Medicine and Anthropology:* Lectures to the Laity, New York Academy of Medicine, International Universities Press, New York, 1959, pp. 108–128. For the psychological impoverishment and stunted emotional development of more "acculturated" Ojibwa Indians, see Hallowell, A. Irving, "Values, Acculturation and Mental Health," *American Journal of Orthopsychiatry,* vol. 20, 1950, pp. 732–743.

3. MacMillan, Allister, and Alexander H. Leighton, "People of the Hinterland: Community Interrelations in a Maritime Province of Canada," in Spicer, Edward H., editor, *Human Problems in Technological Change:* A Casebook. Russell Sage Foundation, New York, 1952, pp. 225–243.

4. Wallace, Anthony F. C., *op. cit.*

5. The account to follow is based directly on Wallace's analysis, *op. cit.*, which it follows closely.
   Wallace's stages of the revitalization process match very closely the stages formulated for the revolutionary process from an independent body of data by Rex D. Hopper, "The Revolutionary Process: A Frame of Reference for the Study of Revolutionary Movements," *Social Forces*, vol. 28, 1950, pp. 270–279. As noted by Ralph H. Turner and Lewis M. Killian (*Collective Behavior*, Prentice Hall, Inc., Englewood, N.J., 1957, p. 309), Hopper's stages, and by implication Wallace's also, can be regarded "as a generalized cycle, applicable to most kinds of social movements in its broad outlines." The same authors define a social movement (*ibid.*, p. 308) as "a collectivity acting with some continuity to promote a change or resist a change in the society or group of which it is a part." As a subcategory of social movement, they define a "cult" as "a collectivity that has the continuity of a social movement, but that makes demands only on the behavior of its members" (*ibid.*, p. 309).

6. Wallace, Anthony F. C., *op. cit.*, pp. 274–275.

7. Mooney, J., *The Ghost Dance Religion and the Sioux Outbreak of 1890*. Bureau of American Ethnology, Annual Report 14, Washington, D. C., 1896.

8. Mooney, J., *op. cit.*

9. Worsley, Peter, *The Trumpet Shall Sound:* A Study of "Cargo" Cults in Melanesia. MacGibbon and Kee, London, 1957.

10. Valentine, Charles A., "Cargo Beliefs and Cargo Cults Among the West Nakanai of New Britain," unpublished manuscript. For a brief published account, see Goodenough, W. H., "Some Observations on the Nakanai," *Papua and New Guinea Scientific Society Annual Report and Proceedings, 1954*, Port Moresby, 1956.

11. Wallace, Anthony F. C., *op. cit.*, p. 275.

12. Reina, Ruben E., personal communication. Reina has described the struggle between liberals and conservatives in one Guatemalan community as its members responded to the opportunities for change and counter-change following the political revolutions of 1944 and 1954, in "Political Crisis and Cultural Revitalization: The Guatemalan Case," *Human Organization*, vol. 17, no. 4, 1958–1959, pp. 14–18.

13. Wallace, Anthony F. C., *op. cit.*, pp. 278–279.

14. Mead, Margaret, *New Lives for Old:* Cultural Transformation—Manus, 1928–1953. William Morrow and Co., New York, 1956, pp. 305–310.

15. Wallace, Anthony F. C., *op. cit.*, pp. 272–273. See also his "Mazeway Resynthesis: A Biocultural Theory of Religious Inspiration," *Transactions of the New York Academy of Sciences*, Ser. II, vol. 18, 1956, p. 638, where he concludes, "Hence the paranoid process and process of mental disorder are to be regarded as opposed in an almost dialectical sense: the disease process is the process of order decrease, the paranoid process is the process of order increase."

16. Wellin, Edward, "Water Boiling in a Peruvian Town" in Paul, Benjamin D., editor, *Health, Culture and Community*. Russell Sage Foundation, New York, 1955, pp. 71–103.

17. Mead, Margaret, *op. cit.*, pp. 190–191.

18. Schwartz, Theodore, *The Paliau Movement in the Admiralty Islands, 1946–1954*. Anthropological Papers of the American Museum of Natural History, vol. 49, part 2, New York, 1962. Our résumé of events is based on this report, on Mead's *New Lives for Old*, and on conversations with Dr. Schwartz.

19. See the comments on this attitude by the United Nations Visiting Mission to Trust Territories in the Pacific, 1956, *Report on New Guinea*, United Nations Trusteeship Council, T/1260, June 20, 1956, p. 79.

20. We have unquestionably greatly oversimplified the Raluana case, which presented a complicated situation with whose details we are unfamiliar. Our admittedly superficial information, however, suggests that our analysis may touch on one of the important factors in the case.

21. Compare the parallel comments on aid to "deserving" and "undeserving" nations by Alexander H. Leighton, *Human Relations in a Changing World: Observations on the Use of the Social Sciences*, E. P. Dutton and Co., New York, 1949, pp. 107–108. See also the questions raised by Henry F. Dobyns regarding selection of American Indian tribes to handle their own affairs in "The Indian Reorganization Act and Federal Withdrawal," *Applied Anthropology*, vol. 7, no. 2, 1948, pp. 35–44.

22. Barnett, H. G., *Anthropology in Administration*. Harper and Row, Publishers, Inc., New York, 1956, pp. 163–165.

23. For an account of a revolution in which the administrator was astute enough to cooperate with the forces of change and channel them in constructive directions, see Leighton, Alexander H., *The Governing of Men*, Princeton University Press, Princeton, N. J., 1945.

24. Our personal knowledge of this example has been supplemented considerably by information supplied by Charles A. Valentine.

25. Barnett, H. G., *op. cit.*, p. 148.

26. See, for example, the discussion of transference by Ruth L. Munroe, *Schools of Psychoanalytic Thought:* An Exposition, Critique, and Attempt at Integration, Dryden Press, New York, 1955, pp. 305–307, 525–530. For a comment on its role in guided social change, see Jacques, Elliott, "Interpretive Group Discussion as a Method of Facilitating Social Change," *Human Relations*, vol. 1, 1948, pp. 533–549.

Chapter 12

FORECASTING THE COURSE OF CHANGE

CHANGE IN ANY PART OF A STABLE SYSTEM sets in motion a series of compensatory adjustments in its other parts and in their mutual arrangements until a new equilibrium is reached. A people's culture and their phenomenal world together form such a system, as we saw in Chapter 10, where we sorted out major subsystems within it and explored their interrelationships. Thereby we outlined in macroscopic terms the ways in which communities may change. We then considered revitalization movements as a natural part of the process by which people mobilize themselves to make deliberate changes on a broad front in either their circumstances or their public culture, or in a combination of both. People feel a need for this kind of effort, we saw, when they are blocked from making compensatory adjustments to changing conditions in gratifying ways, so that accumulating frustration results in more drastic efforts at self-liberation from a condition of mounting emotional stress. As long as people feel able to make needed adjustments in their circumstances and public culture as occasion arises and are able to agree on the adjustments they consider appropriate, long chains of change and compensatory change can occur without leading to the conditions generating revitalization movements. Such movements arise in response to impasses in these chains.

Obviously, development agents would like to know what the consequences of a planned change are likely to be. Will it set in motion a series of further changes leading to impasses or will its consequences allow for ready adjustments leading back to a reasonable equilibrium? Will the change, indeed, require many adjustments? And if so, what will they be? Where adjustments are required, how can they be made so as to minimize the prospect of a need for even greater adjustments? Whether a development program aims at avoiding revitalization movements as one of its consequences or aims at helping such movements win through to new equilibria, it is essential that program planners and executors be able to predict the consequences of the moves they make. Otherwise, they may unwillingly thwart their client's efforts to devise suitable adjustments to the dislocations that planned change will create.

Even within the limitations of present knowledge, a fair degree of prediction and intelligent direction of the course of change is possible. To develop the necessary concepts we must leave the macroscopic plane on which we have been considering change and examine it more minutely.

ACTIVITIES AS UNITS OF ANALYSIS

A useful approach to the analysis of specific changes is to begin with activities. By an activity we mean any action or coordinated grouping of actions that is aimed at affecting existing arrangements in the phenomenal world in some way. These arrangements may be material, social, or psychological. Performing a religious festival, going fishing, building a home, playing a game, teaching a skill, marketing produce, harvesting crops, and undermining the power of a political rival are all obvious examples.

As thus defined, there is a great deal of elasticity in the term "activity." Giving a feast, for instance, may be viewed as a single activity or as a combination of many activities, such as gathering and preparing food, inviting guests, serving guests, making speeches, and so on. We need not concern ourselves with the problem of what are irreducible minima of purposeful action or of what are ultimate as against instrumental ends. The concept of activity is more useful as an analytical tool if kept elastic. At whatever level of specificity we may wish to use it, we can still see the ongoing life of any community as comprising the activities in which its members engage. Because activities are organized with reference to intended goals, they have, like sentences in speech, recognizable beginnings and ends, which make them readily isolable as natural behavioral entities for analysis. Taking activities as our point of departure, then, let us see how we can employ them to help us predict the consequences of change.

THE STRUCTURE OF AN ACTIVITY[1]

Some activities are customary, in that they are designed to accomplish recurring purposes under conditions where the same means for accomplishing them continue to be available. Other activities are *ad hoc* affairs, designed to accomplish unusual ends or to deal with circumstances where the usual means are unavailable. Customary or not, every activity necessarily involves a person or persons, a set of procedures, and one or more purposes or goals. It is linked in many ways to other activities, and its performance has not only an intended but many unintended effects on a community's circumstances. The effects of which people are aware, as we saw in Chapter 3, contribute to the activity's meaning for them; and all of its effects together, whether people are aware of them or not, comprise its function in the total life situation. The interconnections among the structural features of an activity, on the one hand, and the links these features provide among different activities, on the other, are both suggestive for the problem of analyzing change. It will repay us, therefore, to sort out the structural features of activities more precisely.

Purpose

By the purpose of an activity we mean both the objective and subjective states of affairs that the activity is intended to maintain or produce. Obviously, these states of affairs may have value for those who initiate the activity that is quite different from the value they have for other participants, or for nonparticipants, who must reckon with the activity's consequences from different vantage points. The sentiments people have toward an activity must not be confused with its purpose, even though they are not entirely unrelated to it. When we ask people what they are doing, they usually answer by telling us directly or by implication what they intend to accomplish by their actions: "I am making a boat"; "I am going to church"; "I am mending socks"; or "I am giving a party." These answers point to the end in view—creating an object, achieving a destination, restoring things to serviceability, or providing a kind of psychic occasion—because the end is what makes the present behavior intelligible. Our usual response to the answer we receive to our initial question is "Oh, I see!" On occasion we feel called upon to ask the further question, "Then why are you doing it that way? Why don't you do it this way instead?" This question emphasizes that people make sense out of one another's actions only so long as they can relate them instrumentally to an intended consequence. Every activity necessarily has its intended consequences (including simply the fun of performing it), and these constitute its purpose.

The purpose of an activity relates directly to values. There must be something about its anticipated consequences that people want if they are to engage in it. An activity may invite participation for a number of reasons stemming from the private sentiments of its participants, but if its performance is to enjoy public approval, its consequences must be consistent with, and its performance justifiable by, public values. Examining the reasons people give for engaging in their various activities is an important means by which to ascertain their public values. It is obviously more difficult to learn their private sentiments, but these may be even more important than public values in determining a people's readiness to abandon an activity. Indeed, activities that are not supported by public values may be thoroughly institutionalized and widely participated in because of the widespread sense of need for them. We saw, for example, that the people of Truk have private sentiments that lead most of them to engage actively in extra-marital love affairs, an activity they all publicly condemn.

The various wants and value considerations that give shape to the purpose of an activity also set the specifications that the procedures followed must meet if the purpose is to be judged as satisfactorily and praiseworthily accomplished.

Procedures

The procedural aspect of every activity involves a sequence of *operations* on a *medium*, or on several different media. These operations may require the use of *instruments*, and their successful performance necessarily requires some degree of *skill*. The operations and skills may be behavioral or mental. The media may be material, verbal, social, emotional, or ideational. Instruments may be one's own body or a part of it, some convenient object, such as a stick or stone, or another person. They may be verbal expressions, as with a curse, or they may be manufactured objects, the products of other activities.

Depending on the latitude that the procedural specifications allow, there may be little or considerable choice as to the operations to be performed, their sequence, the media to be employed, the instruments used, and the degree of skill required. Some activities are capable of considerable routinization. With others, specific procedures have to be devised to fit the exigencies of each occasion on which they are performed. In warfare, for example, there may be customary strategies defining the goals of war activity, and there may be well-established tactical principles, but how these principles are applied may vary from engagement to engagement.

To the extent that the specifications allow for alternative procedures, the necessity to choose establishes preferences, which reflect values and sentiments. Preferences stemming from the private sentiments of individual performers contribute to differences in personal style. Preferences stemming from public values serve to refine the specifications for an activity's conduct, leading to the formation of a procedural ideal. Once formed, this ideal serves as a model that keeps variations from performance to performance clustered around a mode and, insofar as circumstances permit, well within the minimum specifications set by the more highly valued goals of the activity. But each variation is likely to represent the application of public cultural principles to the unique configuration of problems and opportunities presented by the situation at hand. This may be the case even where some of the minimum specifications for more usual circumstances appear to have been sacrificed. For this reason, wide departure from the public ideal of performance may still be "normative," to use a term frequently encountered in the jargon of social science. The departure represents what any other knower of the public culture might also have done under the circumstances. The degree, then, to which procedures from performance to performance cluster tightly around a mode is a reflection of (1) the extent to which an image of the ideal performance has crystallized in the public culture and (2) the extent to which conditions of performance permitting close approximation to an ideal actually obtain from occasion to occasion.

Time and Space

Whatever the procedures for an activity may be, requirements of time and space follow from them. There is obviously a minimum time required for any one operation. Suitable space is needed. If the operation is lengthy and involves perishable materials, storage facilities may be necessary. Considerations of time and space are obviously related to personnel requirements and have a direct bearing on the occasions for which an activity's performance is scheduled.

Personnel

Some activities have few personnel requirements. They may be such that one individual can perform them satisfactorily by himself without having had much special training. Some activities are more efficiently done by one person than by several people working together. Frequently, however, we observe people engaging collectively in activities that they could perform just as easily alone. In Nakanai, for example, gardening does not ordinarily call for the performance of tasks that require concerted effort. Each woman plants and weeds in her own plot. But women go to the garden in groups and have their gardens side by side for the sake of company. Indeed, the Nakanai undertake in work parties many activities that they could easily do individually because they prefer to work in the company of their fellows. But there is no coordination of effort within these work parties. Each individual performs the same operations as his fellows independently of them.

In any society, on the other hand, there are activities that require cooperative and coordinated effort. In simplest form such coordination does not require the performance of different kinds of tasks, only that the same one be done in concert by several people, as in lifting a heavy log. In more complex activities, different tasks may have to be coordinated. Everyone may know how to perform all the different tasks and thus be interchangeable in the roles they play, or some of the tasks may involve knowledge and skills known only to a few.

For any activity, then, there are minimal and optimal numbers of persons needed to perform it and a minimal and optimal division of tasks. Specialists may or may not be needed, and it may or may not be necessary to have someone in the role of manager or coordinator.

Social Organization

Where it is necessary for several people to work together, conventions are needed governing their organization as a working group. The various tasks to be performed must be categorized. Rights, duties, and privileges must be assigned to each category vis-à-vis each of the others and in relation to the work group as a whole. It may be desirable to lay down certain specifications by which people are eligible to perform this or that task or, for that matter, to participate in the activity at all. Sanctions of some sort are likely to be necessary in order to ensure that participants will observe the conventions.

A problem in any society is to ensure that the minimum manpower needed is available when there is occasion to perform activities requiring the cooperative effort of several people. Activities that are infrequently performed and that have highly flexible personnel requirements may be done by ad hoc work parties. To guarantee the satisfactory performance of many other activities, however, it is more efficient to maintain standing organizations or groups, whose members are accustomed to working together and know their assigned tasks. Such standing groups can be mobilized as needed and go into action immediately.

Occasions

For every activity, finally, there are the occasions in which its performance is adjudged improper, permissible, or mandatory. The propriety of an occasion stems in part from the values that are expressed in the activity's purpose. On the other hand, the effects of its performance may be such as to cause undue hardship under some conditions, as when people decide to suspend feast-giving during periods of food shortage in spite of their social or religious obligations. Indeed, available media, instruments, time, space, and personnel all contribute to the necessary conditions for an activity's performance. But the fact that these requirements are met is not in itself a sufficient condition.

Even when the occasion is suitable in all other respects, the decision to perform an activity may rest with certain individuals who alone are eligible to initiate it. In Nakanai, for example, the death of an important man is a highly appropriate occasion for undertaking a memorial festival—a three-day celebration requiring several years' preparation. These festivals are valued for a wide variety of reasons by the Nakanai, but they can be initiated only by someone among the immediate kin of the deceased, and he can do so only if he commands the resources and following without which so elaborate an undertaking and lavish scale of expenditure is impossible.[2] In every society the decision to initiate some activities is the special privilege of elders, chiefs, or other officials. They may have little or nothing to do with an activity's actual organization and direction, but enjoy absolute control over the occasions of its performance.

This separation of initiating and managing powers is important to remember when we analyze activities. In Nakanai, for example, there are all sorts of occasions when an individual may wish to give a feast for his fellow villagers. By sending a formal invitation in the form of a small gift of tobacco and areca nut to the leader of each group owning a section of net used in pig drives, he in effect initiates a pig hunt. The actual organization and direction of the hunt, however, is in the hands of the leader of one of the net-owning groups—whatever leader is recognized as the most knowledgeable and skillful hunter. In Truk the long cycle of private and public ritual annually performed to ensure a good breadfruit harvest was organized and directed by a ritual specialist. He did not start the ritual on his own initiative, however, but waited until he was asked by his district chief.

Matters of occasion and initiative take us from the analysis of individual activities to their place in the larger pattern of organization relating to the community as a whole. But before we consider the ways in which activities interconnect, let us summarize in tabular form the structural features we have discussed in developing our model of the activity as a unit of analysis.

FEATURES OF ACTIVITIES

1. Purpose

    a. stated goals and their justifications
    b. other gratifications accruing to participants

2. Procedures

    a. operations performed
    b. media used, including raw materials
    c. instruments employed
    d. skills

3. Time and Space Requirements

    a. time required for each operation
    b. time as affected by numbers of participants and their skills
    c. minimum and maximum time requirements
    d. space requirements such as work areas and storage facilities

4. Personnel Requirements

    a. minimal and optimal division of tasks
    b. minimal and optimal number of persons for each
    c. specialists, if any

5. Social Organization

    a. categories of personnel
    b. rights, duties, privileges, and powers and their allocation
    c. management and direction
    d. sanctions
    e. permanence of organization (*ad hoc* vs. standing groups)

6. Occasions for Performance
   a. occasions when mandatory, permitted, and prohibited
   b. processes by which activity initiated
   c. locus of privilege, power, or duty to initiate
   d. relation of initiation to direction
   e. availability of media, instruments, personnel

This outline is obviously capable of considerable refinement. We present it not as an exhaustive treatment but as providing a convenient checklist of things to bear in mind when using activities as points of departure in tracking down the effects of change.

It is obvious that for any activity a change in one of the items listed above may have an effect on a number of the other items. New media may require new skills, may change the numbers of personnel required and the degree of organization needed, or may affect the time and space requirements for the activity's performance. If the purposes for which the activity's operations are performed change, the occasions for their performance will necessarily change also. It is possible, therefore, to take any customary activity and ask how a contemplated change in one or more of its structural features will necessarily affect its other features—provided, of course, we already know how the activity is currently conducted with respect to all of the features we have listed. This is closely analogous to the kind of analysis made by industrial engineers and efficiency experts in order to establish the net gain or loss that will accrue from a proposed reorganization of production methods. The main difference is that we are not so exclusively concerned with monetary costs.

INTERRELATIONS AMONG ACTIVITIES

Orderly living requires that each of the activities in which people engage be organized with reference to the requirements of the others. The purposes of some may allow little latitude in procedure or personnel, so that their organization becomes one of the existing sets of conditions limiting the ways in which other purposes can be conveniently achieved. The net efficacy with which human purposes can be accomplished, as we have seen, depends on the degree to which people have mutually adjusted their various activities. We have already commented on the importance of scheduling in this regard. The several structural features of activities, as we have outlined them, call our attention to other ways in which different activities are mutually interconnected in systems.

Feature Overlap

One kind of interconnection is the sharing of one or more features by several different activities. Activities A and B are designed to accomplish the same purpose under different sets of conditions. Activities X and Y have the same time and space requirements, while Y and Z are the responsibility of the same standing organization of personnel. All groupings of personnel, however varied in numbers and complexity, may be organized in terms of the same principles for allocating authority.

This overlapping of structural features from activity to activity provides one of the important channels by which a change in the conduct of one activity may affect the conduct of others. Where two activities are designed to accomplish the same purpose utilizing different procedures and raw materials, for example, a change that affects the availability of raw materials may have a profound effect on the relative frequency with which people engage in these activities. One of them may drop out of use altogether. Where the same standing group provides the personnel for several different activities, to take another example, and a modification of procedure in one of these activities requires personnel changes to go with it, these personnel changes may result in the appearance of a new kind of standing group, coexisting with the old one, or the organization of the old standing group may be modified accordingly, with resulting procedural adjustments in all the other activities for which the group is responsible.

Feature Complementation

Activities may be systematically interconnected not by the similarity of their structural features but by their complementarity. Activity A exploits one set of raw materials and activity B avoids them, exploiting another instead. This arrangement ensures an adequate supply of materials for both. Special skills required in activities that must frequently be performed concurrently are best acquired by different persons, so that each kind of specialist is available when needed.

Complementation is an exceedingly important organizational principle in connection with raw materials, skills, time and space requirements, personnel, and occasions of performance. A contemplated change in one of these features in one activity must be critically examined to see how it will affect the complementary relationships it has with other activities. For as these relationships are disturbed, freedom to engage in other activities will be affected, and it may become necessary to modify their organization in order to be able to continue to engage in them. Development agents may be sure that their clients will examine proposals for change with such considerations in mind. They are likely to resist a proposal to adopt new procedures in an activity if these procedures require them to use limited resources already being heavily exploited in another activity whose purposes they value highly.

Instrumental Linkage

Activities are also interconnected, in that the purpose of one is to provide conditions necessary to the performance of another. Here the relationship is instrumental.

The value people attach to activities that are essentially instrumental to the performance of others differs from the value they attach to activities that they regard as ends in themselves. Many activities are valued in both ways at once. Fishing is instrumental to eating but may be enjoyed for its own sake as well. Insofar as performing an activity results in states of affairs that are valued as ends in themselves, the activity may be said to have *intrinsic* value. Insofar as it derives value from its interconnections with other activities, its value is *extrinsic*. The instrumental relationship provides perhaps the most important kind of extrinsic value.

Several activities may all be instrumental to the same other activity. Consider, for example, the many activities that are instrumental to the family dinner: working to earn money, shopping, cooking, and so on. The same activity, moreover, may be instrumental to the performance of many others. An important advantage of a monetary economy is that it maximizes the number of other activities for which one activity may be instrumental. It makes it possible to equalize the instrumental value of all activities that result in the same amount of monetary gain per unit of effort, whatever difference there may be in intrinsic value; and it enables people to adjust the instrumental value of any activity relative to its intrinsic value, to the knowledge and skills needed to perform it, or to the expenditure of effort it requires.

Depending on the physical and emotional expenditure involved, people regard those activities that have only instrumental and no intrinsic value for them as tedious or downright onerous. They seek ways of performing them that will provide at least a modicum of immediate gratification and thus impart to them a degree of intrinsic value. Any proposal for change is likely to be welcome if it gives promise of such an effect and is not counter to public values. People will quickly discontinue, moreover, any activities whose value is mainly instrumental, when changes in the activities they served make them no longer necessary. Loss of instrumental value, however, will not result in an activity's demise if it has high intrinsic value as well.

Partial Fusion

Two activities with some procedural requirements in common may be linked, in that a single performance of the common procedures will simultaneously promote the ends of both activities. If the procedures in question are sufficiently onerous so that their single performance for both activities greatly enhances the net efficacy of each, the performance of one may regularly provide the occasion for the performance of the other as well. In Nakanai, for example, there are many social purposes that require killing a domestic pig and distributing pork to neighboring hamlets. The Nakanai frequently find that occasions when they must kill a pig for one purpose are convenient times to undertake other activities for which they must kill a pig also. Thus the sponsor of a memorial feast for a dead kinsman may use this occasion to initiate a junior kinsman into the mysteries of the men's secret society, both activities requiring that he slaughter and distribute pork.

When a change leads people to drop an activity, the net efficacy of any other activities with which its performance has been partially fused is thereby reduced. In this way, discontinuing one activity may leave the performance of others sufficiently devoid of gratification so that they are discontinued as well.

It often happens that in order to kill two birds with one stone an activity may be performed in a manner that would be inefficient if it were not for the still greater compensations deriving from partial fusion. If the activity with which its performance has been fused is discontinued, its procedures will then be revised to make its independent performance feasible or to allow for its partial fusion with some other activity. Any such readjustments necessarily have implications for the overall scheduling of activities.

Net Efficacy and the Problem of Balance

Partial fusion brings us to consider two conflicting considerations between which people seek to strike a balance in designing the tools, skills, and other features of the several activities in which they engage—the conflict between the requirements for efficiently performing any one activity by itself and the requirements of general efficiency or net efficacy of all activities taken together. For a particular activity, for example, it is desirable to have tools designed specifically for the use to which they will be put in that activity. In response to this desideratum, people tend to elaborate their tools into many kinds, each one designed to do one thing as efficiently as possible. Working against this tendency is the need to keep equipment to a practical minimum, so as not to be overburdened with more of it than can be readily maintained or conveniently carried around. The result is that people tend to elaborate equipment in connection with those activities in which they engage frequently and that are performed in a fixed place where equipment can be permanently kept and requires no transportation. But for purposes that arise infrequently or that call for considerable spatial mobility, a few multi-purpose tools are preferable. The average American householder, for example, may have a fairly wide assortment of cutlery in his kitchen, but he does not take it all with him on a camping trip. There, one good multi-purpose knife is what he wants.

The same considerations apply to skills and the organization of personnel. To what extent is it preferable to have people who are highly skilled in a few operations and unable to perform most others as against having people who are jacks of all trades and masters of none? Here the problem is to find the optimal balance between efficiency and flexibility, a balance that is necessarily different for every society and that must be continually readjusted in each society. To what extent is it desirable to have people functioning in many different kinds of groups, each efficiently organized for performing one or two activities, like our own urban fire companies? And to what extent is it desirable to have the same standing group functioning in a wide variety of activities for no one of which its organization is specifically designed, though it serves each reasonably well? We should note that these questions cannot be resolved in terms of the optimum efficiency of groups as productive units alone. Many intangible wants and values must also be considered. For example, there is reason to postulate that the greater the number of groups in which a person participates and the fewer the activities performed by each group, the weaker will be his commitment to membership in any group or to its rules and public values—the less, that is, will membership in any particular group constitute an important feature of his self-image. On the other hand, the fewer the groups to which a person belongs and the greater the number of purposes he accomplishes through any one of them, the deeper his commitment and the fiercer his loyalties and ethnocentric orientation are likely to be.

The problem of balance is one that program planners and development agents must keep constantly in mind. It is easy to get carried away with what looks like the "best" and "most efficient" solution to a particular problem. It is especially easy for us Americans, given the values and habits of thought with which we operate when we begin considering "technical" problems. Too often the most efficient solution, if put into effect, is the most disruptive for the conduct of other activities and the gratification of other wants.[3]

We shall come back to this problem shortly when we consider how the mutual adjustment of activities leads to the development of institutions and look at change in relation to a community's institutional structure. In the meantime it will pay us to see how the concepts we have already presented for analyzing the course of change apply to a concrete case.

FISHING METHODS AND SOCIAL CHANGE
IN THE SOUTHERN GILBERT ISLANDS[4]

The changes to be described occurred during the first half of this century on the atoll of Onotoa in the southern Gilbert Islands. Onotoa is a dry atoll, with an average annual rainfall of only 40 inches, which imposes serious limitations on its agricultural productivity.[5] A careful botanical survey revealed no more than 60 species of vascular plant, domestic and wild.[6] The only crops that grow well enough to play a significant role in the local diet are coconuts, a coarse variety of Cyrtosperma, and Pandanus. The sea is necessarily of vital importance, the daily diet consisting of fish, ripe coconut meat, and a beverage of water mixed with molasses obtained from the sap of the coconut blossom.

In keeping with the importance of fish in their diet, Onotoans have developed a wide variety of fishing activities,[7] calling for different methods and materials and different numbers of participants. Prior to the changes to be recounted here, the fishing activities that contributed most to the food supply and that were in this respect most important economically involved cooperative drives close to shore. There appears to have been need for a permanent organization of men and women who shared a single domestic economy. This cooperating group was an extended family household. Considerations of defense in precolonial times also may have favored this type of family organization. But the only day-to-day economic activities requiring extended families were those connected with in-shore fishing. People worked their land individually.

Among the many fishing methods were several that took place on the open sea entirely outside the very shallow lagoon: torch fishing at night for flying fish, shark fishing, and trolling for large fish. Open-sea fishing, of course, required an outrigger sailing canoe. Given the sparse vegetation, wood suitable for making canoes was scarce and much labor was required piecing together small irregular planks adzed out with shell tools.[8] The number of canoes per capita was necessarily small and the contribution of open-sea fishing to the community's food supply correspondingly slight. Such fishing was primarily a sport to be engaged in occasionally by those who were so fortunate as to command the necessary equipment. As a sport, however, it was highly regarded, and open-sea varieties of fish rated high as desirable food. To own a sailing canoe seems also to have been important in status rivalry.[9]

Following annexation of Ocean Island by Great Britain in 1901, mining operations were rapidly developed there to exploit the island's rich phosphate deposits.[10] Many Onotoans went there to work, and continue to do so. In 1951 about 15 per cent of the atoll's people were away, either as wage-workers or as members of workers' families, most of them on Ocean Island. The great majority of those going there to work went for a period of a year or two, and then came home for several years, after which, depending on their needs, they returned for another year or two. Their main incentive to work, and the chief use to which they put their modest wages, was to acquire the basic equipment for more efficiently carrying on subsistence activities at home, where they have been increasingly caught in a squeeze between limited local resources and an expanding population. (In 1951 Onotoa supported 514 persons per square mile of land.)[11] While Onotoans have also wanted to obtain cloth, cooking utensils, bicycles, tobacco, and a few luxury items, they have given top priority to steel cutting-tools, fish hooks, wire leaders to prevent the loss of fish hooks, and above all to North American redwood with which to build canoes, canvas for sails, and paint to keep their canoes in good condition. In contrast with precolonial times, there were in 1951 two sailing canoes per three adult men in Onotoa.

This change in the availability of sailing canoes is the one whose ramifications we shall consider here. The change is essentially a quantitative one. In 1951 Onotoan canoes were built almost exactly as they used to be. Techniques of fishing were with minor exceptions those of former times. The major material result of work in the phosphate mines, other than small improvements in creature comforts, had been to provide more and better materials with which to make the equipment customarily used in open-sea fishing. What then had been its effects?

Obviously, it enabled many more people to engage regularly in open-sea fishing. Because of the values already associated with this activity, most Onotoans were glad to take advantage of the opportunity. Their desire to do so, along with status considerations, was presumably what motivated them to purchase wood for canoes from their wages. Great increase in the number of people regularly doing open-sea fishing resulted, in turn, in a number of economic and social readjustments.

First of all, as more people spent more time in deep-sea fishing, they devoted correspondingly less time to in-shore fishing. Less equipment for in-shore fishing needed to be manufactured. In 1951 the once carefully maintained stone fish traps on the reef flats were seldom used and were in disrepair. Neglect to maintain the physical equipment needed in in-shore fishing was accompanied by failure to maintain the social system of priorities relating to its exploitation. Once jealously guarded property rights in fishing sites around coral heads within the atoll's lagoon were allowed to lapse. In 1951 the people readily agreed to declare the lagoon public domain, when they adopted by referendum a formal code based on customary property law.[12]

Secondly, unlike most other forms of fishing activity, deep-sea fishing was most efficiently done by two persons working together; it took two to manage the canoe effectually. Increased reliance on this activity resulted in the formation of permanent fishing partnerships of two men, one the canoe owner, who fished together regularly, dividing the catch evenly and sharing the labor needed to maintain the canoe. At the same time, married couples had become less dependent on a large, standing work group, and what in-shore fishing was still done in 1951 was conducted by *ad hoc* working parties of kinsmen.

These changes contributed to two contrasting developments in the traditional social structure of Onotoan communities. One pertained to the extended family and its associated descent group, the *kaainga*, the other to the community and its meeting house, the *mwaneaba*.

Reliance on deep-sea fishing decreased the economic dependence of married couples on the extended family and other kin, so that the extended family was weakened as was the authority of its head. Indeed, it was now possible for couples to reside independently, since in-shore fishing had provided the only economic activities frequently engaged in for which cooperative effort was needed. By signing up to work on Ocean Island, a young man could stake himself to the necessary equipment through which he could become head of his own household early in life. There were undoubtedly pressures from both government and mission to break up the extended family, but they were no greater than in other Pacific islands where extended family organization has persisted in spite of such pressures. A key factor in the almost complete demise of the extended family in Onotoa seems to have been this, the only really marked change in the subsistence economy.

Associated with the extended family in former times was the *kaainga*, a group of people descended from a common ancestor. In the past each Onotoan community contained a number of *kaainga*, which operated as the most important solidary units in matters of law, protection, and revenge. Coming down from the *kaainga's* founder was a tract of land, on which the *kaainga* head lived and where other members of the *kaainga* also had a right to live in the extended family of which he was head, their several houses constituting a distinct hamlet. Newly married couples had a right to live in the hamlet associated with either the husband's or wife's *kaainga*. Their choice determined the *kaainga* membership of their children, who belonged to the one in whose hamlet they grew up. Since the vast majority of couples chose to live in the husband's hamlet of origin, most people belonged to their father's *kaainga*. Nevertheless, people knew what their *kaainga* membership was because of their physical identification with it during childhood and adolescence, and this membership did not change if they moved away as adults. As more and more people resided independently, given the economic opportunity to do so, an increasing number of children grew up uncertain of their *kaainga* membership. This might have led to a change in the rules of membership, had there continued to be pressing reasons for preserving *kaainga* organization. But the prohibition of fighting and of resort to private justice imposed by colonial law had reduced personal dependence on the *kaainga* at the same time that the economic changes we have noted were reducing dependence on the extended family associated with it. As a result, the ambiguities as to *kaainga* membership that followed the increase in independent residence resulted in the *kaainga's* complete demise as a feature of Onotoan social organization within fifty years.

These developments were not without cost, however. Not all the activities for which the extended family and *kaainga* were units of cooperation were discontinued. And there continued to be social and emotional needs and important cultural values that made close identification with a larger kin group important. Dissolution of the *kaainga* as a protective association made neighbor more dependent on the good will of neighbor and increased need for mutual cooperation at the community level.

The community meeting house, *mwaneaba*, was the remaining institution capable of meeting these residual needs. Popular acceptance of Christianity deprived it of some of its traditional functions and meaning, transferring them to the Church, but the *mwaneaba* continues to be of tremendous importance in Onotoan life. In former times the *kaainga* stood between the individual and the community in several important matters, but it does so no longer. The *mwaneaba* is itself organized into a series of seats, *bwoti*, with which community offices are associated. All persons with the right to the same seat are direct descendants of the founding ancestor and together constitute an organized kin group in *mwaneaba* affairs. Principles of *bwoti* membership differ from those of *kaainga* membership, and their operation has not been affected by the changes we have recounted. Nevertheless, they were such as to produce a group whose local membership overlapped considerably with that of the *kaainga*,[13] bringing together much the same kinds of kinsmen. Thus the meeting house was able to provide an organization of personnel ready-made to function as a substitute for the *kaainga* and do so in the context of increased individual dependence on the community as a whole. In this way, the *mwaneaba* has, if anything, gained in functional importance as the *kaainga* has disappeared. Certainly, the seriousness with which Onotoans observe *mwaneaba* protocol attests to its vitality.

To sum up, we have observed in this case the ramifications of what was fundamentally a change in the Onotoan environment such that a scarce raw material, wood for making canoes, became available in unprecedented quantity. This enabled people to procure the equipment needed for deep-sea fishing, so that a food resource hitherto closed to most Onotoans could now be exploited systematically. More time devoted to deep-sea fishing meant less time devoted to other competing activities. The equipment, standing organization of personnel, and system of rights and priorities relating to these competing activities were no longer needed and ceased to be maintained. At the same time new social relationships were formalized, as in the fishing partnership. These developments, together with others resulting from the presence of missionaries and government officers, had a differential effect on institutionalized aspects of Onotoan social structure, promoting the demise of the extended family and *kaainga* and increasing the functional importance of the *mwaneaba* and its *bwoti*.

This may seem like quite a lot to hang on the increased availability of wood. But if we go one step back and consider the sequence of changes in the light of the introduction of money and opportunities to earn it, it immediately becomes evident that the things Onotoans do with the money they earn, other than buying deep-sea fishing equipment, are of little consequence from the standpoint of social and economic change. Other things imported for cash enable minor improvements in the standard of living and in the efficiency of local production, but they have little implication for the balance of activities and social relationships. Cloth, tobacco, bicycles, and sewing machines do not permit Onotoa to support a larger resident population, nor do they make possible any major changes in the subsistence economy or social organization. It is access to more sailing canoes that has opened the way for a chain reaction of change.

We should note, moreover, that the Onotoans responded in this way to the possibilities that working for cash created for them because of the values and aspirations they already had for themselves. In order to have predicted their emphasis on canoes and deep-sea fishing, we would have needed to know the value attaching to canoes as compared with other material things and also the system of preferences attaching to different kinds of fish and fishing activity in the sentiments of the majority of Onotoans and in the overtly stated public value system. Our model of activities and their interrelationships would then have led us to ask most of the remaining questions that our analysis shows us we would have had to ask in order to forecast the sequence of events. This case shows, moreover, that it is not enough to ask these questions only in relation to the particular change whose effects are under consideration. The outcome for any change being considered will be abetted, inhibited, or diverted by the effects of other changes taking place at the same time. That is why forecasting change requires a thorough knowledge of the total social and cultural situation in a community. Models for helping to forecast change can be effectively applied only where there is knowledge. They are not a substitute for it.

The Onotoan case includes some considerations to which analysis of activities inevitably leads us, but which are not readily cared for by looking at activities alone. We found it necessary to talk about social institutions such as the *kaainga* and *mwaneaba* in considering the things affected by change. Institutions such as these are affected not so much by changes in the conduct of an activity as by changes in the mutual scheduling of a number of different activities. We turn now to consider this matter further.

ACTIVITIES AND INSTITUTIONS

The several ways in which activities interconnect all affect both their internal content and the scheduling of their performance. When they can, people try to achieve contents and schedules mutually adjusted so as to permit them to engage in as many rewarding activities as possible at optimal intervals. Helpful to this end are complementary arrangements of activity features, divisions of labor and skill, and effective utilization of overlapping features among activities to fuse their performance into more efficient routines for accomplishing multiple purposes at once.

Fluctuations through time in the availability of material resources, personnel, and skills alternately restrict and expand the possibilities for scheduling activities. People must have alternative recipes for getting things done and alternative schedules, if they are to maintain enough flexibility to adapt their behavior so as to accomplish their purposes in a changing world. But the time and energy expended to learn alternative procedures, develop alternative skills, and do all the things needed to maintain flexibility, deplete the time and energy available for other, more immediately gratifying activities. And the greater the number of alternatives which people must be prepared to take, the more difficult it becomes to arrange their phenomenal world socially and materially so as to enable them to perform any one of the alternatives with ease and efficiency. The more completely conditions permit people to follow one set of alternatives and one schedule of activities, the freer they are to accumulate the necessary raw materials and instruments, to sharpen the particular skills required, and to organize their relations with one another in terms of a given set of principles and standing groups. Under stable conditions, therefore, people commit themselves more and more to particular recipes and to a particular schedule of activities. They pay less and less attention to keeping their world and themselves in a state of readiness to resort to alternatives. Rather they become increasingly concerned to maintain their world so that the need to resort to alternatives will not arise. The recipes, stockpiles, materials and social arrangements, and schedules to which people commit themselves acquire value as ends in themselves. Alternatives are devalued accordingly. These publicly valued procedures and arrangements to which such commitment has been made, and all of the things associated with them, make up a community's *institutions*.[14] There are, for example, many different beliefs, practices, and associated structures and organizations of people by which men seek spiritual comfort, as comparative anthropology makes abundantly clear, but on the broad spectrum of possibilities we in our society have committed ourselves to particular bodies of doctrine, symbols, types of building, ritual procedure, and organizational systems and have established them as institutional aspects of religious activity in American society.

In every society there are areas of activity where flexibility is maintained, where commitment to any particular alternative is low, and where there is little institutional fixity. And in every society there are other areas where commitment is high, flexibility is minimal, and institutions flourish.

Because they develop in the context of increasing the efficiency with which valued ends can be readily achieved, a society's institutions tend to crystallize around the points where activity features overlap and the conduct of activities can be effectively fused. The result is that institutions tend to be highly complex in their meaning and function. Efficiency is served, for example, by developing one or two standing organizations of personnel that go into action whenever an activity calls for cooperative behavior. If, as in our society, there is great reliance on volunteer, *ad hoc* associations when cooperative action is called for, then efficiency is served by having one or two models by which all such associations are organized. So it is that in our volunteer associations we regularly elect a chairman and secretary and conduct business along the lines canonized in *Robert's Rules of Order*. If we have not institutionalized the groups, we have institutionalized their mode of organization.

Because mutuality of expectations is so essential to the orderly conduct of activities involving cooperation, people are under considerable pressure to reduce alternative systems of social organization to a minimum. The emotional stress resulting from conflicting roles also provides strong motivation to fuse personnel organizations for different activities, where possible, and to give complementary scheduling to those activities whose personnel organizations cannot be efficiently fused. The result is that social relationships tend to become highly institutionalized in most societies.

Sheer habituation is another factor promoting the development of institutions. The skills one uses every day, the settings in which one is thoroughly at home, the procedures one has already followed countless times, the rules of conduct one regularly follows, and the people with whom one continually works, all become, in time, fixed points of reference giving stability to one's world. Most gratifications are associated with them, and this gives them special value.

As resort to particular materials, procedural recipes, and patterns of social relationship becomes institutionalized, these things become fixtures with respect to which people seek to adapt the conduct of new activities. They are the things to which people turn first in trying to devise solutions to new problems. It is tempting to speculate that when they can be successfully applied, the resulting solutions are likely to prove minimally disruptive to the conduct of other affairs. But prudence cautions against any such sweeping conclusion. Application of existing institutions to new problems, however, even when it results in serious dislocations, gives people a sense of continuity with the past. Modifications to deal with the dislocations are made in due course and the change process becomes one of successive adjustments rather than a sudden new starting from scratch, though sometimes the latter procedure might have resulted in fewer problems. Because they are fixtures, people tend to order other aspects of their lives in relation to their institutions as given things, which will not presumably change. The result is that people are more willing to contemplate changes in the conduct of activities that are not institutionalized and less willing to contemplate changes in their institutions. Because of their complex relations to multiple purposes it is a safe working principle that change in a society's institutional structure is likely to have seriously unsettling repercussions that ramify widely.

For development agents it is a safe rule that insofar as it is possible to solve a client community's problems by utilizing its established institutions, the solution is more likely to make sense to the community's members and not strike them as threatening. It is also more likely to be one that they can put into operation with minimal initial difficulty, and more often than not with fewer compensatory adjustments later. Where a problem cannot be solved in this manner but requires changes in the community's institutional structure, agents may anticipate that, whatever solution is adopted, a number of new problems are likely to arise in consequence. In the next chapter we examine some of these problems in relation to social control.

SUGGESTED READING

Bascom, William R., and Melville J. Herskovits, editors, *Continuity and Change in African Cultures*. University of Chicago Press, Chicago, 1959.

Cochran, Thomas C., and Ruben E. Reina, *Entrepreneurship in Argentine Culture: Torcuato di Tella and S.I.A.M.* University of Pennsylvania Press, Philadelphia, 1962.

Colson, Elizabeth, "Possible Repercussions of the Right to Make Wills Upon the Plateau of Northern Rhodesia," *Journal of African Administration*, vol. 2, 1950, pp. 24–34.

Epstein, T. S., *Economic Development and Social Change in South India*. University of Manchester Press, Manchester, England (Humanities Press, New York), 1962.

Nash, Manning, *Machine Age Maya:* The Industrialization of a Guatemalan Community. American Anthropological Association, Memoir no. 87, The Free Press, Glencoe, Ill., 1958.

Salz, Beate R., *The Human Element in Industrialization:* A Hypothetical Case Study of Ecuadorean Indians. American Anthropological Association, Memoir no. 85, Menasha, Wis., 1955.

Stanner, W. E. H., *The South Seas in Transition:* A Study of Post-War Rehabilitation and Reconstruction in Three Pacific Dependencies. Australasian Publishing Co., Sydney, 1953.

NOTES TO CHAPTER 12

1. The analysis of activities presented here owes much to the analysis of institutions by Bronislaw Malinowski in *A Scientific Theory of Culture*, University of North Carolina Press, Chapel Hill, 1944, pp. 52–54

2. Goodenough, Ward H., "The Pageant of Death in Nakanai," *University Museum Bulletin* (University of Pennsylvania, Philadelphia), vol. 19, no. 1, 1955, pp. 19–43.

3. The importance of less specialization of technical functions for maintaining industrial flexibility and for developing a corps of devoted employees closely identified with the firm and its fortunes—so important in the early stages of industrial growth—is illustrated clearly by Thomas C. Cochran and Ruben E. Reina, *Entrepreneurship in Argentine Culture:* Torcuato di Tella and S.I.A.M., University of Pennsylvania Press, Philadelphia, 1962.

4. Material for this case comes from a field study of Onotoa's ecology in which we participated in the summer of 1951. The study was sponsored by the Pacific Science Board of the National Research Council, and financed by the Office of Naval Research. This account is adapted from a paper entitled "Ecological and Social Change in the Gilbert Islands," read at the Ninth Pacific Science Congress, Bangkok, Thailand, November 28, 1957.

5. Cloud, Preston E., Jr., *Preliminary Report on Geology and Marine Environments of Onotoa Atoll, Gilbert Islands.* Atoll Research Bulletin no. 12, Washington, 1952, p. 11.

6. Moul, Edwin T., *Preliminary Report on the Flora of Onotoa Atoll, Gilbert Islands.* Atoll Research Bulletin no. 57, Washington, 1957, p. 1.

7. Randall, John E., "Investigation of the Ichthyofauna of Onotoa, Gilbert Islands" in Banner, A. H., and J. E. Randall, *Preliminary Report on Marine Biology Study of Onotoa Atoll, Gilbert Islands.* Atoll Research Bulletin no. 13, Washington, 1952, pp. 43–57.

8. For an account of canoe making, see Grimble, A., "Canoes in the Gilbert Islands," *Journal of the Royal Anthropological Institute,* vol. 54, 1924, pp. 101–139.

9. *Ibid.*

10. British Colonial Office, *Report on the Gilbert and Ellice Islands Colony for the Year 1949.* London, 1950, p. 43.

11. Turpin, R., "Lands Settlement, Onotoa." Unpublished Lands Commission report, Gilbert and Ellice Islands, 1952.

12. *Ibid.*

13. For an account of these principles, see Goodenough, Ward H., "A Problem in Malayo-Polynesian Social Organization," *American Anthropologist,* vol. 57, 1955, pp. 71–83.

14. See Parsons, Talcott, and Edward A. Shils, editors, *Toward a General Theory of Action,* Harvard University Press, Cambridge, Mass., 1959, p. 203. Other writers have sometimes used the term "institution" in a different sense. Thus "an institution is a group of people," according to Carleton S. Coon, *The Story of Man: From the First Human to Primitive Culture and Beyond,* 2d ed., Alfred A. Knopf, Inc., New York, 1962, p. 3.

Chapter 13

CHANGE AND SOCIAL CONTROL

ONE OF THE MOST SERIOUS DISLOCATIONS that can arise in the course of change is the breakdown of a society's social control mechanisms. These mechanisms, if they are to function effectively, must be closely geared to the society's institutional structure and must be largely institutionalized themselves. Social control is, therefore, highly sensitive to any change that affects the usual intermeshing of institutions.

METHODS OF SOCIAL CONTROL

For every society the problem of social control involves the resolution of a paradox. The freedom to act that individuals must enjoy in order to accomplish socially approved ends and to meet their own legitimate desires, gives them opportunities to pursue ends that are socially disapproved. In order effectively to carry out the responsibilities of his office, for example, the President of the United States must have considerable power to act. But the power enabling him to do right also enables him to do wrong. To be in a position to handle the financial affairs of a lodge, club, or other organization, its treasurer must have freedom of action, which also makes it possible for him to abscond with the organization's funds. The freedom that parents in our society must give their teenage children to engage in socially approved activities makes it possible for the children to be delinquent. To restrict people's freedom to the point where they are unable to do wrong is to prevent them from doing what is necessary and right.

Societies control misuses of the power to act in three principal ways. One of them is to offset power with power. This is what we mean when we talk about checks and balances in government. Essentially, it involves keeping power sufficiently distributed so that if any one person or group does something wrong, other persons and groups can retaliate effectively. This approach to social control is based on the assumption that people will misuse power, will act antisocially, if they feel they can at little or no cost to themselves. The object, therefore, is so to structure the relations between persons and groups as to make behavior contrary to the expectations of others too costly. The assumption is that people weigh the advantages and disadvantages of doing right and wrong and rationally decide to do right because in the long run it is to their personal advantage. For this method of control to work effectively, it is necessary to order affairs so that the chances of a person's doing wrong without others knowing about it are minimal. It works only where the individual's actions are subject to the interested scrutiny of others. Once he is in a position where others cannot find him out, this kind of control over his behavior disappears.

The second method by which people control the actions of their fellows is so to condition each one of them when he is young that the prospect of misbehaving makes him feel anxious. He may be free to do something he very much wants to do without being found out, but he is unable to allow himself to do it because of the anxiety he feels in connection with it. And if he does do it, his anxiety will drive him to excessive efforts to cover up his misconduct, efforts that have the effect of directing suspicion upon him. This form of control does not prevent a person from wanting to do wrong, but it effectively inhibits him from doing so and relegates his misconduct to the realm of daydreams. If the anxiety is acute enough, even awareness of a desire to misbehave is repressed.

The third method of social control is to develop self-images in people such that the misconduct in question is inconsistent with their own conception of who and what they are as persons. To do wrong would be to violate their own sense of personal integrity. They are not simply inhibited by anxiety from doing something they want to do; they don't even want to do it. The idea does not attract them.

Each method of social control—the first depending on factors external and the other two on factors internal to the individual —has advantages and drawbacks. Where control is purely external, there are no inhibitions against breaking the rules of conduct, and the individual remains maximally flexible, readily able to alter his conduct realistically in the face of new circumstances and problems even if it means violating existing mores. The drawback is that this flexibility permits of ready antisocial behavior in the absence of external monitors. Where the controls are internal, the reverse tends to be true. They prevent deviant behavior in the absence of external controls, and this is an advantage, but they make the individual less flexible and adaptable. When changing conditions require new forms of behavior, anxiety blocks a person from developing them effectively and makes his response to the exigencies of changing circumstances indecisive and neurotic. When adaptive change requires behavior that is inconsistent with a person's conception of self and that would undermine his integrity, he refuses to make the change. Often enough, he would rather die. The self-image approach to internal control is the most effective and by the same token renders the individual least flexible, insofar as adaptive behavior appears to be destructive of personal integrity. The more the areas of conduct controlled in this way, the more rigid people become. We all know the weaknesses as well as the strengths of what we call a "rigid personality." Where it is important not to compromise, the person becomes a saint; where compromise is necessary, he becomes an intransigent obstructionist.

The Balancing of Control Methods

Every society has the problem of striking a balance among these methods of social control. Where existing social and physical arrangements provide external controls making the abuse of freedom and power impractical, it is not necessary to resort to internal controls, and flexibility is preserved. The exercise of common sense keeps people in line. Social monitoring is often augmented by magical means. In Nakanai, for example, there is supposed to be a form of magic that will seek out and punish a thief whose identity is unknown. In Truk there are divining procedures whereby a thief may be identified. Such practices are widespread and serve to increase the scope of public scrutiny over individual behavior. But even with such techniques, external controls are inadequate or impractical for some areas of behavior. For these, people try to develop internal controls in their fellows. These areas of control, of course, vary from one social system to the next.

For example, all societies prohibit sexual relations between brother and sister (a few make exceptions for royalty). In many, violation of this taboo is prevented by requiring that brother and sister avoid each other's company and sleep in separate houses. For them to be seen together alone is in itself tantamount to incest. Thus, even if a brother and sister want to have sexual relations, there are such effective external barriers that they lack any opportunity without being observed. In our own society, of course, we allow comparatively great intimacy between brother and sister. They have, in fact, frequent opportunities to violate the incest taboo without anyone's being the wiser. They do not violate it because of the great blanket of anxiety in which we wrap not only incest but sex generally. It also inhibits against pre-marital and extra-marital heterosexual relations, though it by no means fully prevents them. At the same time it makes violations, when they occur, impulsive. Efforts at illicit sex are likely to be unsatisfying; and often they are self-defeating. A price we pay for this form of control is that our anxieties tend to carry over into legitimate sexual relationships in marriage, making sex a major source of tension and difficulty in marital relationships. For us, sex is one of the major foci of neurosis, as the clinical evidence overwhelmingly testifies.[1]

As anxieties about sex diminish following marriage in our society, we resort to the self-image method of control in preventing adultery. A woman's integrity as a wife and mother, the major roles about which her identity is constructed in our society, is felt to be compromised by adulterous relations. There is less emphasis of this sort on men, the unwillingness of women providing an external control over them. The controls are, in fact, much more complicated for both sexes; but there is enough truth in this oversimplified statement to present a marked contrast with the Gilbert Islands, where a married woman is never permitted to be alone outside the settlement area or in her house after dark. If her husband must be away from home over night, she sleeps with relatives. She goes to the gardens in the company of another adult woman. Should she go alone into the bush, the chances are that her departure or return will be observed, and the fact that she is unaccompanied will be interpreted as *prima facie* evidence of adultery.

The examples just given should not lead us to conclude that our society places much more emphasis on internal controls generally than other societies. We need only remind ourselves of the many places where we rely largely on external controls. Although we condemn cheating on examinations in our colleges and universities, for example, few schools have found it possible to set up a satisfactory "honor system." Most find it necessary to resort to special seating arrangements and proctors. Our elaborate law enforcement agencies are eloquent testimony to the many areas of activity where we depend on external rather than internal controls. We try to make stealing incompatible with people's self-images, to use another example, but are so ineffectual that we find it better to rely on locks, safe-deposit vaults, night-watchmen, police patrols, statements in quadruplicate, regular inventories, audits, and other external controls in order to prevent theft. In the Southern Gilbert Islands, on the other hand, the self-image control over stealing is more effectively developed. With few locks or hiding places, with gardens unguarded, there are many opportunities for petty pilfering, especially of food resources. Periodic scarcities exacerbate the problem. The Gilbertese, therefore, vigorously aver that anyone who steals is not a proper human being. To steal is not only incompatible with one's conception of self as an honest person; it is incompatible with one's conception of self as a person at all. To see oneself as a thief is to see oneself as inhuman; it is like seeing oneself as a cannibal in our society. In keeping with this position, anyone caught pilfering used to lose his legal standing as a human being permanently. His fate was thereafter a matter of indifference to the community. British colonial law now takes a very different view of theft, one that many Gilbertese say they have difficulty understanding.

All societies, then, rely on a combination of internal and external controls in order to keep their members from misusing the freedom and power they enjoy. A stable social system is accompanied by a particular combination that is reasonably suitable to the control problems inherent in its pattern of institutional arrangements. This means that a set of external controls has evolved and become incorporated into the society's institutions. It also means that techniques for developing needed internal controls have been established as a part of customary child-rearing practices and are reinforced by the established definition of public identities and the public values attaching to each.

Change and the Balance of Control

Any change, cultural or circumstantial, that has the effect of altering existing balances within the community as a relatively stable system is likely to upset the balance of social controls. On the one hand, formerly adaptive internal controls may now impede appropriate adaptations to changed conditions. On the other hand, change may render external controls ineffective or remove them entirely, with a resulting increase in delinquent behavior or other abuses of freedom and power. New methods of external control have to be invented, requiring a number of institutional changes, and people must be freed from old anxieties, acquire new ones, and develop new models for social and personal identities. In time, as conditions stabilize, these adjustments take place; but the process is slow.

Urbanization of rural populations creates perhaps more urgent problems of this kind than any other type of social change. In village communities, where there is no anonymity and where everybody is pretty well aware of everything that is going on, the "goldfish bowl" existence is itself an external control affecting many aspects of life, for which no other form of control is necessary. People observe the social rules not by inner compulsion but because everybody would know it if they did not observe them, and the consequences would be unpleasant. Transported into the anonymity of an urban environment or alien community, these same law abiding citizens find themselves able to do things that they would not dare do at home. For example, Nadel observes that Nupe women in Nigeria tend to be sexually chaste in the rural settlements, where there is little anonymity and the elders are in effective control, and to be less chaste in town. Women who travel widely as traders regularly engage in prostitution as well, although they are chaste at home. Conduct by the same women varies as they move from village to town and from home town to strange town, according to the ability of the persons to whom they are morally responsible to observe their behavior.[2] The conduct of American soldiers in camp towns far from their home communities illustrates the same situation.

This kind of control problem faced the married Gilbertese who worked in the phosphate mines on Ocean Island. We have already observed that when a Gilbertese husband has to be away from home at night, his wife sleeps with relatives. But on Ocean Island, which is far from their home communities, couples often have no close relatives who can serve as chaperones. The problem is more acute, moreover, because work in the mines goes on day and night in two shifts. If a man becomes ill, he is not treated at home, but is removed to the hospital. The solution on which we were told the Gilbertese insisted and to which the government wisely acquiesced, was to provide a special floodlighted, locked compound, resembling a small jail, in which unchaperoned wives may retire to sleep. Wives often do this on their own initiative in order to forestall gossip. Thus the Gilbertese have developed public facilities for chaperonage in the absence of private ones and have redressed an imbalance in their system of external controls occasioned by residence away from home in a pseudo-urban setting. We shall shortly consider other imaginative devices by which they have solved more serious social control problems.

POLITICAL INSTITUTIONS AND SOCIAL CONTROL

The most serious difficulties of a control nature often arise in connection with political power. Political authority, by definition, is the major public instrument of social control. It is charged with the responsibility of erecting suitable external controls over individual behavior, and enjoys the power necessary to punish offenders and otherwise reinforce the control system with appropriate sanctions. The power needed to execute their responsibilities puts political authorities in a position where not only can they violate the rules but they can do so openly without fear of being called to account, unless there is some countervailing power in the community. Different societies have developed different solutions to the problem of control over the controllers.

At one extreme we find societies that grant very little authority to their political leaders. This minimizes the abuse of political power at the expense of a satisfactory instrumentality for social control. Justice under these conditions is largely a private matter, following the vendetta pattern, for example. At the other extreme we find societies with absolute monarchs or dictators, with ample power to maintain order, but with very little to prevent them from abusing their power. Major reliance under these conditions must be on the internal controls or conscience of whoever is in power. A common way in which the political conscience of absolute rulers is promoted is through a council of advisers or through fear of divine disfavor manifested in crop failures or catastrophes. In the period of absolute monarchy in western Europe the court fool is sometimes pictured as a kind of externalized royal conscience. Between these two extremes we find various methods for controlling the abuse of political power. One of the most common methods is to vest authority not in one individual but in a group, all or a majority of whose members must agree before the group can exercise its power. Each member of the group is held in check by the others. If each member is identified with some other interest group or faction in the community, this helps ensure against misuse of power by the governing group as a whole. The separation of powers represents another common approach to the problem. In our own society, of course, we place great emphasis on the separation of judicial, legislative, and executive powers. Some other societies follow the same principle, separating police from military authority, for example, or religious from secular powers.

CHANGE AND SOCIAL CONTROL

Under these conditions the several wielders of authority must cooperate with one another in order to carry out their official duties. Finally, many societies make the possession of political power subject to community approval, as with our own periodic elections.

Change and Political Power

Each of these controls over the abuse of political power is, of course, external in nature. No one or combination of them is feasible under all conditions. As social conditions change, adjustments in the combination of controls are usually needed. For example, change frequently requires that political authorities be given new responsibilities and new powers to go with them. The new powers render existing controls over the abuse of power obsolete. With existing external controls thus rendered inadequate, and with no internal controls (political and social conscience) yet developed to deal with the situation, abuses of power almost inevitably follow, sometimes requiring radical revisions of the whole control system. This problem has been well documented for a New Guinea community by Ian Hogbin.[3]

In former times the leadership of the village of Busama was exercised by two or three "headmen." These offices were not hereditary; they could be achieved only by years of diligent labor in the production of food and other forms of wealth. An ambitious man gained prestige by a constant show of generosity. He always had to have surplus food and material wealth available to give to the needy, to contribute more than his share toward the purchase of a kinsman's wife, and to help underwrite the more important ceremonies calling for large feasts. Every gift called for a return at some time. An ambitious man strove to keep others indebted to him through his generosity. Those unable to repay their debts in kind were morally obliged to give loyal backing to their creditors. The men of Busama were organized, moreover, into several clubs. The club leader had the responsibility for supporting it materially, repairing the building and supplying the food for its ceremonies. An ambitious club leader would try to help other clubs with their affairs until gradually he had succeeded in getting a great part of the community indebted to him. He then was in a position to be initiated into the office of headman, which in turn called for a tremendous outlay by him of wealth and food. As headman it was his duty to continue to underwrite community ceremonies and the feast exchanges between communities. It was also his duty to help keep peace in the community. In this capacity he presided over a village court consisting of the community's responsible elders. In case of dispute, the elders met, heard witnesses, and arrived at a judgment, which the headman announced as his decision. The source of his power lay in the people's sense of indebtedness to him and in the fact that his wealth enabled him to command sorcery against persons who consistently made trouble in the village.

The community had two ways of controlling the headman's misuse of power. First, there was more than one headman, each serving to some extent as a check on the other. Second, a head-man who consistently abused his power was liable to assassina-tion. Moreover, in order to become headman a person had to have led a hardworking and virtuous life for many years. In the course of time, most headmen had developed a conception of themselves as the responsible watchdogs of their community's affairs. Whatever the initial reasons for their ambition, by the time they achieved their goal it would mean a reversal of life-long habit to start abusing the power they had achieved, to the obvious detriment of the community. Some did, to be sure, and having gone too far were duly put to death either by their own families or by concerted community action. Since the cost of power was great and the rewards other than prestige were few, there was considerable reluctance on the part of most men to seek to become even a club leader, let alone a village headman. Often men with desired qualities of character were pushed by their fellows into reluctant acceptance of leadership positions. A few men, however, actively sought power, and their motives, as elsewhere in the world, seem often to have been to put them-selves in a position where they could flout custom with impunity. So long, however, as they continued to be generous, reflected the opinion of the elders in judicial matters, and underwrote the community's feasts, the village was apparently willing to be tolerant of occasional adultery or other abuse of power, if not excessive.

When Christian missionaries came to the village, they succeeded in banning the community feasts and dances whose organization and support was the headman's responsibility and the means by which he confirmed his right to his office. As a result, the office ceased to be filled and was allowed to lapse. The German government, with only a handful of officers to control large areas, reinstituted a kind of headmanship (later continued by the Australian administration) through which to conduct governmental business.

Under the new system, the administrative officer appointed one headman, called a *luluai*, and one or two assistants. The *luluai*, in addition to presiding over the council of elders in the settlement of local disputes, enforced whatever regulations the government sought to impose. He was promised, and received, backing from the government and its police in executing this new duty. The source of his power as headman lay not in his position as creditor of the community but through his being a representative of the District Officer with police backing. In the government's name (though not with the government's approval) he could introduce new regulations of his own devising, whereas the traditional headman had been without legislative power. The way to achieve power as headman was no longer through years of hard work and an exemplary life. The ambitious man must now ingratiate himself with the District Officer and the local Europeans, on whom the District Officer relied for information. In brief, qualification for the office of headman was no longer determined solely by native standards, but by standards that Europeans considered appropriate for natives. This increased greatly the chances for unscrupulous rogues to achieve power in the community. At the same time, the traditional controls that the village had over its headman were removed. There was now only one headman, with no fellow office holder whose rival power served as a check on his actions. Nor could the community any longer resort to assassination. No matter what justification there was for it in the community's eyes, the government could not possibly tolerate the "murder" of its appointed representative. A community's only recourse against an unscrupulous headman was to appeal directly to the District Officer for his removal. In practice, even this was difficult to do. If the District Officer refused the appeal, suspecting that it was motivated by malice, those who made it found themselves at the mercy of the headman whom they had sought to oust. There remained, therefore, no effective controls over unscrupulous headmen. Even well-intentioned people who had been outraged by the abuses of a former *luluai*, when appointed to succeed him, tended in time to be corrupted by the uncontrolled power they now held in their community.

Superficially, changes in the formal political structure of Busama have been slight, but changes in the community's ability to control abuse of political power have been profound. As a result of this and like problems in some other New Guinea villages, the Australian administration has been undertaking new experiments in self-government in native communities.

This kind of problem is by no means confined to New Guinea. The Keesings have noted it arising in Samoa.

> The autocratic use and abuse of their powers is a temptation which particularly faces higher elite leaders today. They are in a position to continue to exercise and take advantage of their Samoan-style authority while truncating their responsibilities and responsiveness to the traditional rights of their adherents. New forms of power have become available in the modern setting—money, commerce, government authority, Christian sanctions, mass communication media—and because these tend to be free-floating and not tempered by restraints and disciplines as they usually are in contemporary Western society, they may be used to build up great personal power. The picture of the autocratic chief has, perhaps surprisingly, more chance of realization in such societies under conditions of modern acculturation than in the closed cultural settings of precontact days. [*4]

As the Samoan example implies, there is almost no kind of change that can take place in a community that does not alter the existing distribution of power within it.[5] What the distribution of power is and what the methods of control within that

---

* Reprinted from *Elite Communication in Samoa: A Study of Leadership* by Felix M. Keesing and Marie M. Keesing, with the permission of the publishers, Stanford University Press, p. 102. © 1956 by the Board of Trustees of the Leland Stanford Junior University.

distribution are, should be carefully analyzed before any program for development is introduced.

The Constructive Use of Existing Political Institutions

Because change of almost any kind disturbs the existing balance of external social controls and because we are inclined to assume that existing political organizations in underdeveloped communities are incompatible with the requirements of more developed economies, development programs frequently include concerted efforts at political reform, patterned after the political institutions in the home country of the developing authority. Such efforts to introduce new forms of political organization can be justified on many grounds. But they often have the effect of exaggerating the very problem they are intended to help solve, because they can work only if there are appropriate internal controls to keep people within the rules at those points where external controls are lacking. Existing internal controls in an underdeveloped community are likely to be geared to its traditional principles of political organization. Therefore, it is often more advantageous to try to adapt these principles to solve political problems in the development situation than to scrap them in favor of completely new institutions based on alien principles.

The aftermath of a postwar strike by Gilbertese labor against the British Phosphate Company over wages in the mines on Ocean Island offers a noteworthy example of the constructive use of native political institutions to solve a serious problem of social control.[6]

The Gilbertese people had never before attempted a strike. They had heard about strikes, however. When the mines reopened after the war, they soon found that the cost of things which they used their earnings to buy had nearly doubled. They would have to work almost twice as long in order to afford the equipment they wanted to take home with them when their contracts expired. Unsuccessful in their attempts to negotiate a wage increase, the Gilbertese struck. Subsequent attempts by government officials to mediate a settlement between the British Phosphate Company and the Gilbertese were seriously impeded by the fact that a group of die-hard strikers were able to intimidate the majority of Gilbertese laborers from accepting reasonable terms. In the end they had to settle for fewer concessions from the Company than they could have obtained earlier.

Quite aside from this, however, the situation revealed the lack of any effective organization within the laboring community whose sanctioned authority would have prevented seizure of power by a small group of extremists. The workers, living away from their true homes for the terms of their contracts, formed a relatively unstructured proletarian community of constantly changing membership. The problem confronting the government and the Gilbertese people was how to develop an effective community organization at Ocean Island's phosphate mines, not only to prevent future coups by small cliques but also to provide authorities acceptable to the Gilbertese who could represent them to the British Phosphate Company and the government. The solution was based directly on the established pattern of community organization in the traditional Gilbertese communities.

The organization of every Gilbertese community centers on its meeting house. In this large open building, all community, as distinct from family, activities take place. Everybody in the community belongs to one of several groups, each of which has its traditional sitting place in the meeting house. Each group is led by a responsible elder, who is the spokesman and executive head. The community's governing body is a committee of these elders. These men discuss every community problem calling for responsible action, and having arrived at a decision submit it to the entire community for approval. They have the power to assess contributions of money, labor, and food from the individual families and sitting groups in the community. Anyone refusing to meet his assessment or other obligations to the meeting house is expelled from meeting-house membership. Expulsion entails loss of the right to participate in any community activities of a political, economic, or recreational nature.

An agreement was reached between the government, the Gilbertese communities providing most of the labor, and the British Phosphate Company to extend this political system into the laboring compound. With every contingent of labor from a village there now went one of the village elders. The Company paid him a minimum wage whether or not he did any work (most of them performed work that they were physically capable of). In the labor compound, workers from the several villages of one island were organized like a single village at home, and the elders who accompanied them formed a local meeting-house type of governing committee. Failure to fulfill one's obligations to this transplanted community might result in expulsion from the meeting house at home on one's return. Though laborers came and went, they were always answerable to their fellow citizens for their conduct and were no longer free to exploit the relative lack of formal organization formerly characterizing the labor compound. (This system was applied to the large community of short-term contract labor. A small community of Gilbertese making a career of work with the Company remained physically and politically separate.)

This solution had several distinct advantages. It met with the full approval of the Gilbertese. Because it utilized native principles of organization, its mechanics were immediately understood by the Gilbertese. No long period of learning a new system was required, and it became effective immediately. It introduced into the labor community the same system of external controls that people already respected and that was suitably complemented by existing internal controls. That is, it fit the standards of honor by which the Gilbertese already operated and the existing system of mutual obligations for which their self-images and anxieties were geared. Finally, it did not make the mistake of using the local political organization as a model while filling its offices with men who were unqualified to occupy them according to that model. Offices were held by already proven and qualified elders from the home communities, bona fide members of the home councils of elders, people who by native standards were to be respected and reckoned with. The fact that they were too old to work in the mines was wisely disregarded as irrelevant to the political problem. Since the inception of this arrangement, negotiations between the British Phosphate Company, the government, and the Gilbertese laboring community have proceeded in a more orderly fashion. It is our understanding that Gilbertese labor has acquired a stronger and more effective voice by virtue of its now being, in effect, organized labor.

In this instance we cannot say whether the particular procedure adopted was first suggested by the Gilbertese or by colonial administrators. In either case, the administrators had to approve it and persuade the British Phosphate Company's management to go along with it, since it involved hiring and paying elders whose work output in all probability would be minimal. For the administrators to approve it, and even more so for them to initiate it, required that they already have an intimate knowledge of, and respect for, the native system of local government. This case illustrates how indispensable such knowledge is for development planning.

The case also demonstrates what can be accomplished if development agents make a genuine and intelligent effort to utilize existing institutions in solving social and political problems arising in the wake of economic and other kinds of change. Left to themselves, of course, people normally try to solve new problems by applying to them the devices and institutions they already know. By following this normal adaptive process, administrators in the Gilbert Islands were able to find a remarkably effective solution to one of the most vexing problems in the industrialization process, that of community organization and social control in the newly formed settlements of industrial workers. If the reader now says to himself, "But in the areas with which I am familiar, the problems are different, and the Gilbertese solution is therefore no help to me," he is missing the point. The problems are always different; and the solutions, if they are to be good ones, must always be different, too. To try seriously, not just superficially, to find what in native institutions may provide a solution to problems of political and social organization is always to be recommended.

To arrive at such solutions, however, requires the exercise of creative imagination as well as a thorough understanding of local institutions and how they work. Workable solutions of this kind are not likely to be readily apparent to agents of change or to the community's members. To be found, they require that agent and community work closely together in both the formulation and organization of a program. Students of development projects have come to insist on this type of cooperation for sound, practical reasons. Members of the community, when they put their minds to it, are at least as likely as the development agents to be aware of the organizational possibilities within their existing institutional structure. They are at least as likely to suggest courses of action that will result in a minimum of unnecessary and irrelevant dislocation and readjustment. If, finally, the community is, in fact, without organizational resources of its own that are suitable to meet the problems confronting it, this lack will become more fully apparent to all concerned if agent and community work together in the search for a solution.

LEGISLATION AND SOCIAL CONTROL IN CHANGE

Legislation, the definition of rules of conduct by constituted authority, is a necessary feature of social change. It is often used as a means of inducing people to change existing practices and to engage in new kinds of activity. The imposition of a head tax in New Guinea originally had the purpose of providing the native population with incentives to work on European-owned plantations and to shift from subsistence to cash-crop gardening. Community development ideally seeks the voluntary cooperation of its clients, but that does not diminish the importance of legislation in the change process. Any kind of community action necessarily requires that the community's authorities make decisions regarding its future and that these decisions be binding on the community's members. When people are committed to radical reform, moreover, as in the revitalization process, they want rules of conduct laid down for them, as we have observed, feeling a need to know how they should conduct themselves in the new identities they are seeking collectively to develop. Under these conditions, legislation is needed to define and consolidate changes that people are already committed to making. Furthermore, as development progresses, unforeseen problems arise whose solution requires some modification of existing rules of conduct. The course of change inevitably calls for legislative action of some kind in order to maintain a viable social order.

Legislation can be effective only to the extent that people willingly comply with its provisions. No rules can work well if people are unwilling to accept them. To make legislation effective in their work, development agents must understand the conditions that militate for and against popular acceptance of a society's rules and voluntary compliance with them.

By way of introduction, we should observe that regardless of their present level of development, all societies possess rules of conduct that are recognized by their members as obligatory, in that their observance is a condition of membership in their society in good standing. In every society, moreover, some of its rules are an object of conscious attention and concern, or even dispute, whereas others are so taken for granted that people have not bothered to try to give them explicit formulation. Indeed, in areas of conduct where there is consensus as to what the rules are, a desire to honor them, and opportunity to do so without social, moral, or emotional conflict, in such areas there is no more need for a community to codify its rules through formal legislation than to codify its language's grammar. People learn them as they do their grammar, without self-consciousness, having their specific mistakes corrected and the mistakes of others pointed out to them, without the rules themselves ever being precisely or even explicitly stated. Given an organized system of rules, moreover, its integrating and unifying principles—which form a society's basic public values and for which its members gradually acquire a "feel"—serve to make unthinkable a number of actions. There is no need to legislate against cannibalism in our own society, for instance, nor to legislate against homosexuality in Truk.

Because human attention concentrates on rules that are not readily complied with or whose occasional breach raises widespread anxiety, we tend to overlook the fact that the vast majority of people voluntarily comply with most of their society's rules most of the time. As we shall see, deliberate legislation often fails to meet the conditions that promote such compliance. Understanding these conditions can greatly increase the effectiveness of legislation in the development process.

The Conditions of Voluntary Compliance

In the light of what we have already discussed at length in this and earlier chapters, several propositions come to mind about the degree of voluntary compliance a rule is likely to enjoy.

1. Compatibility with Other Rules. Other things being equal, to the extent that observing one of a society's several rules does not militate against observing another, compliance will be voluntary. Where there is mutual inconsistency, the rules will become a matter of conscious concern and there will be pressure toward their revision and explicit formulation. When new legislation is introduced without reference to the content of the existing body of rules, it frequently proves to be inconsistent in some way with that body, or a part of it, and thus presents an enforcement problem. Legislators who are thoroughly familiar with existing rules, whether they have been codified or not, are most likely to sense what will be consistent and what not. Without such familiarity, their chances of getting voluntary compliance are small.

2. Consistency with Basic Values. To the extent that a rule is compatible with the unifying principles for the body of rules as a whole, compliance will be voluntary. For example, there are in the island of Truk many specific rules governing people's relations with their fellows. All of these rules are such, however, as to be consistent with a principle that husband and wife are socially equal. In all social relationships that a man has through his wife he is subject to the rules that govern his wife. She, in turn, follows the same principle in dealing with people who have close ties with her husband. The equivalence of spouses serves as one of the guidelines in the structuring of social relationships in Truk.

As with the first condition, new rules tend to be inconsistent with such underlying principles when a legislative authority does not belong to the community for which it legislates, or belongs to a subcommunity whose values and principles do not coincide with those of other subcommunities within the larger society. The resulting conflict of values tends to foster rejection of incompatible rules and makes for nonvoluntary compliance.

3. Consistency with People's Self-Image. When compliance with a rule befits the view people have of themselves, it will tend to be honored voluntarily. Conversely, people will tend to resist complying with rules that are at odds with their view of themselves, that serve to make them feel unworthy, or that do violence to their sense of personal integrity. Colonial ordinances based on an official image of the underdeveloped native as a "child" are not likely to find favor with the native. Discriminatory rules based on the assumed inferiority or undesirability of some racial or cultural group are regularly subverted by members of those groups. Regulations whose existence implies that people are dishonest insult those who think of themselves as honest. Administrators not infrequently assume, and often for good reason, that they know better what is good for their clients than their clients do. But any action, including the laying down of rules, that conveys this impression to their clients will be resented, as long as their clients do not also accept the idea that the administrator knows best.

It frequently happens, of course, that people become dissatisfied with their present conditions and the view of themselves that those conditions promote. This impels them to achieve new conditions that will be consistent with the self-image to which they aspire. This is usually the case, as we have seen, in communities whose members are involved in revitalization movements. Rules that appear to promote the achievement of the desired state will enjoy voluntary compliance, and those that appear to block its achievement will be resisted. Certain it is that the convert or other enthusiast happily embraces and conforms to the rules laid down by his religious or political leaders. At the same time he openly defies those rules of his larger society that appear to him to stand in the way of the achievement of his personal salvation.

4. Applicability. If the realities of a person's circumstances make a rule readily applicable, he will tend to honor it voluntarily. But insofar as it is unrealistic, compliance will be reluctant or even refused.

At one extreme, of course, is the situation where compliance taxes one's physical or mental powers, or one's emotional, social, or material resources beyond their capacity. When this happens one cannot comply no matter how much one tries; and when this is the prospect, there is reluctance even to try.

Less extreme is the case where compliance is within the limits of one's resources and capacities but puts a severe enough strain upon them (or appears that it will do so) as to outweigh the penalities of noncompliance. Each individual has his own wants and needs whose gratification must frequently be suspended in order that others may have their turn in caring for theirs. Since the regulation of gratifications is one of the principal ends rules serve, they not only provide opportunities for gratification and are in this respect rewarding, they also frustrate gratification and are in this way punishing. The balance of gratification and deprivation for any rule, moreover, differs from person to person, not only according to their position in the social order but also according to the immediate circumstances in which they find themselves as a result of their own past actions and the actions of others. For example, to comply with the rule against cheating on an examination carries few adverse consequences for the student who has studied his lessons, but it can be very punishing to the student who has neglected his lessons and whose non-cheating is likely to be rewarded with a failing grade. When an opportunity to cheat presents itself in the latter case, compliance hinges on the rule's consistency with the student's self-image and basic values.

The fact that such psychological and emotional factors can outweigh considerations of material advantage calls our attention to the importance of the emotional or inner realities. Obviously, in the absence of anger one has no difficulty observing the rule that one must not physically assault another; but the greater one's anger, the harder it is to comply. Contrariwise, it may be hard to apply a rule strictly to persons toward whom one has feelings of obligation and guilt. Fear, hate, love, pity, remorse, anxiety, any emotional state, as we explicitly recognize at places in our own law codes, affect the applicability of a rule fully as much as external conditions.

Individuals who are severely disturbed emotionally may find the whole system of rules too burdensome and deliberately adopt forms of behavior that inform their fellows not to expect the usual rules to apply to them, as is evidently the meaning of the bizarre and offensive behavior of some psychotics.[7] To try to control the behavior of such persons by insistence on the rules or by the imposition of more rules, as well we know, serves only to make more desperate their attempts to find exemption from them. It is with good reason that we recommend relief from the normal demands of everyday activity for persons who have suffered a "nervous breakdown." There are times when the members of a community as a group are under sufficient strain, as may occur under conditions of rapid change, that they begin to find many of the rules that they formerly accepted too burdensome emotionally. Attempts to introduce new rules serve only to complicate life further. The greater the pressures in the form of new rules and coercive measures to ensure compliance with them, the more likely are the community's members to be attracted to extreme cultistic movements that emphasize bizarre or offensive acts.

5. *Commitment to the Social Group.* Regardless of the ease or difficulty of compliance with specific rules, as long as a person is committed to membership in a social group, he will seek to honor the body of rules governing its members' conduct and thereby to maintain his good standing in the group. Should he, for some reason, wish to declare his membership in the group at an end, he may deliberately violate its rules, especially those peculiar to the group in question, thereby communicating to all his separation from it. This is the obvious interpretation when a member of a religious sect openly begins to do things prohibited by it. Increased drinking during prohibition symbolized for many their refusal to be identified with the social and religious groups that favored prohibition. To take an extreme example, moreover, some of the apparently senseless murders in our society, especially those where the choice of victim appears incidental and where there is no serious attempt at concealment, can be interpreted as acts of social suicide by which those who commit them choose to place themselves beyond the pale of membership in human society and thus to accomplish the destruction of their former identities. Where there is rejection of a

social group or of one's self-image as a member of a group, flagrant violation of its rules is likely to be deliberate.

Conditions Promoting Formal Jural Institutions

In every society these conditions for acceptance and voluntary compliance are adequately met for at least some of its rules. And in every society there are some of its rules for which these conditions are insufficiently met. The latter rules are the ones on which public attention tends to focus. They tend to be explicitly formulated as commandments and to be accompanied by specific sanctions to help enforce compliance.

In a small, homogeneous community, not in the throes of rapid change, the conditions for voluntary compliance obtain for a relatively high proportion of its rules. The self-image of the community's members and their basic values are likely to be sufficiently similar as to allow for the development of a body of rules that are fairly compatible with them and that are sufficiently consistent with each other as to form a coherent and orderly system. Commitment to the local group and its rules is likely to be automatic, since there are few, if any conceivable alternatives, and the relative stability of local conditions allows the rules to evolve a form that gives them maximum applicability.

The larger the society, the greater the number of its subgroups, and the more pluralistic the cultural backgrounds of its members, the greater the proportion of its rules for which the conditions of voluntary compliance do not universally obtain. Where there are caste and class distinctions, and legislators tend to come from one caste or class, for example, the images they have of other groups in the society are likely to be at variance with the images these groups have of themselves. Their values are not likely to be the same as the values of the other groups. As it becomes necessary to make more of its rules explicit, moreover, there is a greater likelihood that mutal consistency among the rules will break down. This is enhanced by the fact that as soon as a rule is given explicit formulation, its objectivization makes it easier to think about changing it. It becomes a target for different interest groups, which can now perceive how modifications can work to their immediate advantage. The resulting modifications lead to a breakdown of the mutual consistency between rules, requiring further emendations and codifications. The greater the rate of change in the external realities, moreover, the greater the difficulties in applying existing rules, a condition that also leads in the direction of greater concern with rules and their explicit definition. Change and social complexity together promote the development of institutions for formulating and amending the rules and for enforcing compliance with them.

Implications for Development

Legislating new rules, we have said, is a necessary part of community development. Development agents, moreover, are committed to winning the cooperation of their clients; and when rules are involved, cooperation is expressed in voluntary compliance. The degree to which new rules find acceptance and voluntary compliance depends directly on how well they meet the conditions we have outlined.

Several obstacles to achieving these conditions are obviously built into the development situation. The agent's basic values are not likely to be the same as those of the community's members. His image of the community is not likely to be the same as the community's image of itself. He is likely to have inadequate knowledge of the real conditions affecting the applicability of the community's rules, and to have incomplete knowledge of the body of rules that the community already possesses. The community's members are likely to have a stronger commitment to the local group of which they are members than to the larger social entity to which both they and the agent belong. Clearly, to the extent that the agent attempts to legislate for the community, he minimizes the chances of voluntary cooperation with his program by the community's members. To the extent that he allows the community's members to legislate for themselves, he maximizes the chances of voluntary compliance with whatever new rules are necessary to implement development.

We must bear in mind, of course, that anything that enjoys maximum voluntary compliance is not always in the best interests of the community. It is not our recommendation that development agents take no part in legislative processes in the course of their work. But the part they play will have an effect on the kind of cooperation they get. Of one thing we may be sure. If voluntary compliance with new rules is something development agents value, then it is essential that whoever makes the rules be as familiar as possible with the existing body of rules, the basic values, the self-image and the self-aspirations of those for whom he would legislate. Otherwise any predictions he may make about the kind of cooperation he is likely to receive will be figments of his own preconceptions.

SUGGESTED READING

Apthorpe, Raymond, editor, *From Tribal Rule to Modern Government:* The Thirteenth Conference Proceedings of the Rhodes-Livingstone Institute for Social Research. Lusaka, N.Rh., 1959.

Bohannan, Paul, *Justice and Judgment Among the Tiv.* Oxford University Press, London, 1957.

Fortes, A. Meyer, and E. E. Evans-Pritchard, editors, *African Political Systems.* Oxford University Press, London, 1940.

Gluckman, Max, *The Judicial Process Among the Barotse of Northern Rhodesia.* Manchester University Press, Manchester, 1955.

LeVine, Robert A., "The Internalization of Political Values in Stateless Societies," *Human Organization,* vol. 19, no. 2, 1960, pp. 51–58.

Podgorecki, Adam, "Law and Social Engineering," *Human Organization,* vol. 21, no. 3, 1962, pp. 177–181.

NOTES TO CHAPTER 13

1. That this is not so in all societies is indicated by the findings of Allan R. Holmberg in *Nomads of the Long Bow:* The Siriono of Eastern Bolivia, Smithsonian Institution, Institute of Social Anthropology, Publication no. 10. Government Printing Office, Washington, 1950.

2. Nadel, S. F., *A Black Byzantium:* The Kingdom of Nupe in Nigeria. Oxford University Press, London, 1942, pp. 333–334.

3. Hogbin, H. Ian, *Transformation Scene:* The Changing Culture of a New Guinea Village. Routledge and Kegan Paul, Ltd., London, 1951.

4. Keesing, Felix M., and Marie M., *Elite Communication in Samoa:* A Study of Leadership. Stanford University Press, Stanford, 1956, p. 102.

5. For a discussion of similar problems in Africa, see Ashton, E. H., "Democracy and Indirect Rule," *Africa,* vol. 17, 1947, pp. 235–251; also Forde, Daryll, "Government in Umor: A Study of Social Change and Problems of Indirect Rule in a Nigerian Village Community," *Africa,* vol. 12, 1939, pp. 129–161.

6. I am indebted to Paul B. Laxton and Harry E. Maude for information relating to this incident. Needless to say, I am solely responsible for any errors of fact or interpretation concerning the matter as it is here presented.

7. Goffman, Erving, "The Nature of Deference and Demeanor," *American Anthropologist,* vol. 58, 1956, pp. 495–496.

Part 2

PRACTICE

Chapter 14

PROBLEMS OF PRACTICE: THE AGENT

IN PART I WE HAVE DISCUSSED at length the problem of cooperation in change in general theoretical terms and with our attention
primarily on the client community. We turn now to consider the
development agent.

Obviously, his job is anything but an easy one, calling for a
combination of capacities that many of us lack. From their study
of Americans in overseas assignments, Cleveland, Mangone, and
Adams conclude that five major attributes are essential to success:[1]

1. *Technical Skill.* The expert has to be more flexible and creative in the application of his skills in development work overseas
than in their routine application at home.

2. *Belief in Mission.* The development worker overseas has to
have enough commitment and enthusiasm to work effectively
without close supervision from above and in the face of manifold
social pressures to slacken his efforts.

3. *Cultural Empathy.* The capacity to look at different cultures
with interest and respect is obviously essential.

4. *A Sense of Politics.* The development worker must be sensitive to the local political climate and be able to discover and
reckon with political currents and cross-currents.

5. *Organization Ability.* The technical expert's job is less one of
directly practicing his skill in building bridges, growing crops,
healing the sick than it is one of developing local organizations
that can do these things effectively; and this requires the capacity
to develop viable organizations within the framework of the local
social system.

These attributes are needed by Americans who work overseas, regardless of whether they are working as development agents. It is obvious from our discussion that a development agent also needs a solid understanding of cultural, social, and psychological processes. First and foremost, however, he must possess a general attitude of mind toward himself and his clients. What was referred to above as "cultural empathy" is a by-product of this attitude, but it does not properly describe it. It will repay us to consider more specifically what this attitude of mind includes, even at risk of occasionally repeating the obvious.

THE NECESSARY ATTITUDE

Basically, the attitude of mind we speak of is an agent's willingness to accept other people generally as fellow human beings, as entitled to the same respect for their wants, beliefs, felt needs, customs, values, and sense of personal worth, as he expects for his. Virtually everyone accepts his friends and relatives in this way; but ethnocentrism tends to reduce our acceptance the farther we get from those we consider to be most like ourselves. To accept the members of a client community when they are of different race, language, culture, and condition of life is something that many of us find difficult. But acceptance is essential, if a development agent is to respect their right to be the kind of people they want to be. His acceptance of and respect for his clients as fellow men, moreover, must be unconditional. He is not likely to gain the confidence and trust of his clients if he makes their acceptance of what he wants for them a condition of their status as human beings.

From this attitude of mind important things follow. For instance, experience has amply demonstrated that people are much readier to cooperate with development agents if they are treated as partners in the change process and given the opportunity to do as much as possible for themselves. Resistance to changes in practice in a clothing industry, for example, was effectively lowered when "group participation in planning for the changes" was actively stimulated.[2] Governor Muñoz tells of the enthusiasm and pride in accomplishment of people in an isolated village in Puerto

Rico who, having been shown how by a government technician, went ahead and built their own road to connect their village with the highway.[3] But if we are to make our clients partners in the development process, we must respect their autonomy. If we accept the view that community development is aimed at "helping people to help themselves," we must be willing to let our clients make their own decisions; we must want to allow them the courtesy of making their own mistakes and learning for themselves.

If we are unable to accept our clients as fellow men, moreover, we shall be unprepared to see the value of their strange customs and beliefs from their point of view; we shall tend to be impatient with their concerns; and we shall be unable to react with sympathetic understanding to their changing moods in the course of development.

An agent's failure to accept his clients cannot be concealed. He may protest to the contrary, but his actions will belie him. For accepting others in principle is not the same thing as accepting them in practice. Even with a considerable degree of sophistication, it is still a difficult job to know and control all of one's own attitudes affecting one's acceptance of others. So many of our reactions are based not on private prejudices, peculiar to our individual selves and arising from our individual emotional needs, but on attitudes that we share with other members of our society. These reactions are expressions of the socially shared values and attitudes in our own culture. We may never have had occasion to question them, and it is difficult to call them into question, so much do they seem the proper, indeed the only, way of viewing things. Many of our physical reactions are thoroughly conditioned by these values and attitudes. Even with the best will in the world, for example, it is sometimes impossible to keep one's nose from wrinkling at what it interprets as an unpleasant smell, even though other people may accept the odor as familiar and not at all unpleasant. Experience with the lives of other people is a good corrective for these unconscious standards by which we react to people and the things associated with them, for they become emotionally less absolute the more they are called to conscious attention in the presence of working alternatives.

This attitude of mind then—the willingness to accept others unconditionally as one's fellow men, with all that that implies— is not a trivial thing. It is not something easily assumed and just as easily discarded. It ties into our most fundamental psychological orientations; and even when these are appropriate, our culture may intervene to impose serious limitations on its expression. The circumstances in which development agents must work, moreover, may be more or less demanding of their own emotional resources, so that as their emotional needs are intensified or gratified, as they become more or less preoccupied with self, their ability to maintain the requisite attitude changes. In the sections to follow, we consider some of the things that directly relate to this necessary attitude of mind.

STEREOTYPES

To organize experience, it is essential to categorize it. As we have seen, inventories of types of experience are an essential part of culture. Important among them are the categories of identity, the identity features, in terms of which we perceive others and with reference to which we adjust our behavior and attitude toward them. As long as our behavior and attitude accords with their own self-image, there is no problem in our relationship; but to the extent that it does not, difficulties and misunderstandings arise. To accept others as human beings like ourselves we must do our best to relate to them with due respect for their individuality, and we must seek to understand and respect their image of themselves, even when this image does not appear to us to be very realistic.

We try to do this as a matter of course for people with whom we have close and intimate relations. A wise parent seeks to deal with his children in ways best suited to meet each one's particular needs and to cultivate each one's particular abilities. The more remote people are from us, however, the less concerned we become with their individuality and the broader and more general the identity categories into which we lump them. Not being in close contact with them, we have little opportunity to refine our stereotyped image of their identity. Ethnocentrism, moreover, may make us uninterested in modifying our stereotypes when we do have occasion to deal with them more closely.

A development agent going into a strange community for the first time inevitably brings with him a whole series of stereotypes of underdeveloped communities. For adjusting to the concrete realities of a particular local group, however, stereotypes are likely to be of little use to him. A case of record, for example, shows how inappropriate in Palau was the behavior of the labor expert from the Philippines, who regarded all "natives" from whatever part of the world as alike.[4] In the light of what we have been saying, it is obvious that development agents must try to see each community in all its individuality. To do this, they must take the time to get to know it, its members, and its customs well.

If it is important for a development agent to avoid dealing with the client community in terms of his own stereotypes, it may be equally important that his clients do not respond to him in terms of their stereotypes for outsiders. The experience of under-developed communities with Europeans and Americans varies, of course. But in most instances it has been limited to dealing with officials, missionaries, employers, tourists, and soldiers. There will have been individuals in all these categories who managed to establish excellent relations with the local population, but they are not likely to have had community development in the modern sense of that term as their sole or even primary responsibility. In some measure they will have come to represent coercive author-ity, police power, economic exploitation, religious evangelism, or sheer indifference in the stereotypes the community's members have of them. Attached to these stereotypes, moreover, there is likely to be considerable resentment.[5]

The first thing a development agent's clients will want to know about him is where they are to place him in their stereotypes. Whatever one they put him in, they will proceed to deal with him accordingly and weigh everything he has to say from the point of view that their stereotype presents. The agent's profession of dis-interested altruism may well be dismissed as a front for what are really more sinister purposes. Members of a nutrition research team in Latin America, for example, had the experience of being seriously believed to be cannibals who specialized in eating babies.[6] The belief in this case was fostered by persons hostile to them and their work, but it was not without precedent in the customary attitudes that people in the community regularly took of foreigners. Strangers were customarily represented to children by their parents as cannibalistic bogeymen. To suggest that their interest in infant nutrition was a cover for more diabolical motives was to take advantage of an established stereotype.

Another way in which agents may find themselves stereotyped by their clients is in respect to the categorizations they have for themselves, as distinct from those they have for foreigners. We can illustrate this from personal experience. In Onotoa in the Gilbert Islands, the entire population is nominally, at least, either Protestant or Catholic. Within each denomination there are those who take their church seriously and those who do not. Because of the things that missionaries used to stress, another classification has developed that cuts across the first one. Regardless of his denomination, a person is also either a "missionary" or a "pagan." If the former, he does not smoke, drink, or consort with women and is, consequently, a member of the Church in good standing (if he is a Protestant). A "pagan," on the other hand, being one who enjoys tobacco, liquor, and sex, is not in good standing with his parson. When we undertook an ethnographic study of an Onotoan community, one of the first things people wanted to know was whether we were Protestant or Catholic—Catholics formed a minority against whom there was strong feeling—and whether we were "missionaries" or "pagans." In Onotoan eyes we had to be, as they were, one or the other of the latter pair in precisely the same way that we had to be one or the other of the former. Our work made it preferable that we be neither "pagans" nor "missionaries"; but we doubt that our efforts to develop a third category were successful.

An agent cannot hope to remain unclassified and hence in some sort of limbo. Unless he makes a special effort, moreover, he is likely to be classified in terms of stereotypes that effectively undermine the kind of relationship he wants to have with his clients. To get past their stereotypes of him, the agent must give his clients an opportunity to know him well, so that he becomes a distinct individual for them. They must, therefore, have the opportunity to deal with him and see him in operation under a variety of conditions, for it is only our more intimate acquaintances whose individuality we can be fully aware of. Whatever the difficulties, and there are bound to be many, a development agent must strive for a comparable intimacy, not just so that he may have the kind of knowledge and understanding of the community that he needs, but so that its members may have an equally intimate knowledge of him and what his presence can mean for them. It is far better for an agent to expose his weaknesses and thereby gain acceptance as a true human being than to hold himself aloof and remain somewhat like the local bogeyman.

If we are to accept our clients as fellow human beings, we must give ourselves an opportunity to know them well; and if our clients are to accept us we must give them a similar opportunity to see what manner of men we are.

FLEXIBILITY

As an expert in soils, health, or technology—whatever it may be—a development agent may naturally assume that it is his job to try to impart his technical understanding to his clients and to show them his "right" way of doing things. His clients have their own understanding of their problems, based on the ideas and beliefs of their culture. Although the understanding that his professional point of view gives him enables him to make a more sophisticated diagnosis of the nature of his clients' problems, their beliefs may make it almost impossible for him to share this diagnosis with them. To insist on their adopting his view as a necessary condition of remedial action is to demand something difficult and often quite unnecessary for successful development. This does not mean that his clients may not have to modify their view of their problems. Much more often than not, they do. But all that is needed is a view that permits of realistic ameliorative action, whether or not it coincides with the agent's.

In our own political arena, for example, we repeatedly observe how necessary it is to formulate a program in popularly meaningful terms for it to get support. Those who so formulate it may actually predicate their program on a somewhat different understanding of the realities. If capacity to reformulate in terms that are meaningful to others is indispensable in politics, it is equally so in planning and executing development projects.

A development agent, then, must try to understand how his clients see their problems. His efforts to help them clarify their problems must be couched in what they regard as common sense terms. As we have seen, the different cultural backgrounds of agent and community make what is ordinary common sense to one not necessarily so to the other. By talking over the problem with the client community's members, by judiciously asking key questions that they have not thought to ask themselves, an agent can lead them to new insights more in line with his own diagnosis. But he is wise to let the insights be theirs and to keep his own diagnosis to himself. Only negative results are likely to come, for example, from telling people that their fear of ghosts is keeping them from fully utilizing their resources, however much he may see this as being an important aspect of their problem. It is better for him to try to lead them to discover this for themselves, to see that they have before them possibilities that only the ghosts are preventing them from realizing. Ghosts then become for them a real part of their problem; and they are now in a position to entertain the possibility of laying them. The outlook they develop that makes this possible for them will probably not correspond to the agent's. They may continue to believe in the reality of ghosts. If through new rationalizations or exorcisms they can find a way to remove this obstacle to a more rewarding life, it need be of no further concern to the agent that their view of things differs from his. If the agent tries to make himself a propagandist for a particular set of beliefs or course of action, he will not be in a position to appreciate the genuine possibilities for constructive development as they arise, but will find himself actually resisting them as obstructions to the imposition of his own beliefs and the enactment of his own will. Thus, with the best of intentions, he can destroy the basis for constructive development.

Yet it is extremely difficult not to be doctrinaire. We have to be firmly convinced of the rightness of our own understandings and procedures if we are to presume to use our knowledge in the service of others. Because we are convinced, it is almost impossible for us to see how they can appear unreasonable to anyone else.

Certainly, it can't do any harm to try to explain the real situation to others. Our job, after all, is to educate them, isn't it? Insofar as we can do so, yes! But there are ways and ways to educate. Education by indirection, by asking questions that lead to new insights is better suited to the problem of achieving cooperation in change than is education by lecture and precept. The latter approach is likely to build up walls of resistance to further learning quickly, but the former helps keep the doors to learning open.

Again we come back to what it means to accept others fully as persons. We do not ask of those whom we accept unconditionally that they believe as we do, we want only that their lives be as productive and rewarding in the light of their wishes as their capacities will allow.

In addition to being flexible in the ways in which he formulates a community's problems, a development agent must also be flexible in his role as development agent. Not only must he be able to adapt his role to the needs of the particular client community, he must also be able to change his role as development progresses and his clients' needs change. For example, the declared aim of Britain's colonial administration in the Gilbert Islands is to make the Gilbertese people as self-governing as possible. As the development of local self-government continues and more and more responsibility is vested in the Gilbertese people, the role of British administrators must change accordingly. As has been aptly observed in connection with administrative failure in Japanese Relocation Centers during World War II,[7] an authoritarian administration, if it wishes to develop local self-government, must be prepared to relinquish its authority, must even welcome as a sign of growing democratic awareness demands that it do so, rather than respond to such demands as rebellions to be crushed.

Similarly, in any development program in which the local population is to become responsible for continuing the new techniques or for operating and maintaining the newly introduced equipment, if the agent is unwilling to let his clients handle the equipment (for fear they will break it), practice the new techniques (for fear they won't perform them correctly and will spoil some part of the project), or plan and organize on their own (for fear they will make a mess of things), he demonstrates a lack of just the kind of role flexibility that development requires. He must be able to let others do things, so that they can learn by their mistakes—they will not learn any other way. Like colonial administrators in the Gilberts, he must work to put himself out of a job. To do this, he must play progressively different and progressively less important roles in the community's affairs.

To be free to adjust his conduct to fit the needs and circumstances of the client community requires that a development agent not be bound closely by restrictive policies and directives from his superiors in the agency he represents or, equally, by his own preconceived plans. To be able to relate well to the community at all stages of his work and to gear his work to the community's capacities and understandings, an agent must be free to develop his program from day to day. Overall objectives and a general strategy he should have, but only in broad terms. The rest he must work out as he goes along. Very often he can only state the problems and the directions in which it seems worth trying to go. Elaborate plans and itemized budgets cannot realistically be projected far ahead. Flexibility of action is as necessary as flexibility of mind.

But in order to be flexible, one must be sensitive to the needs of others as they change in the course of development. It is others, not oneself and one's own needs, that one must keep in mind. But if we are to keep the needs of others in mind, they must be important to us, have value for us as persons like ourselves. This means that we must be in close contact with them so that we are ever mindful of their presence and the reality of their changing needs in the development situation. If it is difficult for a field agent to develop and maintain the close contact that keeps the reality of his clients' needs clearly before him, it is almost impossible for other agency personnel in administrative positions to do so. They are often the makers of policy and major decisions, however, a fact posing such important problems for success in community development as to warrant separate consideration in Chapter 16.

COMMUNICATION

From what we have said, it is obvious that a development agent cannot get to know the community and its changing problems well or dispel his stereotypes and be realistically flexible if he fails to maintain good communication with his clients. In practice, this involves a number of things.

When people communicate, they do more than exchange mutually intelligible words. An important purpose of communication is to share experience, or to enlarge the area of mutual understanding between persons whose experiences differ. When the degree of such difference is slight and the desire to share is strong, as with well-adjusted married couples, communication is almost automatic, requiring little conscious attention. The words and gestures of each partner are familiar to the other, immediately revealing to each the changing moods of the other. Basic areas of agreement (or sometimes disagreement) are known and taken for granted, and we frequently observe between such persons the signs of their accord in the way either one is able to finish the unfinished thoughts of the other. But communication is never completely effective even under optimum conditions. There are always some areas of experience, even for the most compatible spouses, that remain resistant to communication. The husband's life work may be chemical engineering, about which his wife knows next to nothing, or she may find it impossible to interest him in her intensive club activities, however absorbing they may be to her. If lack of communication about these things, and the mutual understanding resulting from it, sometimes creates crises in the lives of well-adjusted spouses, it is clear that where differences between people include differences in every aspect of experience, in social and cultural background, and even in language itself, communication becomes a major problem.

Not the degree of difference alone, but the strength of the desire to compose it, to share experience, is important for successful communication. When both parties share the same goals and are eager to achieve them, both will presumably make whatever effort is needed to bridge the differences between them in order to get on with the job. When communications break down for some reason, both will seek to restore them; they will not immediately conclude that the breakdown reflects the other's indifference or welcome it as an excuse to stop further cooperation. But when two parties have different goals or lack enthusiasm for those mutually held, neither is likely to make any great effort to resolve the existing differences. How much or how little mutuality of goals there is between a development agent and his clients will greatly affect the ease with which they can communicate. But irrespective of the degree to which he and they share particular goals and desire for their achievement, the responsibility for composing the differences between them is the agent's. It is his responsibility to work toward greater mutuality of goals as well as to enlarge the area of understanding between himself and his clients.

Again we see the crucial importance of the agent's attitude of mind. The most important single step he can take in establishing a climate for effective communication is to try to understand and appreciate the community's goals for itself and to make them in some real degree his own. Without taking this step he cannot expect the community's members to concern themselves with his goals for them, however beneficial they may be in the abstract. To make their goals and aspirations for themselves his own is to identify himself with them, and identification in this sense is one of the major ends of effective communication.

To achieve the community's goals, however, may call for outlays of labor and wealth that are beyond the community's resources, or may require modifications of living habits that people in the community are unable to accept. In this respect their goals may be unrealistic. Furthermore, it is a common human failing to confuse means with ends. Thus people's ultimate desire for improved health may lead them to decide that they need a hospital, when, in fact, it might be far less practical as a means to their basic goal than better sewage disposal, telephone communication to the area's existing medical facilities, or a road to give existing medical authorities ready access to their community. But having the hospital may be so joined in their minds with the goal of improved health as to make them unwilling to consider alternative proposals. Although it is vital for a development agent to identify with the community's members by making their goals his own, he has also the practical problem that some of these goals may be unrealistic or require modification. It is also important, therefore, for his clients to be able to identify with the agent in the sense that they can adopt as their own some of the goals he has for them.

This aspect of agent-community relations is usually stressed in community development practice: the problem of educating the local people to see their circumstances as the agent does, so that they will accept his plans for them. This is all very well in its place, but it is futile to expect the members of a community to identify with the agent until he has first identified with them. When they are confident that he is in full sympathy with their aspirations for themselves, when they can feel sure that points of disagreement between them tend to be over matters of effective means, they will be better prepared to consider his proposals as the constructive suggestions of an expert and not as expressions of alien self-interest.

Learning the Client Community's Language

These aspects of the communication problem are fully present even when the agent and client community both use the same spoken language. How much more of a problem is communication to the development agent as he tries to get across the barriers of difference in experience and culture through a language that he does not know! Ability and willingness to learn the language of his clients is essential. But social and cultural considerations may provide serious barriers to an agent's willingness to learn his clients' language.

Although they come from a country that has absorbed millions of non-English speaking people in a few generations, most middle-class Americans have had little more than superficial acquaintance with a spoken language other than their own. The reason for this lack of language facility would appear to be a basic attitude toward foreign languages and foreign things in general that has characterized middle-class America in the recent past. Happily, however, it now shows signs of changing. Because assimilation of large numbers of immigrants was so important, pressures were exerted upon them that discouraged their use of foreign ways and languages. Strong positive value was attached to learning to speak like native Americans. The burden of making themselves understood fell upon the non-English speaking immigrants, while native Americans developed scornful attitudes toward foreign accents and languages, and the complacent feeling that where languages differ it is up to the other fellow to make the effort. This attitude, of course, has become a great handicap to many Americans whose work takes them abroad. Faced with what seems an impenetrable wall of gibberish, the American agent is easily tempted to retreat to the familiar technical aspects of his job while he confidently waits for the members of the client community somehow to resolve the language difference.

Even where the value of learning the local language is fully appreciated in the abstract, American attitudes that have developed in relation to immigrant populations work in subtle ways to inhibit learning. To learn another language requires that one speak it. This means making all kinds of mistakes that are amusing to the native speakers. Immigrants to America, having had to learn English, have been the butt of all kinds of humor, good and ill-natured, over their inability to speak without an accent. It is a very unpleasant feeling to find oneself providing others with the same kind of amusement that one has long enjoyed at home at the expense of the Hyman Kaplans.[8] American development agents find themselves having to make fools of themselves, as they see it, because they have habitually laughed at others for speaking broken English and because of the derogatory associations they have with foreign sounds and mannerisms in speech. French phonetics, for example, are associated in the minds of many Americans with an affected manner. The German manner of speaking, the Spanish, Swedish, Italian, Chinese, each has its derogatory associations in present-day American culture. It is somehow a violation of one's identity as an American seriously to try to imitate these foreign manners of speech. Thus it is easy for Americans to feel that they are damned if they do and damned if they don't: to feel foolish for speaking the local language brokenly and equally foolish to think of themselves speaking it correctly. The result is what has come to be known as the "language block" so common among Americans. Fortunately, new methods of language instruction in schools and colleges, with much more emphasis on spoken skills, are beginning to remove this block. For the fact is that we may provide others with some amusement, but we will never appear to them as fools, if we seriously try to learn. We seem most foolish when we make only the half-hearted effort.

Learning another language is, of course, a strenuous effort, but there is reward in it beyond the better grasp of reality it gives. There are subtle ways in which rapport improves simply because the agent makes the effort to learn his clients' language, quite apart from the proficiency that he attains. People identify their language with themselves and feel, often quite rightly, that they would lose their ethnic identity without it. A foreigner who has frequent dealings with them and who yet makes little effort to learn their language is, wittingly or not, guilty of slighting them. They will rarely attribute his failure to the mental inertia or psychological block that are probably responsible for it, but will surmise that for some reason he refuses to learn it. The reasons that will occur to them will be related to their feelings about themselves; the more sensitive they feel about their status as a people in relation to the agent and his own ethnic background, the more likely they are to attribute slurring or disdainful motives to him. Conversely, an agent who sets out to learn the community's language offers a subtle compliment to its members that few of them will fail to appreciate. What is just as important, it gives them a chance to help him from their superior position as initiates in the language. Benjamin Franklin observed that if he particularly wanted someone to like him, he would arrange for the other to do him a favor. There are all too few situations where the members of underdeveloped communities are in a position to do the agent favors, so for this reason, too, it is important to make an effort, at least, to learn their language. By this alone, the agent may become a friend rather than a stranger, a welcome guest and not an intruder.

Interpreters

To make an effort is one thing. To learn enough of the community's language to be able to carry on the elaborate communication necessary to many aspects of a development program is another. Often enough it is impossible to do so. The alternative is, of course, to use an interpreter, one who knows both the agent's and the community's languages well enough to mediate communication between them.

Relying on an interpreter greatly decreases a development agent's control over what is going on. Much depends on the fitness of the interpreter for his job. Since it is he who forms the communicating link between the program and the people, his position in relation to both is of great importance. The ideal arrangement is one where the interpreter is a member in good standing of the client community and at the same time is himself identified through training and interest with the development program's objectives. But even with such a person there will be some unavoidable distortions in communication, simply because the interpreter is by virtue of these identifications unrepresentative of his home community. With the type of interpreter much more commonly found, one who knows little about the development project and cares little for its fate, all kinds of distortions creep in. Perhaps his knowledge of the agent's language is too limited to permit him to understand fully what he is to translate, or perhaps he feels that he should edit the utterances of both parties to avoid possible offense. Not infrequently he will hold his responsibilities as an interpreter subordinate to his private ambitions and may then manipulate what is said on both sides to protect or further his own interests or those of his family and friends. In many countries where development programs are undertaken in rural communities, the interpreter may come from a class or ethnic group that looks down on the community's members and habitually insults them or deals with them arrogantly. Even when the interpreter approaches the ideal, the development agent's ignorance of the local language is likely to lead him to phrase things in ways that are difficult to translate.

The best check on distortions is provided by whatever the agent has managed himself to learn of the client community's language. Indeed, the more he knows, the more useful in some ways an interpreter can become, as we once had an opportunity to observe in connection with the operation of land courts in the Gilbert Islands. Even those colonial officials who had nearly perfect speaking knowledge of Gilbertese used an interpreter when they presided at courts adjudicating land disputes. The reason given was that the interpreter provided a check on the officer's and the people's mutual understanding of what was going on. Testimony given in Gilbertese was followed closely by the officer. Then the interpreter repeated it to him in English. If this did not accord with what the officer thought he had understood from the Gilbertese, he would then check with all concerned until the misunderstanding was cleared. Similarly, the officer addressed the court and announced his decisions in English. He then listened carefully to make sure that there was complete understanding while the interpreter translated into Gilbertese. This procedure helped ensure that the import of testimony and the intent of a decision was perfectly clear in both languages of record. The Gilbertese interpreter's failings in English and the officer's failings in Gilbertese were both thrown into relief and kept from being an uncontrolled source of misunderstanding.

This example illustrates how important it is for development agents to learn at least something of the local language. The contrast between the Gilbert Islands, under British rule, and the Trust Territory of the Pacific as administered by the United States in 1947 was remarkable in this respect. At that time, there was in Truk not a single government official who knew more than a few words of Trukese. Not one of Truk's ten thousand people could communicate with any American officer except through a handful of interpreters, the only Trukese who knew any English at all; and none of these few interpreters knew very much English. There was, in effect, no direct communication between the government and the people, and there was no check on the reliability of interpretation. Later it became the policy to require that one official, the district anthropologist, learn the language of his district in the Trust Territory so that he could function as liaison between the people and the administration, but unfortunately no other officials were required to learn a native language. The position of district anthropologist, moreover, is increasingly rarely filled. Improved communication is almost entirely a result of native schooling in English. In the Gilbert Islands, by contrast, every new government officer is required to pass an examination in the native language within a period of two years. His appointment in the Colonial Service is not fully confirmed until he meets this requirement. Furthermore, he is not eligible for promotion to higher grades until he has passed a "higher standard examination" in the native language. This examination includes a government communication containing mistakes of grammar and vocabulary, which the examinee is required to note and correct; it also requires writing an essay in Gilbertese on some aspect of native life, such as village meeting-house organization and protocol or the construction and sailing of outrigger canoes. Every government officer of more than two years' residence can communicate directly with any Gilbertese. The outstanding record of administration in the Gilberts, which includes successful programs for transplanting populations to new islands, would have been impossible without the easy communication resulting from this requirement.

Learning the Culture Through the Language

When he attempts to learn the language of the community in which he works, a development agent will discover that he is doing more than learning an alternative set of verbal symbols. He is also absorbing new experiences that form the background of meaning for the language. He may learn, for instance, a word that at first seems literally to translate our word "family," and then discover as he tries to use the word that it may include a maternal uncle but not a father (if the society is organized along matrilineal lines). The people of Truk, indeed, have taken over the English word "family" as *faameni*, by which they mean a matrilineal lineage. A father and his sons belong to different *faameni*, as also do a husband and wife.

To learn another language is, of course, to learn the meanings, the categories of thought and systems of ideas for which the language is a code. Without such knowledge it is virtually impossible to understand what one's clients are thinking and why. And it is only as one tries to learn their language and undertakes to use it on all possible occasions that one has a chance of gaining such an understanding.

In our own work on Truk, for example, for a long time we were baffled by two words that seemed at first to correspond roughly to the English words "love" and "like." But efforts to use them proved this assumption about their meaning to be wrong. It finally turned out that one of them, *togeej*, meant "the positive affect one feels for another person (or animal) because of one's ability to fill the other's need" and the other, *saani*, meant "the positive affect one feels for another person or thing because of the other person's or thing's filling one's own need." A person can properly only *togeej* his children, and because he *togeej* someone in trouble, he helps him; he can *togeej* and *saani* his sweetheart; and he can only *saani* a beautiful work of art. The words distinguish, in effect, between what we sometimes refer to as "altruistic" and "selfish" love. There are, of course, no reàl English equivalents, nor are there any real Trukese equivalents for English *like* and *love*.

Because the meanings in one language are not homologous with the meanings in another, but only analogous, and because they often relate to very different bodies of experience, no language can be entirely learned from a book. To a considerable extent it must be learned in the context of living experience.[9] To come to share the client community's experience in this way is far more important for effective communication than to develop a faultless accent. People will forgive a somewhat mangled pronunciation of their tongue if the speaker shows a comprehensive and sensitive knowledge of its categories of meaning.

Communicating with All Parts of the Community

Development agents must not only communicate effectively, they must do so with the right persons. It will not serve their purposes well to be able to communicate effectively with the local trouble-maker but not with the local leaders. A development agent in one of our own communities would have little chance of success if he failed to communicate satisfactorily with the local mayor, newspaper editor, parson, labor leader, and political boss. Every community, no matter how "under-developed," no matter whether in Central Africa, the Amazon basin, a Pacific island, or rural Minnesota, has its influential members, its leaders of public opinion. Some of them may occupy local political offices or hold official titles, but others may not. It is crucial to know who these people are and to be in communication with them. In order to do this, of course, a development agent must learn how the community is organized, who the key figures in it are, and the nature and extent of their influence.[10]

Important as it is to communicate with the community's leadership, it is also important to have direct communication with as many of the community's members as possible. To deal only with the leaders is, in effect, to make them one's interpreters and to invite all the distortions that are entailed. A development agent's presence is likely to precipitate a wave of talk in the community, with everything he says being passed from person to person along the channels of gossip. Unless he can communicate directly with the community's members at large, all kinds of problems are likely to arise. This is especially a problem in complex communities, as Leighton and Longaker observe in connection with the introduction of psychiatric clinics in North American communities.

> As a consequence of the distortions that develop in the course of communication, many people in the community will perceive the goals and functions of the clinic in terms that are very different from those of the innovators themselves. This discrepancy, furthermore, is apt to be underestimated by the innovators. It is natural for them to assume that they have communicated to the majority of the people after they have repeated themselves to exhaustion in public and private statements and in pamphlets and newspaper articles. As a result they may tend unrealistically to think of "the community" when they should be thinking of variation in different parts, or of "the people" when it would be more accurate to think of many different kinds of people with many different kinds of viewpoints.[*11]

In our own home community, people seeking to introduce civic improvements, after talking to all the clubs and church and civic groups and after going the rounds of informal neighborhood meetings, often find themselves confronted at the first formal public hearing with a large and hostile citizen turnout representing segments of the community that do not belong to the clubs, or to the church and civic groups, and that do not customarily attend informal neighborhood meetings. They have their own

* Reprinted by permission from Alexander H. Leighton, John A. Clausen, and Robert N. Wilson, editors, *Explorations in Social Psychiatry*. Basic Books, Inc., New York, 1957, p. 370. Copyright by Basic Books, Inc.

channels of communication, and those not in the know have their work cut out to learn what they are and how to use them.

But an agent cannot talk to everybody himself. He often has to rely to a considerable extent on the community's leaders. How, then, can he minimize the problem of distortions? Distortions are likely to be most serious if he tries to use the community's leaders merely as persons through whom to communicate with others, as links (interpreters) in a communication chain. The practical solution is to try to work out in partnership with the community's leaders a program that they are themselves enthusiastic about and that they see as their own. Then, in their full understanding of the project, they can help to communicate it effectively to the rest of the community, calling upon their superior knowledge of its communication channels. It is not for idealistic reasons alone that those who are experienced in community development work emphasize the necessity of taking the community's leaders and members into partnership. As a matter of practical politics, it is a great help in coping with communication problems. But to be able effectively to take them into partnership calls once more for an appropriate attitude of mind in the agent.

When working with and through a community's leaders, development agents should be prepared for what otherwise may be disconcerting surprises in the communication process. Community leaders are likely to formulate a program's objectives and to rationalize proposals for meeting them in unexpected ways. A development agent may jump to the conclusion that they have misunderstood him or are perverting the program's aims. His natural impulse is to jump in with counter-statements of his own addressed directly to the public and intended to correct what he assumes is incorrect information. In yielding to this impulse, however, an agent may be his own worst enemy. He may say things that the community's leaders avoided saying because they knew they would be impolitic. And by spoiling their play, an agent will cause them to lose face and will alienate them from cooperating with him further. Thus his action will have betrayed his own mistrust of the community's leaders and his lack of respect for them as persons. The way to avoid this situation is to discuss carefully with the community's leaders what they understand to be the human problems they must solve if they are to enlist the rest of the community's cooperation in a development project. Merely reaching an understanding with them about the aims and technical aspects of development is not enough. Understanding and consensus on the tactics of communication are also essential.

"The Silent Language"

Words are, of course, not the only things that communicate. As Edward T. Hall has vividly stated,[12] the public culture of any community provides a great many other conventional signs for and routings of behavior. People have no more self-conscious awareness of many of them than they have of the sound units and grammar of their spoken language. Yet display of these signs and conformity with these routings has high communicative value. A great deal of cross-cultural misunderstanding occurs in consequence. The length of time it is permissible to keep someone else waiting before it connotes an insult, for example, is very different in Latin America and the United States. The physical distance appropriate to a private conversation is likewise different. Hall's account of the North American backing away from his Latin-American counterpart, as the latter struggles to get within what is for him appropriate and comfortable conversation distance while the former seeks to protect himself from what feels to him like an intrusion on his person, reveals beautifully how the "silent language" of culturally standardized behavior communicates in ways provocative of misunderstanding and false stereotypes. Latin Americans think we are "distant or cold, withdrawn and unfriendly," and we "are constantly accusing them of breathing down our necks, crowding us, and spraying our faces."[13]

Differences of this sort are perhaps most disconcerting when we encounter them among peoples who seem to be otherwise culturally much like ourselves. We cannot put our finger on the problem in our relations. They just make us uncomfortable, that is all, and hence appear to be "difficult" to deal with. We are likely to attribute the difficulty to something in their character, when it actually reflects only a small but irritating cultural difference. These differences are irritating because what appears to be familiar behavior to both parties means different things to each of them. Once the real nature of the difference is recognized, it quickly ceases to be an irritant.

Anyone seeking the cooperation and good will of other peoples must pay close attention to the standardized behaviors and meanings that lie outside the threshold of self-consciousness. They are an important potential obstacle to successful cross-cultural communication.

"CULTURE SHOCK"

The term "culture shock" has become widely known to people concerned with overseas development work. Kalervo Oberg first used this expression to refer to the emotional stress of adjusting to a new cultural setting.[14] Culture shock is a consequence of being suddenly removed from familiar settings in which a person knows all the little things needed to get along: how to greet people, how to say no without offending, how to deal with people in subordinate positions, how to take care of intimate bodily needs. It is a product of ignorance of both the local culture and the local language. It can be a very disturbing thing to have all the little things one has taken for granted suddenly removed. Some people react to this situation positively as an adventure; others are terrified and incapacitated. Few, however, do not find it stressful to be continually operating in ignorance of the meaning to others of their own actions or of the meanings they should attribute to the actions of others.

What do we do, for example, when a local acquaintance nudges us and tells us to say something to a passerby in words we do not understand? Is our acquaintance seriously trying to help us do the right thing? Is he pulling our leg, having some innocent fun? Or is he using us in some way that will make us appear at a disadvantage, perhaps deliberately trying to get us into trouble? Suppose we say what he told us to say, and suppose that our hearers laugh. Are they laughing at us or at something else in the situation, perhaps the reaction of the passerby, who is surprised and himself caught off balance by being politely addressed in his own language by someone who presumably knew no word of it? Suppose the passerby reacts with apparent indignation, giving us and our acquaintance a tongue-lashing, while at the same time a gang of spectators goes into paroxisms of laughter; and then suppose our acquaintance nudges us, as the irate passerby starts to walk away, and whispers to us to call something else to him. The whole episode may represent no more than the standard byplay between cousins or brothers-in-law in an institutionalized joking relationship in which we were being invited to take part in good fun. Our reaction, however, is almost certain to be one of fury at having been put in such a situation. Our acquaintance probably is unaware of how thoroughly he has shattered the dignity we have been struggling to maintain in the face of so many uncertainties. An experience or two like this may well make us want to get away from "these horrid people" as fast as we can and go back to the certainties of home. This is especially likely if we have no strong commitment to stay.

Experiences of this particular kind are less likely to befall us if by local standards our years and rank make us persons of consequence. But even then, the uncertainties remain, and as soon as we make a serious effort to deal with local people, we will find ourselves in all kinds of situations where we must depend upon the advice of local acquaintances. We are likely, moreover, to be an object of great curiosity. People will point at us, then say something to their companions, who will laugh, and then they will all look at us again and laugh some more. We often do the same thing ourselves to visiting foreigners who excite our curiosity without, of course, meaning any harm by it.

Those who are truly stimulated to learn the language and get oriented will find that problems of this kind gradually become fewer. Their severity, moreover, depends to some extent on a person's attitude. If he has accepted the local people from the beginning as friendly and trustworthy, the uncertainties that he suffers will be less terrifying. He will assume that the laughter he seems to evoke is friendly laughter and he will laugh, too. But someone who is oversensitive, who is not secure in himself, who tends to be suspicious of other people and their motives, even at home, will find the experience intolerable.

Significantly, reports indicate very little culture shock among the first groups of Peace Corps volunteers. The low pay and other working conditions of the Peace Corps make it attractive to people who are more likely to have a suitable attitude of mind to begin with. Rigorous screening can eliminate many more who would be unlikely to handle well the problems of initial exposure to an alien setting. Finally, even an intensive short course in the language of one's clients before actually going among them can greatly reduce the amount of culture shock.

EMOTIONAL ISOLATION

The field conditions under which development agents work obviously vary considerably. To gain an intimate knowledge of the client community and its people, an agent must live in fairly close association with them. Insulating himself in a special residential quarter for Euro-American aliens with all the material conveniences of home—often with more conveniences than he is accustomed to at home—is a sure way to erode the attitude of mind necessary for community development. Indeed, it is prima facie evidence that the proper attitude of mind is lacking. Intimate experience with other people and their way of life, once the necessary adjustments to alien customs have been made, is extremely rewarding in many ways, as anthropologists can testify. At the same time, if it extends over a long period it is likely to subject a development agent to a new set of strains, especially if he is cut off from other members of his own society. The anthropologist Elenore Smith Bowen has recounted with great sensitivity some of the emotional distress that isolated field workers almost inevitably experience.[15]

No matter how mature emotionally a field agent may be, as a human he has needs that his emotional well-being requires be met. He needs familiar human companionship—the sort of company in which he can relax, be drawn out of himself and his concern with his work. He needs to be important to someone; he needs to belong; and he needs to be indulged occasionally by someone else. If he is alone in a strange social and cultural world, his needs, which life at home has met so well, become increasingly acute. In time they can exert a dominating influence over everything he does. The effects usually take one or a combination of several forms.

Persons who find it impossible to fill emotional needs by establishing intimate and rewarding relations with members of the local community tend to become increasingly depressed and morose. In time, they may come to hate the place and its people, who could perhaps help meet their needs if given an opportunity. Withdrawal, often through alcoholic drinking, may become habitual. This response produces the classic picture of the European deteriorating in the tropics or any other place that his attitude has turned into a "Godforsaken hole."

Another response is to try to establish close relations with members of the local population. The tendency is to try to find among them substitutes for those who in the past have been most important in filling one's needs: a close friend, a father figure, a man "Friday," an adopted child. For a mature man, of course, one of the greatest needs is for the combination of gratifications that stems from a satisfactory domestic relationship with a woman. Hence the not uncommon phenomenon of the isolated European with his "native" wife or mistress. A report on the Peace Corps in Tanganyika notes that women are likely to be a major problem for the volunteers.

"It gets quite lonely out there, you know," an agricultural expert with twenty years' experience told the volunteers as a preface to his warning against "going native" to the extent of taking an African wife or mistress. *[16]

Apart from the problem of women, people sometimes feel that they can fill their needs if they "go native" to the extent of adopting those local forms of conduct that they expect will provide them fuller entry into the community and to the kinds of relationships they seek. This approach creates difficulties in their relations with other persons of European background with whom they must also have dealings. Furthermore, not having fully mastered the local culture, their efforts at "going native" are likely to appear to the community's members as amusingly inappropriate and as far from the real thing, as do our children's efforts to play the grownup. Such efforts, however, may not be entirely out of

* Reprinted by permission from John P. Nugent, "The Peace Corps Comes to Tanganyika," *The Reporter*, vol. 26, February 1, 1962, p. 36. Copyright by The Reporter Magazine Co.

place. Local reactions will depend largely on what people sense are the motives for trying to "go native." They may respect the effort, if they see it as reflecting a genuine concern to master the local language and culture. But if they see it as a sign of emotional weakness, they will be inclined to scorn it.

Indeed, an essential feature of the attitude of mind that a development agent must cultivate is not to be overly concerned with being liked by his clients. This is not to say that he should be unconcerned about whether or not he tramples on their feelings. Quite the contrary! But he should exhibit such concern because of the respect he feels for them as persons and not because his own feelings of adequacy and security depend on his winning their affection. A person who is anxiously dependent on the friendship and good will of others cannot help his friends if their preoccupation with their own need of the moment makes them indifferent to his dependency on them. This observation applies equally to the nations that agents represent. Efforts by the government of the United States to woo the friendship and allegiance of newly emerging nations, whose governments are necessarily preoccupied with what they see as their own problems, are doomed to failure. Aid programs to these nations can be successful as instruments of governmental policy only if given out of our understanding of and respect for their own concerns. Otherwise we appear to be trying to take advantage of their needs so as to use them to gratify wants of our own. All of us have known people who have tried to use us in this way. We do not number them among our friends.

For a development agent, of course, "going native" for personal reasons is, in effect, to put his own needs ahead of the needs of his clients. When he meets with resistance from his clients to a suggestion he has made, instead of being able to deal with it as a symptom of some factor in the development situation that needs further investigation and clarification, he will interpret it as personal rejection by people whose affection, acceptance, and indulgence he is seeking in his loneliness. He will be inclined to see his clients' behavior not as a normal response to the stresses of change but as a personal betrayal, and he may easily conclude that his clients are fickle, calculating, and untrustworthy.

Instead of trying to find acceptance as one of themselves by "going native," an isolated worker may try to get closer to his clients by rejecting his identification with the social groups from which he comes. A common way to express this is to link all other alien outsiders in the area with the social background he is rejecting and to champion all community causes and complaints, real or fancied, against them, making evident in word and deed his hostility to government officials, missionaries, and representatives of outside commercial interests. Often coupled with this approach to meeting his emotional needs is a super-dedication to serving the community, in the hope of thereby earning the love, respect, and gratitude of its members. This predisposes a development agent to feel that he has a moral right to the community's acceptance and cooperation. He necessarily interprets any problems that arise in his relations with his clients as evidence of their ingratitude. He may soon conclude that they are unworthy and beyond redemption.

As these examples suggest, an agent's growing emotional needs become a problem not only because they render his actions compulsive and inflexible, but also because they generate in him delusions about the nature of his relations with his clients. He interprets people's reactions to him according to how they seem to fill his own needs. He sees an ordinary act of courtesy by someone in the community as an expression of extraordinary affection. A negative reaction to something he has said or done becomes a crisis rather than a small matter to be straightened out. As our needs become severe, we tend increasingly to see things in terms of extremes, as very good or very bad. We tend more and more to alternate between elation and despair. We project our ever more desperate hopes and increasingly acute fears into all situations, progressively losing touch with their realities.

His emotional needs make an isolated field worker more easily victimized by precisely the persons whom he is most anxious to avoid: the rogues, the ruthlessly ambitious, the ostracized—the little collection of individuals in every community who feel that they have much to gain by getting close to him. The local outcast may be even more hungry for friendship than the field worker. Those who feel they can profit by making their fellows think that they are "in solid" with the agent will quickly find out what they can do to make the agent feel good about himself, how they can effectively indulge him and make themselves indispensable to him. Insofar as his relations with the community are dominated by his own emotional needs, therefore, an agent increases the likelihood that he will form his closest contacts among those of the community's members who are most likely to make trouble for him in the conduct of his work. They will make it harder for him to develop good working relations with responsible members of the community.

The needs that give rise to the kinds of reactions just outlined are present in all of us. Persons who have never managed to meet them satisfactorily at home and who, therefore, come into the field situation already hungry will find their hunger intensified. Some will be strongly inclined to look upon the client community as a new field to exploit in trying to satisfy it. They are obviously poor risks as development agents. But what can an agent who has been relatively well adjusted do to avoid the traps into which his developing needs are likely eventually to lead him?

First, he must accept the idea that he will have emotional needs and that they will become increasingly acute. If he chooses to think that he will be an exception or that he will be strong enough to keep his needs from compromising him in his work, he does himself a disservice. He renders himself unable to admit that he has problems when they arise—as almost inevitably they will —and therefore unable to do something constructive about them. It is only by admitting to our frailty that we free ourselves to look for something constructive to do about it.

Although "going native," trying to be accepted by the community as one of its own, represents an unsatisfactory solution, an agent will find it helpful if he allows himself to have the kinds of contacts with the community's members from which warm personal relationships can develop. In time he will discover persons whom he finds and who find him congenial. The resulting friendships can fill some of his needs as well as help him conduct his work, but an agent must not expect too much of them. His friends, if they are of the right kind, will all have loyalties to other persons in the community that take precedence over their regard for him. For this reason alone, the community can meet the agent's emotional needs only in a limited way, at best.

It becomes important, therefore, for a field agent to cultivate satisfying relationships with such of his fellow Americans and Europeans as may be located in the area. To the extent that he looks to them for gratification of his emotional needs, whether successfully or not, he keeps these needs less of an issue in his relations with the community, the most immediate object of his professional concern.

In the long run, however, there is no substitute for one's own family. It is advisable for any agent who is to be in an isolated community for more than a few months to have his family with him. To the extent that his wife has adequately filled his emotional needs in the past he ensures that these needs will continue to be filled if she accompanies him. But taking his family along can also raise problems. Both the agent and his wife will find themselves having to operate together in a strange environment. The routines and adjustments they have worked out in their relationship are bound to be partially disrupted. The wife may be unable to adjust. Her emotional vulnerabilities may be exposed by the isolation and strange conditions of living, and the husband's work may prevent him from filling his wife's needs. Her lack of commitment to her husband's work may make the wife a ready victim of culture shock. Thus her presence may be a hindrance rather than a help. Moreover, an agent's wife and children are important factors in his relations with his clients. As her husband's social alter-ego, the wife functions as a development agent herself. No matter how successfully her husband may meet the requirements of the local situation, if she generates resentment and mistrust in the community by her conduct, agent-community cooperation may be impaired. Development agents need their wives in the field, but development requires that their wives be as qualified in attitude of mind as are the agents themselves.

SELECTING FOR ATTITUDE

The attitude of mind we have been talking about is not something that can be developed in a short indoctrination course. It is as much a product of an untroubled personality as anything else. Anxious persons who face the prospect of an assignment in development work with immediate and intense concern about their health, the food, drinking water, and cleanliness are unlikely to have the requisite attitude of mind when compared with those who react to it as an interesting adventure.

In their study of overseas workers, Cleveland, Mangone, and Adams found that they were readily classifiable, on the basis of tests, into five personality types: (1) "anxious-defensive ('wary,' 'tense,' 'worrying')"; (2) "passive-conformist ('conservative,' 'restrained')"; (3) "narcissistic-indulgent ('charming,' 'good-looking,' 'impulsive')"; (4) "constricted ('formal,' 'painstaking,' 'awkward')"; and (5) "positive-bouyant-overt-resourceful-active." It was the last that seemed to be regarded most highly by supervisors overseas.[17]

Highly significant, moreover, was another finding by these authors. The capacity for what they call "cultural empathy" seemed to be most frequently exhibited by those workers abroad who had already had considerable "environmental mobility."[18] They had had experience with many different kinds of people, had knocked about a bit, and had developed in this way a feeling for people in different walks of life. Those who had never learned to live with any but "their own kind," who had avoided doing so, and who had organized their lives with single-minded concentration on their own personal "success" were less able to meet the requirements of overseas work satisfactorily.

One plant pathologist we interviewed was rated "high" on both his technical competence and his attitudes toward foreign nationals. It turned out that as a boy he had heard many stories from his mother about her two brothers who lived and worked abroad. He had gone to a private, all-scholarship school that combined practical farming with intensive academic studies, and at 17 years of age, with $200 saved, he simply took off for Europe, eventually landing in Leningrad, unable to speak a word of Russian. Making his way to Moscow, he visited an agricultural trade show, met an English-speaking geneticist, and accepted an offer to operate a tractor in the Ukraine for the summer. At the end of the summer he decided to continue his education in Moscow for a year; he enrolled in an academy, lived with Russian students, learned Russian, and shared with his friends both their rigid studies and their off-time visits to concerts, ballets, and the countryside. The United States contains many plant pathologists, but few whose records of environmental mobility prepared them so well as this one was for service abroad.

Another American presents a contrasting case. He has been working for the government overseas for almost a dozen years; now employed in his specialty by the ICA, he deals with local officials at the highest level. He says with complete candor:

"The only reason I got into government was because, after college, a guy came up and offered me a job in Europe. . . . If a young man getting out of college asked me for advice, I would tell him, first, don't get into government and, second, don't go overseas. If he wants to get ahead financially, he shouldn't do either of these things. . . . If I were single, I would quit the government immediately. . . . My wife would like to go back to the United States. . . . She was quite unhappy out here, mainly worrying over the children, their health, and other dangers to their general welfare. Most American families in this neighborhood have been robbed. . . . We're not interested in running around very much. Life, for us, is pretty much a matter of home and family and the children. We don't have much contact with the local nationals. . . . It's so much better to sit down at home and have a beer and read the paper. As far as language is concerned, I don't myself feel that in two years, even if I knocked myself out, which would hurt my job, I would end up knowing it very well. Then I would leave and in the future it would never be of any benefit. So why should I do it: I've been able to get along without the language."

This case typifies hundreds of others in which the individual, empty of goals and incentives, concentrates upon the inconveniences and the discomforts, the bother of getting about in a strange milieu, the nuisance of learning a foreign language. Why do people feel this way? In this case, at least, family background and limited environmental mobility seem to have set the stage for an unimpressive and joyless overseas performance. "We lived a normal sort of suburban life," he said, "except we had a lot of financial trouble." From caddying at a golf club (which he detested) to the selection of courses at college the whole focus was on "the idea of making a lot of money and getting out of the bind I was in." He worked hard with an eye toward success, and even his several extracurricular activities were calculated with the cold eye of ambition rather than the joy of the activity. He ruefully admitted, "I knocked myself out because I thought I had to be successful."*[19]

Clearly, much has yet to be learned about the screening of personnel suitable for development work in alien cultural settings. In the light of these considerations, however, it would seem useful in recruiting for development work that appeals be made to a sense of social responsibility, to the spirit of adventure, and the ideal of service, rather than to extraordinary pay, vacation style living, and social privilege. The position taken by the Peace Corps in this respect is clearly in the right direction.

CONCLUSION

Whatever problems may arise in his relations with his clients, responsibility for resolving them falls primarily on the agent. To hold these problems at a minimum and to do the things that are needed to cope with them as they arise, an agent must be prepared to accept his clients unconditionally as fellow human beings and to respect their persons in every way that such acceptance implies. Without such an attitude, moreover, it is difficult to overcome preliminary stereotypes, to make a serious effort to learn the language and customs of the client community, and to be undoctrinaire and flexible in action. An appropriate attitude toward people in general, and his clients in particular, can greatly reduce "culture shock" and lead an agent to develop relations with his clients that help sustain him emotionally. Of the many things that affect the course of community development, perhaps none is more important than the attitude of the development agent himself.

SUGGESTED READING

Adair, John, and Kurt Deuschle, "Some Problems of the Physicians on the Navajo Reservation," *Human Organization*, vol. 16, no. 4, 1958, pp. 19–23.

Bowen, Elenore Smith, *Return to Laughter*. Harper and Bros., New York, 1954.

Bunker, Robert, and John Adair, *The First Look at Strangers*. Rutgers University Press, New Brunswick, N. J., 1959.

* Reprinted with permission of the publishers from *The Overseas Americans* by Harlan Cleveland, Gerard J. Mangone, and John Clarke Adams. Copyright © 1960 by the McGraw-Hill Book Company, Inc., New York, pp. 177–179.

Cleveland, Harlan, Gerard J. Mangone, and John Clarke Adams, *The Overseas Americans*. McGraw-Hill Book Co., New York, 1960.

Dexter, Lewis A., "O.P.A.: A Case Study in Liberal Priggishness," *Applied Anthropology*, vol. 4, no. 1, 1945, pp. 32–33.

Foster, George M., *Traditional Cultures: And the Impact of Technological Change*. Harper and Row, Publishers, Incorporated, New York, 1962.

Hall, Edward T., and William Foote Whyte, "Intercultural Communication: A Guide to Men of Action," *Human Organization*, vol. 19, no. 1, 1960, pp. 5–12.

Joseph, Alice, "Physician and Patient," *Applied Anthropology*, vol. 1, no. 4, 1942, pp. 1–6.

Whyte, William Foote, "The Social Role of the Settlement House," *Applied Anthropology*, vol. 1, no. 1, 1941, pp. 14–24.

NOTES TO CHAPTER 14

1. Cleveland, Harlan, Gerard J. Mangone, and John Clarke Adams, *The Overseas Americans*. McGraw-Hill Book Co., New York, 1960, pp. 123 ff.

2. Coch, Lester, and John R. P. French, "Overcoming Resistance to Change," *Human Relations*, vol. 1, 1947–1948, p. 531.

3. Muñoz Marin, Luis, "We Can Save Latin America from Castro," *This Week Magazine*, December 17, 1961, p. 15.

4. Useem, John, "South Sea Island Strike: Labor-Management Relations in the Caroline Islands, Micronesia" in Spicer, Edward H., editor, *Human Problems in Technological Change: A Casebook*. Russell Sage Foundation, New York, 1952, p. 157.

5. See, for example, the account of the reception given Gerald D. Berreman in an Indian village as he reports it in *Behind Many Masks: Ethnography and Impression Management in a Himalayan Village*, Monograph no. 4, Society for Applied Anthropology, Ithaca, N. Y., 1962.

6. Adams, Richard N., "A Nutritional Research Program in Guatemala" in Paul, Benjamin D., editor, *Health, Culture, and Community: Case Studies of Public Reactions to Health Programs*. Russell Sage Foundation, New York, 1955, pp. 448–450.

7. Wax, Rosalie, "The Destruction of a Democratic Impulse: A Case Study," *Human Organization*, vol. 12, no. 1, 1953, pp. 11–21.

8. Ross, Leonard Q. [Leo C. Rosten], *The Education of Hyman Kaplan*. Harcourt, Brace and Co., New York, 1937. Also Leo Rosten's *Return of Hyman Kaplan*, published in 1959 by Harper Bros., New York.

9. See, for example, the comment by Ronald M. Berndt, *Excess and Restraint: Social Control Among a New Guinea Mountain People*, University of Chicago Press, Chicago, 1962, p. viii: "The bizarre, the exotic, the unknown quality, the air of having entered an alien world—that is to say, feelings arising from ignorance of the situation and the people—had, within such a short period (a year), almost completely evaporated. In its place had come some knowledge of the society and culture, some comprehension of the significance of events, some understanding of the meaning of what we saw and heard. And the only way this state of affairs could have been brought about was through learning the local language and not relying solely on interpreters."

10. For an excellent illustration of this aspect of the communication problem, see Whyte, William Foote, "The Social Role of the Settlement House," *Applied Anthropology*, vol. 1, no. 1, 1941, pp. 14–24. See also Loomis, Charles P., and Douglas Ensminger, "Governmental Administration and Informal Local Groups," *Applied Anthropology*, vol. 1, no. 2, 1942, pp. 41–59; Oliver, Douglas L., "A Case of Change in Food Habits in Bougainville, British Solomon Islands," *ibid.*, pp. 34–36; Kimball, Solon T., and John H. Provinse, "Navajo Social Organization in Land Use Planning," *Applied Anthropology*, vol. 1, no. 4, 1942, pp.18–25.

11. Leighton, Alexander H., and Alice Longaker, "The Psychiatric Clinic as a Community Innovation" in Leighton, Alexander H., John A. Clausen, and Robert N. Wilson, editors, *Explorations in Social Psychiatry*, Basic Books, Inc., New York, 1957, p. 370.

12. Hall, Edward T., *The Silent Language*. Doubleday and Co., New York, 1959.

13. *Ibid.*, p. 209.

14. In *Consultation in the Brazil-United States Cooperative Health Program 1942–1955*. Division of Health, Welfare and Housing, United States Operations Mission to Brazil, The Institute of Inter-American Affairs, Rio de Janeiro. See also the discussion by Cleveland, Mangone, and Adams, *op. cit.*, pp. 26–45; and by Foster, George M., *Traditional Cultures: And the Impact of Technological Change*, Harper and Row, Publishers, Incorporated, New York, 1962, pp. 187–194.

15. Bowen, Elenore Smith, *Return to Laughter*, Harper and Bros., New York, 1954. Although Miss Bowen portrays the emotional strains of field work very well, the reader should not assume that her fellow anthropologists would be happy unreservedly to endorse her ways of dealing with such strains or her concept of the role of the field anthropologist.

16. Nugent, John P., "The Peace Corps Comes to Tanganyika," *The Reporter*, vol. 26, February 1, 1962, p. 36.

17. Cleveland, Mangone, and Adams, *op. cit.*, p. 174.

18. *Ibid.*, p. 176.

19. *Ibid.*, pp. 177–179.

Chapter 15

PROBLEMS OF PRACTICE: SOCIAL CONSIDERATIONS

So far we have considered problems of community development exclusively from the standpoint of the agent and his relations with the client community's members. We have treated these problems as if the relevant system of social relationships involved essentially two parties, the community and the agent. There are many situations in which this is actually the case. A lands commissioner in the Gilbert Islands—working on the problem of developing a complete register of real property on an atoll, codifying its customary land law, developing land courts competently staffed by local personnel and inducing the villagers to adopt such modifications of their customary law as seem advisable for orderly administration and adjudication— may spend up to two or three years on an atoll where he and his family are the only resident Europeans, except possibly for a missionary. Within the limits his clients impose, the lands commissioner is free to establish whatever relationships with the Gilbertese community seem best calculated to accomplish his development mission. There is no third party to be reckoned with. The social setting provides him with only the members of a culturally homogeneous client population to consider. It is obviously an ideal context in which to undertake development, for it imposes the fewest restrictions on an agent in the conduct of his work. In many instances, however, development must be done in more complicated social settings.

Social complications take two basic forms. In one there are other members of the agent's own society present in the development situation—people with whom he normally identifies himself and to whom he habitually looks for his everyday social gratifications. The other complication involves the presence of a series of interdependent social entities, such as communities, classes, castes, or ethnic groups, of which the client community or population is but one. They may be culturally heterogeneous and may have antithetical political and economic interests. Both generic kinds of complication often present themselves simultaneously, with the added complication that the agent himself belongs to one of the social groups in the larger social system.

THE STATION COMMUNITY

The picture we portrayed in the preceding chapter of the development agent living isolated from anyone who shares his own cultural background, where his sole daily contacts are with members of the client community, does not represent what is often the situation in fact. It frequently happens that development agents reside and maintain their headquarters at an administrative station of some kind, equipped with various facilities for housing resident European aliens. Several other families representing the agent's own society are also housed there. They may all be directly associated with the same development project in which the agent is himself engaged, or they may have business with the client population of a different sort. Often, for example, an agricultural development agent is a civil servant who is assigned to a field station where there are other civil servants with different administrative responsibilities: a physician in charge of the local hospital and clinic, a supervisor of schools, a director of works, a chief of police, all forming a part of the staff of a general civil administrator (governor, resident commissioner, superintendent, and so on).

These station personnel and their families, together with a few other people of similar ethnic and cultural background in the area, tend to form a distinct social enclave, which we may call a station community. They will identify a development agent assigned to the area as "one of us." They will expect him to live in the manner in which they live, to participate in their closed social round, to join "the club." They will make it very hard for him to do anything else. Over and over again, people have gone out with some kind of development mission only to find that the values of the station community to which they attach themselves and the demands that its members make upon them effectively prevent them from developing the relationships with their clients that their work requires. They never do get around to the intimate observation of, and participation in, the client community's affairs that success in their work requires. Their efforts to learn the local language make little progress because they are not in a situation where they have to use it constantly. Their social relationships are established primarily with other members of the station community, so that they assimilate its dominant attitudes and conventions, including its stereotypes regarding the client community.

Those who do make the effort in the face of these obstacles and establish good working relations with their clients may find themselves criticized by other station personnel. They will be accused of "relaxing standards" or even "going native." The adjustments in the development agent's living that enable him to get closer to his clients are likely to require that he live in a style that is unconventional from a middle-class European or American point of view. How to strike the right balance in this "conflict between their obligations to be empathic with the local population and their need to get along with their fellow workers" is often a major problem facing development agents.[1]

Even when all of its members are dedicated to community development work, a station community of even a few families inevitably becomes a separate social world built on the common cultural background of its members, and to the extent that it does so it becomes cut off from the client community. The station community is, like one's home, a place apart, where one can "be oneself" and relax from the strains of one's work. As such, it has a place. But insofar as development work requires a fuller involvement with one's clients than existing patterns of station life are geared for, the station can serve as an important obstacle to successful development work. Station communities—whether on our Indian reservations or in colonial areas—are, in fact, notoriously insular. Their members have dealings with their administrative clients in such narrowly limited contexts, either on official business or as masters to domestic servants, that they may be almost totally ignorant of the language and culture of their clients after years of residence among them. Few of us in the professional classes in our home towns, where we have lived most of our lives, really know much about the people there whose way of life is different from ours, even though we have daily contact with many of them as medical patients, welfare clients, or pupils in school. When we go abroad to work with people in underdeveloped areas, unthinkingly we may organize our lives in station communities so as to maintain the same social distance as existed at home in dealing with our clients. In consequence, although we may learn a great deal about them professionally, what we know is usually much less than we need to know in order to be effective in development work.

THE LARGER SOCIETY

In most of the world, the community that is the primary object of development is but one of a larger aggregation of social units linked together in a political and economic order. This larger order may be a nation state, a colony, or a territory under United Nations trusteeship. In each case the larger order is composed of different classes, castes, or ethnic groups, each with its own cultural characteristics, and all participating unequally in a system of power relationships.

In the Trust Territory of New Guinea, for example, we can see the several components of the larger order in bold relief. In any area there are native village communities on the one hand and a small European community on the other. Each can be divided into several interest groups and subcommunities. The native villages, for example, may cluster into several distinct groups, each with its own language and culture. The Europeans are likely to include missionaries, planters, government officials, and (in the towns) clerks and store managers. The Europeans and natives form two distinct social castes, between which there is almost no social mingling or intermarriage. Relations across caste lines are largely confined to contexts of business exchange, work, domestic service, formal education, and government. In the towns there is an intermediate caste. It includes Chinese and other persons of oriental ancestry, the descendants of oriental-occidental and (where the children have been reared outside the native community) European-native unions. Within this caste there are, as among Europeans, class distinctions. Educated natives who have adopted a European mode of dress and living mingle more readily with this intermediate caste and some of the wealthier and educated orientals mingle more readily with the Europeans. But the three castes maintain well-defined social boundaries and territories.

In New Guinea, development programs have been sponsored by government and have native welfare as their primary concern. But planters and missionaries cannot be ignored. Their resistance to an agent can spoil his efforts to get cooperation from the native community. In one area in which we worked personally, efforts to establish a producer's cooperative were effectively sabotaged by a local missionary's opposition. Missionaries and planters wield real power in the form of religious and economic sanctions. The missions constitute a powerful pressure group which the territorial administration must be wary of offending. Both groups have institutionalized ways of dealing with the native community, enjoy certain privileges, pay for services at certain fixed rates, and have their spheres of influence (both real and presumed) in native affairs. If the changes that an agent hopes to effect in the native community appear to threaten their privileges and influence, missionaries and planters are likely to be hostile both to the agent's program and to him personally. In many areas the government operates at a disadvantage in its development efforts, in that its personnel are not permanently located in the communities to be developed but the mission stations and plantations are. Government projects come and go but the missions and plantations remain, it would seem, forever. Their power is an ever-present factor in the community's life. Mobilized against a development project, it can effectively block the project within the client community itself.

In many other parts of the world similar problems exist. A big problem in economic development in many parts of the Middle East, for example, is the opposition of a small class of great estate owners—the landlords—to anything that will substantially improve the lot of the peasant communities. A major problem in some parts of Latin America is the rigid class lines separating the aristocracy, the middle class, and the peasants, and the caste barriers separating Indians from non-Indians. Set patterns of relationships among these groups have led to stereotypes and attitudes that reinforce a feudal type of social *status quo* and that stand in the way of most efforts at economic and social development.[2] In other parts of the world the different social groups may be less obvious for an outsider to identify, and their power to complicate the development situation may be less readily apparent. But the chances are good that wherever development is undertaken, planners and field agents will have to take careful account of the conflicting interests in the larger social order.

Usually, the people whose welfare is to be improved belong to the segment of the larger society that is most in need, the one with the fewest privileges, with the least political, economic, or other power, and with the least prestige. It is likely to be the group that is regarded as most "backward" or "degenerate," like "animals," by the other groups in the larger social order. Some of the problems that this situation raises for development agents are avoidable, once they are recognized; others are less easy to overcome.

Development as a Threat to Privilege

The first and most obvious problem is connected with the threat to privilege that a development program is likely to represent. In some instances it may be possible to argue that in the end greater benefits will .accrue through general economic improvement, but frequently program administrators face the necessity of getting sufficient power behind them so that they can provide the client community with immunity from reprisals by hostile privileged groups. Such immunity cannot always be achieved. Often agents may find it necessary to enlist the voluntary cooperation of privileged groups before they approach the community with which they intend to work. Members of a privileged group are often key figures in the program's execution, as when they control the issuance of permits for new business enterprises, have power over essential transportation facilities, or otherwise constitute a vital link in the network of expanding economic relations whose growth the program is designed to stimulate. Short of a complete political and social revolution, their cooperation is essential in areas where a *rentier* class controls the fate of peasant communities, and in countries and colonies where governmental functions above the village level are in the hands of a privileged group such as a hereditary aristocracy, a group of industrial magnates, an educated class of bureaucrats, a cabal of army officers, or a distinct ethnic group. Cornell's now famous project in Vicos, Peru, for example, aimed at transforming the life of Indian peons on a large hacienda, would not have got off the ground unless it had the full backing and support of government authorities.[3]

The power of privileged groups obviously imposes genuine limitations on the kinds of program that can be undertaken with their acquiescence. Even within these limitations, getting their cooperation may be every bit as difficult as getting the cooperation of the client community itself, so much so, that development agents may be misled into thinking that once their cooperation is achieved, the whole problem of consent and cooperation is solved. It is easy to develop a picture in one's mind of the community eager for the benefits that one hopes to bring them and of the privileged group representing the only barrier to the program's successful execution. But as the experience at Vicos, Peru, reveals, after the government's consent had been obtained and the hacienda owner had been persuaded to rent his hacienda to Cornell University with economic development in mind, then came the long hard job of gradually gaining the confidence and cooperation of the Vicoseños themselves.

After privileged groups have given their consent to a development project, they may subsequently become a source of difficulty to change agents for reasons other than fear that they will lose their political or economic privileges. For example, an agent may incur criticism because he does not pattern his dealings with the community's members along the lines already established by the privileged group. If, in the interests of cooperation, he treats village elders with respect for their dignity, has them sit down with him to discuss village problems (rather than stand at attention as required by government officials in some parts of the world), sits down to eat with them, and allows them to approach him freely and thereby take liberties with his time and comfort, he may appear to the privileged group to be undermining the whole social order. To the extent, moreover, that by such behavior he is successful in getting cooperation of a kind that the members of the privileged group have not been able to achieve, he is likely to incur their hostility because of jealousy.

Privileged groups have a vested interest in their established pattern for dealing with subordinate groups in the social hierarchy. They have elaborate rationalizations as to why these patterns are appropriate and just. For these rationalizations to carry weight, they must stem from the privileged person's superior knowledge of the character and nature of persons in the subordinate groups. The New Guinea planter, for example, is sure that he "knows all about natives." But he usually restricts his dealings with them to a very limited set of situations in which his interests are paramount. He demands a show of subservience at all times. He is very bitter about "cheeky" natives. He resents "crazy anthropologists" who go out and live in native villages for a few months or a year and then go home and "write a book telling everything about the natives." An anthropologist not only deals with natives in ways that violate the pattern for white-native relations, but in doing so he may learn much more about them in a short time than the average planter learns in a lifetime of seeing and dealing with natives every day. In order to achieve success in his work, a development agent will necessarily be doing very much the same thing. He is likely to be resented for the same reasons. The need to operate in a different way from that of the privileged group implies that the latter's way is inadequate for any but the limited situations in which its members deal with persons in the subordinate group, an implication they are likely to resent.

This poses a problem for development agents. On the one hand, they must deal with members of the underdeveloped community in ways calculated to earn their trust and cooperation, and on the other hand, in doing so, they must try not to alienate the good will of persons in superordinate groups.

They can, of course, try to make it clear to the latter from the outset that since they are aiming to do things that are different from the usual, they must resort to unusual tactics. We have found privileged persons willing to accept our different role as anthropologist when it was rationalized as a calculated tactic rather than being presented in moral terms, which by implication passed adverse moral judgment on their own patterns for dealing with natives. As long as we did what we did for practical reasons and not out of personal inclination or ethical principle, they were willing to accept us, believing that we were not traitors to the privileged group with whom they identified us as fellow white men and scientists.

The Social Position of the Agent

Frequently agents of community development are themselves members of the privileged group. Often where development is contemplated on a large scale, as under UNESCO or American foreign aid programs, American or European agents do little work directly at the community level, but go to another country in order to train its nationals to be the actual agents of community development. Often, too, governments have their own development programs, with their own nationals as program administrators and agents.

Where an agent is a member of the privileged group, his natural tendency in dealing with underdeveloped and subordinate communities is to do so within the framework of established patterns of privilege. He is likely to be responded to, in turn, by members of the subordinate group according to their own stereotypes of the privileged group.[5] The result can be much like that described by Simmons for a health center in Chile.[6] The physicians in the center belonged to the privileged social class and the patients were members of the working class. The physicians dealt with their patients and were responded to by them in class terms, to the detriment of the health program. Similarly, investigation showed that a major reason for difficulties in the development of rural India could be explained as follows:

Most of the government representatives . . . have always assumed an authoritative, paternalistic attitude toward the villagers. As government employees they kept themselves aloof. The maintenance of a respectable distance from the ruled has frequently been considered by officialdom one of the important methods of perpetuating control over them. When the representatives of the nation-building departments (Education, Public Health, Agriculture) appeared on the scene, they followed in the footsteps of the police and the tax collector in their behavior and attitude toward the villagers.[7]

In the Chilean case just cited, the nurses at the health center had class backgrounds closer to those of patients and were able to communicate with them and gain their confidence to a far greater degree than were the physicians. Because they also understood what the physicians intended, they were indispensable as intermediaries, interpreting the physicians to the patients and the patients' needs and problems to the physicians. Because of the attitude of government officials toward villagers in India, and in order to minimize differences in social background, the planners of a project there

. . . decided to recruit as few government employees as possible. Therefore, the personnel of the project came to the job with none of the stereotypes about themselves and the villagers that are often present in the minds of government officers. Almost all the field workers were young graduates, fresh from schools and colleges. In making the selection much emphasis was laid on their aptitude for the job and their understanding of village life. Familiarity with the habits, attitudes, and thinking of the village people, which they had derived from their own rural background, was an important factor in their selection.[8]

Local Assistants

This points to one of the ways in which it is often possible for project administrators and outside agents of change to resolve the dilemma arising from their need to gain the cooperation of both a privileged, power-wielding group and the underdeveloped community. The agent may be able to train one or two persons from within the community as assistants, and they, in turn, can maintain many of the more intimate relations with the community's members without evoking comment from the privileged group. At the same time this frees the project administrator to make more concessions in his public conduct to the prejudices of the privileged class.

There are other advantages to such an arrangement. Problems of agent-community communication can be greatly diminished as his assistants interpret the community to the outside agent and also interpret him to the community. Nor is it without utility when members of the community identify the agent with prestige figures in their own larger social order. Analysis of the reasons that some people did and others did not adopt the practice of boiling drinking water in a Peruvian town, for example, showed that for at least one woman it was the endorsement of the visiting physician that finally led her to break with tradition and adopt the new practice. She accepted the arguments of the local health worker, a woman of her own social class with whom she was on good terms, but could not cite her as an authority in order to justify her adoption of the new practice to critical neighbors. The physician, however, was a proper authority whom she could cite with finality. It was the health worker who persuaded her of the value of boiling water and the physician who provided her the acceptable public authority for doing so.[9]

In this vein, a personal experience of the writer may be illuminating. When he first went abroad to make an anthropological study of a Pacific Island community, he was a student member of an expedition including several fellow students and led by a professor of maturer years. As leader of the expedition, the professor was accorded great respect and held in some awe by our employees and informants. They felt a bond with us students, however, who also were in the position of looking up to the professor. They were willing to confide to us many things that they would not mention in his presence. At the same time, because of his position as leader, he was taken more seriously by the community's leaders, and his opinions carried more weight. The writer, who had foolishly prided himself on the greater intimacy he enjoyed with informants on this occasion, found himself some years later leader of a similar expedition in another community. Now it was his students who enjoyed the confidences of informants, and it was he who was treated with the reserve appropriate to an important person. The point, of course, is that to the extent that a development agent enjoys prestige and is respected and looked up to by members of the community, he may be listened to more but will be told less. It is advisable that he have associated with him intimately persons with whom the community's members can feel more relaxed and in whom they will confide more readily.[10]

The use of members of the local community (or persons of similar social and cultural position and background) as agents of change is, of course, standard practice all over the world where missionaries, government officials, and economic adventurers are attempting to change local conditions to accord with their respective ends. Throughout New Guinea, for example, it is the native pastor-teacher and the native catechist who have the direct intimate contacts with villagers by which their conversion and, more importantly, the consequent changes in their way of life are very largely achieved. Similarly, the native policeman, not just the white official, is a major agent through whom uncontrolled villages are brought under government control. It is perhaps significant, moreover, that as of 1954 the two most successful spontaneous attempts at self-development by native communities in the New Guinea territory had been led by former native police sergeants, one with the government's blessing and help by Simogun in the Sepik River district and the other without that blessing by Paliau in the Admiralty Islands.

There are obvious problems that can arise from the use of local assistants as agents of a development program. Carefully selected and trained, however, they can be indispensable.[11] Through them the community can have a sense of fuller participation in the technical aspects of the program. Most important, however, is the fact that in situations where it is necessary to present different faces to different social groups in order to maintain their cooperation, a lone worker may be less effective than several persons who can front for each other according as their diverse social backgrounds equip them to deal with one or another group.

In selecting assistants whose backgrounds place them on an equal social footing with the community's members, certain principles may be applied:

1. If the community is divided into two prominent factions, the assistant should not be identified with either faction. If possible, two assistants, one representing each faction, should be selected. An assistant from another community of similar culture and social position may be advisable as one who is neutral in factional disputes.

2. An assistant should be of a social status that will allow for his ready acceptance by the majority of the community's members as someone with whom they can talk freely, as one of their own kind.

3. He should qualify in age and experience as someone whose views are to be taken seriously.

4. His personal background and needs should be such that he will not be inclined to use his participation in the program as a means of self-aggrandizement or a way of wresting from the community privileges that it would not accord him otherwise. Someone whose position within the community's social system is already relatively secure is preferable. If he already enjoys a position of leadership and influence within the community, so much the better.

THE VICOS EXPERIENCE

Reference has already been made to the deservedly famous Cornell University experiment in community development at Vicos, Peru. It provides a model of accomplishment in a situation presenting all of the problems we have been discussing in this chapter. Over a period of ten years the hopelessly impoverished Indian peons of a large, run-down hacienda have become economically productive, have learned to manage their own affairs with responsible local self-government, have created fine educational and public health facilities for themselves, and are exporting their new-found "know-how" to neighboring communities. We cannot review here the many facets of this remarkable undertaking.[12] But we should note the success of that project's leaders in promoting better relationships and mutual respect between Indians and *mestizos* in the area—a matter of vital importance to the project as a whole. Holmberg's account of this problem and the several approaches to it deserves quotation in full.*[13]

The barriers to communication between Indians and *mestizos* are a major factor isolating the Indian villages from the influences of the outside world. The dominant *mestizo* group, standing between the Indians and the nation, has served to block communication, not facilitate it. Even a partial lowering of this barrier would lead to an increased involvement and participation by the Indian communities in the national society. Furthermore, no effort to develop the wellbeing of the indigenous villages and to retain potential leaders within their *sierra* villages can work if by staying there they must also remain forever at the bottom of the social ladder.

One approach to improving intergroup relations stresses the need for changing the behavior of the minority or depressed group, with the expectation that this will gradually modify the attitudes of the majority or dominant group. The assumption made is that present attitudes stem from the behavior of the minority and that altering this behavior will result in removing the prejudices of the majority group. It can, however, be argued on strong grounds that the unfavorable attitudes of the dominant group are often transmitted from one generation to the next without reference to the actual situation and that the "improvement" of the minority group will not necessarily create a more favorable attitude toward it. Indeed, the emphasis placed upon improving the status of the minority may actually cause the dominant group to feel that its superior position is being threatened and it may react even more negatively to evidences of that improvement.

An alternative approach is to tackle the problem of changing the attitudes of the majority group. The variety of techniques which have been studied range from formal programs of education to the creation of situations in which contact takes place between members of the two groups either voluntarily or under some degree of compulsion. Many of these methods have created more favorable attitudes toward the minority group. In such an approach, however, too little attention is paid to effecting changes within the minority. In the *sierra* of Peru, for example, it will be necessary to bring about changes in the behavior of both *mestizos* and Indians.

Still a third approach is to create new situations for which there is no set pattern of behavior, and in which each person must decide for

* Reprinted with permission from *Social Change in Latin America Today:* Its Implications for United States Policy by Richard N. Adams and others. Harper and Row, Publishers, Incorporated, 1960, © Council on Foreign Affairs, New York, pp. 102–104.

himself how to act. In making his decision, the individual takes into account a number of new factors present, apart from his general attitude toward the minority group. These new factors may include the appropriateness or inappropriateness of discrimination as applied in other situations, the need for securing the cooperation of the other person, the relevance of laws or strongly held values forbidding discriminatory behavior, or the presence of other people who would disapprove of such conduct.

Whatever approach is stressed, it is clear that, as the process of modernization gets under way, a great improvement can be brought about in relations between *mestizos* and Indians in the *sierra*. This can be hastened, however, if new situations are arranged so as to bring members of both groups together in a way that will minimize discriminatory behavior. This is possible in schools, in developmental projects, in recreational events, and so forth, provided they are based on real needs of both Indians and *mestizos* and therefore elicit the cooperation of both groups in order to achieve shared ends.

Holmberg has indicated[14] that this last approach was the one actively pursued at Vicos. Projects of genuine interest to *mestizos* and Indians alike, such as improved education, establishment of a medical clinic, a motion picture theater, provided the occasions for bringing *mestizos* and Indians together under conditions of mutual need and hence of equality. A planning committee of Indians and *mestizos* would eat together—something members of the two groups would not otherwise do. *Mestizos* and Indians would sit beside each other in the unsegregated theater, because their desire to see movies outweighed their commitment to maintaining traditional barriers. The gradual multiplication of new contexts for *mestizo*-Indian interaction beyond traditional contexts is having a noticeable effect on the attitudes and stereotypes of both groups. Early in this book we indicated that the basis for cooperation between an agent and his clients lay in their having felt needs which made their cooperation a value to both. The same holds for the problem of promoting cooperation and respect in the relations between any two social groups.

Also important in the Vicos project was the active participation in it by Peruvian nationals of professional background. Schoolteachers, health workers, and others, as they became involved in the growth and development of Vicos, were drawn into the newly emerging pattern of community organization as the project had fostered it. As they made the necessary adjustments to the new social realities, they experienced the peasants in new ways with important effects on their attitudes toward them. Through the project, Pèru is acquiring nationals with new understanding of the Indians and with experience in the human aspects of development work that eventually may make a real difference in the social progress of the nation. To be sure, the Vicos project is but one community experiment in a vast ocean of increasingly impatient need. It shows, nonetheless, what can be done when sophisticated attention is given to the things we have been discussing in this book.

SUGGESTED READING

Adams, Richard N., and others, *Social Change in Latin America Today:* Its Implications for United States Policy. Harper and Row, Publishers, Incorporated, New York, 1960. (Also available in paperback as a Vintage Book, Random House, New York, 1961.)

Berreman, Gerald D., *Behind Many Masks:* Ethnography and Impression Management in a Himalayan Village. Monograph no. 4, Society for Applied Anthropology, Ithaca, N. Y., 1962.

NOTES TO CHAPTER 15

1. Cleveland, Harlan, Gerard J. Mangone, and John Clarke Adams, *The Overseas Americans.* McGraw-Hill Book Co., New York, 1960, p. 155.

2. Adams, Richard N., and others, *Social Change in Latin America Today:* Its Implications for United States Policy. Harper and Row, Publishers, Incorporated, © Council on Foreign Affairs, New York, 1960.

3. Holmberg, Allan R., "Changing Community Attitudes and Values in Peru: A Case Study in Guided Change" in Adams, Richard N., and others, *op. cit.*, pp. 63–107.

4. *Ibid.*

5. See the comments in this vein by I. T. Sanders, "The Folk Approach in Extension Work," *Applied Anthropology,* vol. 2, no. 4, 1943, pp. 1–4.

6. Simmons, Ozzie G., "The Clinical Team in a Chilean Health Center" in Paul, Benjamin D., editor, *Health, Culture, and Community.* Russell Sage Foundation, New York, 1955, pp. 325–348.

7. Singh, Rudra Datt, "The Village Level: An Introduction of Green Manuring in Rural India" in Spicer, Edward H., editor, *Human Problems in Technological Change.* Russell Sage Foundation, New York, 1952, p. 61.

8. *Ibid.*, p. 62.

9. Wellin, Edward, "Water Boiling in a Peruvian Town" in Paul, Benjamin D., editor, *op. cit.*, pp. 84–86.

10. See the revealing experiences in this regard reported by Gerald D. Berreman, *Behind Many Masks:* Ethnography and Impression Management in a Himalayan Village, Monograph no. 4, Society for Applied Anthropology, Ithaca, N. Y., 1962.

11. See, for example, the conditions in which American Indians have been successfully used as health workers, as reported by John Adair, "The Indian Health Worker in the Cornell-Navaho Project," *Human Organization*, vol. 19, no. 2, 1960, pp. 59–67.

12. In addition to the already cited essay by Allan R. Holmberg, *op. cit.*, the interested reader should consult his paper "The Research-and-Development Approach to Change: Participant Intervention in the Field" in Adams, Richard N., editor, *Human Organization Research:* Field Relations and Techniques, The Dorsey Press, Homewood, Ill., 1960, pp. 76–89. See also the symposium "Community and Regional Development: The Joint Cornell-Peru Experiment," *Human Organization*, vol. 21, no. 2, 1962, pp. 107–124.

13. Adams, Richard N., and others, *op. cit.*, pp. 102–104.

14. Personal communication.

Chapter 16

THE PROBLEM OF
ADMINISTRATIVE RELATIONS[1]

COMMONLY A FIELD AGENT working directly with an under-developed community is at the end of an administrative chain or hierarchy. He is employed by an agency and is charged with accomplishing the agency's objectives in the operational arena. His relations to others in the agency's administrative hierarchy obviously have direct bearing on the ease with which he can perform the role that the realities of the field situation require of him. In view of his need for flexibility of operation, the kinds of commitments he is likely to have to make in order to obtain cooperation, and the knowledge he must have at his disposal, we may properly ask to what extent our customary patterns of administering may be realistically applied to community development and to what extent they may be a source of difficulty themselves.

Administrators and students of administrative processes are familiar with the analyses of Barnard and Simon.[2] We shall not attempt to review systematically their important contributions to the development of a science of administration. Here we shall confine ourselves to aspects of administration for which community development raises special problems.

TWO VIEWS OF THE ADMINISTRATIVE PROCESS

The administrative process has been characterized as "a cycle which includes the following special activities: A. Decision-making, B. Programming, C. Communicating, D. Controlling, E. Reappraising."[3] It is seen in theory and structured in practice as one in which responsibility for these activities is primarily at the top of the administrative hierarchy. That is, the top administrator makes the ultimate decisions, and decisions are made by those below only as he delegates authority downward. If his decisions are to be properly executed, he must translate them into a program of action, and he must communicate this program downward to those who will actually do the work. Since a top administrator is responsible for the accomplishments of his organization, controlling the behavior of subordinates who carry out the program is necessarily one of his major concerns. It is no accident that "the concept of authority has been analyzed at length by students of administration."[4] Reappraising, again, is a task of the top administrator. While it depends on communication upward from below, either step by step by way of the administrative chain or more directly by way of studies or inspections that bypass it, reappraising remains the top administrator's responsibility. Certainly, in the view of administrators and students of administration, the locus of responsibility in an enterprise is seen to be at the top of the administrative hierarchy.[5]

From another point of view, the administrative process has to do with facilitating the accomplishment of some kind of objective in which the activity of a number of persons must be coordinated by someone in a position to observe the total situation. The administrator as coordinator may be seen as a clearinghouse of information from one worker to another to enable each to adjust his actions to the actions of the other. As facilitator, it is the administrator's duty to supply the workers with the necessary services that they cannot supply for themselves. By this view the administrator coordinates, channels information, directs traffic, and services operations, and the locus of ultimate responsibility is with the worker, the operator, who must actually get the job done.

If the first picture of administration represents the administrator's view, the second represents the operator's. The two "theories" of administration follow from the respective responsibilities and concerns of administrators and operators. To the extent that a person is charged with responsibility for operations that he cannot perform by himself and whose performance he must therefore delegate to others, he is concerned with controlling their behavior, retaining authority over them, and reserving to himself the power to make decisions and map strategy. To the extent that a person is charged with the responsibility for accomplishing an objective through the direct application of his own knowledge and skills, he is concerned with preventing restrictions on the free exercise of his skill, with maintaining maximum freedom to adjust his tactics to the realities of the immediate situation, with being able to veto strategies that call for unrealistic applications of skill, and with being able to demand such services as are necessary to implement accomplishing his operational objectives.

The administrator's view of his responsibilities reflects their essentially social and lay character, the fact that he must answer to some nonprofessional individual or group of individuals for organizing the efforts of others to accomplish a desired objective. He looks to the stockholders, the electorate, the chief of state, or persons higher in an administrative hierarchy as the critical judges of what is accomplished, critical because in our social system they have the power to reward or punish him. The operator's view of his responsibilities is essentially technical and professional. He is identified with a craft or profession which has standards of its own. His self-respect and future economic security depend as much, if not more, on his standing among his fellow craftsmen as on sanctions to which his administrative employers are usually able to subject him.

The greater the amount of knowledge and the greater the degree of skill that the operator commands, the freer he can be of administrative controls and the closer he comes, in administrative eyes, to being a "prima donna." For the operator whose skills permit him to achieve such a degree of autonomy, an administrative organization functions essentially in a supporting and servicing role. Hospitals present an outstanding example of organizations where those engaged in operations largely command the administrative structure rather than being commanded by it. The relation of staff physicians to hospital administrators comes very close to realizing in practice the operator's or worker's theory of administrative organization. The physicians command the services of the hospital, not the reverse (except in the case of interns and resident physicians, who are still in training, and who significantly are usually young physicians as yet without much standing in their profession). This is a situation that administrators tend to find distasteful. They like to think of operational personnel as their instruments, not as their masters.

The conflict of interests between administrators and operators in our larger enterprises, whether private or public, has been resolved largely in the administrator's favor. We are not concerned here with the reasons this should be so. Suffice it to say that in most enterprises it is the administrator who is held generally responsible for their outcome by some kind of public, while the operator is held responsible only for the proper application of his skill to the specific task assigned. In order to eliminate the possibility for skilled operators to be free of administrative authority and controls, administrators have sought to break operations down and reorganize them in such a way as to eliminate the need for skilled operators as much as possible. By emphasizing programming and other procedural controls, administrators have sought to mold operations to be as much an instrument of their will as the nature of the operations would permit.[6] To this end, administrators tend to feel they must enjoy unquestioned authority and have power to invoke strong sanctions. This has been the case especially where those engaged in operations do not have people as the object to which they apply their skills, as in industry and, except in shooting wars, the army. Automation now brings the administrator's ideal one step closer to fruition by presumably eliminating operators entirely, leaving no one but the maintenance man between the administrative programmer and the machine. The push-button world may not inappropriately be labeled the administrator's Utopia.

The operator's theory of administration tends to apply more in those enterprises where a high degree of professional skill is required of the workers; where the workers operate directly on people, to whom both they and the administrators are responsible, as in hospitals, schools, and public entertainment; or where those engaged in operations have to cope with conditions that they cannot control technically, to which they must constantly adjust tactics, and in which success or failure is governed as much by factors beyond their control as by their own technical qualifications. Military operations in time of war are perhaps the classic example for the last type of situation. Despite the authoritative atmosphere in which army rules and regulations are administered in peacetime, in war field personnel are necessarily accorded great freedom to ignore them in order to deal as effectively as possible with the exigencies of combat. Anyone who has experienced the United States Army in both war and peace knows the difference in practice between an administrator's and an operator's theory of administration.

THE CONFLICT OF VIEWS IN DEVELOPMENT PROGRAMS

Community development is an enterprise that offers all three major conditions in which the operator's view of administration tends to assert itself in practice. The field agent must have a high degree of skill and knowledge. We have been at pains in this book to show that his work requires a professional level of knowledge and skill. Secondly, a field agent operates directly on people, to whom he owes responsibilities similar in some respects to those that a physician owes his client and in other respects to those that a politician owes his followers. Finally, he has to cope with conditions over which he has limited social and technical control and that call for great flexibility of tactics.

Ideally, then, we should expect community development operations to have some of the character, in slower motion, of military operations in war. We should expect to find those in the field largely commanding the resources of the larger organization. We should look for emphasis on getting professionally competent men of good judgment into field operations, where they must have great freedom to make their own tactical decisions, and corresponding de-emphasis on administrative channels and procedural controls. Once the planning stages are over and operations have commenced, we should expect administrators to be concerned primarily with providing the kind of support that field personnel find they need and with keeping information and supplies flowing freely. Just as physicians and university professors are deemed the proper judges of what they need in order to do their jobs, administration having the job of supplying these needs, so we would expect experienced field agents to be able to make the best assessment of their needs and agency administrators to regard it as their duty to do what they can to take care of them.[7]

While we often find operations conforming in part, at least, to these expectations, often, too, we do not. What we frequently find instead is a situation in which administrators regard their field personnel as professionally less competent than themselves to judge the tactical requirements of the field situation and look upon them as disorderly, wasteful, sloppy in their bookkeeping, and constantly disturbing administrative routines by their sudden shifts in tactics. We find them insisting on strict accountings for everything, imposing unrealistic procedural controls, and possessing and wielding authority over operational personnel of a sort appropriate to the view that operators are properly only instruments of the administrator's will. We find, in short, that in spite of the fact that community development presents the conditions appropriate for practicing the operator's theory of administration, the administrator's theory is frequently the one in effect.

One reason for this, of course, is that field operations in many aspects of community development have not yet been professionalized, especially where human relations are concerned. Field personnel may well have no more understanding than administrators have of the human side of their work and what it involves; and where they do, they cannot invoke a degree in applied social science or an established reputation within a professional group of fellow clinicians in community development. Although an even chance for success in their work requires a professional level of knowledge and skill in human relations as well as in technical matters, this fact has not yet become generally recognized. But even in those agencies where it is recognized, there is another factor working in favor of what we have called the administrator's type of organization.

We noted earlier that the administrator's theory of administration tends to prevail in practice when the administrator and not the operator is held directly responsible by the organization's public for the outcome of operations. In industry, for example, it is managers and not workers who are held responsible by the stockholders for an enterprise's earnings and by the general public for the quality of its products. In medicine, on the other hand, it is the surgeon who is directly responsible to the public for the success of his operation, not the hospital's board of managers. The administrator, we have seen, is responsible to the operator when the operator is directly responsible to the public, while the operator is responsible to the administrator when the administrator is directly responsible to the public.

In the case of community development, where the developing agency is not itself a part of the community being developed, there are at least two publics instead of one. The administrator is primarily responsible to one, the public supplying the money and technical resources for the development program; and the field agent is primarily responsible to the other, the underdeveloped community. Because the administrator, removed from the actual scene of operations, has to answer to the public supplying the money and technical resources, he is under pressure to judge operations from the point of view of that public. Similarly, the field agent, having daily to answer to the community's members, tends to take the community's point of view. Thus conflicts of viewpoint and interest between those establishing and supporting a development program and those who are its intended beneficiaries find expression in the relations between administrator and field agent, each seeking to persuade the other of both the rightness and practical necessity of his position.

In this conflict of interest between administrator and operator, the administrator tends to hold the trump cards, as long as operators remain nonprofessional and are not conscious of being occupationally different from administrators. This is especially the case where field operators are organizationally classed as junior administrators under the direct authority of administrative seniors and are completely dependent on senior administrators for promotions, pay increases, and efficiency ratings, with their performance as field men judged by persons who are not field men. What happens where administrators have this kind of advantage is that in the conflicts of view between them and the field men, the field men lose. An administrator can simply order otherwise, withhold the necessary support, or transfer a field man to another job. Insofar as their disagreement arises from a conflict of interest between the two publics of a development program, it is the public comprising the underdeveloped community that inevitably loses.

The situation is analogous to one that would obtain if psychiatrists in the United States were members of an organization established and maintained by funds appropriated annually by, say, the Japanese government or made available through subscription by the Japanese public. The administrators of this fund being answerable to the Japanese public or government would be in a position, as the administrative superiors of the psychiatrists they employed, to dictate the kind and extent of psychiatric treatment any patient would receive. This dictation would be not from the standpoint of the patient's needs as understood by the psychiatrist but from the standpoint of the Japanese public's needs. The point is not that the Japanese public should have its needs frustrated, but that for the patient's needs to be frustrated in every instance where they failed to fit in with the Japanese public's interests of the moment would be to negate the purpose for which the latter ostensibly established the psychiatric program in the first place. The situation is not different if we substitute our own national and state legislatures for the Japanese government in our hypothetical example.

In administering development programs we tend in practice to create an organizational structure that produces this kind of result—inevitably so when those responsible for setting up the organization do not go out of their way to guarantee that its operating personnel enjoy sufficient status and autonomy within the organization to make it impossible for administrators to dictate to them the resolutions of the conflicts of interest between their respective publics. Ideally, we hasten to add, field personnel should not be in a position to dictate such resolutions to administrators either. Rather, it is preferable that administrators and field men both have sufficient autonomy so that such conflicts can be resolved only by both sitting down and together working out the best possible solutions. This is what administrators and field personnel are supposed to do in theory in any organization, but they rarely do so in practice, except where there is a clear-cut and fairly equal division of power and authority between them.

We encountered a situation where just such a division of power and authority was functioning effectively in a development project in the Gilbert Islands. The purpose of the project was to register property, codify native property law, adjudicate all existing property disputes, and establish workable lands courts run by native personnel. Government affairs in the Gilbert Islands were handled by a line organization consisting of junior administrative officers, district officers, and a Resident Commissioner, who was chief administrative officer of the Gilbert and Ellice Island Colony. He was, in turn, responsible for all governmental operations within the colony to the High Commissioner for the Western Pacific. When the "lands" program was established, responsibility for its conduct was made independent of the administrative authority of the Resident Commissioner. The lands commissioners, as the program's three field personnel were called, were responsible to the Resident Commissioner for their personal conduct and for other matters having nothing directly to do with the lands program, but they were authorized to organize and conduct the program without interference, and the Resident Commissioner was required to provide the necessary facilities.

To ensure this, the senior lands commissioner was brought in from outside the colony with a civil service rank *equal* to that of the Resident Commissioner, a fact of great administrative significance for rank-conscious British public servants.[8] He was given complete authority to organize and conduct the program for as long as needed to bring it to completion. After conducting a pilot project on one atoll, the lands commissioner received and trained two additional field men, who were responsible directly to him, each of them subsequently carrying out similar projects on their own on other atolls in the colony.

Each resided on the atoll in which he worked for the duration of his project (from eight months to a year and a half). The lands program was his sole responsibility throughout. While he might perform other governmental functions, he was expected not to do so when their performance might in any way jeopardize the lands project.

From what we observed of the program, it was accomplishing its objective to an extraordinary degree. The three field men doing the job were able to give it their full attention, knew they were not going to be moved out to do something else in the middle of the project, and were not forced by a tight administrative schedule to get everything done within a set time. While the time needed for each atoll was estimated and tentative deadlines were set as working goals, they were flexible at the discretion of the man doing the job. Although there were certain overall procedures that had been worked out in the pilot project, they were open to revision as needed to adapt to local conditions. In keeping with this approach, a uniform code for all atolls was not insisted upon, however desirable such uniformity might have been from an administrative point of view. Each atoll was free to have its own code in keeping with local custom, and properly so, for if the Gilbertese were to be responsible for their own legal affairs, they could be expected to be more successful if operating within the framework of their own traditional law.

In this example, the autonomy of the lands commissioners resulted from recognition of the need to keep development operations independent of the more usual governmental operations, which are often more coercive and authoritarian in nature. The result was that the lands commissioners were free to take a *professional* view of their job and to deal with it in terms of its own requirements. They could do this because no elaborate agency was set up to deal with land matters. Such services as the lands commissioners required were furnished by existing governmental organizations. But obviously, independence from governmental operations is not in itself enough when development becomes the domain of a vast administrative structure of its own. For then the professionals on the line need to be free to negotiate effectively with their own administrators.

We should not close this discussion without reference to the conflict between what Simon has called social and organizational values and to the implications of this conflict for what are administratively "correct" decisions.[9] His concern was that decisions that were good for the organization or for its immediate objectives might not be in keeping with the general social purposes for which the organization was created by its supporting public. Our point here has been that agencies concerned with community development may be faced with a further conflict between two different sets of social values. These conflicting organizational and social values are expressed in the interests of the agency itself as an organization to be maintained, in the interests of its supporting public, and the interests of the underdeveloped community.

While conflicts that arise between an organization and its supporting public are usually negotiated by representatives of the organization and the public, conflicts between the interests of the two publics which development agencies serve have in practice been negotiated within the agency itself. We do not find representatives of the two publics negotiating solutions to their differences and presenting the agency with an agreed-upon set of social values. Instead, the two publics are represented, one by the agency's administrators and the other by its operatives. As long as this continues to be the practice, agencies are faced with an organizational problem of how to structure the lines of authority and responsibility within them so that these negotiations can be conducted on equal terms.

The conflict between the two publics to which such agencies are responsible has, furthermore, an obvious bearing on administrative attitudes toward organizational loyalty. Both administrative and operative personnel may be loyal to their organization and to its avowed purposes and yet in their roles as representatives of conflicting publics each may feel the other to be disloyal, with the operator regarding the administrator as disloyal to the ultimate purpose of the organization, and the administrator seeing the operator as disloyal to him personally, to the agency of which he is administrative head, and even to the public by whose will the agency was created. To perceive legitimate conflicts of interest and social value in terms of loyalty and disloyalty is to becloud the real issues with *ad hominem* irrelevancies.[10]

While it remains for students of administration to find satisfactory ways of restructuring organizational relationships between administrators and field personnel, we can suggest that a more equal division of responsibility and authority between them may prove helpful.

FIELD AGENTS AND THE SYSTEM OF REWARDS

The "lands" program in the Gilbert Islands illustrates another matter in addition to the importance of autonomy for field personnel. There was no fixed civil service rank for the lands commissioners below that of the highest administrative officer in the colony. They were there to do a job and stay with it until it had been completed. In the course of the years in which they were engaged in it, their civil service standing was open to advancement without their having to be shifted to a new post with each advancement. This seemed to be true in the case of the junior lands commissioners, at least. These men could be rewarded by promotion for doing a good job and go on performing the same job. This in effect accorded their work a professional status, with rewards for professional competence and in recognition of previous service, independent of position in an administrative hierarchy.

By contrast, in many organizations engaged in community development, especially governmental organizations, field personnel are rewarded according to administrative rather than professional standards. Post A calls for a technician in grade 1 and post B calls for one in grade 2. If the man at post A has done a good job and accumulated enough seniority for promotion, he cannot be promoted to grade 2 and left at post A to carry on with the work he has handled so well. He must be transferred to post B because that is a grade 2 post (a bigger post in number of operations and *administrative* importance). Here his experience at post A will not help him; he must become familiar with a new situation and a new set of problems. His successor at post A must learn what he has already learned and repeat the same mistakes. In order to get recognition for himself, moreover, he is under pressure to undo what his predecessor has done, seek to improve it in some way, or drop it entirely in favor of developing something else; that is, he is under pressure to give the operations at post A the stamp of his own personality, make them his own accomplishment. This system of having promotion require transfer to a new assignment before completion of the first one has led one observer of agricultural development in the tropics to comment:

> The ingredient that seems lacking is the constancy of leadership and inspiration. No revolutionary system of farming can be evolved, let alone proved and preached, in one or two tours of duty; nor can the inspiration of one man be transferred to another merely by an order of promotion. The great need today is for any agricultural officer who shows originality and inspiration in developing a system of mixed tropical farming to be kept at his station and given every promotion there on the spot in order to work out his system to its logical end.[11]

What is here said in relation to agricultural technicians is equally applicable to community development workers generally. A system that rewards skilled clinicians by removing them from the clinic into ever higher administrative positions or transferring them from one clinic to another before they can accomplish anything of value in any one is wasteful indeed. The scale of promotions and monetary rewards for agents of community development should be independent of the posts to which they are assigned or the degree of their administrative responsibility. In a well-run university a professor does not have to become an administrator in order to get a promotion in rank or an increase in salary. He need only demonstrate his competence as a teacher and scholar. After twenty years he may still be teaching the same subjects to the same number of students and yet have moved steadily from an instructorship to an endowed professorship with comparable increases in salary.

It is our conviction that a similar type of arrangement in organizations concerned with community development would have many desirable features. In addition to the advantage already suggested, it would help greatly to professionalize community development as an applied or clinical science in human relations, for it would allow those engaged in it to make a career of it. Otherwise, they will continue to see their work primarily as a stepping stone to a career in public administration or as an opportunity for young scientists and technicians to pick up a year or two of field experience before retiring permanently to the library or laboratory. The disadvantages of the latter situation are obvious. There is an added difficulty to the former. Where field work in community development is viewed as the first step in an essentially administrative career, the field worker is perforce concerned that he be recognized mainly for his administrative rather than his professional skills. He is tempted, therefore, to build up his work in terms of administrative responsibilities, to try to expand operations for the purpose of acquiring assistants, and otherwise to engage in the game of empire building. He is going to orient his work essentially toward the end of pleasing his administrative superiors at the expense, if necessary, of getting a workmanlike job done. A student of the British civil service, for example, has noted that,

> The service is so graded and its salary scales so adjusted that failure to cross a particular promotion bridge at more or less the expected time may well represent a serious set-back, not only financially, but socially and personally; and the fact that, as we have seen, many of the opportunities for promotion that are available to the average civil servant come by way of internal selection means that his conduct and the quality of his work are frequently conditioned by the need to convince his superiors that he is well fitted for promotion from his existing grade.[12]

He adds in this connection, "Like generally prefers like, and it is naturally enough an excellent qualification for promotion to resemble, or at least to appear to resemble, one's supervisors in make-up, approach to the work and general outlook."[13]

We conclude, then, that an administrative system that treats agents of community development as junior administrative officers, whose careers depend on their being promoted to essentially administrative rather than operational assignments, is bound to impose upon community development in practice the orientations, attitudes, and values of administrators and the public to which they are responsible and to ignore the realities of the community's circumstances and its interests as a second public whose channel of communication with the agency is through its field personnel.

Standards of Personal Success

There tends also to be a difference between professional and administrative values in connection with rewards and ideas as to what constitute the marks of a successful career.

In administrative eyes the measure of success is the degree to which one has managed to ascend the administrative ladder toward the top post of an organization. Of equal importance is the size of the organization to which one belongs; it is a mark of distinction to move from a post in a small organization to an equivalent post in a large one. Thus, in an autobiographical sketch, Benjamin Fairless says of his decision to leave the Republic Steel Corporation for the United States Steel Corporation:

> At this point I had to make the hardest decision of my life. . . . Should I stay on in the top job at a smaller corporation but one which I knew thoroughly, or should I gamble on a lesser job in a bigger corporation of which I knew nothing? . . . I was faced with a perplexing decision: whether to keep the bird in the hand or go after more birds. I am happy to see, with the benefit of today's hindsight, that I made the right choice.*[14]

As Fairless clearly expresses it, the administrator sees his career in terms of movement up an established hierarchy. The new worlds to conquer consist of opportunities to assume more responsible administrative positions within an organization, to assume positions of wider scope in larger organizations, or to expand the scope of one's own organization. The administrative system of rewards is structured accordingly, consisting of an ever more limited number of prizes for which there is competition at all levels.

This means that for the administrator the only form of recognition that really counts is recognition from above and the only sanctions that can seriously injure him are those imposed

* *Life*, October 15, 1956. Copyright, 1956, Time Inc.

by his superiors. Of the variety of ways in which recognition from above may be expressed, none is sweeter to an administrator than to have his recommendations accepted as policy. This is, of course, important to him as an earnest of further tangible rewards, but more than that it is a public demonstration of his influence within the organization and an affirmative expression of confidence in his ability. It is small wonder that administrators tend to become personally identified with their own proposals and attach strong emotions to them.

Leighton has called attention to the intense rivalry that exists where alternative proposals are presented by middle-position executives who are competing for recognition.[15] He rightly emphasizes that such rivalries for recognition create a poor atmosphere for objectively weighing the merits of alternative proposals. A middle-rank administrator is likely to be less concerned with getting what is objectively the best proposal than with getting his own proposal adopted. Not infrequently, too, this atmosphere of jealous partisanship interferes with the transmission of proposals up the administrative line, as when a subordinate transmits a proposal to his immediate superior that is better than one the superior has already formulated and sent on to higher administrators for consideration.

Thus the system of rewards and punishments, the kinds of liability to which administrators are subject, while motivating them individually to high standards of personal performance, serve at the same time to block communication between the lower and upper ends of the hierarchy and to put considerations of personal recognition ahead of loyalty to the objectives of the organization as such. This accounts for the interests that top executives have in finding "good organization men" to fill administrative positions of middle rank.

There is, of course, another reason why top administrators like "good organization men," and why junior administrators, however competitive they may be for recognition and advancement, also tend to exhibit great loyalty to the organization employing them. Organization is their business in life, not operations. What an organization does and how well it does it is less important than that it continue to prosper as an organization. The organization is like a host from which the administrator parasitically draws his own sustenance, spiritual as well as material. As the organization prospers, so does the administrator; and as the administrator can find ways of improving on its organizational structure, he proves his importance and satisfies his creative urges. When the organization's continued existence is threatened, he seeks to preserve it by whatever means appear prudent. This means, among other things, that he will sacrifice operations. Few administrators, for example, will liquidate their organization when given insufficient funds to accomplish its operational objectives adequately. Doing it right or not at all, while a value, is not one to compete with the value of saving the organization. While it may be that an inadequate postal or transportation system is preferable to none, it is seriously to be questioned whether an inadequate development program is better than none. An inadequate dose of penicillin may be worse than no dose at all.

For a professional person, by contrast, success depends in part on recognition from fellow professionals for the competence with which he meets professional standards of performance. In part also it depends on the extent of lay recognition and consequent demand for his services. There is little emphasis here on organizational loyalty and more on professional integrity. The professional tends to feel uncomfortable when placed in an administrative hierarchy in which the welfare of the organization as such comes ahead of craftsmanlike performance, where he is constantly called upon to violate his professional standards to meet budgetary or other administrative requirements. Professional men are used to concentrating on the cultivation of their own knowledge and skills as the surest way to personal recognition and financial reward. Concern with winning recognition from above or with being "good boys" as defined by an immediate organizational superior tends to be secondary.

This means that for professionally minded persons, the best jobs are not necessarily those with the highest administrative rank or those that command the best salaries, albeit they have allure, but those that allow the greatest scope for practicing their professions.

In an organization where professionally trained persons are needed to carry out its operations, or some important part of them, serious problems can arise if they are subject solely to an administrative system of rewards. What may happen can be illustrated in connection with the use of anthropologists in the Trust Territory of the Pacific. Barnett describes its administrative organization as follows:

> The United States Trust Territory is administered through its principal executive officer, the High Commissioner. He is advised and assisted by a deputy and a staff of departmental officers who are charged with the supervision of certain activities and the implementation of policy respecting them. Those departments most directly concerned with the Micronesians are Education, Public Health, Economics, and Political Affairs. The senior anthropologist for the Territory, whose title is Staff Anthropologist, is for administrative purposes assigned to the Political Affairs Department, a division whose functions are much more diverse than its name implies.
>
> In general, and to the extent that it is appropriate, the organizational scheme at headquarters is duplicated in the administrative subdivisions of the Territory. Each group of islands constituting a subdivision is the responsibility of a District Administrator. He is assisted by heads of departments like those at headquarters and by special project managers. The counterpart of the Staff Anthropologist at this level is the District Anthropologist. There are five of them, one for each of the districts of Palau, Yap, Truk, Ponape, and the Marshall Islands. *[16]

In accordance with usual administrative procedure, the position of Staff Anthropologist has a considerably higher rating than does the position of District Anthropologist. The District Anthropologist conducts studies of Micronesian communities within his district and is charged with obtaining as intimate a knowledge of the local language, customs, sentiments, and conditions as he can, so that he can advise his District Administrator and district departmental heads in connection with the various development programs for which they are responsible. At the district level, the anthropologist is employed in a more

* Reprinted with permission from *Anthropology in Administration* by H. G. Barnett, Harper and Row, Publishers, Incorporated, New York, 1956, p. 86.

fully professional capacity to do those things for which his professional training best fits him. His usefulness, moreover, depends on his staying in his district for considerably longer than one two-year tour of duty. Within so short a time, he is only beginning to acquire the kind of intimate knowledge of his district that can make him truly effective. The Staff Anthropologist is located in the Territorial Office in Guam (now in Saipan). His only personal contact with the Micronesians about whom he is supposed to advise the High Commissioner and territorial department heads is the little he can acquire on quick tours of the districts. He is dependent on reports coming in from the District Anthropologists, whose work he supervises from the purely professional standpoint. While he coordinates and advises on the research of others, he does little research himself. His location and duties prevent it.

Anthropology is a profession in which the opportunity to engage in field research is highly valued. Recognition professionally depends almost exclusively on the quality of one's researches. A job that provides opportunities for research into other people's customs is valued, while one that does not provide such an opportunity is valued less. Thus the administratively less desirable post of District Anthropologist is professionally more desirable. There has been little difficulty in filling it with capable young anthropologists eager for a chance to engage in field research. By contrast, it is with considerable difficulty that the Territory has been able to prevail upon more mature anthropologists to take the administratively higher position of Staff Anthropologist. While several District Anthropologists have been willing to stay on for a second two year tour of duty, only one Staff Anthropologist has been willing to remain for a second appointment. Those who have consented to take the position have done so largely out of a sense of duty and with the express understanding that it was on a temporary basis only while on leave from their university posts. Yet the pay is considerably better than that received by some persons who refused the staff position.

It should be noted, moreover, that the several District Anthropologists are relatively young men. Already several of them have left the Trust Territory to pursue their professional careers in museums and universities where advancement in pay and status is open within the profession itself. They have looked upon their service in the Trust Territory as a good opportunity to get professionally useful experience, but they have not been able to think in terms of a professional anthropological career within the Territorial Service. The reason for this is simple; the post of District Anthropologist is fixed at a given civil service rating in the Territorial table of organization. To advance in the service, the anthropologist must be promoted out of anthropology into administrative positions in which he ceases to pursue a professional career, at least as an anthropologist. Already several District Anthropologists have made this shift into administration. The result is that District Anthropologists will normally be relatively young men, among whom the more gifted will, after a tour or two of duty, leave the service for professionally greener pastures or accept promotion into administrative posts at the very time when they have accumulated enough experience to make their future service as anthropologists of far greater value than before. An opportunity for professional advancement and promotion within the position of District Anthropologist would help the territory develop a professionally outstanding staff of anthropologists with enough job continuity to ensure the specialized knowledge of their districts without which their general professional training is largely useless.[17]

What we have had to say about Trust Territory anthropologists should be applicable to the problem of developing competent staffs of field agents of community development. They, too, can be of maximum service only after they have invested enough time in a given locality to learn its specific ways and problems, its language and customs. Whatever their professional background in human relations generally, it cannot be of service in the vacuum created by ignorance of the local scene. To promote men out of the field, to provide them no inducements to stay in the field, or to downgrade them in relation to administrators is to deny an organization the services of professionally mature field personnel.

WHO SHOULD MAKE POLICY?

It is sometimes asserted by social scientists and laymen alike that social scientists should administer programs where human relations enter critically into operations. Anthropologists, for example, should administer the Trust Territory of the Pacific, hold the major policy and decision-making positions. Often enough, professional men working in advisory positions in administrative organizations have come to feel that only if they themselves assume administratively responsible positions will decisions in keeping with operational as distinct from administrative objectives be properly made. While there are times when this works out as anticipated, more often this is not the case. If a professional turns administrator he must in truth turn administrator and look upon his work with at least one administrative eye. He has to enjoy administration for its own sake. Otherwise he will be a misplaced operator, impatient and unhappy in what he is called upon to do, emotionally unable to make the compromises and arbitrary decisions that successful administration often demands. As administrator he will have to concern himself with the organization as such as well as with implementing its operational goals.[18]

The fact is that in practice neither the operator's nor the administrator's point of view can entirely dominate the scene. In industry if either the production or accounting departments entirely dominate an enterprise difficulties are likely to arise. The successful enterprise strikes a balance between them. Usually the best administrators are persons who have had experience in the work of more than one department and who can, therefore, establish policy and make decisions with an eye to their consequences for the organization as a whole. They are, furthermore, men who respect what their technical advisers have to tell them. Although ultimate decisions may properly belong to the top administrator of an undertaking, if he makes those decisions in disregard of what is fiscally, mechanically, or psychologically practical, even though he may be making a smart choice politically, at least for the moment, he will not achieve the objectives for which he is responsible. The president of an industrial firm ignores his production engineers at his peril. He assumes that they are competent engineers and limits his decisions to one of the choices within the limits beyond which, in their estimation, desired production results cannot be obtained. For him to pretend that he knows more about their area of technical competence than they do is obvious folly.

The position of professional field agents of community development *vis-à-vis* administrators should be similar to that of production engineers. They should be invited to participate in discussions leading to the formation of policy decisions so that the decisions which result will not transgress the limits of what is operationally feasible from the standpoint of human relations and social processes, as well as from other technical standpoints. When called upon to report on the social situation in a community in which they have been working for some time, their report should be respected even though it be at variance with the less-informed opinions held by the administrator who will make the ultimate decisions.

It is a matter of record, for example, how a careful assessment of the state of Japanese morale in early 1955 by social scientists hired to make that assessment was ignored by top policy-makers in our government in World War II. The report did not accord with their preconceived opinions, which were without systematic foundation. The decision-makers preferred to follow their less-informed opinions rather than to take seriously the findings of their own hired experts, with the result that the war with Japan was continued for some months longer than need have been the case. The findings of the experts were confirmed after the war.[19]

If an industrial policy-maker chose to ignore the findings of his engineers, regarded engineers as untrustworthy crackpots, he would be judged a fool. It is still common for administrators to regard social scientists as crackpots and to ignore their recommendations, even when they are based on a solid body of accumulated and verified knowledge, in favor of their own uninformed opinions and intuitive hunches. Sometimes it is possible for intelligent administrators to do this successfully, provided decisions have to do with their own society, about whose workings they have necessarily acquired considerable practical knowledge in the course of a life successfully lived in it. But this knowledge can be of little help in making decisions about other societies.

It is because of this frequent disregard by administrators of the findings and recommendations of social scientists that the latter are sometimes driven to conclude that scientists should themselves take over administrative responsibility and authority in undertakings where human relations and social processes are critically involved. This can provide no long-range solution to the decision-making problem, however. Competent professional or technical men often have limited administrative ability, just as competent administrators are often limited in professional or technical understanding.

In formulating policy and making decisions, then, it is necessary that both administrators and technicians, including field personnel in community development, be aware of their respective limitations. There is in this regard a special burden on the technician, who, because he knows much more about some things than the administrator, may be inclined to patronize the administrator intellectually. There is, likewise, a special burden on the administrator, who, because he has greater authority and power in the organization and is, therefore, by his standards "more successful," may assume that he is generally superior to the technician and that his intuition or uninformed opinion is by virtue of his greater administrative authority likely to be sounder than an informed contrary opinion by a technical subordinate. As Leighton has observed, too often technical experts are engaged not to ascertain what is practicable or to deal with a problem on its merits, but to add the weight of their professional authority to a position upon which an administrator has already decided without benefit of prior professional consultation.[20]

SUGGESTED READING

Barnett, H. G., *Anthropology in Administration*. Harper and Row, Publishers, Inc., New York, 1956.

Green, James W., "Success and Failure in Technical Assistance: A Case Study," *Human Organization*, vol. 20, no. 1, 1961, pp. 2–10.

Leighton, Alexander H., *Human Relations in a Changing World*. E. P. Dutton and Co., New York, 1949.

Mosher, Arthur T., *Technical Cooperation in Latin-American Agriculture*. University of Chicago Press, Chicago, 1957. See especially Chapter 17.

Richardson, F. L. W., *Talk, Work, and Action:* Human Reactions to Organizational Change. Monograph no. 3, Society for Applied Anthropology, Ithaca, N. Y., 1961.

Wilkening, Eugene A., *The County Extension Agent in Wisconsin:* Perceptions of Role Definitions as Viewed by Agents. Research Bulletin 203, University of Wisconsin, Madison, 1957.

NOTES TO CHAPTER 16

1. Portions of this chapter were presented in substantially their present form at a meeting of the Association of Management in Public Health in Miami, Fla., October 18, 1962, in a symposium entitled "Scientific Decision Making—Fact or Fiction?"

2. Barnard, Chester I., *The Functions of the Executive*, Harvard University Press, Cambridge, Mass., 1938; and Simon, Herbert A., *Administrative Behavior: A Study of Decision Making Processes in Administrative Organization*, Macmillan Co., New York, 1947.

3. Litchfield, Edward H., "Notes on a General Theory of Administration," *Administrative Science Quarterly*, vol. 1, June, 1956, p. 12.

4. Simon, Herbert A., *op. cit.*, p. 11.

5. See the similar comments by Herbert A. Simon, *op. cit.*, p. 10, on "responsibility."

6. This trend is clearly reflected in labor union organization with the emergence of so-called vertical unions under the old C.I.O. The idea of industry-wide as distinct from craft organization followed the industrial trend of programming operations so as to eliminate the need for skilled personnel as much as possible.

7. For an example of how a conscious effort to operate within this view of the administrator's role effectively served the ends of social and economic development, see Green, James W., "Success and Failure in Technical Assistance: A Case Study," *Human Organization*, vol. 20, no. 1, 1961, pp. 2–10.

8. See, for example, Dunnill, Frank, *The Civil Service:* Some Human Aspects, George Allen and Unwin, Ltd., London, 1956.

9. Simon, Herbert A., *op. cit.*, pp. 199–204.

10. How moral considerations prevent understanding and the possibility for realistic appraisal in administration is thoroughly discussed by Alexander H. Leighton in *Human Relations in a Changing World*, E. P. Dutton and Co., New York, 1949, pp. 155–161.

11. Jolly, A. L., "A Third Revolution in Tropical Agriculture?" *South Pacific*, vol. 8, March–April, 1956, p. 238.

12. Dunnill, Frank, *op. cit.*, p. 61.

13. *Ibid.*, p. 63.

14. Fairless, Benjamin, "It Could Happen Only in the U. S.," *Life*, October 15, 1956, pp. 174–176.

15. Leighton, Alexander H., *op. cit.*, pp. 174–176.

16. Barnett, H. G., *Anthropology in Administration*. Harper and Row, Publishers, Inc., New York, 1956, p. 86.

17. As this book goes to press, all the anthropologist positions in the Trust Territory have been vacated, apparently as a matter of policy.

18. See Leighton, Alexander, *op. cit.*, pp. 140–142.

19. *Ibid.*, pp. 120–127.

20. *Ibid.*

Chapter 17

PITFALLS OF CULTURAL IGNORANCE: EMOTIONAL CONCERNS

IN ADDITION to the social and psychological factors that interfere with a development agent's ability to play his role successfully in the development process, the fact that his clients have a culture with which he is initially unfamiliar also provides a series of submerged reefs on which his mission may easily founder. We have already seen how important it is for a development agent to learn the culture of his clients in order to be able to design intelligent programs for change and foresee the new problems that change will bring. His ability to learn the culture is enhanced, however, if he has some idea of what to expect. Furthermore, he has in practice to establish working relations with his clients before he has had an opportunity to learn much of their culture. It is in this early period when he is still learning their culture that an agent is also developing his *modus vivendi* with his clients. It is important, therefore, to have some warning of the kinds of cultural difference that exist in fact and of the pitfalls to understanding and communication that they create.

A famous episode will illustrate. Official ignorance precipitated a costly war that could easily have been avoided in what is now Ghana, West Africa. The British governor, Sir Frederick Hodgson, in a speech to the assembled Ashanti chiefs, demanded the right to *sit* on the sacred Golden Stool on the grounds that he was now the ruler of the Ashanti nation. As Edwin W. Smith comments:

> A singularly foolish speech! An excellent example of the blunders that are made through ignorance of the African mind! The Governor

453

regarded the Stool as a kind of Stone of Scone upon which the kings of Ashanti were seated at their accession, a symbol of supreme authority, and hence, as the representative of Queen Victoria, he naturally expected to have it brought out as his throne. As a matter of fact, no King of Ashanti had ever sat upon it. It was held in reverence by the people as being, not an appurtenance of the kingly office, but the embodiment of the nation's soul. If the Governor had known the real significance of the Stool in the mind of the people he would not have reproached the chiefs in this manner. This much may be said in his defense—he blundered in ignorance.

The speech was received by the assembly in silence. But the chiefs returned home to prepare for war. Within a week fighting had commenced.[*1]

Since the problem of cultural differences stems from the contrast between the respective cultures of agent and client, our discussion will necessarily have reference to the attitudes and values that agents bring into the development situation from their own culture. We shall take the culture of middle-class Americans to represent the agent's culture. Most Americans who work as agents of community development are of middle-class background, and in their mode of life and social relationships they usually express the attitudes and values of this class.

The questions we shall consider, then, are: (1) What are the more likely booby traps resulting from cultural differences? (2) How do middle-class American attitudes and values contribute to their formation? (3) How different are the values, attitudes, and social patterns of others likely to be? (4) What kinds of problems in agent-client relations do these differences create? (5) What can an agent do to avoid them?

ETIQUETTE

We have already noted in Chapter 8 the importance of etiquette as a means whereby people pay respect to one another's social identities. The problem for development agents is that the rules of etiquette vary so, similar actions having entirely different social significance in different cultures. As Lado notes, for example,

* From *The Golden Stool* by Edwin W. Smith. Published by Doubleday and Company, Inc., New York, 1928, p. 7.

A wink from a man to a woman in Spain might be a bold suggestion. From a woman to a man it might be even more of a suggestion. In the United States a wink does not normally have such
meaning. It is difficult for the Spanish individual not to react to a
wink in the United States the way he might in his own culture.*[2]

When the agent and his clients are used to different conventions,
have habitually observed different forms in their interpersonal
dealings with their fellows, the possibilities for misunderstanding
are obviously great.

All societies have standards of comportment, definitions of
what is good and bad form in particular situations. The situations they distinguish are many and varied, and an outsider is
not expected to know about them all or to be familiar with the
fine points of conduct within them. All societies, however, possess
some forms that are generally applicable, that signify cordiality
of relations among those observing them. They are the "common
courtesies." Failure to learn them can have serious consequences,
for they are among the most important criteria by which people
judge one another. People are always pleased when an outsider
coming among them tries to learn what these common courtesies
are.

One problem in not knowing the conventions by which people
observe common courtesies with each other is, of course, the
possibility of inadvertently giving offense. Thus Useem speaks of
the labor relations expert called in to help settle a strike in the
Palau Islands:

> He acted "informally" in the presence of natives, joking and
> teasing in the American style, shadow boxing, fondling children, be-
> ing generous to natives in need. One of his ingratiating gestures to
> indicate he was a "good Joe" was to put his arm around the shoul-
> ders of ranking native men while laughingly tousling the hair on
> their heads. This is the equivalent in our society of opening a man's
> fly in public as a joke, for in Palau the head is a sensitive zone.[3]

On the other hand, it is equally possible for an agent to be
offended where no offense is intended. People in the community

* Reprinted by permission from Paul L. Garvin, editor, *Report of the Seventh Annual
Round Table Meeting on Linguistics*, no .9, Georgetown University, Washington, 1957,
p. 7. Copyright, 1957 by Georgetown University Press.

may appear to take liberties with him and his person on occasion in the same way. For example, in many Pacific Islands the standard greeting is "Where are you going?" or "Whence coming?" To westerners this seems like an unwarranted prying into one's personal affairs and also to require lengthy explanations, annoying when one is in a hurry. It is a help to know that the perfectly proper reply is "North!" or "South!" or "Inland!" and that the question has no more significance than the standard American greeting "How are you?" Each expression, the American's and the Islander's, serves the purpose of acknowledging the presence of someone with whom one has cordial relations.

The Palauan example illustrates a tendency Americans may find it necessary to guard against. Egalitarian friendliness is a strong American value that evokes positive responses in many parts of the world. It is accompanied by a high valuation on informality in social relationships, which is symbolized by dispensing with the more polite and reserved forms and by taking minor liberties with others. The salesman's techniques are perhaps the most highly developed, with backslapping, the off-color joke, and relating very personal experiences. These are standard parts of American culture and, as such, the *formal* things Americans do to put their fellows at ease. They are not the things one does to put people in other societies at their ease. A higher degree of formalism by American standards (without lessening evidence of friendliness), being on one's "best behavior," can do much more to put others at ease and give them a sense that their feelings and sensibilities are a matter of concern.

Beyond the simple formulas for casual encounters, there is the proper display of manners between guest and host, a relationship in which change agents are not unlikely to find themselves. To convey the possibilities for misunderstanding and offense in this area, we cannot do better than to repeat Sir Arthur Grimble's delightful story of his first lesson in politeness in the Gilbert Islands, when he went to the home of a village headman for instruction in native custom.

> . . . I went to the kaubure's house place in the village an hour or so before sunset on the day arranged.

A little golden girl of seven, naked save for a wreath of white flowers on her glossy head, invited me to mount the raised floor of the *mwenga*. As she spread a fine guest mat for me to sit upon, she told me her name was Tebutinnang—Movement of Clouds. Seated cross-legged on another mat, she explained with gravity that her grandfather had charged her to entertain me with conversation, should I arrive before his return from fishing. He would not be very long now; would I like to drink a coconut while she went on entertaining? When I said yes, please, she climbed down from the floor, brought in a nut which she had opened under the tree outside with a cutlass almost as long as herself, sat down again, and offered it to me cupped in both hands, at arm's length, with her head a little bowed.

"You shall be blessed," she murmured as I took it. I did say, "Thank you," in reply, but even that was wrong; I should have returned her blessing word for word, and, after that, I should have returned the nut also, for her to take the first sip of courtesy; and at last, when I had received it back, I should have said "Blessings and Peace," before beginning to drink the milk. All I did—woe is me!—was to take it, swig it off, and hand it back one-handed, empty, with another careless "Thank you."

She did not rise and run off with it as I expected, but sat on instead, with both arms clasping the nut to her little chest, examining me over the top of it. "Alas!" she said at last in a shocked whisper. "Alas! Is that the manners of a young chief of Matang?"

She told me one by one of the sins I have confessed, and I hung my head in shame, but that was not the full tale. My final discourtesy had been the crudest of all. In handing back the empty nut, I had omitted to belch aloud.*[4]

If an agent of change is ignorant of local niceties and, as is not unlikely, is called upon to perform before he has an opportunity to learn what they are, what is he to do then?

In the great majority of communities in which he is likely to work, people will be aware that his customs differ from theirs. They will be prepared to make allowances for this. Their major concern will be that their efforts as hosts or as gift givers, whatever they may be, are treated with the consideration that they feel they deserve. An agent can use the formalities he associates with such occasions in his own culture, provided he does so with appropriate spirit. When we are unacquainted with what is

* Reprinted with permission of the publishers from *We Chose the Islands:* A Six-Year Adventure in the Gilberts by Sir Arthur Grimble. William Morrow and Company, Inc., New York, pp. 47–48. © 1952 by Sir Arthur Grimble.

expected of us in strange situations we tend, it seems, to disclaim responsibility for holding up our end in them. To be diffident is to seem not to care and is, in fact, to be less concerned about the feelings of others than about one's own. This can give hurt.

Beyond this is the tendency of many middle-class Europeans and Americans to regard others as outside the social circle within which the usual courtesies are given and received. Too frequently they fail to observe the simplest amenities when speaking to persons of alien and peasant background. A few years ago, for example, some of the Gilbertese employees of Pan American Airways on Canton Island went on a one-day strike. The reason they gave for this demonstration was their desire that their immediate bosses use some of the common courtesies in dealing with them, rather than keep relations entirely on a "do this" and "do that" basis with never a "please" or friendly "good morning." This, we understand, was their grievance.

One may ask why we should emphasize the importance of such common courtesies, why one shouldn't expect agents of change to observe them as a matter of course. One of the problems is that these simple courtesies are very important symbols of social acceptance. Their omission is a reminder that one discriminates among human beings as entitled to different degrees of consideration. In many parts of the world, where there are marked distinctions of social class or where there is a small minority of European administrators, missionaries, and businessmen in positions of political and economic dominance, members of the privileged group may make a regular practice of refusing courtesies to those whom they regard as their inferiors. They call this "showing them their place," quite aptly, because they are indeed showing them what they think of them. Change agents coming in to such areas will be shown the ropes for dealing with "natives" by the resident privileged group with which they will be identified. Members of the privileged group will usually object to efforts by agents to conduct themselves in a different manner. Change agents may thus find themselves subject to strong social pressure from "their own kind" to comport themselves in ways that are detrimental to achieving cooperation in change.

Beyond the problem of ordinary courtesies as between fellow human beings, there is the subject of ceremonialism and formalism in connection with special occasions. The degree to which people emphasize form and ceremony in the conduct of public affairs, for example, varies considerably. The kinds of stances that ceremony may require one to take are also varied. In connection with Samoa, for example, the Keesings write:

> By Western standards the ceremonial contexts of elite communication involve a leisurely and measured, as well as correctly ordered, sequence of events which is likely to tax even the most patient European. What the latter judges as slow action, repetition, long intervals, are to the Samoan an essential part of his savoring of the occasion. . . . It also adds an appreciated note of eliteness, unusualness, at times virtual sanctification, to what otherwise is the rather commonplace familiar round of community and kin affairs. So any speed-up or short cut in the long-drawn timing and tempo would verge on sin.[*5]

The same authors comment on the strongly contrasting values of Samoans and New Zealanders in this regard.

> The writers have on record numbers of public ceremonies, for example, with the parts played by New Zealand officials clipped to an irreducible minimum, underplayed with close-lipped precision and sharp, restrained motions; the corresponding parts played by Samoan elite, with elaborations of status exhibition, leisurely oratory, superb staging and gestures, full play of emotional content and artistic expression and lavish hospitality and displays of gifts; the slow, dignified, rollingly fluid, and graceful gestures of the Samoans in speech and in action setting off the angular, quiet, often nervously tense behavior of the New Zealanders. The contrasts tend to be sharpest in relation to the lesser New Zealand personnel: the top officials, as a result of diplomatic or comparable training and experience, cope better with this cross-cultural situation.[*6]

They conclude that this contrast was an important factor in the desire of Samoans to have "seconded" officials from New Zealand replaced by Samoan counterparts as rapidly as possible.

[*5,6] Reprinted from *Elite Communication in Samoa: A Study of Leadership* by Felix M. Keesing and Marie M. Keesing, with the permission of the publishers, Stanford University Press, Stanford, pp. 85, 192–193. © 1956 by the Board of Trustees of the Leland Stanford Junior University.

As for Americans, while not averse to ceremony under certain conditions, they pride themselves in "getting on with the job." Administrators and executives like to make a show of efficiency by speedily rendering decisions, leaving off the "frills" in negotiating and quickly "getting down to business." At the same time we like to be relaxed and informal in our dealings with others. This is part of the American style of doing things. It requires special effort, therefore, to adjust one's expectations to a different style, such as the Samoan one. And in no other part of the world will Americans find their style exactly duplicated. It is tempting to judge as inefficient people whose styles are different, to regard their underdeveloped condition as a result of this difference in style, and to conclude that only a liberal injection of American "get-up-and-go" will promote community development. Experience makes it clear that the only efficient way to proceed in other communities is in accordance with the style that comes naturally to its people. To do otherwise is to introduce unnecessary complications, asking them to make all kinds of adjustments and changes that are incidental to a program's objectives.

FOOD

Development programs very often have as one of their main objectives improvement of the local diet. Regardless of their objectives, however, agents of change will find that food is a sensitive matter that is likely to have a marked effect on their relations with their clients. Food is inevitably associated with deep-rooted values and attitudes, not only for the community in which an agent is working but for the agent as well. It is so for the simple reason that among all men eating is an intensely gratifying activity. In all societies, moreover, gratification is associated with a few foods, specific as to source, manner of preparation, appearance, taste, smell, and feel. (Why do we prefer yellow to white oleomargarine, for example?) The pleasure men derive from eating, moreover, is associated with certain physical and social surroundings and with regular times in the customary daily routine. The physiological pleasure of eating promotes in all of us a set of positive attitudes toward what we habitually eat and the circumstances under which we eat it.

There is another side of the picture, however. All men also have to learn that it is dangerous to eat certain things. One of the most important lessons for small children to learn is that they cannot put everything in their mouth. Men develop, therefore, great anxiety about eating anything that has not been certified as fit for human consumption by those whose authority they trust. The result is that every society has standards as to what is edible and what is not. People tend to react with disgust to anything as food that fails to measure up to their standards of taste, source, smell, texture, and appearance. The problem for interethnic relations is, of course, that these standards vary from society to society. While none considers edible things that are in scientific fact inedible, virtually every society considers unfit to eat some things that are actually quite suitable as food. It is here that standards vary.

As a result, men everywhere—and agents of change are no exception—observing other people eating food of a kind or in a manner which by their standards they consider disgusting, tend to regard them as disgusting people. The European's shudder at the sight of a native of the Gilbert Islands sucking the eyes out of fish heads is matched by the latter's shudder at the sight of the same European eating eggs. Because of the strong ideas all people have about what is fit and unfit for human consumption, food can be a stumbling block to the formation of good working relations between agent and community. By deprecating the food that the community's members enjoy eating, an agent offers them insult; for the implication is clear that people who eat what he regards as unfit for human consumption must somehow be subhuman.

It can be difficult not to give offense in this regard. Field workers and administrators are often offered food as a gesture of friendship and hospitality. What is offered may be unappetizing or unhealthy from their point-of-view. Whether they are in a position to refuse it or not, they should keep their anxieties to themselves and remember their manners. A slight wrinkle of the nose in disgust may be all that is necessary to betray an attitude that will be resented. In our experience, thoughtlessness with regard to the feelings of other people about their food is one of the commonest failings of Euro-Americans. The attitude from which this thoughtlessness stems is well illustrated by the questions we and our anthropological colleagues are frequently asked when the subject of our field studies comes up in conversation with our lay acquaintances: "You didn't eat their food, did you?"

As a general rule it is wise for agents and administrators to consider themselves the guests of the community in which they are working and to be prepared, as such, to eat the food that is offered them by local hosts. If there are compelling reasons for not doing so, they should find out the local conventions by which such invitations may properly be declined without causing offense. All too often offense is given for the simple reason that the visitor does not know how to say no politely.

As simple and obvious as the foregoing remarks may appear, it is worth noting that in several areas in which we have ourselves done ethnographic field work we were forcibly struck by the intensity of feeling revealed to us in response to our willingness to eat local food. Over and over again we were told, much to our surprise, that this was exceptional. Their experience of Europeans was such that local people expected negative attitudes from them toward their food. They explicitly said that this was one of the things they most resented in Europeans: the implication that what they ate was unfit and that what they prepared was dirty.

In most societies, food is the symbol par excellence of hospitality and fellowship. Not to offer the visitor food is to declare him unwelcome, and not to accept food offered is to declare one's unfriendliness to the giver. Clearly, whether one's work as an agent of change is directly with dietary problems or not, food can be a source of misunderstanding and ill-feeling between agent and community.

In projects where the objective is to improve the local diet, the foregoing considerations take on added significance. It is difficult, indeed, to avoid the implication that the project administrator disapproves of the local foods when he tries to introduce new ones "in order to improve the diet." The very existence of the project may be an implied insult, and taken as such. In promoting his program, therefore, the administrator may find it politic to emphasize that he is concerned with ways of increasing the quantity rather than the quality of available food, or again that he is interested in helping people obtain a greater variety of foods rather than in substituting a better food for the present inferior one. It is often possible to introduce new ideas about food by expressing a positive attitude toward those foods already in use. The Nakanai natives of New Britain, for example, use lime juice in some of their taro cooking recipes. Were an agent to seek to increase the amount of vitamin C in Nakanai diet, he would do well to build on their use of limes and other vitamin C bearing foods. By praising them for their wisdom in recognizing the virtue of such food, he may find them more willing to listen to the suggestions he has to make.

Food and Basic Values

The symbolic role of food in the life of most people extends beyond its connection with hospitality. With most of the world's peoples, food and eating tend to be invested with both social and religious values. Food taboos, for example, enhance the sense of purpose and dedication people seek to achieve in their spiritual life. They invest the intangibles with concrete meaning and provide tangible means for achieving intangible ends, as with fasting during Lent or Ramadan. The primary values associated with human activity are, in the last analysis, rooted in physiology. The degree to which man will endure hunger, thirst, pain, and sexual deprivation is the ultimate measure of the emotional value he attaches to things and ideas. To require deprivation as a means of achieving the social and religious goals which a community's customs define as important for its members is to enhance the value of their achievement. In most societies, therefore, food or abstinence therefrom is intimately linked with ceremonial life and with those values that are nearest and dearest to people. In his thorough account of the place of food in native life on the Melanesian island of Tanga, for example, Bell states:

> In all those situations which involve the intervention of the super-natural, such as the employment of magic in gardening, canoe building, love making, fighting, fishing, voyaging and a host of other activities the ultimate outcome of which is shrouded in fear, danger and uncertainty, there is an accompanying prohibition against the consumption of food by the operator and often by the other persons

participating. In like manner, wherever there is the likelihood of food-stuffs having come into contact with the evil spirits . . . or with a menstruating woman, the head of a male or the buttocks of a female, there is strict prohibition on consumption.[7]

The wise administrator will seek to know not only what existing food habits are, but how food is utilized in the religious and ceremonial life of the people. In some societies eating is itself a religious rite. Under such conditions, what to the administrator appears to be a proposal to change eating habits may appear to the community as a proposal to change religious practices.

The role of food in helping to make a success of social gatherings is something with which the reader is already familiar from his own experience. That it can be important in the transaction of public business is perhaps, less obvious. Thus the Keesings[*8] report that:

> Westerners are apt to underestimate the extent to which the feasting itself and associated ceremonial is important to Samoans. The European outsider is likely to consider them "wasteful" or "unnecessary." Such a viewpoint comes out even in official documents, as reports of the United Nations Missions in Samoa. While interest is expressed in these enjoyable Samoan customs, there is an anxiety to get ahead with the "serious business." In Samoa feasting is always serious business, for Samoans "say it with food."

In the realm of social relations, it is important to know whether there are exclusive rights to certain foods (or taboos against them) that mark differences in social class, rank, cult, or clan membership. Thus, in the Caroline Islands, native navigators cannot eat food that is not separately prepared and served from food intended for laymen, even within their own families. And in Samoa, according to the Keesings[*9]:

> Titled people of appropriate rank eat together. Women and un-titled men eat separately, usually later, and children usually last on the remaining pickings. This status distinction in commensal usages comes to have deep emotional context. The writers have seen a Samoan chief ask a younger untitled man to join them and him, in

*8,9 Reprinted from *Elite Communication in Samoa:* A Study of Leadership by Felix M. Keesing and Marie M. Keesing, with the permission of the publishers, Stanford University, Stanford, pp. 80, 79. © 1956 by the Board of Trustees of the Leland Stanford Junior University.

an informal meal on a modern egalitarian basis as being "all educated people." The younger man tried again and again to swallow food but it would not go past his throat so that he almost choked on his respect, and finally the chief said: "You had better go and finish your meal with the women and young men."

In many societies it is forbidden for certain kinds of relatives to eat from the same pot. The great depth of moral feeling about these prohibitions has been well illustrated by Bell who describes the difficulties of a Tangan boat crew lost at sea:

> The crew consisted of Tengpwunpwun, who was my informant's mother's brother, Milasiaro his father, Kiapselin his brother, and Neda his mother's brother's son. Four coconuts only were taken as emergency rations, and as the voyage lasted five days and the canoe drifted 160 miles before stranding on the Carteret group, one can imagine how the little band suffered from hunger and thirst. When they came to the last coconut, my informant drank first and then handed it to his brother. Kiapselin then passed the nut to Neda, but although the latter was almost dying of thirst, he refused to drink from a nut with which both his cross-cousins had made contact.[10] They pressed him to drink, however, and after crying at the disgrace of his action, he gave in. Tengpwunpwun then took the nut from his son Neda and after a little coaxing, he too took his fill. There remained Milasiaro, but he refused to drink as the nut had been pressed to the lips of his wife's brother Tengpwunpwun. He said that he preferred death to the shame of such an action. Eventually, after hours of pleading, he broke down and, to the accompaniment of much weeping and self-condemnatory wailing, drank.[11]

A problem agents may encounter is that less nutritious foods have the highest prestige as the things rich men eat. We heard a story recently about university students in an oriental country where rice formed the staple food. According to this story some of the students would have to drop out of class periodically for medical treatment against beriberi. They knew the cause of beriberi and far from considering the illness a disgrace looked upon it as something of which to boast. Only the wealthy could afford to live on polished white rice. To suffer from beriberi, like having a Cadillac in front of one's door, was valued as a form of conspicuous ostentation. Under these conditions where prestige foods are less nutritious, a rise in the affluence of the community can lead to a reduction in the standard of health. We are not without such problems in the United States.[12] Conversely, in parts of the Solomon Islands where pork (practically the only meat) is something of a luxury, it is reserved for adult men. Women and children get practically no meat in their diet at all. To change eating habits so that those who most need protein can get it requires changing the social system as well. Under conditions such as these, agents may find it easier to introduce new high protein foods that do not have social symbolic importance than to try to effect a redistribution of traditional foods.

Some societies fail to make full use of their available food resources for religious or social reasons. The refusal of Hindus to eat beef is a well-known example, despite the availability of cattle. Many of the cattle-keeping people of East Africa fail to make efficient use of their herds for food and resist orders to reduce their herds in order to eliminate rinderpest. Here the reasons are social rather than religious. Social prestige and wealth are based on the size of a man's herds. Cattle also play an important role in the exchanges at marriage. To kill cattle for medical reasons or to provide food is to diminish one's social standing.

There are societies, on the other hand, especially in parts of Indonesia and the Pacific Islands, where production of food is the major means of getting and maintaining social prestige. The ambitious man expends tremendous effort to raise quantities of food in excess of his immediate needs, and with it to entertain the community with large feasts or to underwrite the feasts connected with important religious ceremonies. In some areas this becomes quite competitive, with several families vying with each other to see which one can provide the most lavish entertainment. Customs of this kind may be either a hindrance or a help to agents of change, depending on how they approach them. Once they understand local attitudes and values associated with food and food resources, agents can sometimes appeal to them directly in order to gain acceptance of their proposals.

Any project designed to produce an improvement in dietary standards, then, is a delicate operation. It is likely to require adjustments in taste, work habits, and social and religious values.

Even such a simple thing as the texture of a new food may cause its rejection, as is dramatically illustrated in a case reported by Apodaca for New Mexico.[13] A new variety of maize giving a much higher yield was introduced into a Spanish American community only to be rejected by the housewives because it produced meal whose texture made it impossible to make what they considered proper tortillas. Obviously, it is essential to know the place of food, with all its ramifications, in community life before seeking to introduce changes.

Finally, it should not be necessary to emphasize the importance of first evaluating the necessity for change at all. Careful analysis of the nutritional content of local foods as locally prepared should be a routine part of the planning phase of every program contemplating dietary change. An important result of a survey of native nutrition and health in New Guinea, for example, was the discovery that native methods of cooking, however strange to European eyes, were about as good as could be devised from the standpoint of preserving the nutritional value of food. While there were some serious dietary deficiencies, they had nothing to do with cooking methods. Indeed, native practices in this regard were often better from a nutritional point of view than those of most European and American housewives.[14]

In assessing the dietary habits of other peoples, moreover, it is important to guard against erroneous judgments resulting from the use of one's own culture as the frame of reference. The problem is well illustrated by Lado:

> For some time it was puzzling to me that on the one hand Latin American students complained that North American meals abused the use of sugar while on the other hand University dietitians complained that Latin Americans used too much sugar at meals. How could these contradictory opinions possibly be true at the same time? We can observe that the average Latin American student takes more sugar in his coffee than do North Americans. He is not used to drinking milk at meals, but when milk is served he sometimes likes to put sugar in it. The dietitian notices this use of sugar in situations in which North Americans would use less or none at all. The dietitian notices also that the sugar bowls at tables where Latin Americans sit have to be filled more often than at other tables. She therefore feels quite confident in making her generalization.

The Latin American student for his part finds a salad made of sweet gelatin, or half a canned pear on a lettuce leaf. Sweet salad! He may see beans for lunch. He sits at table, all smiles; he takes a good spoon full and, sweet beans. They are Boston baked beans. Turkey is served on Thanksgiving Day, but when the Latin American tastes the sauce, he finds that it is sweet—it is cranberry sauce. Sweet sauce for broiled turkey. That is the limit. These North Americans obviously use too much sugar in their food. And whatever secondary meanings attach to the abuse of sugar in the native culture are tagged to the foreign culture. *15

SEX

About the only generalizations that can safely be made with regard to sex are that all societies prohibit sexual relations and marriage within the immediate family as incestuous, that all permit sexual relations between married partners, and that all regulate sexual relations in other contexts in some way; but what that way is varies greatly.

Many societies allow premarital relations as an appropriate part of courtship behavior, while others disapprove of them entirely. Many societies also permit some extra-marital relations, usually between brother-in-law and sister-in-law, while at the same time outlawing other extra-marital unions as adulterous. Few societies confine sexual relations as proper only to married couples. Some communities, moreover, have few restrictions on sex relations between their own members, but consider relations with foreigners a terrible thing, and other communities take just the opposite position. The great range of differences in attitudes toward sex among different societies seems to be a common source of confusion in interethnic relations. It is furthermore a topic about which the average European and American is likely to have many misconceptions.

As comparative studies reveal,[16] what we may call middle-class American attitudes toward sex are of a rather extreme nature, as compared with those found in many other parts of the world. The only relationship among ourselves in which coitus is socially

* Reprinted by permission from Paul L. Garvin, editor, *Report of the Seventh Annual Round Table Meeting on Linguistics*, no. 9, Georgetown University, Washington, 1957, pp. 145–146. Copyright, 1957 by Georgetown University Press.

approved is the marital one. The social consequences of having sexual relations under any other circumstances are potentially, at least, serious. While we train our young women in ways generally consistent with this viewpoint, our young men are educated (specifically by slightly older men) in a manner which is incompatible with it. They are led to consider sexual experience a necessary requisite to achieving man's estate, quite independent of marriage. Young men, therefore, value sex positively and are actively interested in having experience while at the same time expecting and finding young women to have, at least overtly, a rather negative orientation. Our double standard motivates young men sexually and at the same time inhibits them from realizing their desires, which being thus frustrated find expression in a fantasy world filled with attractive women who are themselves as actively interested in sex as the men who dream of them. This fantasy world is given all kinds of spurious reality in cover-girl art, the burlesque theatre, and pulp literature. These serve only to increase the frustration, because they give unattainable substance to what would otherwise remain idle dreams. While most men make a reasonably satisfactory adjustment to this situation, they are poorly equipped to maintain a sense of proportion when they find themselves in a society where the standards governing sexual expression are different. Indeed, one of the serious problems in this regard is the myth that in other societies women are like those who populate our fantasies. The popular misconceptions of Parisian and Polynesian women are obvious examples.

The result of all this is that when American men find themselves in societies where the code of sexual conduct differs from ours, their past frustrations plus their mistaken ideas about foreign women have a tendency to get them into trouble. Because one of the chief sources of restraint at home was the presumed attitude of American women, the presumed different attitude of foreign women unleashes the dammed up desires. Men frequently find it impossible to exercise their normal self-control under these conditions, and in consequence may find themselves acting the fool not only in their own eyes, but, what is far more important for interethnic relations, in the eyes of the community's members as well. Finding the community's standards different, they may conclude that the community has *no* standards and quickly run afoul of the standards that do in fact exist, and about which the local people feel just as strongly as we do about our own.

In Truk, for example, it is not at all uncommon to observe extremes of sexual horseplay going on publicly between a man and woman. The visitor is, in fact, an ideal foil for such horseplay precisely because he is *not* a member of the community. During our residence there, young men frequently recited to us in the presence of the woman they were talking about, the details of her anatomical charms, with the obvious intent of embarrassing her. In every instance where such public horseplay occurred, however, the woman was a sister-in-law of the man and there was no one present who was sister to the man or brother to the woman. Only between siblings-in-law of opposite sex was such "kidding around" permissible. How easy for the stranger to conclude that sexual joking was freely permitted on Truk and that the Trukese were "without morals!" How easy, in the interest of establishing friendly relations with the Trukese, to try to joke with them in the manner thus observed! Yet sex may never be mentioned in the presence of brother and sister. So strict is the feeling in this regard, that after puberty brother and sister may not even sleep under the same roof. As in America, there are times when a sexual joke is welcome and appreciated, and there are equally times when it is not. As in America also, no one will be condemned for *not* talking about sex wherever and with whomever he may be.[17] Indeed, the cardinal rule for all outsiders establishing relationships in a community is to take no liberties of any kind, sexual or otherwise, until one has fully ascertained from trustworthy informants what the proprieties are.

The last point is worthy of special emphasis, because if the American code is extremely restrictive regarding coitus it is extremely permissive by comparison with other societies concerning many other forms of sexual behavior. The open "necking" which is so common in America, for example, would be shocking in many parts of the world. By the standards of most Pacific Islanders, the public kissing of American husbands and wives is lewd.

Suppose a change agent with no marital ties discovers that it is quite within the bounds of local propriety for him to seek to have sexual relations with certain women in the community. He has carefully learned the proprieties and studiously observes them. What then? He can still make an egregious fool of himself, for the very reason that emotionally his attitudes and values are those of a different social milieu, one for example in which sex is not taken casually. He is very likely, therefore, to become emotionally involved in ways that are not intelligible to the community's members or that strike them as evidence of gross immaturity. In societies where there are fewer barriers to sexual expression, people learn to exercise restraint for esthetic and other reasons and interpret evidence of such restraint as indicative of the individual's maturity of judgment. Their confidence in an agent of change as a mature and responsible person can be seriously shaken if, because of his different background, he strikes them as lacking in restraint or being improperly oriented emotionally in sexual matters.

Agents may sometimes be in the position where women are offered to them by the community authorities as a gesture of hospitality. A courteous decline on the grounds that the agent's customs forbid his sleeping with other than his wife, while it may seem strange to them, will be respected. Indeed, in many communities in which agents are likely to be working, the people are well aware that western customs differ from their own in sexual matters. They will not condemn a westerner for observing his own customs, provided that in doing so he does not violate their own moral code.

That sex is a source of trouble in relations between Americans and other people springs in large measure from our own customs regarding it. As a general rule it is wise for administrators living in alien communities to be accompanied by their wives, if possible. This not only helps to reduce the physical tension they would otherwise experience, but also keeps them in direct touch with important restraints on irresponsible behavior with which they are familiar. If his wife is with him, moreover, an agent is much less likely to be offered opportunities for sexual involvement by the community's members themselves.

FRIENDSHIP

In every society there are a number of standardized types of social relationship. Each involves a definite set of mutual expectations, which must be met if the relationship is to be maintained satisfactorily. The number of types and the expectations characterizing them, however, differ considerably. In this connection, friendship as conceived by North Americans of middle-class background is not a relationship with which other peoples are necessarily familiar or in which they can readily function. Because a development agent necessarily depends heavily on the "friendly" relations he establishes with his clients, failure to recognize cultural differences in the area of friendship can create serious problems.

Some people structure all relatively intimate relationships in terms of kin relationships. In Truk, for example, when two unrelated men wish to be "close friends," to recognize a special trust and mutual dependency or freedom with each other, they become "brothers." Their relationship is patterned after the brother relationship and includes such things as sharing immediate personal property and permissive sex relations with one another's wives. In other societies, there are categories of relationship apart from kinship that crudely resemble our idea of friendship, but the expectations (rights, duties, and privileges) in these relationships may be quite different.

For example, Reina found friendship patterns among Ladinos and Indians in Guatemala to be so different—to involve such different values and to have such different emotional and social functions—that "a cross-'race' friendship is unworkable."[18] These differences caused him personally a great deal of difficulty in his relations with Indian informants before he learned the Indian friendship pattern. Even then, it created problems for him in that it was difficult to accommodate their intense, exclusive, jealous "friend" relationship to the demands of anthropological research.

> . . . The keeping of a permanent and reliable informant was not an easy matter. The procedure was painful for both the investigator and the informant. To keep a particularly good informant, it was necessary to give him a very careful explanation of the role of the

investigator and his need for maintaining contact with everyone in the community. It took a long while for the informant to become accustomed to this type of relationship, and he would often point out with disturbed feelings that he had seen "so and so" come to the house and stay all afternoon, or that he had been told some undesirable member of the community dropped in seeking a camarada puesto [Indian type of friendship]. At times he felt elated and happy, but on other occasions he felt hurt and distant. It took constant effort to keep him stimulated to serve as informant and, most of all, to think of his relationship in these terms while many in the community were advising him to withdraw. After several months of insecurity, he found his own puesto [adjustment to the investigator], became secure, and turned out to be a desirable informant who brought many acquaintances and relatives for intensive interview.[19]

Samoans may have trouble in their friendships with Americans for different reasons.[20] Relationships in Samoa depend heavily on the balance of favor and return. When A consistently does more for B than B can return, he indicates that he is willing to assume responsibility for B, and B responds by becoming a dependent of A, free to look to A for a sheltering wing and rendering loyal support in return. A generous American is likely to put his Samoan acquaintances or employees in a position where they begin to relate to him as dependent to patron, with the American finding himself cast in a role he does not wish to play. Furthermore, every Samoan has to find and maintain an appropriate balance of equality and dependency relations with his fellows, especially with his kinsmen and kin group leaders. Samoans help each other to keep balances appropriate to their respective stations in their local social system. An American outsider, with different approaches to social relations, may not put appropriate brakes on his dealings with his Samoan friends, involving them in commitments (as they see it) that seriously disrupt the balance of their relations with kinsmen and other associates. For the Samoan, moreover, the degrees of intimacy in social relations are different from what they are for Americans. Thus, as he becomes an American's "friend," the American will allow him intimacies which from the Samoan point of view permit other intimacies that Americans do not accord them. As they begin to act accordingly, the American rebuffs them, the Samoan then sees his relationship as being defined as much less intimate than the American wants it to be. Each may conclude that the other is unpredictable and untrustworthy and put subsequent dealings on a footing of mutual exploitation.

As these considerations suggest, different social systems generate different social and emotional wants in people. Different kinds of friendship patterns arise accordingly, and different people evaluate relationships of similar behavioral content differently. It is one hundred per cent certain that a development agent will bring to any relationships he forms with his clients a different set of values, wants, and emotional strengths and vulnerabilities than his clients will bring to them. At least some misunderstanding and hurt feelings on both sides are inevitable. Wise and understanding clients can be of great help. But the responsibility for wisdom, understanding, and patience lies with the agent. He must be sensitive to the possibility of difficulty in friendships and work at devising ways of dealing with it.

RELIGION

We have already discussed human belief at some length, but a few words on magic, superstition, and religion may be appropriate, given the values that we attach to these labels and the consequent difficulties we inadvertently make for ourselves when dealing with peoples in underdeveloped countries.

Any thoughtful development agent is prepared to respect what he perceives to be the religious convictions of other people, but he may have a different attitude toward what he regards as mere superstition or magic. In the thinking of most Europeans and Americans religion is a different thing from magic and superstition. A fairly sizable body of literature has been devoted to the task of precisely differentiating magic from religion.[21] The fact remains that these attempts have proved to be little more than interesting exercises in taxonomic hair-splitting aimed at justifying a view of religious phenomena peculiar to our own culture. As one discussant of the matter notes, our use of these terms tends to be based on subjective and evaluative criteria rather than objective ones:

. . . "magic" implies any approach to religion, even within our own faith, which appears to us unworthy, that is, which we have rejected for ourselves. Our books today are written largely by people who hold themselves above the use of talismans and incantations, who profess to have no belief in ghosts, demons, devils, and the rest, and so in our literature the words "superstition" and "magic," which describe such beliefs, or such practices of self-protection, are almost always words of condemnation, if not scorn, usually set off against "true religion," or "true" levels of our own religion.[22]

The sociology of religious phenomena has received considerable attention, especially from British anthropologists,[23] whose studies demonstrate the various ways in which a people's beliefs and rites (whether we chose to call them magical or religious) may help to promote social solidarity, to uphold social and legal codes, and to formalize the handling of personal and social crises. This work, however, does not seriously inquire into the nature of the phenomena as expressions of processes within individual human beings in response to the hopes and fears that they individually experience. On the other hand, studies that have dealt with institutionalized procedures for giving symbolic expression to emotional problems have not tried seriously to develop a functional definition of religion (or functional typology of religious experience) out of their findings.[24] Obviously, we cannot undertake such a task here. But it can make a great deal of difference in our thinking and attitudes if we face the implications of the ways in which we intuitively speak of religion when we are not self-consciously trying to define it.

For one thing, we unhesitatingly talk about a society's customs and institutions as being "religious" or "economic" or "political" or "recreational." We treat these and other such categories of custom as if they are somehow complementary, as if they classify human activity in terms of a single general frame of reference. What makes a custom economic, political, or recreational, as we define these terms, are the kinds of problems the custom solves, the conscious and unconscious ends for which it serves as means and the ways in which it otherwise functions in the fabric of a people's existence. If customs are economic, political, or recreational to the extent that they function in economic, political, or recreational ways, then a custom is presumably religious to the extent that it functions in religious ways. From this point of view, what we seem to mean by religion is not a belief in the supernatural, or any specific kind of belief at all, but any set of practices and accompanying beliefs that have what we are prepared to designate as religious functions.

Intuitively, we recognize practices and beliefs as being in some way religious by virtue of the emotional investment people have in them. Regardless of how we may wish more precisely to define religious functions, they certainly have to do with the handling and control of emotions in those contexts in which emotions are a problem. In earlier chapters we have already talked about the emotional problems arising from the frustration of wants. We discussed psychological techniques by which people privately and collectively seek to live with the emotions resulting from their frustrations so as not to impair their ability to maintain desired relationships with their fellows and to achieve and maintain the kinds of public images and self-images they desire. We illustrated these techniques with an account of Trukese beliefs and practices relating to the soul—beliefs and practices that we would not hesitate to include in a description of religion in Truk. The matters we discussed in connection with identity goals, personal worth, and the emotional problems attending identity change clearly related to things that we conventionally associate with religion, for example "salvation." Insofar as they are concerned with people's identity problems, revitalization movements are recognizably religious movements. And we readily perceive the religious functions of such devices as prayer, talismans, and oracles by which we keep our emotions from getting in our way under conditions of stress, mobilize our inner resources to deal with difficult situations, or resolve the dilemmas of life without risk to our self-esteem.

Obviously, we cannot here attempt a serious discussion of how we are precisely to define the kinds of emotional problem whose solution or attempted solution gives a belief or practice a religious function. But some further comments are in order.

First, the same belief or practice need not have religious functions for everyone. One man in our society may join the Church for religious reasons and another join it for political ones. A rabbit's foot may have religious value for one and not for another. It follows, then, that public approval is irrelevant for determining whether or not a particular belief or practice functions in a religious way. A religious rite is no less religious because its devotees conduct it furtively. It can even be argued that the emotional problems of some individuals are such that they can find religious or saving value only by resort to practices that their fellows do not condone. Such individuals may be regarded as emotionally ill, but that is beside the point.

Furthermore, just as a proper study of a community's economics requires us to examine all of its customary activities, beliefs, and institutions with an eye to how they function economically (some being more preponderantly economic in function than others), a study of religion in a community requires us to examine all of its activities, beliefs, and institutions with an eye to their religious functions. The Church in our society obviously has economic and political as well as religious functions. By the same reasoning, the World Series in baseball, consulting one's psychiatrist, veterans' organizations, and political parties and elections may have significant religious functions for at least some Americans. We know personally a number of people who would rather change their church affiliation than their political party. Achieving the symbols of personal "success" would seem to be one of the major devotions in the private religious life of many Americans.

In conclusion, then, it would seem that whatever we may finally decide to mean by religion, we must define it in functional terms. The functions we designate as religious relate largely to individual emotional needs and problems, which may or may not be widely shared. Furthermore, what is religion in the life of a given people is going to have only a partial resemblance to what our own cultural values have normally led us to include under the term.

But where does magic fit into our discussion? Malinowski observed that what we ordinarily think of as magic tends to be elaborated at those points in technological procedures where technical control of the outcome is incomplete.[25] This is pretty well substantiated in the experience of other anthropologists. If we stop worrying about just what we mean by magic for the moment, we can state with reasonable confidence that compulsive, ritualistic behavior tends to develop in those situations where people have doubts about their control of the important factors (including self-control) and the outcome is a matter of concern to them. Concern, moreover, is the really critical thing. When there is little concern, lack of technical control is unlikely to produce ritualistic behavior. When emotional concern is great, there is likely to be considerable ritual even in the presence of good technical control. The fixation on food as a symbol of emotional concern to most Trukese makes intelligible their elaborate rituals to ensure a good harvest of breadfruit (*the* food) in spite of their admission that breadfruit harvests are pretty dependable anyway. They simply feel much more comfortable when the ritual has been performed. If the death of a king raises great concern about the future of the social establishment of which he is the prime symbol, we may expect elaborate ritual to accompany his funeral and/or the installation of his successor. The Coronation of Her Majesty Queen Elizabeth II was a magnificent, solemn, and at the same time joyous affirmation of the durability and stability of nearly everything of value to Britons and a promise of continued progress toward the realization of their most cherished aspirations.

What we are saying, in effect, is that ritual arises not so much in response to lack of technical control *per se*, but in response to the emotional investment people have in the outcome or resolution of situations confronting them. If they have realistic things to do, they will do them. If they have no very realistic things to do, they will do unrealistic things. If the realistic things to be done are inadequate as expressive vents to their concern, extra and unnecessary things will be done in addition. If their concern is caused by lack of technical control, ritual may well develop; but ritual also appears where concern is due to other than simple lack of control.

If these propositions are correct, then it follows from our comments on the nature of religion that if ritualistic behavior arises in response to emotional needs, it has religious functions. As compulsive, ritualized acts, then, what we usually call magical behavior falls within the range of religious behavior. From this point of view, concern about the outcome of technological processes need not alone define the sphere of magic. As we have observed, chronic concern about the annual harvest is likely to produce agricultural rites. Our own cultural bias inclines us to call them religious if the forces believed to be involved are personified as deities, and to dub them magical if the same forces are conceived in impersonal terms. To make such a distinction is to focus on the mythological rationale and to obscure the emotional value of the rites for those who perform them. For example, prayer and mechanical rain-making cannot be meaningfully separated, one as religious and the other as magical, in the following case reported in the *Manchester Guardian*.[26]

> Prayers for rain were offered . . . in churches of all denominations in County Durham where from 8 a.m. today water will be rationed for the five hundred thousand people supplied by the county water board. Mr. C. F. Grey, M.P., joined in prayers from Easington Lane Independent Methodist Church.
> Mr. Grey, who has had no reply to his request to the Air Ministry to send rainmakers to Durham, said, "I believe in prayer, we have not just to sit back. If we can get rain by artificial means, so much the better. I shall catch an early train to London in the morning and get in touch with the Air Ministry to urge them to act."

Concern about one's ability to play the roles expected of one in life, to achieve in practice standards of conduct and performance compatible with the image of self to which one aspires, is equally likely to result in ritual activity—in compulsive addiction to acts that provide reassurance and a sense of renewed strength, whether they be touching a potent object or withdrawing for quiet meditation and prayer. Everyone cultivates practices to this end and cherishes the beliefs that rationalize them. We may derogate such of our addictions of this sort as impair our ability to deal successfully with other things in life; we may find it difficult to rationalize some of them in terms of other beliefs that we also cherish. To deny their religious function for such reasons, however, is to reduce our chances of understanding the nature of religious phenomena.

From a practical as well as a scientific point of view, then, superstitions are religious beliefs in which we who call them superstitions do not believe, provided they do not seriously threaten us. If they threaten us they are heresies or anathemas. Magic, likewise, is any religious practice or rite based on what we who label it magic consider to be false beliefs, that is, superstitions. The "laying on of hands" in the Christian rite of confirmation is a magical act or not, depending on one's personal beliefs and values.

If follows that when people from Christian societies deal with non-Christians they tend to recognize as religion only those parts of other religions that contain ethical, doctrinal or ritual elements similar or analogous to those of Christianity. Other aspects of alien religions are "superstition and magic" and, by the peculiar alchemy of our thinking, not therefore to be respected as religion at all. If development agents are prepared to be circumspect and tactful as regards Islamic shrines or the Hindu doctrine of reincarnation, they must be equally prepared to be circumspect and tactful as regards amulets or belief in demons as the cause of sickness. The latter may be every bit as much religious objects and beliefs as the former, regardless of what one's personal evaluation of them may be. When an agent of change has the problem of coping with beliefs and practices that strike him as superstitious or magical, he will find it repays him to assume that what he is really dealing with is someone else's religious belief and ritual.

Indeed, the little rites, the talismans, and the demonic beliefs are usually of greater religious significance in the everyday life of ordinary people than are the pantheons, temples, and intellectualized belief systems of the professional priests and theologians. The little Sunday morning ritual of polishing the new car seems to do more for some Americans' peace of mind, self-confidence, and assurance of worth than going to church. Our tendency to think of religion in terms of its more elaborate institutional expressions can blind us to the important religious functions of many customs and institutions. Public institutions may persist for political and economic reasons long after losing the religious functions that promoted their original development; and a people's real religion may be tied to private areas of activity that we are inclined to overlook.

SUGGESTED READING

American Values and Attitudes

Lantis, Margaret, special editor, "The U.S.A. as Anthropologists See It," *American Anthropologist*, vol. 57, 1955, pp. 1113–1295.

Williams, Robin M., Jr., *American Society:* A Sociological Interpretation. Alfred A. Knopf, Inc., New York, 1952.

Etiquette and Allied Subjects

Goffman, Erving, *The Presentation of Self in Everyday Life.* Doubleday Anchor Books, New York, 1959.

Hall, Edward T., *The Silent Language.* Doubleday and Co., Inc., New York, 1959.

Keesing, Felix M. and Marie M., *Elite Communication in Samoa.* University of Stanford Press, Stanford, 1956.

Food

Bell, F. L. S., "The Place of Food in the Social Life of the Tanga," *Oceania*, vol. 17, 1946, pp. 139–172, 310–326; vol. 18, 1947, pp. 36–59, 233–247; vol. 19, 1948, pp. 51–74.

Read, Margaret, "Cultural Factors in Relation to Nutritional Problems in The Tropics," *Proceedings of the International Congress on Tropical Medicine*, Washington, D. C., 1948, reprinted in *Education and Social Change in Tropical Areas*, London, 1955, pp. 6–13.

Report of the New Guinea Nutrition Survey Expedition 1947. Department of External Territories, Canberra.

Scott, H. S., "Education and Nutrition in the Colonies," *Africa*, vol. 10, 1937, pp. 458–472.

Sex

Ford, Clellan S., and Frank A. Beach, *Patterns of Sexual Behavior.* Harper and Bros., New York, 1951.

Hoch, Paul H., and Joseph Zubin, editors, *Psychosexual Development in Health and Disease.* Grune and Stratton, New York, 1949.

Friendship

Reina, Ruben E., "Two Patterns of Friendship in a Guatemalan Community," *American Anthropologist*, vol. 61, 1959, pp. 44–50.

Religion

Malinowski, Bronislaw, *Magic, Science, and Religion.* The Free Press, Glencoe, Ill., 1948; Doubleday Anchor Books, Garden City, N. Y., 1954.

Firth, Raymond, *Elements of Social Organization,* Philosophical Library, New York, 1951. Chapter 7.

Goode, William T., *Religion Among the Primitives.* The Free Press, Glencoe, Ill., 1951.

Goodenough, E. R., *Jewish Symbols in The Greco-Roman Period.* Pantheon Books, New York, 1953–1958. 8 vols.

Howells, William, *The Heathens:* Primitive Man and His Religions. Doubleday and Co., Garden City, N. Y., 1948.

Lowie, Robert H., *Primitive Religion.* Grossett and Dunlap, New York, 1924; 1952.

Radin, Paul, *Primitive Religion:* Its Nature and Origin. Dover Publications, New York, 1957.

NOTES TO CHAPTER 17

1. Smith, Edwin W., *The Golden Stool:* Some Aspects of the Conflict of Cultures in Modern Africa. Doubleday and Co., New York, 1928, p. 7.

2. Lado, Robert L., "Problems in Learning the Culture" in Garvin, Paul L., editor, *Report of the Seventh Annual Round Table Meeting of Linguistics and Language Study.* Monograph Series on Language and Linguistics, no. 9, Georgetown University. Georgetown University Press, Washington, 1957, p. 144.

3. Useem, John, "South Sea Island Strike" in Spicer, Edward H., editor, *Human Problems in Technological Change:* A Casebook. Russell Sage Foundation, New York, 1952, p. 157.

4. Grimble, Sir Arthur, *We Chose the Islands:* A Six-Year Adventure in the Gilberts. William Morrow and Co., New York, 1952, pp. 47–48.

5. Keesing, Felix M., and Marie M., *Elite Communication in Samoa.* Stanford University Press, Stanford, 1956, p. 85.

6. *Ibid.,* pp. 192–193.

7. Bell, F. L. S., "The Place of Food in the Social Life of the Tanga," *Oceania,* vol. 19, 1948, p. 57.

8. Keesing, Felix M., and Marie M., *op. cit.,* p. 80.

9. *Ibid.,* p. 79.

10. It was taboo for a man to eat food with which a cross-cousin (that is, the child of a paternal aunt or maternal uncle) or brother-in-law had been in contact.

11. Bell, F. L. S., *op. cit.,* pp. 56–57.

12. See, for example, Raper, Arthur, and Pearl Wheeler Tappan, "Georgia Share Croppers," *Applied Anthropology,* vol. 2, no. 3, 1943, pp. 3–11.

13. Apodaca, Anacleto, "Corn and Custom: Introduction of Hybrid Corn to Spanish American Farmers in New Mexico" in Spicer, Edward H., editor, *op. cit.,* pp. 35–39.

14. *Report of the New Guinea Nutrition Survey Expedition 1947*. Department of External Territories, Canberra, pp. 25, 100–101.

15. Lado, Robert L., *op. cit.*, pp. 145–146.

16. See Ford, Clellan S., and Frank A. Beach, *Patterns of Sexual Behavior*, Harper and Bros., New York, 1951; also, Murdock, George P., "The Social Regulation of Sexual Behavior" in Hoch, Paul H., and Joseph Zubin, editors, *Psychosexual Development in Health and Disease*, Grune and Stratton, Inc., New York, 1949.

17. For sexual customs in Truk, see Gladwin, Thomas, and Seymour B. Sarason, *Truk: Man in Paradise*, Viking Fund Publications in Anthropology, no. 20, Wenner-Gren Foundation for Anthropological Research, New York, 1953; also, Goodenough, W. H., "Premarital Freedom on Truk: Theory and Practice," *American Anthropologist*, vol. 51, 1949, pp. 615–620.

18. Reina, Ruben E., "Two Patterns of Friendship in a Guatemalan Community," *American Anthropologist*, vol. 61, 1959, p. 50.

19. *Ibid.*, p. 49.

20. I am indebted to Gloria Cooper for information on the problems of American-Samoan friendships.

21. Notably, Sir James Fraser, *The Golden Bough:* A Study in Magic and Religion, abr. ed., Macmillan Co., London, 1947; and Malinowski, Bronislaw, "Magic, Science, and Religion" in Malinowski, Bronislaw, *Magic, Science and Religion and Other Essays*, Doubleday Anchor Books, Garden City, N. Y., 1954.

22. Goodenough, E. R., *Jewish Symbols in the Greco-Roman Period*. Pantheon Books, New York, 1953–1958, vol. 2, p. 160.

23. Evans-Pritchard, E. E., *Witchcraft, Oracles, and Magic Among the Azande*, Clarendon Press, Oxford, 1937, and *Nuer Religion*, Clarendon Press, Oxford, 1956; also, Nadel, S. F., *Nupe Religion*, The Free Press, Glencoe, Ill., 1954.

24. For some beginnings, see Goodenough, E. R., *op. cit.*, vol. 4; Goodenough, E. R., "Religion and Psychology" (unpublished manuscript); Wallace, Anthony F. C., "Revitalization Movements," *American Anthropologist*, vol. 58, 1956, pp. 264–281; Wallace, Anthony F. C., "Mazeway Resynthesis: A Biocultural Theory of Religious Inspiration," *Transactions of the New York Academy of Sciences*, Ser. II, vol. 18, 1956, pp. 626–638.

25. Malinowski, Bronislaw, *op. cit.*

26. Quoted in *The Health Education Journal*, vol. 15, 1957, p. 77.

Chapter 18

PITFALLS OF CULTURAL IGNORANCE: ECONOMIC AND SOCIAL ORGANIZATION

MOST DEVELOPMENT PROJECTS are directly concerned with economic and social matters. Regardless of development objectives, moreover, the enactment of a program necessarily involves the established procedures by which business in the client community is conducted, its system of political and social relationships. Cultural differences in these areas may not be as immediate a source of hurt feelings and emotional heat in the personal relations between an agent and his clients as the areas considered in the previous chapter. Nevertheless, the client community's existing patterns of economic and social organization are so vital to the strategy and tactics of program enactment that any false stereotypes can lead to serious blunders. In this chapter, therefore, we shall examine some important aspects of these topics on which most people are poorly informed.

ECONOMIC ORGANIZATION

Work

A widely held value in Euro-American society, especially among middle-class people, is that work is a good thing in and of itself. Idleness is sinfulness, or something close to it. The responsible person, when he has nothing to do, looks around for something to do.[1] Made-work is a common phenomenon in our business establishments and government bureaus, because we feel that it is wrong for people not to be busy. Among many of the world's societies, however, work is not valued as an end in itself; rather it is seen as a means to an end. There are certain things that have to be done in the routine of living, and one does them. When there is nothing that has to be done, it is proper to relax. From this point of view made-work is an absurdity. Given this attitude, any work whose relevance to recognized and valued ends is not clear appears to be made-work, and is reacted to negatively.

A great part of the work connected with development projects is rightly the responsibility of the community's members. Unless they understand clearly how it relates to the achievement of goals that they themselves value, their performance is likely to be desultory. The chances are that they will not work simply because they consider it good to be busy. We remember, for example, the way in which some administrative personnel referred to Truk's people as hopelessly lazy because they used to lie down on the job of cutting grass around the administrative headquarters area with bush knives. Much of the grass cutting was made-work. They were on a payroll, and if there was nothing else for them to do at the moment, the standing order was that they be kept busy cutting grass. These workers were the same men who in their own villages often put in long hard hours of labor on jobs that were important to them. They were not generically lazy, but could see no point in expending a lot of energy doing something that, as far as they could see, made not a particle of difference to anyone.

This example leads to another point. In industrial societies most work is organized in relation to a clock. In our complex business and industrial system, work is broken down into a series of distinct operations that continue without beginning or end indefinitely. The work is there to do, and people are employed to put in so many hours a day at it. The stage of the work has little to do with quitting time. At five o'clock a worker stops, wherever he happens to be, and picks up again the next morning or is replaced by another worker on the next shift. In nonindustrial societies work is not clock-oriented but task-oriented. To finish a particular job requires a certain amount of time. If more time is required than is feasible without a break, the overall task is broken down into convenient parts. A plantation manager in New Guinea once told us that he found it better to set a quota of work for each man for each day than to require his employees to work a given number of hours. As soon as a man filled his quota, he was through for the day. He found that his employees measured work in terms of the amount to be accomplished and not in terms of being busy for a fixed amount of time. By task-orienting the work, he increased production and improved his relations with his employees. No longer was it necessary to police the work to see that the men were not "soldiering" on the job. No longer was the natives' indifference to exact time as measured by a clock a source of irritation. That they began at six in the morning or at ten in the morning was no concern provided at the day's end they had completed the day's quota of work. What this plantation manager, in effect, had discovered was that it was better to let his local hands organize the work to be done in a way that fitted their working habits and made sense to them. Not only was the work more congenial when placed on this footing, but they had a greater sense of responsibility. These considerations apply not only to Melanesians in New Guinea, but to virtually any nonindustrial population. To try to organize the work of such people on a strict eight to five o'clock basis is very frequently to create a situation that is irritating both to the administrator and to the local community.

Another problem that may occur in connection with work done by the client community's members results from the kinds of tools made available. In all societies people are used to using certain kinds of equipment and have established muscular habits appropriate thereto. While a short-handled hoe may seem to be a back-breaker to some, those used to it may prefer it and work more efficiently with it than with a strange long-handled hoe that calls for the use of different muscles in different patterns of coordination. Throughout most of the South Seas, to cite another example, the long heavy machete that is the American stock in trade is regarded as too large and unwieldy for most operations and therefore disliked. A short, light bush knife is preferred, and the people are highly skilled in its use. Although in some projects the community's members must adjust to new kinds of equipment, agents should remember that such adjustment may itself be a source of irritation and dampen people's enthusiasm.

The social aspects of work also vary from society to society. Many people prefer to do work in the company of others even though it can readily be performed in individual isolation. Not looking upon work as morally good for its own sake, they customarily make social occasions out of their work. What would otherwise be long and tedious tasks are turned into a community or family party. We are familiar enough with this attitude in connection with the "bees" that until recently characterized work in our own rural communities. Many nonindustrial people similarly seek to make fun out of work whenever possible. Local interest in community projects, where this attitude prevails, may be considerably increased if the work is organized as a social event along customary lines. In many societies any community project properly culminates in a feast. Important projects are therefore planned for such times as the community has sufficient food. Allowance for this by agents may make a considerable difference in the success of their projects.

In many communities there already exist cooperative work groups and clubs, such as the *dokpwe* of Dahomey in West Africa.[2] By inviting them to organize the work for community development projects, change agents can save themselves much wasted effort and have greater confidence that the work will be organized in ways meaningful to the community's members. Such traditional cooperative labor groups, however, tend to lose value for a community's members as they shift increasingly from a subsistence to a cash economy. Increasing prosperity often makes people reluctant to spend time fulfilling labor obligations to their neighbors and community when they can now afford to pay cash wages and cash taxes instead. As development progresses, it is likely that a community's cooperative work groups will become increasingly less usable as a resource for getting development work done. Nor can it be assumed that all underdeveloped peoples are cooperative by nature regardless of circumstance.[3] But where local cooperative organizations already exist, they can be of great value as long as cash remains generally scarce.

Administrators, finally, must take care to gear their work expectations to accord realistically with the energy level of the population. In many areas of the world, energy levels are low because of inadequate diet or endemic disease. People ridden with malaria and hookworm cannot be expected to meet the same standards of work output as healthy people. The same is true of people whose diet is low in protein. Where administrative expectations of work output are not met, it is important to consider whether they are set too high in view of the prevailing energy level, or whether, as indicated above, the purpose of the work has been made both clear and reasonable and the conditions of work are compatible with local attitudes and habits. In any community there are bound to be a few individuals who by personality and temperament are lazy, by local standards as well as by the administrator's, but whole populations are not inherently lazy. When a community performs in a desultory manner, something is wrong with the health of its members or with agent-community relations, but not with the collective character structure of the local population.

Wealth and Incentives to Production

Some change agents report that the kinds of economic incentives with which they are familiar and on which western entrepreneurship is based appear to be absent in the under-developed communities in which they have worked. This has frustrated their efforts to stimulate local production and thereby raise material standards of living.[4] Since societies differ considerably in their values and in the relative weight they give to similar values—with what seems worthwhile and important to the members of one appearing unimportant to people from another—change agents have to learn what the local values are and adjust their objectives to accomplishing things that the local incentive system will sustain.

Much more information will have to be accumulated by anthropologists with training in economics before an adequate and well-tested theory of work or production incentives can be developed. Enough has been done, however, to indicate that economic considerations of material self-interest are only one of a number of factors involved.[5] Other considerations include social prestige, pride of craftsmanship, social obligations of kinship and neighborhood, political loyalties, and moral values concerning the kinds of things that people can rightfully demand of one another and their natural environment.

One way to learn about local incentives is to inquire into the reasons why respected persons in the community enjoy prestige. Thus in our own society, an important indicator of social position is the possession of wealth. In keeping with this fact, the acquisition of wealth is taken for granted as one of the major aims in life. Furthermore, we seek to acquire it with the intention of spending it on ourselves so that we may acquire the material symbols of high social position. These symbols emphasize living luxuriously. We tend to assume that other people are similarly motivated, that they will seize any opportunity to increase their material wealth for the same reasons.

Many other societies also emphasize the accumulation of wealth, but with different ends in view, direct personal consumption not being the object at all. In many Melanesian communities, for example, the production and acquisition of wealth is for the purpose of underwriting bigger and better festivals whose termination leaves the underwriter materially impoverished, but socially much respected. Another reason for acquiring wealth in Melanesia and adjacent areas is to meet one's social obligations and parental responsibilities in elaborate ceremonial and marital exchanges. These exchanges also provide a means of putting others in one's debt and thereby building up a loyal political following, thus acquiring power in community affairs.

In Palau, for example, the important thing is to be a broker through whose hands large sums of native money pass. Investment is not for the purpose of accumulating more wealth for one's own consumption but in order to be in a position to make even more impressive investments in the future. The entire emphasis, in short, is on being a "big time operator" who successfully engineers "big deals" within the local context. Rather than emphasizing the simple possession of wealth, Palauans stress its movement.[6] The American Indians of the Pacific Northwest coast are famous for a somewhat similar orientation toward wealth.[7]

Important in these societies is the way in which tokens of wealth used in prestige-giving exchanges relate to western forms of money. Economic development usually presupposes that increased production will bring more money into the community and will enable the community's members to purchase more of whatever they want. A problem in Melanesia and Palau, and presumably in some other parts of the world also, is that western money may not buy the things people value most. These things must be bought with local wealth tokens or with food produced in one's own garden. In time, to be sure, western money may acquire greater liquidity locally, but this is not something likely to be accomplished within a time span that will help specific projects aimed at stimulating production.[8]

The relative nonliquidity of western money in many under-developed communities has led to some unfortunate stereotypes. One is the idea, common among Europeans with respect to local labor in tropical areas, that the native's wants are few and simple, that he will work only in order to satisfy these wants, and that once they are satisfied he will go home and loaf. As Belshaw indicates in his critique of this view, it has served as a rationalization for low-wage policies in colonial areas.[9] Furthermore, it makes assumptions about local wants as measured by people's desire for western money, which may have relatively little liquidity in the local economy. If there are only a few things that a local person values and that outside money will buy, he may prefer to expend his energies working within the traditional local economy for personally more rewarding ends; and if he is blocked from doing this, he may decide to take it easy.

Life in the Melanesian communities in which we have worked was not characterized by doing a little work to meet fixed and limited wants. Where wants were largely traditional, great energy was expended to achieve them, but little time was spent earning money. In communities where European commodities were desired ahead of traditional ones and where personal well-being and worth were increasingly measured by their possession, great attention was given to schemes for earning money. At-tempts to take advantage of these interests, however, and to develop cash cropping or other forms of enterprise must be gauged in relation to the new wants and the possibilities for satisfying them. Furthermore, new wants are not necessarily substitutes for old ones, which only traditional activities will meet, but may be additions to them. A community may express a strong desire to have help in developing ways of satisfying its new wants, only to find its enthusiasm waning when traditional wants go unsatisfied in the resulting competition for time and energy.

Another consideration complicating the problem of incentives is that many societies forbid anyone who has them to deny the necessities of life to those who are without them. There are some societies in which this attitude includes more than the bare necessities. In the Gilbert Islands, for example, there is a custom whereby no request or favor should be refused, especially to a kinsman, if it is within one's personal power to grant it and granting it does not interfere with one's personal survival needs or with one's obligations or prior commitments to others. As soon as someone begins to accumulate luxury goods, he is bound to have to share them with others who ask for them. Customs such as this tend to render impractical any idea of accumulating significantly more in the way of material wealth than is also available to one's fellows. Improvement in living standards must be on a community rather than an individual basis.

Property

There is a widely held idea that in many underdeveloped and in most "primitive" societies there is no such thing as private property in our sense of that term, that what prevails is some form of collective ownership by clan or community. This assumption has a corollary that the local chief or clan head has the authority to dispose of the collectively owned land or other possessions of his group. It is also frequently assumed that in communities where cursory investigation shows there are individual property rights, these rights must be like those found in our own society. In sum, it is supposed that people have either private or collective ownership, and that all societies with private ownership are basically similar in their ideas and practices, as are all those with collective ownership. That property systems even among so-called "primitive" peoples are likely to be complicated and variable is an idea that seems to be alien to western thought, except among the few administrators and students of society who have taken the trouble to give them serious first-hand study. Such studies have rarely been undertaken, however, so that even our scholarly literature is replete with the false assumptions noted above. Even anthropologists have until fairly recently been among those scholars who actively promoted the myth of "primitive communism."[10] The fact of the matter is that almost any community in which agents of change are likely to work possesses a clear-cut and fairly elaborate system of customary law relating to property, a system that in many respects may be unlike anything agents are expecting, and of which others who have already had considerable experience with the community have little or no understanding.

What the local system of property law is and how it works is something the agent will have to learn himself. Property law is so variable that it is impossible to make valid generalizations about it, given our present state of knowledge. What we can do, however, is to illustrate some of the important differences and provide a few concepts that are helpful in analyzing any property system.

By property, first of all, we do not mean the things that are in some way or other owned. We mean, rather, the kinds of rights, privileges, powers, duties, and liabilities characterizing the relations between people "with regard to some subject matter and governing the use and enjoyment of the latter."[11] The right of physical possession or tenure is only one of many different kinds of rights. What the specific rights, privileges, and powers of property relations are vary from one society to the next. Within the same society, moreover, these may be combined in several different ways with respect to different subject matters. Each combination of rights, privileges, and powers represents a specific kind of *title* within a property system. In our society, for example, "eminent domain" is one kind of title and "fee simple" is another. In most societies the property system recognizes more than one kind of title. In Truk it is necessary to distinguish three distinct kinds of title, one of which does not include the right of physical possession, and no one of which is exactly like any with which we are familiar in our property law.

Societies also differ in the kinds of transactions recognized as lawful in property relations. A transaction is an act that transfers a title regarding some subject matter from one party to another or that results in some other change in the existing social distribution of rights, privileges, and powers relating to it, as in our own transaction of "leasing." In Truk there are two distinct kinds of transaction that approximate, but are far from being identical with, what we mean by "gift." The social implications and legal results of the two are very different. Any agent working there would soon be involved in at least one of them, as he began to receive the customary small gifts of food and handicrafts. Not to understand the meaning of these gifts and the obligations his acceptance of them places upon him could seriously affect his relations with the Trukese.[12]

Another important area of difference in property law stems from the local definition of what is its subject matter. The air we breathe is not a part of the subject matter of property relations in our society. Its use is unregulated. In Truk this is true of fresh water resources, but not of salt water fishing sites, which are subject to ownership by individuals and family groups.

Just as we recognize property rights to some intangibles through patenting of ideas and techniques and copywriting utterances, most nonwestern communities also recognize various "incorporeal" or intangible matters as part of the subject matter of property law. Groups or individuals may have exclusive title to rites, songs, stories, spells, professional skills, or religious and political offices.

Trukese practices regarding land illustrate how different local definitions of the subject matter of property can be. Truk's people adhere strictly to the idea that everyone is sole owner of any product of his own labor or husbandry, even when it is an improvement on something owned by someone else. A man owns the house he builds, the trees he plants, or the garden he cultivates, though all be on someone else's land. One man may own the soil of a plot of land but not the corresponding space or territory. Whereas we think of real estate as a unitary segment of terrestrial space including everything under it and on it, the Trukese see it as a composite of many freely separable parts. A foreigner seeking to purchase land in Truk usually finds that he must pay not one but many individuals and groups, each having one of three distinct kinds of title to several distinct things in the same plot. Trukese law allows for a greater number and variety of "encumbrances" in connection with real estate than does our own.[13]

Truk calls attention to another important point about property in technologically underdeveloped societies. We sometimes speak of our concept of the corporation (as a group or social body that is the legal equivalent of an individual) as if it were a fiction in law peculiar to our own civilization. This is by no means the case. The majority of real property in Truk, for example, is held by lineages (in which membership is based on matrilineal descent) that in Trukese law possess exactly the same entitlements and engage in exactly the same transactions as do individuals. A lineage even has its "children," who are its natural heirs when its membership in the female line dies out. Corporate ownership, in which the group is a legal party to property relationships independent of its members, is a characteristic of many underdeveloped societies, where it is often confused with "communal" ownership by western observers. It was so confused in Truk by most observers until after World War II.

The only assumptions that development agents can safely make about property in their client communities are: (1) there is a definite property system of entitlements and transactions of some kind; (2) it may be complex; (3) any assumptions they make about it are likely to be in error; and (4) it will merit careful study.

FAMILY AND DOMESTIC ORGANIZATION

Our family structure, which we take so much for granted, plays so small a role in community organization in western industrial society that we are often unprepared for the importance of family and kinship in community affairs elsewhere in the world. The consequences of development for family life, moreover, are productive of much resistance to change and of social disorganization in the wake of change. Nor is planning helped by our many false stereotypes about other people's forms of family organization.

Human reproduction, with long periods when infants are fully dependent on their mothers, has important social consequences. It makes women periodically unable to engage in some kinds of activity during their child-bearing years; and endangering the lives of women is more injurious to community survival than endangering the lives of men. Presumably for these reasons, all societies seem to have found it expedient to divide responsibility for at least some activities and tasks between men and women, with a consequent differential development of skills. To women go those tasks that are less likely to result in serious injury or death and that do not otherwise drastically interfere with childcare. In all societies, therefore, we find men and women dependent on one another for much more than the gratification of sexual wants alone, joined in relationships involving an exchange of all kinds of goods and services. The division of responsibility, labor, skills, and knowledge between the sexes makes it necessary, moreover, for men as well as women to participate in the physical maintenance, socialization, and education of children.

There is no natural reason why a woman should cooperate with the same man for daily exchange of goods and services, for sexual gratification, and for purposes of reproduction. Nor is there any natural reason why a child should look to the same man and woman for his physical care, legal sponsorship, socialization, and education. Arrangements concerning these matters are, indeed, highly varied from one society to the next. There are some further generalizations that can be made, however.

For reasons that are still not entirely clear, all human societies prohibit sexual relations between close siblings.[14] This means that a woman has two potential kinds of partner for cooperation in economics and childcare, her brother and her sex partner; and a child can look to either his mother's brother or his mother's sex partner as legal sponsor, provider, teacher, and disciplinarian, but only to his mother's sex partner (or partners) as his progenitor. Because of the uneven ratio of sexes born to any one woman, moreover, any relationships that call for a one-to-one pairing of a man and a woman as an efficient and balanced cooperative unit cannot regularly involve brothers and sisters. But when one-to-one pairing is not necessary, the sibling or (by extension) cousin relationship can serve as the basis for domestic cooperation between the sexes just as well as the sex-partner relationship can. A few societies, like the land-owning Nayar castes in Southwest India of a century or two ago, invest everything in the sibling relationship, leaving only sex and procreation to the conjugal (sex-partner) relationship.[15] Some societies, like our own, go to the other extreme, putting on the conjugal relationship the whole load of cooperation between the sexes in domestic matters. Many more societies range between these two extremes, giving some weight in domestic affairs to both relationships, so that a woman cooperates in some matters with her husband and in other matters with her brother.

Obviously, when community development involves domestic economic relationships or changes in the routines by which children are trained and educated, development agents must be alert to the possibility that considerable responsibility in these matters rests with the brother-sister rather than the husband-wife relationship. In Truk, for example, the joint interests of siblings invariably take precedence over those of husband and wife. A woman expects to dissolve her marriage if there is a serious quarrel between her husband and her brother. The freedom of married couples to make decisions affecting domestic matters in Truk is exceedingly limited by comparison with our own society. Similarly limited is a father's freedom to make decisions affecting the education of his children.

Finally, we should note that in societies where the conjugal relationship is emphasized, close cooperation between a woman and her husband in economic matters and in the care and training of children depends on the degree to which men are actually able to assume their responsibilities. In many parts of the Caribbean area and among depressed urban populations in the United States, men are often unable to find employment sufficiently remunerative to permit them to play the husband-father role as they conceive it. The resulting so-called "matrifocal" family organization is one in which a woman and her children form the basic unit.[16] The woman enters into a sexual liaison with a man without his necessarily assuming any financial responsibility for her or her children. His financial contribution roughly governs the extent to which he is entitled to act as husband-father in the family. Such financial assistance as men can give to women they tend to give to their sisters and mothers.

The husband-wife relationship, however it is structured, contrasts with the brother-sister relationship in that it is essentially contractual, whereas the latter is not. When large segments of a population find themselves unable to fulfill the obligations of the marriage contract, as established in their public culture, they cannot in practice maintain a conjugally based family structure and must develop other, substitute arrangements.

Plural Marriages

The ratio of the sexes ensures that in any society the majority of people are in monogamous conjugal unions at any one time. In some societies, people are monogamous as a matter of convenience, but permit polygamous arrangements for those who want and can manage them. Truk is an example.

In a very few societies, polyandry is customary, one woman having several husbands at once. Under such an arrangement, the division of labor by sex must give the major responsibility for productive economic activity to men. Women in polyandrous societies—contrary to what many Americans assume—have few responsibilities of importance and tend to suffer a corresponding diminution of value.

Polygyny, where one man has several wives, is looked upon with favor in a great many of the world's societies—widely in Africa, for example. In some places, polygyny is permitted only with women who are sisters or who come from the same family (a condition known as *sororal* polygyny). In others, wives are permitted or even required to come from different families (producing *general* polygyny). In the latter event, each wife usually is given a separate hut or apartment of her own, in which she is undisputed mistress, and relations between co-wives are governed by a strict code of authority and etiquette.

Polygyny can be practiced extensively only in societies where the division of labor and/or responsibility between the sexes gives women more than an equal share of the load. For this and other reasons, Europeans and Americans often assume that polygyny is degrading to women. But, in fact, polygyny is not incompatible with high status for women. Whatever their status in the larger community may be, moreover, women tend to have real power and importance in domestic matters in polygynous societies, because they carry a large burden of responsibility and do most of the productive work.[17]

A striking difference between polygyny and polyandry reveals what for purposes of analysis must be regarded as the basic family: a woman and her children. Polyandrous families are not subdivided into discrete units according to the different husband-fathers in them. They are elementary conjugal families in which the husband-father position is filled by several men at once. By contrast, polygynous families are invariably subdivided, each wife-mother and her children forming the nucleus of a discrete elementary family, with the same man occupying the husband-father position in more than one such family at a time.

Compound Family Structures

When frequently recurring domestic economic activities require a cooperating work group larger than can be supplied by most elementary families, complex households containing several elementary units provide the necessary standing domestic work force. Anthropologists have discerned several different structural types.

A *compound consanguine household* is composed of a set of kin-related women and their children, who make up the elementary family units, with male roles filled by the women's brothers. The kin connections by which the men and women are linked together are necessarily through women. The women have sexual liaisons with men who are not members of the domestic unit.[18]

Compound conjugal households appear in many societies in a wide variety of forms. Existing anthropological classifications are based on a typology of kin alignments that fails to do full justice to the range of organizational principles encountered.[19] These principles govern the various ways in which conjugal pairs become associated in compound households. They regularly involve considerations of kinship. One consideration is whether the significant kin ties are properly the husband's, the wife's, or optionally those of either. Cross-cutting this consideration are others having to do with the nature of the kin tie itself. It may be a personal tie to some relative, in which case the kind of relative may be specified (for example, the husband's or wife's father), or any one of several kinds of kin connection may serve. The tie, on the other hand, may be to an already established social group, instead of a kinsman. This may be some kind of descent group, unilinear or nonunilinear (see below), which owns a landed estate, the couple joining other members of the husband's (or wife's) lineage who with their spouses already reside on the estate. In such cases, the household group is based on ties its constituent couples have to some other kind of group. In some societies, on the other hand, the composite domestic group itself is the significant object of reference, the married couple joining the group among whom the husband (or wife) grew up. In all of the foregoing, moreover, the significant kin connections may either impose a duty or confer a right upon the married pair. In Nakanai, for example, a couple has the duty to reside with the husband's father as long as he lives. A Trukese couple has the right to join the household of origin of either the husband or the wife, but has no right to any other.

The nature of the activities in which they engage and the extent of the resources available to them give compound households an upper size limit beyond which they divide into smaller groups of more manageable size. What this limit is varies greatly. In some societies we encounter large extended family households. In others, three or four couples are optimal. In some, like the Iban of Western Borneo, compound families tend to consist of only two couples, one in each generation.[20] A couple joins the household of the bride or groom, depending on the number of siblings each has in his or her household of origin, and adoption serves as a common device for pairing couples in junior generations with those in senior generations. These so-called "stem families" represent the minimum size possible for compound conjugal households.

Whatever their specific form, compound families tend to play a more important role in community organization than do independent elementary families such as we have in the United States. Our type of family has no permanence, lasting only for the duration of a single marriage, but compound families may be relatively permanent fixtures, lasting for generations. Their permanence and larger membership enable them to accumulate estates and to function as standing groups for numerous economic, political, and religious activities. As we might expect, therefore, compound families tend to put more emphasis on internal solidarity; and they also tend to enjoy greater autonomy as important segments within the community.

These tendencies have important implications for community development. In communities with compound families, individual interest in new ways of doing things may mean little in itself, because individuals will not act on their own but only as their families are prepared to act. A young mother in a large household, for instance, may be personally willing and even eager to adopt new methods of baby care proposed by public health agents, but may be restrained because the other women in her household are unsympathetic to the idea. In this example we see one of the chief causes of failure in many development undertakings, for too often agents work entirely with individuals isolated from their families. They establish maternity clinics, to carry our example further, in which they seek to educate expectant mothers in prenatal and postnatal care, oblivious of the fact that expectant mothers have next to no say at home as to what is actually done. They should be educating the mother-in-law or grandmother, all the important relatives of the expectant mother who, in fact, determine the kind of care she and her baby receive. To deal with expectant mothers alone works better in our society, because they are the mistresses of their households and can dictate the procedures to be followed therein. Because this approach works in our society, we tend to assume that it will work equally well elsewhere, without stopping to think that women of child-bearing age are likely to have little control over the conduct of affairs in compound family households.

Extensions of Compound Family Organization

Principles similar to those by which married couples aggregate themselves into compound households may also serve to aggregate households, whether compound or elementary, into larger local groups: hamlets, neighborhoods, villages, and barrios or wards within larger towns. A Yoruba city in Nigeria, for example, is described as divided into a number of "compounds," each the property of a lineage in which the men of the lineage reside together with their wives and children. Some compounds contain hundreds of people.[21]

KIN GROUPS AND KIN RELATIONSHIPS

Social groupings based on kinship ties are by no means confined to households or larger local units. Kin groups of this more general sort can be conveniently subdivided into two major types: descent groups and kindreds.

Descent Groups

A descent group is any kind of social group consisting of all or some of the descendants of some ancestor (or mythological being) as their fixed point of reference. Their organization in other respects, as well as their functions, varies greatly from society to society. Descent groups do not ordinarily include all of the descendants of the original ancestor, because in time all of a community's members would be descended equally from all of its founders and the resulting descent groups would become coterminous with the community itself. Membership, therefore, is usually restricted to some descendants, others being excluded. The criteria used to restrict membership in descent groups in a society represent its rules of descent (for purposes of group affiliation as distinct from inheritance and other matters to which considerations of descent may also apply).

The most common means of restricting membership in descent groups is to include as new members only the children of existing members of one sex. If only the children of male members are included, the descent group is *patrilineal;* if only the children of female members, the group is *matrilineal*. In some societies, membership in his mother's or father's group is optional with the individual, who can choose one or the other but cannot belong to both. In other societies, membership is restricted on the basis of other criteria such as the residence of one's parents or the inheritance of shares in particular estates. Membership in descent groups may be determined by one criterion for men and a different criterion for women.[22]

It frequently happens that a society will have several sets of descent groups, each with different functions. These different sets may all be governed by the same descent rules, one set nesting inside another, or they may be governed by different descent principles, one set being patrilineal, for example, while another is matrilineal. Anthropologists tend to refer to descent groups of more limited scope (as when all the members can actually trace their descent from the founding ancestor several generations back) as *lineages* and to those of wider scope (as with major divisions of a society) as *clans* or *sibs*.[23]

There are two popular misconceptions about the meaning of descent rules as they apply to membership in social groups. One is that where membership is matrilineal, men are subordinate to women and so-called matriarchy prevails. Very few of the world's societies with matrilineal descent groups even remotely approach conditions that could be characterized as matriarchal.[24] The other misconception is that the rule of descent reflects primitive ideas about reproduction: that in matrilineal societies the father is not regarded as a relative at all, but is simply the mother's husband. These erroneous ideas are survivals of an outmoded and disproved theory of the evolution of the human family. A rule of descent serves simply to differentiate those of one's kinsmen who are fellow members of the same social group from others who, while still one's kinsmen, are in different social groups. If, for example, membership in a political party in our society were based strictly on a rule of patrilineal descent, it would not follow that a man who was a Republican because his father was a Republican would claim no kinship with his Democratic mother, and her Democratic father and Democratic brothers and sisters. Patrilineal descent in this case would apply to political party membership and not to biological relationship as such.

Almost all societies where descent groups occur prohibit marriage within the same lineage and clan. Actual kinship ties, therefore, cut across these groups and help to bind them together by virtue of mutual kinship obligations. Kinship serves as a cement holding together the several descent groups as a community.

Descent groups may be corporate bodies, in that they are themselves parties to social and legal relationships (as distinct from the individual members). Descent principles may also be used to divide a society into a series of segments that function in other ways, such as channeling hospitality rights or defining the boundaries of incest in marriage. It is as corporate bodies, however, that descent groups tend to be of greatest moment for agents of community development. They are often the significant constituents of the political order, for example. They may hold property and enjoy specific economic, political, or religious privileges and rights. Clans often have labor or ritual specializations. Clearly, development agents cannot ignore a community's lineages and clans. Important decisions in the community may be made on a clan basis. Clan leaders are frequently important persons without whose cooperation agents can expect to make little progress. No individual is likely to change his way of doing things where clan affairs are concerned, unless his fellow clansmen are prepared to do the same.

Personal Kindreds

Personal kindreds contrast with descent groups, in that technically they consist of the people who have a relative in common and who consequently share certain rights and duties in relation to him.[25] A person's cousins on his father's side may have no kin connection with his cousins on his mother's side, but together form a part of that person's kindred. Unlike descent groups, which have continuity through time, kindreds can exist only for the life of the individual who is their focus. Since they are bounded by degree of relationship rather than by a descent principle, no two persons, except full siblings, have exactly the same personal kindred; and a person belongs to as many different kindreds as he has different relatives. Although frequently unreported for societies with elaborate descent group structures, it is probable that personal kindreds are operative in most societies, regardless of what other kind of kin group organization may also be represented. In some societies where descent groups are absent, personal kindreds play a significant role in the business of community life, as among the Kalingas of Luzon in the Philippines, where kindreds have been the units of vengeance and redress.[26]

Kin Relationships

Societies show wide differences in the way they structure kin relationships. In western society we are used to a classification of these relationships that is suitable to the minor role of kinship in community organization and to the existence of independent elementary families and the absence of anything resembling lineages or clans. Except between very close kinsmen, we have few social obligations or established modes of conduct that are specifically linked to kin relationships. In most nonindustrial societies, kin relationships are much more widely extended and are associated with many different kinds of obligation and diverse modes of conduct.

One thing that is often baffling to Europeans and Americans is the local method of classifying kinsmen. To illustrate the problem, let us look for a moment at the method of classification employed by native speakers of Pidgin English in the Territory of New Guinea. (See accompanying chart.) Although most of the words are derived from English, their meaning is quite different. In the Pidgin classification, for example, I distinguish siblings according to whether they are of the same ("brother") or opposite ("sister") sex to me. My parents and their siblings of same sex I class together as my "papa" and "mama," but their siblings of opposite sex, my paternal aunt and maternal uncle, I class together as my "country." The terms "papa" and "mama" similarly include all of my parents' cousins whose sex is the same as theirs, while "country" includes all of their cousins whose sex is opposite to theirs. Similarly the children of my siblings of same sex are

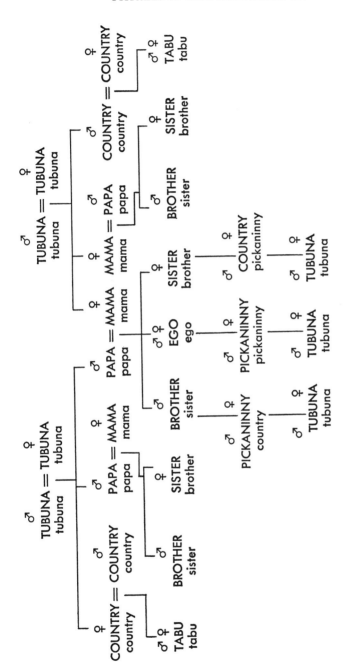

PIDGIN ENGLISH KINSHIP CHART

All terms in capital letters are as used by a male ego, in small letters by a female ego. In various parts of New Guinea there are minor variations on this system, which is the one in use on the north coast of New Britain Island. Those terms of English origin are given the English rather than the Pidgin spelling for the reader's convenience. In many areas the aunts and uncles shown here as *papa* and *mama* are referred to as *small papa* and *small mama*.

classed with my children as "pickaninny," while the children of my siblings of opposite sex are my "country," just as I am their "country." Cousins who are children of siblings of the same sex are, like children of the same parents, "brother" and "sister," but cousins who are children of siblings of opposite sex are "tabu" to one another. All my grandparents, grandchildren, and other kin in their respective generations are classed together as my "tubuna." Strange as the Pidgin system of kinship nomenclature may seem to us, its type is frequently encountered. It is no more natural or unnatural than our system but differs from it, in that its uses different criteria for classifying relatives, stressing the degree of generation removal and the similarity and difference of sex among sets of siblings on the genealogical tree rather than the degree of collateral removal, the seniority of generation, and the sex of the relative, as in standard English nomenclature.

The subject of kinship classification is complicated and technical. Most people who encounter its elaboration by anthropologists are appalled by what strikes them as an overconcern for social trivia. Why, indeed, should we bring the matter up at all in a discussion of this kind?

We can readily answer this question by citing the complaint of a European resident in New Guinea about the untrustworthiness of his native household servants. He was incensed at how one of them had apparently tried to pull the wool over his eyes. The employee had asked leave to go attend the funeral of his "papa." The leave had been granted. A few months later he had again asked leave to attend the funeral of his "papa." The European immediately assumed that his employee was lying to him, and either must have been very stupid to try to play the same father's funeral trick within the space of a few months or else he must have held a very low opinion of his employer's intelligence. The European's assumptions were, of course, wrong on all counts. The employee had, in fact, a number of people who were "papa" to him, and they had reached an age when they were dying off. Because of the importance of kin relationships in most nonindustrial communities, agents of change will inevitably find knowledge of how these relationships work necessary to their understanding of what is going on locally.

Kinship, we have noted, also involves specific obligations and modes of conduct. We have already mentioned in another context the sexual joking relationship between brother-in-law and sister-in-law in Truk. Usually an individual has a distinct set of obligations toward each type of relative; he has one set of obligations to all those who are "papa" to him and another set of obligations to those who are "country" and so on. Licensed joking relationships are a common phenomenon. In many societies there are also avoidance relationships between certain classes of kinsmen. We have seen how brothers and sisters avoid one another's company on Truk. In many societies, moreover, a man may have nothing to do with his mother-in-law. It is also common for younger brothers to have to render strict obedience to older brothers. Agents unfamiliar with the local conventions in this regard are likely to get themselves and others involved in embarrassing situations. One does not invite relatives who must avoid each other to be guests in one's home at the same time, for example, or expect them to work side by side on the same construction job.

How easy it is to jump to wrong conclusions can be illustrated by the comment of a Naval administrator about the people of Puluwat in the Pacific Islands. During a mass medical check there, he noticed that women were constantly crouching down as they saw men approach and sit down. He learned that they did so because it was forbidden for them to be physically higher than these men. He concluded that the men of Puluwat really "ruled the roost" as far as their women were concerned. In actual fact, however, the only men in whose presence women exhibit this behavior are their brothers (or clan brothers). They would not think of crouching in the presence of their husbands or any other man, except the local chief. To deal with the Puluwatese on the assumption that men generally had complete control over women would be a serious error. Not aware of the pattern of kinship relationships and how social behavior was conditioned by it, the administrator completely misinterpreted the implications of what he observed and was preparing to deal with the Puluwatese on the basis of this misinterpretation.

An education officer in Rabaul once told us how baffled he had been by the behavior of one of his most trusted native school-teachers. The leader of a local faction that was organizing resistance to the government's program to establish local self-government called for and received the active support of this teacher, who had previously indicated to the education officer that he did not sympathize with the faction he was now supporting. A well-known British anthropologist, who was visiting Rabaul at the time, suggested that the two native men were close kinsmen, probably "brothers," and that this was why the teacher had supported the leader of a cause with which he had declared himself out of sympathy. When forced to choose sides in a conflict between his brother and the government for which he worked, his values required that he choose his brother, right or wrong. Inquiry proved this to be the correct explanation (the leader of the political faction was the teacher's true brother) and made it possible for the education officer and the teacher to resume their relationship of mutual trust and respect.

It is for reasons of this kind that kinship can be an important source of difficulty in agent-community relations.

LEADERSHIP AND AUTHORITY

There seem to be two common stereotypes of the political organization of primitive or underdeveloped communities. One is the idea that if there is a headman or chief, he has unlimited authority. The other is that if there is no chief, no clearly defined locus of authority and no real political structure exist. Anthropological study shows both of these stereotypes to be false. Where there has been careful investigation of political institutions, it is clear that even so-called primitive peoples may have political theories and philosophies of government, coherent principles of community organization, and established procedures for making and executing decisions.

For example, each community in Truk contains several lineage groups, whose members trace descent through women from a common ancestress. Each group is a property-holding corporation, whose executive head is its eldest male member. In accordance with native political theory a community's territory was originally owned by one lineage. This lineage made grants of its land to the children of its male members from time to time, who, in turn, became the founders of new lineages in the community. The original lineage thus theoretically "sired" all the other lineages. The headman of the original lineage is, therefore, the symbolic "father" of the other lineages. Since the other lineages obtained their land from the original lineage, they owe it payments of food, and the original lineage retains certain residual rights in the land it has given them. As headman of the original lineage, the community's chief is administrator of these residual rights. Except as titular father and executor of the original lineage's territorial interests, he is without power. He must submit any proposal for community action to the heads of all the other lineages, who must also give their approval. Though he leads the community in war, he cannot coerce any individual to take part in battle. We have in short a customary definition of the responsibilities and powers of a chief, an established theory of the relations between chief and follower from which these responsibilities and powers legitimately derive, and a clear demarcation of the limits beyond which a chief may not seek to extend his powers. In other words, the people of Truk have a constitution, albeit an unwritten one. They resent violations of their constitution fully as much as we resent violations of our own.[27]

This example from Truk presents but one of the many varied forms of political organization among the world's societies; and no two societies are identical in this regard. Many communities do not have a chief or headman at all, but are governed by a council of elders or family heads. It is common to find leadership roles in different activities in the same society calling for quite different persons and offices. The adjudicator of disputes is not likely to be the leader in war, for example. Rarely does a headman have more than administrative and judicial powers. In few communities where there are headmen do they have legislative power, the power to change established custom in order to deal with new problems and circumstances. Such power more commonly resides with the community at large, with a council of family heads, or is split up among different offices according to whether the matter is economic, religious, or social in nature. In some societies leadership is hereditary and in others it is achieved by virtue of wealth, magical power, or military skill. In some communities, as in Truk, the powers and prerogatives of leaders are explicitly set forth and circumscribed. In others, a leader's influence depends largely on his personality and the respect with which the community regards him.

There are, then, very few generalizations that may be made about political organization in underdeveloped and nonurban communities. Development agents must find out how each local system works and whether the presumed leaders are front men only or wield real authority. They must learn what are the limits of the leaders' authority and know the native political theory that sanctions this authority.

In many areas where agents of change are likely to work, the local political situation may be complicated by the presence of headmen who are appointed by colonial, regional, or national governments, with little regard to the prevailing form of local government. While the appointed official serves as the local representative of the higher government to the community, the community is likely to handle its internal affairs through its own political officials who are not recognized by the higher government. Under these conditions an agent of change may be faced with the problem of having to work through official representatives who have no real standing in the community and at the same time work through unofficial leaders who do have standing. If he ignores the official representative in favor of the *de facto* authorities, the former can cause serious trouble because of his connection with higher governmental authorities outside the community. But if an agent ignores the real leaders in the community, he is likely to be identified with the outside authorities, who may not be liked and with whom the community may cooperate as little as possible. Thus an agent may be faced with the problem of keeping on good terms with what amounts to two rival governments in the same community.

Anthropologists frequently have the same problem in connection with their work. They usually find the following the safest general principle to follow. On making initial contact with the community it is best to deal with the official representatives, regardless of how the members of the community regard them. Thus one avoids alienating them from the outset. At the same time one makes an effort to find out who, if any, are the other leaders in the community and to clear one's moves with them also. Anyone undertaking a community project in the United States, for example, must give recognition to, and enlist the interested support of, the local clergyman, banker, labor union head, newspaper editor, and other informal leaders as well as the mayor.

There are times when a community is split into factions, between which rivalry is so intense that it is impossible to win the approval of one faction without automatically losing the approval of the other. Agents should scrupulously avoid being identified with any one faction, if possible, but there are times when it is impossible. Inevitably agents will occasionally become completely identified with the wrong faction and, as a result, will be unable to promote any kind of community development. When this happens, it may be wise for the agent to withdraw from the scene entirely in favor of a successor who, profiting from this experience, can make more appropriate contacts in the community. As in any other endeavor, initial failure is often a necessary preliminary to ultimate success.

Decision-making

For a decision to have legitimacy in some communities, it must be arrived at in accordance with procedures and rituals without whose observance no decision is binding. Thus in the United States our legislative bodies must follow certain rules and rituals in order to have their actions accepted by the community. In some other communities it is not so much the procedure followed in arriving at a decision that is all important, but the source of the decision in whose name it is rendered.

In stratified communities, moreover, with different levels of authority, certain kinds of decisions may be regarded as appropriate to particular levels. It is reported for Samoa that

> . . . it would demean higher elite persons, and shame their adherents, for them to take action on matters appropriate to decisions by those lower in the hierarchy. When one of the "royal" chiefs gave a radio talk promoting

some improvements in taro culture there was a strong Samoa-wide reaction, a resentment that he was lowering his dignity by talking of such matters, and also that he was "not an expert" in this agricultural field and didn't "know anything about taro growing!" [*28]

This example also illustrates that high socio-political office does not necessarily entitle one to speak with authority on all subjects, but only on those for which the office has a socially recognized "right" to speak.

In the United States we are accustomed to majority rule. A proposal for community improvement comes up for a vote, and the minority is expected to yield to the majority and cooperate with it in executing the decision arrived at. In many societies community action is decided by the principle of unanimity rather than by majority rule, which is not unlike the practice in the Society of Friends, where decisions require discussion by the Meeting until a "sense of the meeting" is arrived at. This is the case in the otherwise very different societies of the Papago Indians of Arizona and the Samoan Islanders. Writing about the former, Dobyns emphasizes that achieving unanimity often requires considerable time; where it is not achieved, no action is possible. "When outsiders demand fast action," he concludes, "not allowing time to achieve unanimity, Papagos are disturbed." [29] A former administrator in the New Hebrides islands in Melanesia comes to a similar conclusion.

> When I was a District Officer in the Pacific Islands I used to get very annoyed because people would take a long time to decide anything. I then found that this was because they were not content with majority rule. They required unanimous consent to anything which concerned the village. So that if one person disagreed, that would mean the veto on the project. I still didn't fully understand until reading in anthropology made me realize that this was a consequence of the small size of the community. Everyone knew everyone else; furthermore nobody had anywhere else to go. An open quarrel would be a very serious thing, probably resulting in violence with all sorts of ramifications. So that it was highly important for the people to avoid any cause for quarrel, and any underlying hostility. [30]

* Reprinted from *Elite Communication in Samoa: A Study of Leadership* by Felix M. Keesing and Marie M. Keesing, with the permission of the publishers, Stanford University Press, p. 126. © 1956 by the Board of Trustees of the Leland Stanford Junior University.

Political maneuvering where the unanimity principle operates must follow different lines from those required in western society. Since local leaders are much more likely to comprehend the right way to proceed under these conditions, a change agent is wise to follow the advice of those leaders who are sympathetic to his proposals in his efforts to win the support of others.

One procedure that is always safe to follow, is to discuss one's proposals with the various community leaders privately before presenting them to the community officially for public decision. Once a leader has taken a public stand, he is likely to stay with it regardless of how his personal opinions may subsequently change. Having committed himself publicly, he would lose face to admit that he was wrong. The community's leaders should have the opportunity to have their objections met and their misconceptions clarified privately. Those who are sympathetic to the project can work privately on those who are initially opposed to it.

Such procedures take time, to be sure, but impatience with them is self-defeating. To initiate a program by asking the community to change its customs with respect to decision-making is to invite failure, for one slashes at the very heart of the community's political structure. Sometimes an agent can successfully move into a community, assemble its people to a public meeting, submit his proposals for their approval, and get a sympathetic response. However, this more often results in a negative response or in the immediate cleaving of the community into pro and con factions, which having publicly taken their stand cannot now change their opinions without suffering loss of face or political recognition. As in our own society, it is very difficult for political leaders to admit they have been wrong and continue to be respected as political leaders. By splitting the community into pro and con factions, agents of change effectively destroy the conditions for community cooperation as far as their program is concerned.

An observation by the Keesings is important for agents working in communities where unanimity principles prevail. They point out that in Samoa, since there is no room for an "organized, out-in-the-open opposition minority party," there is inevitably a great deal of undercover frustration and dissatisfaction. When it becomes sufficiently widespread, a small personal grievance voiced by anyone may serve to coalesce dissatisfied elements into a concerted movement against the established authorities.[31] Such movements find unity in everyone's being against the same authority figures; but since the reasons are highly varied, positive formulations of goals are necessarily general and vague, often couched in mystical terms and utilizing slogans whose words have wide appeal only because they have different meanings for different people. A serious problem facing agents of change is the ever-present possibility that acceptance of a project by the established authorities within a community may provide the occasion for bringing into the open all of the previously unexpressed dissatisfactions toward those authorities. Thus a project can be doomed for reasons that are completely incidental to its merits or the change agent's own methods of approach. To assess such dissatisfactions before they break into the open is obviously very difficult, if not impossible. Just as preliminary study of a target community's physical and cultural resources is needed before a program can be designed, preliminary study of the existing emotional attitudes toward the established leadership is also essential.

Regardless of the procedures by which decisions are made, it is important to bear in mind that those leaders (even when their positions are hereditary) who have the right to make them are usually responsible to a body of followers or electors whom they represent. Consequently they are rarely in a position to make on-the-spot decisions. They need time to ascertain the sentiments of the groups they represent, especially when the decisions involve departure from custom or novel ideas. The Keesings stress this for Samoa.

> This fact is surprisingly little realized by government officials and others. . . . Too often they expect outright answers on new problems from an elite assembly during its session. They assume or imply that the representatives have the authority delegated to them on such specifics, or are in a position to exercise arbitrary authority. . . . In the reorganized Legislative Assembly of Western Samoa the problem arose immediately of how long Samoan members should be

given to frame their comments on motions after their introduction: officials wanted to allow one day only, but the Samoans asked for a longer period and in the end the decision was made to give at least seven days' advance notice of motions. *[32]

The Distribution of Authority by Age and Sex

In every society important distinctions are made regarding the eligibility of men and women to participate in specific activities. Certain activities are women's exclusive responsibility; others are men's; while still others may be the responsibility of either sex. But these activities vary considerably. Also variable is the social position of the sexes relative to each other, although there are virtually no societies in which men are in an overall subordinate position to women. In most societies, however, women have decision-making authority in connection with the activities for which they are responsible, while men have authority in activities that are their responsibility. As the failure of efforts to introduce a high-yield corn into a Spanish-American community reveals,[33] agents are not likely to get very far with proposals to change activities in the women's sphere if they have only masculine approval for them. In parts of West Africa, to use another example, where marketing is done by, and is under the control of, women (whereas production is under the control of men), attempts to bring about changes in marketing must have the approval of women and the women's market organizations if they are to succeed. Wide variation in the distribution of authority between the sexes requires agents to be wary.

Age is also likely to have implications with which an agent is unfamiliar. In western society old people "retire," for example. They turn over the management of family, business, and governmental affairs to younger men and women. The affairs of our society are dominated largely by persons of "middle age" rather than by "elders." In many of the world's communities this is not the case. We should not expect the decision-makers of another community to be in the same age group with those in our home

* Reprinted from *Elite Communication in Samoa: A Study of Leadership* by Felix M. Keesing and Marie M. Keesing, with the permission of the publishers, Stanford University Press, pp. 123–124. © 1956 by the Board of Trustees of the Leland Stanford Junior University.

town. Our customary values and attitudes do not equip us very well to look to old men and women as the wielders of ultimate authority, as indeed they are in many societies.

Agents of change, moreover, may find themselves called upon to play the role of an elder, although they may feel that their age alone does not justify it. An agent who is relatively young may find that this is a handicap in his relations with clients who are unused to seeing younger people in positions of responsibility and, indeed, assume that younger people are not fitted for such positions. Under these conditions, an agent has an added burden of proof placed upon him, his very age being a strike against him in his attempt to establish himself as a responsible person in his clients' eyes. If at the same time he shows a preference for dealing with younger people in the community—that is, with his age contemporaries—as would be more appropriate at home, this may be interpreted by the community as demonstrating the agent's relative immaturity. While he may be well liked and respected as a young man, he may not be respected as a responsible agent of community development. Some African societies, indeed, are rigidly organized into distinct age strata, each stratum having a distinct legal status in the community.[34] Clearly, the age of a development agent can be sufficiently vital to his program's success as to make it an important factor governing his job assignment.

Assessing Public Opinion

Another politically important way in which communities differ culturally concerns the public expression of opinion. Among ourselves we assume that every citizen has a right to have an opinion and to express it freely on any subject whatsoever. In planning community projects it is possible to sound out public opinion on the ideas and issues involved and to adjust one's policies and tactics accordingly. There are many communities, however, where this is difficult. In Truk, for example, serious matters involving the community are a matter of public concern to family heads and older people. Younger adults are not supposed to voice vigorous opinions on them, because they have not yet learned all the relevant facts in the community's history, demonstrated their responsibility and dependability, or had the breadth of experience prerequisite to sound judgment. Matters in which one has little or no legitimate voice are matters on which one is likely to be reluctant to express an opinion.

This is most apropos of highly stratified and rank-conscious communities. The Keesings' account of Samoa spells out the difficulties change agents may encounter in assessing public opinion on matters which it is the traditional right of leaders to decide.

> *It is rarely possible in . . . Samoa to get a public expression of individual opinion or minority opinion on any issue that has been "processed" through the elite leadership system; and any secret polling would be resented. Elite subjects must be dealt with through elite channels.* Thus, of Samoans who have testified before the various government investigatory bodies on political affairs in each territory, only a handful have expressed points of view that differed from the standard patterns as voiced by the leaders, and these in virtually every case were individuals who have lived outside of Samoa, and who were markedly deviant in Samoan terms. In relation to the self-government petition to the United Nations sent by the leaders of Western Samoa in 1947, the only strong opposition by any group came from one whole district, Falealili. Throughout Samoan history this particular district has had a traditional right and duty to voice opposition where it deemed appropriate. In the old Samoan policy it was a *Tumua* area with special "opposition" rights—the district is known ceremoniously as the "conscience of the 'Malietoa' "; so that this was part of an expected pattern.

> Outsiders who are used to a ready formulation of individual judgment find particularly disconcerting the wall of inhibition here. It is a rare, socially deviant individual even among the elite who would be prepared to express his personal opinion outside the proper communication channels on any issue that has been or is due to be "processed" through the group leadership system. For a non-elite person to yield a considered personal judgment in this way to an outsider would be virtually unthinkable. In such a milieu an opinion poller can obviously have thin pickings only, and random sampling response techniques on any public question would be ruled out. Should a subject of elite concern be raised, it would be passed off in some polite way or the interrogator referred to the appropriate titled person.

An investigator needing information must obviously go to the persons who not only command it but also have the right to impart it, i.e., a purposive and controlled rather than a random type of sampling.*[35]

CONCLUSION

The materials presented in this and the preceding chapter hopefully demonstrate how wide and deep the pitfalls of cultural ignorance can be. No responsible military commander cares to mount an attack without information on his enemy's numbers, weaponry, disposition, fortifications, channels of supply, troop morale, and so on, especially if this information is accessible to him. Similarly, no responsible development agency can afford to launch a development project without being informed as to the client community's culture in all of its aspects, especially its principles of economic, social, and political organization. Nor can it afford to be ignorant of the emotional climate of the community's members. Unlike a military commander, moreover, who often has great difficulty gaining the information he feels it is crucial to have, a development agency is rarely in a position where it cannot find out what it ought to know if it is willing to take the time.

The record shows, however, that development agencies seldom take advantage of their opportunities. Their efforts are not entirely fruitless, of course, but to say that actual accomplishment averages as much as 15 per cent of plan is being generous. By contrast, the Vicos project in Peru shows how much of plan can be realized when the developing authority not only respects the dignity of its clients and assumes an attitude of patience, but also takes the necessary time to study the client community beforehand and then closely follows every step of the development process, so that day-to-day decisions are informed ones and the tactics of program enactment can be changed as needed to adapt them to the changes taking place within the client community.[36]

* Reprinted from *Elite Communication in Samoa:* A Study of Leadership by Felix M. Keesing and Marie M. Keesing, with the permission of the publishers, Stanford University Press, pp. 128–129. © 1956 by the Board of Trustees of the Leland Stanford Junior University.

With such examples as Vicos before us, continued failure by development authorities to make serious efforts to overcome cultural ignorance will constitute *prima facie* proof of their essential indifference to the wants and needs of their clients.

SUGGESTED READING

Economic Organization

Belshaw, Cyril S., *Changing Melanesia:* Social Economics of Culture Contact. Oxford University Press, Melbourne and Wellington, 1954.

Bohannan, Paul, "The Impact of Money on an African Subsistence Economy," *The Journal of Economic History*, vol. 19, 1959, pp. 491–503.

Conklin, Harold C., *Hanunóo Agriculture:* A Report on an Integral System of Shifting Cultivation in the Philippines. Food and Agriculture Organization of the United Nations, Rome, 1957.

Erasmus, Charles J., "Work Patterns in a Mayo Village," *American Anthropologist*, vol. 57, 1955, pp. 322–333.

Firth, Raymond, *Malay Fishermen:* Their Peasant Economy. K. Paul, Trench, Trubner and Co., Ltd., London, 1946.

Herskovits, Melville J., *Economic Anthropology:* A Study in Comparative Economics. Alfred A. Knopf, Inc., New York, 1952.

Symposium, "Economic Motivations and Stimulations in Underdeveloped Countries," *International Social Science Bulletin*, vol. 6, 1954, pp. 369–476.

Property

Goodenough, Ward H., *Property, Kin, and Community on Truk*. Yale University Publications in Anthropology, no. 46, New Haven, 1951.

Hoebel, E. A., *Man in the Primitive World:* An Introduction to Anthropology. McGraw-Hill Book Co., New York, 1949, chap. 23.

Samkalden, I., "Land Tenure and Land Reform" in Ruopp, Phillips, editor, *Approaches to Community Development:* A Symposium Introductory to Problems and Methods of Village Welfare in Underdeveloped Areas. W. Van Hoeve, The Hague, 1953, pp. 153–170.

Family and Kin Organization

Adams, Richard N., "An Inquiry into the Nature of the Family" in Dole, Gertrude E., and Robert L. Carneiro, editors, *Essays in the Science of Culture in Honor of Leslie A. White*. Thomas Y. Crowell Co., New York, 1960, pp. 30–49.

Murdock, George P., *Social Structure*. Macmillan Co., New York, 1949.

Murdock, George P., editor, *Social Structure in Southeast Asia*. Viking Fund Publications in Anthropology, no. 29. Quadrangle Books, Chicago, 1960.

Radcliffe-Brown, A. R., and Daryll Forde, editors, *African Systems of Kinship and Marriage*. Oxford University Press, New York, 1950.

Schneider, David M., and Kathleen Gough, editors, *Matrilineal Kinship*. University of California Press, Berkeley, 1961.

Political Organization

Apter, David E., *The Goldcoast in Transition*. Princeton University Press, Princeton, N. J., 1955.

Fortes, Meyer, and E. E. Evans-Pritchard, editors, *African Political Systems*. Oxford University Press, New York, 1955.

Keesing, Felix M., and Marie M., *Elite Communication in Samoa:* A Study of Leadership. Stanford University Press, Stanford, 1956.

Leach, Edmund R., *Political Systems of Highland Burma:* A Study of Kachin Social Structure. G. Bell and Sons, Ltd., London, 1954.

Oliver, Douglas L., *A Solomon Island Society:* Kinship and Leadership Among the Siuai of Bougainville. Harvard University Press, Cambridge, Mass., 1955.

NOTES TO CHAPTER 18

1. Williams, Robin M., Jr., *American Society:* A Sociological Interpretation. Alfred A. Knopf, Inc., New York, 1951, pp. 394–396.

2. Herskovits, Melville J., *Dahomey:* An Ancient West African Kingdom. J. J. Augustin, New York, 1938, pp. 71–75.

3. For a good discussion of assumptions about cooperative behavior as they relate to community development, see Erasmus, Charles J., *Man Takes Control:* Cultural Development and American Aid, University of Minnesota Press, Minneapolis, 1961, pp. 89–91.

4. McClelland, David C., "Community Development and the Nature of Human Motivation: Some Implications of Recent Research." Paper prepared for the Conference on Community Development, Center for International Studies, Endicott House, Massachusetts Institute of Technology, December 13–15, 1957.

5. Herskovits, Melville J., *Economic Anthropology:* A Study in Comparative Economics, Alfred A. Knopf, Inc., New York, 1952, p. 111. For important new contributions to motivational theory relating to economic and social development, see Erasmus, Charles J., *op. cit.*; Hagen, Everett E., *On the Theory of Social Change:* How Economic Growth Begins, The Dorsey Press, Homewood, Ill., 1962; McClelland, David C., *The Achieving Society*, D. van Nostrand Co., Princeton, N.J., 1961.

6. Barnett, H. G., *Palauan Society:* A Study of Contemporary Native Life in the Palau Islands. University of Oregon Press, Eugene, 1949.

7. Codere, Helen, *Fighting with Property:* A Study of Kwakiutl Potlatching and Warfare, American Ethnological Society Monograph 18, New York, 1950. Compare Benedict, Ruth, *Patterns of Culture*, Houghton Mifflin Co., Boston, 1934, pp. 173–222; also, Murdock, George P., *Rank and Potlatch Among the Haida*, Yale University Publications in Anthropology, no. 13, New Haven, 1936.

8. For a vivid account of the relation of European to local currency, see Davenport, William, "Red-Feather Money," *Scientific American*, vol. 206, March, 1962, pp. 94–104.

9. Belshaw, Cyril S., *Changing Melanesia:* Social Economics of Culture Contact. Oxford University Press, Melbourne and Wellington, 1954, pp. 118–132.

10. In his *Primitive Economics of the New Zealand Maori* (G. Routledge and Sons, Ltd., London, 1929, pp. 351–359), for example, Raymond Firth finds it necessary specifically to refute the impression given by earlier students of the Maori that their property system was "communistic."

11. See the statement by George P. Murdock and others, in *Outline of Cultural Materials*, 3d ed. rev., Human Relations Area Files, Inc., New Haven, 1950, p. 51.

12. See also Held, G. J. (*The Papuas of Waropen*, Martinus Nijhoff, The Hague, 1957, pp. 35–36), who comments: "Gratitude in our sense of the word will not be found in this potlatch-society. The gift is accepted without a word of thanks. It would be highly improper to show how much one enjoys the present or how much one needs it. This does not mean to say that therefore there would be a complete lack of appreciation. If the giver states frankly what he wishes to receive in return, nobody considers this unseemly. Small friendly presents like some tobacco or a few areca-nuts a man of position may ask without damage to his prestige, whilst of people of lower status this would be considered as begging. By means of a present which is excessively large according to Papuan standards, or which is not offered in a dignified fashion, one insults the recipient. For the investigator the giving of presents is a delicate point which he has to watch carefully."

13. For a full account of Trukese property, see Goodenough, Ward H., *Property, Kin and Community on Truk*, Yale University Publications in Anthropology, no. 46, New Haven, 1951, pp. 29–64.

14. Our own traditional belief that incest is likely to result in unhealthy offspring cannot be used to explain the universal presence of its prohibition, as has been clearly shown by George P. Murdock, *Social Structure*. Macmillan Co., New York, 1949, pp. 289–290.

15. Schneider, David M., and Kathleen Gough, editors, *Matrilineal Kinship*. University of California Press, Berkeley, 1961, pp. 298–384.

16. Adams, Richard N., "An Inquiry into the Nature of the Family" in Dole, Gertrude E., and Robert L. Carneiro, editors, *Essays in the Science of Culture in Honor of Leslie A. White*. Thomas Y. Crowell Co., New York, 1960, pp. 30–49.

17. See the discussion of polygyny by Ralph Linton in *The Study of Man*, D. Appleton-Century Co., New York, 1936, pp. 183–187.

18. For an example, see the account of former Nayar land-owning castes in Southwest India, in Schneider, David M., and Kathleen Gough, editors, *op. cit.*, pp. 298–384.

19. Anthropologists commonly classify domestic units as follows: (a) *patrilocal household*, an aggregation of couples in which the husbands are related to one another through their fathers; (b) *matrilocal household*, an aggregation of couples in which the wives are related to one another through their mothers; (c) *avunculocal household*, an aggregation of couples in which the husbands are related to one another through their mothers; (d) *bilocal household*, an aggregation of couples related to one another through either the father or mother of either the husband or wife; (e) *consanguine (duolocal) household*, in which the members of both sexes are all blood relatives, husbands and wives remaining in their respective households of origin after marriage and not jointly participating in a common domestic establishment; (f) *fraternal joint household*, an aggregation of couples in which husbands (or senior generation of husbands) are brothers; (g) *stem family household*, an aggregation of only two couples, one parental to the other; (h) *neolocal household*, a single couple with unmarried children.

20. Freeman, J. D., "The Iban of Western Borneo" in Murdock, George P., editor, *Social Structure in Southeast Asia*. Viking Fund Publications in Anthropology, no. 29. Quadrangle Books, Chicago, 1960, pp. 65–89.

21. Schwab, William Bear, *The Political and Social Organization of an Urban African Community*. Ph.D. dissertation, University of Pennsylvania, Philadelphia, 1952.

22. Goodenough, Ward H., Review of *Social Structure in Southeast Asia*, edited by George Peter Murdock, in *American Anthropologist*, vol. 63, 1961, pp. 1341–1347. See also Davenport, William, "Nonunilinear Descent and Descent Groups," *American Anthropologist*, vol. 61, 1959, pp. 557–572.

23. Readers of anthropological literature will often encounter the terms "clan" and "sib" as synonyms. In his *Social Structure* (Macmillan Co., New York, 1949) George Peter Murdock gives "clan" a special meaning, using it to refer to a descent group in which married couples rather than individuals are the immediate constituents. In older literature "clan" may refer to matrilineal descent groups only and *gens* to patrilineal descent groups.

24. The Iroquois of New York are the only group for whom anything approaching matriarchy is attested. That this was a recent development in response to special conditions resulting from prolonged and disastrous warfare seems evident from a review by Cara B. Richards, "The Role of Iroquois Women Through Time" in *Cultural Stability and Cultural Change*, edited by Verne F. Ray, Proceedings of the 1957 Annual Spring Meeting of the American Ethnological Society, University of Washington Press, Seattle, 1957, pp. 36–45.

25. For a review of the anthropological concept of the kindred, see Freeman, J. D., "On the Concept of the Kindred," *Journal of The Royal Anthropological Institute*, vol. 91, 1961, pp. 192–220.

26. Barton, R. F., *The Kalingas:* Their Institutions and Custom Law. University of Chicago Press, Chicago, pp. 70–71.

27. For a fuller account, see Goodenough, Ward H., *Property, Kin and Community on Truk*, pp. 135–140.

28. Keesing, Felix M., and Marie M., *Elite Communication in Samoa:* A Study of Leadership. Stanford University Press, Stanford, 1956, p. 126.

29. Dobyns, Henry F., "Experiment in Conservation: Erosion Control and Forage Production on the Papago Indian Reservation in Arizona" in Spicer, Edward H., editor, *Human Problems in Technological Change: A Casebook*. Russell Sage Foundation, New York, 1952, p. 213.

30. Belshaw, C. S., from a talk quoted by Keesing, Felix M., and Marie M., *op. cit.*, p. 116.

31. Keesing, Felix M., and Marie M., *op. cit.*, pp. 120–121.

32. *Ibid.*, pp. 123–124.

33. Apodaca, Anacleto, "Introduction of Hybrid Corn to Spanish American Farmers in New Mexico," in Spicer, Edward H., editor, *op. cit.*, pp. 35–39.

34. See, for example, Wilson, Monica, *Good Company:* A Study of Nyakyusa Age-Villages, Oxford University Press, New York, 1951.

35. Keesing, Felix M., and Marie M., *op. cit.*, pp. 128–129. On this problem in Africa, see Marwick, M. G., "An Experiment in Public-Opinion Polling Among Preliterate People," *Africa*, vol. 26, 1956, pp. 149–159.

36. Holmberg, Allan R., "Changing Community Attitudes and Values in Peru: A Case Study in Guided Change" in Adams, Richard N., and others, *Social Change in Latin America Today*, Harper and Bros., New York, 1960, pp. 63–107.

INDEX

INDEX